A SHORT HISTORY OF
CHINESE PHILOSOPHY

中國哲學小史

馮友蘭著

[The Chinese title by Mrs. Fang Chao-ying]

A SHORT HISTORY
OF CHINESE
PHILOSOPHY

FUNG YU-LAN

Edited by Derk Bodde

THE FREE PRESS, *New York*
COLLIER-MACMILLAN LIMITED, *London*

CONTENTS

EDITOR'S INTRODUCTION

In spite of the innumerable books that have been written about China in recent years, it is remarkable how little really authentic knowledge we in the West have about the philosophy of that country. Even most well-educated Americans, if asked to list some of China's major philosophers, will, unless they are China specialists, be unable to name more than Confucius and possibly Lao Tzu. This statement, I suspect, applies almost as strongly to the average professional teacher of philosophy as it does to the layman.

Books and articles in English on the subject are not lacking, to be sure, but with few exceptions they are either too specialized to be popular or too popular to have much value. The present volume, indeed, is the first in English that attempts to give a really comprehensive and systematic account of Chinese thought as a whole, from its beginnings with Confucius to the present day. The fact that it is the work of a Chinese scholar who is generally acknowledged by his countrymen to be supremely well qualified for the task, makes its appearance all the more significant.

As we read this book, we see that Chinese philosophy is far wider in scope than either Confucius or Lao Tzu, or even the Confucian and Taoist schools with which they are linked. In the course of some twenty-five centuries, Chinese thinkers have touched upon well-nigh all the major subjects that have engaged the attention of philosophers in the West, and though the schools to which they have belonged have often borne the same name through many centuries, their actual ideological content has changed greatly from one age to another. Could Confucius, for example, have been reincarnated through a Buddhist process of metempsychosis so as to meet his great twelfth century follower, Chu Hsi, he would probably hardly have guessed

xi

that the ideas preached by the latter were the orthodox "Confucianism" of that time.

Beneath this diversity, however, we find certain themes occurring and reoccurring; one of them is what Dr. Fung describes in his first chapter as that of "sageliness within and kingliness without." How to acquire the *Tao* or Way to become an inner sage and outer king? This, understood in a somewhat figurative rather than strictly literal sense, has been a central problem of Chinese philosophy, and gives it, as Dr. Fung points out, its dual quality of being both this-worldly and other-worldly. It is this point that Dr. Fung took as the main thesis of his recent book *The Spirit of Chinese Philosophy*. I shall not spoil his story at this point except to suggest that this same quality, half-consciously perceived by the West, has perhaps helped to create that common impression of China as a land peopled both by mystic sages, who sit in eternal meditation on mountain peaks below pine trees, and by exceedingly practical and somewhat matter-of-fact men of affairs.

During the 1930's, when I began my study of Chinese philosophy and other aspects of Chinese culture in Peiping, one of my happiest contacts came in 1934-35 when I attended Dr. Fung's class on Chinese philosophy at Tsing Hua University. He had then just published the second volume of his monumental *History of Chinese Philosophy*, which speedily became the standard work in its field. One day when I came to class, Dr. Fung asked me whether I knew of anyone who would be willing to translate his book into English. As a result, I agreed to undertake the task, and my translation of the first volume was published in the summer of 1937, just after the outbreak of the Sino-Japanese war. At the time, I hoped to translate the second volume within two or three years.

Meanwhile, however, my work took me from China, the long years of war followed, and many other tasks intervened. Aside from a few sporadic efforts, therefore, it was only with the coming of Dr. Fung from China to the University of Pennsylvania in the autumn of 1946 as Visiting Professor of Chinese that I was able to begin anew. Since then I have translated a series of individual chapters from volume two which have already appeared, or will probably appear, in the *Harvard Journal of Asiatic Studies*, a publication of the Harvard-Yenching Institute in Cambridge, Mass. A list of them will be found in the bibliography at the back of this book, and when completed they will be published as a single volume. Under a grant recently awarded to me under the terms of the Fulbright Act, providing for the sending of American scholars and teachers to China and other countries, I expect to leave shortly for a year in Peiping, where I hope to complete the translation of the entire second volume by the autumn of 1949.

Last year, however, while I was beginning this work in Philadelphia, Dr. Fung decided that he would himself like to write in English a shorter version of his original *History*. For this he enlisted my aid as editor, and the present book is the result.

In subject matter this book for the most part follows the original Chinese work fairly closely. Its first sixteen chapters correspond roughly to the latter's volume one, and its remaining chapters to volume two. It is, however, considerably shorter, as is evident from the fact that my translation of the first volume of the original *History* covers 454 rather large pages, and the Chinese edition is in turn 50 pages shorter than volume two. This shortening has been achieved for the present book by omitting entirely some of the lesser thinkers dealt with in the original *History* and reducing the space allotted to the remainder. Footnotes have also been largely avoided, and such matters as detailed bibliographical references, discussions on the dating and authenticity of various texts, and much biographical data have been eliminated. Yet the resulting volume is a product of solid scholarship, which may be relied on as a remarkably acccurate and well-rounded account of its subject.

There are other features, too, which distinguish it from the usual abridgement. In the first place, it has been written with the Western reader specifically in mind, which means that its treatment and subject matter are not always the same as they would be in a book intended solely for a Chinese public. Such is the case with its first two chapters, for example, which do not occur in the original *History* at all, and the same is true of a good part of its chapter twenty-seven.

In the second place, it embodies a number of conclusions and points of emphasis which were arrived at by Dr. Fung only after the publication of his original *History* in 1934. The third chapter, for example, summarizes a theory that was first published by Dr. Fung in Chinese only in 1936, in a separate *Supplement* to his original *History*. The final chapter, devoted to Dr. Fung's own philosophical ideas, is also necessarily new, since these ideas were first expressed in a series of creative philosophical books which he wrote during the war years. Likewise, the treatment of Neo-Taoism and Buddhism in chapters nineteen to twenty-two has been considerably changed from that in the *History*. (The corresponding chapters in the latter work, however, are to be revised by Dr. Fung along similar lines before I translate them into English.)

The choice of subject matter, treatment, and actual writing of the present book are, of course, almost entirely the work of Dr. Fung himself. My own contribution has been primarily that of editing his manuscript with the needs of the Western reader in mind, so as to make its English correct and readable. Many of the quotations from original texts have been borrowed, with occasional trifling changes, from my translations of the same passages in the longer *History*, when available, but in other cases Dr. Fung has prepared renditions of his own for key terms or passages, or has used those contained in E. R. Hughes' translation, *The Spirit of Chinese Philosophy*. Many other quotations, of course, are entirely new. The Bibliography and Index have been compiled by me.

The general reader may find it helpful to be given a brief résumé of the course of Chinese history, before concluding this introduction. Traditionally, the history begins with a series of sage-kings, said to have reigned in the latter part of the third millennium B.C. It is the uncritical acceptance, both by Chinese and Westerners alike, of the stories about these men, that has created the erroneous widespread impression regarding the excessive antiquity of Chinese civilization. Today, however, scholars are generally agreed that these sage-kings are little more than mythical figures, and that the stories about them are the idealized inventions of a much later period. The historical existence of China's first dynasty, the *Hsia* (trad. 2205-1766 B.C.), is likewise uncertain, though it may some day be confirmed by future archaeology.

With the *Shang* dynasty (trad. 1766-1123 B.C.), however, we reach firmer historical ground. Its capital, which has been partially excavated, has yielded an abundance of inscriptions carved on bone and tortoise shell. It is these inscriptions that were prepared in conjunction with the method of divination described in chapter twelve.

Coming to the *Chou* dynasty (1122?-256 B.C.), we have abundant historical records, and the Chou is also the golden age of Chinese philosophy. During its early centuries, a large number of small states, most of them grouped around the valley of the Yellow River in

North China, were linked together through common ties of allegiance to the Chou royal house in a feudal system roughly analogous to that of medieval Europe. As time wore on, however, this feudal system gradually disintegrated, resulting in the eclipse of the Chou royal power, the steady increase of bitter warfare between the now independent states, and other violent political, social, and economic upheavals. It was men's efforts to find answers to the resulting pressing problems that confronted them, that caused the appearance of the first Chinese organized philosophical thought, which constitutes the cultural glory of the age. Confucius (551-479 B.C.) was the earliest of these philosophers, and was followed by a host of others belonging to widely differing schools of thought. Most of the subject matter in chapters three to sixteen of the present book is concerned with these schools. Politically, the same centuries following Confucius are appropriately known as the Period of the Warring States.

The state of Ch'in, from which the name China is probably derived, brought this age to an end in the year 221 B.C. by annihilating the last of the other opposing states, thus for the first time creating a really unified Chinese empire. The resulting Ch'in dynasty replaced the old feudal aristocracy by a centrally appointed nonhereditary bureaucracy, thus instituting a form of government that has since set a pattern for all later dynasties. With the sole exception of the creation of the Chinese Republic in 1912, these events marked the greatest single change in China's political history.

The very harshness exercised by the Ch'in to achieve this end led to its speedy overthrow. Its work of unification was continued, however, by the politically powerful Han dynasty (206 B.C.-A.D. 220), under which the empire was expanded to include most of present day China proper, together with much of present Chinese Turkestan. This political unification was accompanied by a corresponding unification in the field of thought. Most of the Chou philosophic schools disappeared as separate schools, though many of their ideas were absorbed into Confucianism and Taoism, which now became dominant. These developments are described in chapters seventeen to eighteen.

Following the four hundred years of Han rule, there came another four centuries which may be termed the Period of Disunity (A.D. 221-589), during much of which China was usually divided between a series of short-lived dynasties in the south, and another series of equally short dynasties in the north. Several of the latter were ruled

by non-Chinese nomadic groups, who during this period succeeded
in forcing their way past the Great Wall. For the Chinese people as
a whole these centuries, sometimes referred to as China's dark ages,
were ones of frequent suffering. Culturally, nevertheless, they were
outstanding in many ways, and philosophically they were marked by
the temporary eclipse of Confucianism, and the dominance of Neo-
Taoism and Buddhism. These two latter philosophies are the subjects
of chapters nineteen to twenty-one.

The *Sui* (590-617) and especially *T'ang* (618-906) dynasties, however, brought renewed unity and political strength to China, and in
many ways marked a high-water mark in cultural achievement. Under the T'ang, Buddhism reached its peak, and one of its schools,
Ch'anism, is treated in chapter twenty-two. Afterwards, however,
Buddhism entered the gradual decline which it has ever since followed; Confucianism, on the contrary, began once more a rise which
brought it to eventual supremacy. The early steps in this revival are
described in the beginning of chapter twenty-three.

The collapse of the T'ang was followed by an uneasy interlude of
fifty odd years. Then came the *Sung* dynasty (960-1279), which
though politically weaker than the T'ang, was culturally equally brilliant. In the field of thought, it was marked by the greatest recrudes-
cence of Confucianism which had been seen since the Han dynasty.
This movement, known to the West as Neo-Confucianism, is described in chapters twenty-three to twenty-five.

The *Yüan* dynasty (1280-1367), which replaced the Sung, is notable as the first under which all of China was ruled by an alien group,
the Mongols. Culturally, however, it was comparatively unimportant.
The *Ming* dynasty (1368-1643) which followed restored the country
to Chinese rule, but though it was a pleasant period in which to live,
it contributed little to culture that was radically new. In philosophy,
however, it was notable as the dynasty under which the school in
Neo-Confucianism known as that of Universal Mind reached its
culmination. This development is described in chapter twenty-six.

Under the following *Ch'ing* dynasty (1644-1911), all of China
again fell under non-Chinese rule, this time that of the Manchus.
Yet until the beginning of the nineteenth century it was one of the
most prosperous periods of Chinese history, and also one which saw
definite advances in certain cultural fields, though declines in others.
Politically, the empire was extended even beyond the frontiers which

it had achieved under the Han and T'ang. Beginning in the early nineteenth century, however, Manchu power steadily decayed, and China's resulting internal weakness unfortunately coincided with the growing political and economic pressure of the industrialized West. The ways in which these various developments influenced the field of thought are described in chapter twenty-seven.

The overthrow of the Manchus in 1911, resulting in the abolition of the oldest monarchical system in the world, marks a turning point in Chinese history. During the decades following the establishment of the Republic in 1912, China has been faced with the need of simultaneously making sweeping changes in her social, political, and economic fabric alike. We in the West have required some three centuries to pass through similar changes. It is scarcely surprising, therefore, that long years of political and intellectual disorder in China— disorder greatly aggravated by fierce aggression from the outside— have been the result. Indeed, as we look around us at the Western nations today, it is obvious that among them, too, gigantic changes are still in the making, the outcome of which no man can predict. Little wonder, then, that in China the future looks dark and uncertain. Yet Chinese history shows us that repeatedly in the past, though often at untold cost in human suffering, the Chinese have succeeded in surmounting and recuperating from the crises that have faced them. They can do so again, but only provided that the world as a whole learns quickly to accept the same cosmopolitanism that has been prominent in much of Chinese political thinking. (See chapters sixteen and twenty-one.) In the changes that China is yet to make, a good deal of her past ideology must inevitably be discarded. Some of it, however, will survive as a permanent contribution to future world philosophy. Possible ways in which this contribution may be made are suggested by Dr. Fung in his final chapter.

DERK BODDE

May, 1948
Philadelphia, Pa.

AUTHOR'S PREFACE

A short history of any subject should not simply be an abridge-ment of a larger one. It should be a picture complete in itself, rather than a mere inventory of names and "isms." To achieve this, the author should, as a Chinese expression says, "have the whole history in his mind." Only then can he give the reader an adequate and well-rounded account within his chosen limited scope.

According to Chinese historiography, a good historian must have wide scholarship in order to master all his materials, sound judgment to make proper selection of them, and literary talent in order to tell his story in an interesting way. In writing a short history, intended for a general public, the author certainly has less chance to display his scholarship, but he needs more selective judgment and literary talent than he would for writing a longer and strictly scholarly work.

In preparing this work, I have tried to use my best judgment in selecting what I consider the important and relevant from materials which I have mastered. I was very fortunate, however, to have as editor Dr. Derk Bodde, who has used his literary talent to make the style of the book interesting, readable, and comprehensible to the Western reader. He has also made suggestions regarding the selection and arrangement of the material.

Being a short history, this book serves as no more than an introduction to the study of Chinese philosophy. If the reader wishes to know more about the subject, I would refer him to my larger work, *A History of Chinese Philosophy*. The first volume of this has been translated by Dr. Bodde, and he is now translating the second one; also to my more recent work, *The Spirit of Chinese Philosophy*, translated by Mr. E. R. Hughes of Oxford University. Both works are mentioned in the bibliography compiled by Dr. Bodde at the end of the present book. Acknowledgements are due to both Dr. Bodde and Mr. Hughes, from whose books I have borrowed some translations of the Chinese texts appearing herein.

In publishing this book, I welcome the opportunity of expressing my thanks to the Rockefeller Foundation for the grant which made it possible for me to come from China to the University of Pennsylvania as Visiting Professor during the year 1946-47, and which resulted in the writing of this book. Also, I wish to thank my colleagues and students in the Department of Oriental Studies for their cooperation and encouragement, and especially Dr. Bodde, Associate Professor of Chinese. I am likewise grateful to Dr. A. W. Hummel, Chief of the Asiatic Division, Library of Congress, for his encouragement and help in making arrangements for the publication of the book.*

FUNG. YU-LAN

June, 1947
University of Pennsylvania

* Dr. Bodde is now Professor of Chinese at the University of Pennsylvania, and Dr. Hummel has become Chief Emeritus at the Library of Congress.

A SHORT HISTORY OF
CHINESE PHILOSOPHY

CHAPTER 1

THE SPIRIT OF CHINESE
PHILOSOPHY

THE place which philosophy has occupied in Chinese civilization has been comparable to that of religion in other civilizations. In China, philosophy has been every educated person's concern. In the old days, if a man were educated at all, the first education he received was in philosophy. When children went to school, the *Four Books*, which consist of the *Confucian Analects*, the *Book of Mencius*, the *Great Learning*, and the *Doctrine of the Mean*, were the first ones they were taught to read. The *Four Books* were the most important texts of Neo-Confucianist philosophy. Sometimes when the children were just beginning to learn the characters, they were given a sort of textbook to read. This was known as the *Three Characters Classic*, and was so called because each sentence in the book consisted of three characters arranged so that when recited they produced a rhythmic effect, and thus helped the children to memorize them more easily. This book was in reality a primer, and the very first statement in it is that "the nature of man is originally good." This is one of the fundamental ideas of Mencius' philosophy.

Place of Philosophy in Chinese Civilization

To the Westerner, who sees that the life of the Chinese people is permeated with Confucianism, it appears that Confucianism is a religion. As a matter of fact, however, Confucianism is no more a religion than, say, Platonism or Aristotelianism. It is true that the *Four Books* have been the Bible of the Chinese people, but in the *Four Books* there is no story of creation, and no mention of a heaven or hell.

Of course, the terms philosophy and religion are both ambiguous. Philosophy and religion may have entirely different meanings for dif-

1

ferent people. When men talk about philosophy or religion, they may have quite different ideas in their minds concerning them. For my part, what I call philosophy is systematic, reflective thinking on life. Every man, who has not yet died, is in life. But there are not many who think reflectively on life, and still fewer whose reflective thinking is systematic. A philosopher *must* philosophize; that is to say, he must think reflectively on life, and then express his thoughts systematically.

This kind of thinking is called reflective because it takes life as its object. The theory of life, the theory of the universe, and the theory of knowledge all emerge from this type of thinking. The theory of the universe arises because the universe is the background of life—the stage on which the drama of life takes place. The theory of knowledge emerges because thinking is itself knowledge. According to some philosophers of the West, in order to think, we must first find out what we can think; that is to say, before we start to think about life, we must first "think our thinking."

Such theories are all the products of reflective thinking. The very concept of life, the very concept of the universe, and the very concept of knowledge are also the products of reflective thinking. No matter whether we think about life or whether we talk about it, we are all in the midst of it. And no matter whether we think or speak about the universe, we are all a part of it. Now, what the philosophers call the universe is not the same as what the physicists have in mind when they refer to it. What the philosophers call the universe is *the totality of all that is*. It is equivalent to what the ancient Chinese philosopher, Hui Shih, called "The Great One," which is defined as "that which has nothing beyond." So everyone and everything must be considered part of the universe. When one thinks about the universe, one is thinking reflectively.

When we think about knowledge or speak about knowledge, this thinking and speaking are themselves knowledge. To use an expression of Aristotle, it is "thinking on thinking"; and this is reflective thinking. Here is the vicious circle which those philosophers follow who insist that before we think we must first think about our thinking; just as if we had another faculty with which we could think about thinking! As a matter of fact, the faculty with which we think about thinking is the very same faculty with which we think. If we are skeptical about the capacity of our thinking in regard to life and the universe, we have the same reason to be skeptical about the capacity of our thinking in regard to thinking.

Religion also has something to do with life. In the heart of every great religion there is a philosophy. In fact, every great religion *is* a philosophy with a certain amount of superstructure, which consists of superstitions, dogmas, rituals, and institutions. This is what I call religion.

If one understands the term religion in this sense, which does not really differ very much from common usage, one sees that Confucianism cannot be considered a religion. People have been accustomed to say that there were three religions in China: Confucianism, Taoism, and Buddhism. But Confucianism, as we have seen, is not a religion. As to Taoism, there is a distinction between Taoism as a philosophy, which is called *Tao chia* (the Taoist school), and the Taoist religion (*Tao chiao*). Their teachings are not only different; they are even contradictory. Taoism as a philosophy teaches the doctrine of following nature, while Taoism as a religion teaches the doctrine of working *against* nature. For instance, according to Lao Tzu and Chuang Tzu, life followed by death is the course of nature, and man should follow this natural course calmly. But the main teaching of the Taoist religion is the principle and technique of how to avoid death, which is expressly working *against* nature. The Taoist religion has the spirit of science, which is the conquering of nature. If one is interested in the history of Chinese science, the writings of the religious Taoists will supply much information.

As to Buddhism, there is also the distinction between Buddhism as a philosophy, which is called *Fo hsüeh* (the Buddhist learning), and Buddhism as a religion, which is called *Fo chiao* (the Buddhist religion). To the educated Chinese, Buddhist philosophy is much more interesting than the Buddhist religion. It is quite common to see both Buddhist monks and Taoist monks simultaneously participating in Chinese funeral services. The Chinese people take even their religion philosophically.

At present it is known to many Westerners that the Chinese people have been less concerned with religion than other people are. For instance, in one of his articles, "Dominant Ideas in the Formation of Chinese Culture," * Professor Derk Bodde says: "They [the Chinese]

* *Journal of American Oriental Society*, Vol. 62, No. 4, pp. 293-9. Reprinted in *China*, pp. 18-28 (H. F. MacNair, ed.), University of California Press, 1946.

are not a people for whom religious ideas and activities constitute an all important and absorbing part of life. . . . It is ethics (especially Confucian ethics), and not religion (at least not religion of a formal, organized type), that provided the spiritual basis in Chinese civilization. . . . All of which, of course, marks a difference of fundamental importance between China and most other major civilizations, in which a church and a priesthood have played a dominant role."

In one sense this is quite true. But one may ask: Why is this so? If the craving for what is beyond the present actual world is not one of the innate desires of mankind, why is it a fact that for most people religious ideas and activities constitute an all-important and absorbing part of life? If that craving is one of the fundamental desires of mankind, why should the Chinese people be an exception? When one says that it is ethics, not religion, that has provided the spiritual basis of Chinese civilization, does it imply that the Chinese are not conscious of those values which are higher than moral ones?

The values that are higher than the moral ones may be called super-moral values. The love of man is a moral value, while the love of God is a super-moral value. Some people may be inclined to call this kind of value a religious value. But in my opinion, this value is not confined to religion, unless what is meant here by religion differs from its meaning as described above. For instance, the love of God in Christianity is a religious value, while the love of God in the philosophy of Spinoza is not, because what Spinoza called God is really the universe. Strictly speaking, the love of God in Christianity is not really super-moral. This is because God, in Christianity, is a personality, and consequently the love of God by man is comparable to the love of a father by his son, which is a moral value. Therefore, the love of God in Christianity is open to question as a super-moral value. It is a quasi super-moral value, while the love of God in the philosophy of Spinoza is a real super-moral value.

To answer the above questions, I would say that the craving for something beyond the present actual world is one of the innate desires of mankind, and the Chinese people are no exception to this rule. They have not had much concern with religion because they have had so much concern with philosophy. They are not religious because they are philosophical. In philosophy they satisfy their craving for what is beyond the present actual world. In philosophy also they have the super-moral values expressed and appreciated, and in living according to philosophy these super-moral values are experienced.

According to the tradition of Chinese philosophy, its function is not the increase of positive knowledge (by positive knowledge I mean information regarding matters of fact), but the elevation of the mind —a reaching out for what is beyond the present actual world, and for the values that are higher than the moral ones. It was said by the *Lao-tzu*: "To work on learning is to increase day by day; to work on *Tao* (the Way, the Truth) is to decrease day by day." (See ch. 48.) I am not concerned with the difference between increasing and decreasing, nor do I quite agree with this saying of *Lao-tzu*. I quote it only to show that in the tradition of Chinese philosophy there is a distinction between working on learning and working on *Tao* (the Way). The purpose of the former is what I call the increase of positive knowledge, that of the latter is the elevation of the mind. Philosophy belongs in the latter category.

The view that the function of philosophy, especially metaphysics, is not the increase of positive knowledge, is expounded by the Viennese school in contemporary Western philosophy, though from a different angle and for a different purpose. I do not agree with this school that the function of philosophy is only the clarification of ideas, and that the nature of metaphysics is only a lyric of concepts. Nevertheless, in their arguments one can see quite clearly that philosophy, especially metaphysics, would become nonsense if it did attempt to give information regarding matters of fact.

Religion does give information in regard to matters of fact. But the information given by religion is not in harmony with that given by science. So in the West there has been the conflict between religion and science. Where science advances, religion retreats; and the authority of religion recedes before the advancement of science. The traditionalists regretted this fact and pitied the people who had become irreligious, considering them as having degenerated. They ought indeed to be pitied, if, besides religion, they had no other access to the higher values. When people get rid of religion and have no substitute, they also lose the higher values. They have to confine themselves to mundane affairs and have nothing to do with the spiritual ones. Fortunately, however, besides religion there is philosophy, which provides man with an access to the higher values—an access which is more direct than that provided by religion, because in philosophy, in order to be acquainted with the higher values, man need not take the roundabout way provided by prayers and rituals. The higher values with which man has become acquainted through philosophy are even purer than those acquired through religion, because they are not mixed with imagination and superstition. In the world of the future, man will have philosophy in the place of religion. This is consistent with Chinese tradition. It is not necessary that man should be religious, but it *is* necessary that he should be philosophical. When he is philosophical, he has the very best of the blessings of religion.

Problem and Spirit of Chinese Philosophy

The above is a general discussion of the nature and function of philosophy. In the following remarks I shall speak more specifically about Chinese philosophy. There is a main current in the history of Chinese philosophy, which may be called the spirit of Chinese philosophy. In order to understand this spirit, we must first make clear the problem that most Chinese philosophers have tried to solve.

There are all kinds and conditions of men. With regard to any one of these kinds, there is the highest form of achievement of which any one kind of man is capable. For instance, there are the men engaged in practical politics. The highest form of achievement in that class of men is that of the great statesman. So also in the field of art, the highest form of achievement of which artists are capable is that of the great artist. Although there are these different classes of men, yet all of them are men. What is the highest form of achievement of which a man *as a man* is capable? According to the Chinese philosophers, it is nothing less than being a sage, and the highest achievement of a sage is the identification of the individual with the universe. The problem is, if men want to achieve this identification, do they necessarily have to abandon society or even to negate life?

According to some philosophers, this is necessary. The Buddha said that life itself is the root and fountainhead of the misery of life. Likewise, Plato said that the body is the prison of the soul. And some of the Taoists said that life is an excrescence, a tumor, and death is to be taken as the breaking of the tumor. All these ideas represent a view which entails separation from what may be called the entangling net of the matter-corrupted world; and therefore, if the highest achievement of a sage is to be realized, the sage has to abandon society and even life itself. Only thus can the final liberation be attained. This kind of philosophy is what is generally known as "other-worldly philosophy."

There is another kind of philosophy which emphasizes what is in society, such as human relations and human affairs. This kind of philosophy speaks only about moral values, and is unable to or does not wish to speak of the super-moral ones. This kind of philosophy is generally described as "this-worldly." From the point of view of a this-worldly philosophy, an other-world philosophy is too idealistic, is of no practical use and is negative. From the point of view of an other-worldly philosophy, a this-world philosophy is too realistic, too superficial. It may be positive, but it is like the quick walking of a man who has taken the wrong road: the more quickly he walks the further he goes astray.

There are many people who say that Chinese philosophy is a this-world philosophy. It is difficult to state that these people are entirely right or entirely wrong. Taking a merely superficial view, people who hold this opinion cannot be said to be wrong, because according to their view, Chinese philosophy, regardless of its different schools of thought, is directly or indirectly concerned with government and ethics. On the surface, therefore, it is concerned chiefly with society, and not with the universe; with the daily functions of human relations, not hell and heaven; with man's present life, but not his life in a world to come. When he was once asked by a disciple about the meaning of death, Confucius replied: "Not yet understanding life, how can you understand death?" (*Analects*, XI, 11.) And Mencius said: "The sage is the acme of human relations" (*Mencius*, IVa, 2), which, taken literally, means that the sage is the morally perfect man in society. From a surface point of view, with the ideal man being of this world, it seems that what Chinese philosophy calls a sage is a person of a very different order from the Buddha of Buddhism and the saints of the Christian religion. Superficially, this would seem to be especially true of the Confucian sage. That is why, in ancient times, Confucius and the Confucianists were so greatly ridiculed by the Taoists.

This, however, is only a surface view of the matter. Chinese philosophy cannot be understood by oversimplification of this kind. So far as the main tenet of its tradition is concerned, if we understand it aright, it cannot be said to be wholly this-worldly, just as, of course, it cannot be said to be wholly other-worldly. It is both of this world *and* of the other world. Speaking about the Neo-Confucianism of the Sung Dynasty, one philosopher described it this way: "It is not divorced from daily ordinary activities, yet it goes straight to what antedated Heaven." This is what Chinese philosophy has striven for. Having this kind of spirit, it is at one and the same time both extremely idealistic and extremely realistic, and very practical, though not in a superficial way.

This-worldliness and other-worldliness stand in contrast to each other as do realism and idealism. The task of Chinese philosophy is to accomplish a synthesis out of these antitheses. That does not mean that they are to be abolished. They are still there, but they have been made into a synthetic whole. How can this be done? This is the problem which Chinese philosophy attempts to solve.

According to Chinese philosophy, the man who accomplishes this synthesis, not only in theory but also in deed, is the sage. He is both this-worldly and other-worldly. The spiritual achievement of the Chinese sage corresponds to the saint's achievement in Buddhism, and in Western religion. But the Chinese sage is not one who does not concern himself with the business of the world. His character is described as one of "sageliness within and kingliness without." That is to say, in his inner sageliness, he accomplishes spiritual cultivation; in his kingliness without, he functions in society. It is not necessary that the sage should be the actual head of the government in his society. From the standpoint of practical politics, for the most part, the sage certainly has no chance of being the head of the state. The saying "sageliness within and kingliness without" means only that he who has the noblest spirit should, theoretically, be king. As to whether he actually has or has not the chance of being king, that is immaterial.

Since the character of the sage is, according to Chinese tradition, one of sageliness within and kingliness without, the task of philosophy is to enable man to develop this kind of character. Therefore, what philosophy discusses is what the Chinese philosophers describe as the *Tao* (Way, or basic principles) of sageliness within and kingliness without.

This sounds like the Platonic theory of the philosopher-king. According to Plato, in an ideal state, the philosopher should be the

king or the king should be a philosopher; and in order to become a
philosopher, a man must undergo a long period of philosophical training before his mind can be "converted" from the world of changing
things to the world of eternal ideas. Thus according to Plato, as
according to the Chinese philosophers, the task of philosophy is to
enable man to have the character of sageliness within and kingliness
without. But according to Plato, when a philosopher becomes a king,
he does so against his will—in other words, it is something forced on
him, and entails a great sacrifice on his part. This is what was also
held by the ancient Taoists. There is the story of a sage who, being
asked by the people of a certain state to become their king, escaped
and hid himself in a mountain cave. But the people found the cave,
smoked him out and compelled him to assume the difficult task. (*Lü-
shih Ch'un-ch'iu*, I, 2.) This is one similarity between Plato and the
ancient Taoists, and it also shows the character of other-worldliness
in Taoist philosophy. Following the main tradition of Chinese philosophy, the Neo-Taoist, Kuo Hsiang of the third century A.D., revised this point.

According to Confucianism, the daily task of dealing with social
affairs in human relations is not something alien to the sage. Carrying on this task is the very essence of the development of the perfection of his personality. He performs it not only as a citizen of society,
but also as a "citizen of the universe," *t'ien min*, as Mencius called
it. He must be conscious of his being a citizen of the universe, otherwise his deeds would not have super-moral value. If he had the
chance to become a king he would gladly serve the people, thus performing his duty both as a citizen of society, and as a citizen of the
universe.

Since what is discussed in philosophy is the *Tao* (Way) of sageliness within and kingliness without, it follows that philosophy must
be inseparable from political thought. Regardless of the differences
between the schools of Chinese philosophy, the philosophy of every
school represents, at the same time, its political thought. This does
not mean that in the various schools of philosophy there are no
metaphysics, no ethics, no logic. It means only that all these factors
are connected with political thought in one way or another, just as
Plato's *Republic* represents his whole philosophy and at the same
time is his political thought.

For instance, the School of Names was known to indulge in such arguments as "a white horse is not a horse," which seems to have very little connection with politics. Yet the leader of this school, Kung-sun Lung, "wished to extend this kind of argument to rectify the relationship between names and facts in order to transform the world." We have seen in our world today how every statesman says his country wants only peace, but in fact, when he is talking about peace, he is often preparing for war. Here, then, there is a wrong relationship between names and facts. According to Kung-sun Lung, this kind of wrong relationship should be rectified. This is really the first step towards the transformation of the world.

Since the subject matter of philosophy is the *Tao* of sageliness within and kingliness without, the study of philosophy is not simply an attempt to acquire this kind of knowledge, but is also an attempt to develop this kind of character. Philosophy is not simply something to be *known*, but is also something to be *experienced*. It is not simply a sort of intellectual game, but something far more serious. As my colleague, Professor Y. L. Chin, has pointed out in an unpublished manuscript: "Chinese philosophers were all of them different grades of Socrates. This was so because ethics, politics, reflective thinking, and knowledge were unified in the philosopher; in him, knowledge and virtue were one and inseparable. His philosophy required that he live it; he was himself its vehicle. To live in accordance with his philosophical convictions was part of his philosophy. It was his business to school himself continually and persistently to that pure experience in which selfishness and egocentricity were transcended, so that he would be one with the universe. Obviously this process of schooling could not be stopped, for stopping it would mean the emergence of his ego and the loss of his universe. Hence cognitively he was eternally groping, and conatively he was eternally behaving or trying to behave. Since these could not be separated, in him there was the synthesis of the philosopher in the original sense of that term. Like Socrates, he did not keep office hours with his philosophy. Neither was he a dusty, musty philosopher, closeted in his study, sitting in a chair on the periphery of life. With him, philosophy was hardly ever merely a pattern of ideas exhibited for human understanding, but was a system of precepts internal to the conduct of the philosopher; and in extreme cases his philosophy might even be said to be his biography."

The Way in which Chinese Philosophers Expressed Themselves

A Western student beginning the study of Chinese philosophy is instantly confronted with two obstacles. One, of course, is the language barrier; the other is the peculiar way in which the Chinese philosophers have expressed themselves. I will speak about the latter first.

When one begins to read Chinese philosophical works, the first impression one gets is perhaps the briefness and disconnectedness of the sayings and writings of their authors. Open the *Confucian Analects* and you will see that each paragraph consists of only a few words, and there is hardly any connection between one paragraph and the next. Open a book containing the philosophy of Lao Tzu, and you will find that the whole book consists of about five thousand words—no longer than a magazine article; yet in it one will find the whole of his philosophy. A student accustomed to elaborate reasoning and detailed argument would be at a loss to understand what these Chinese philosophers were saying. He would be inclined to think that there was disconnectedness in the thought itself. If this were so, there would be no Chinese philosophy. For disconnected thought is hardly worthy of the name of philosophy.

It may be said that the apparent disconnectedness of the sayings and writings of the Chinese philosophers is due to the fact that these sayings and writings are not formal philosophical works. According to Chinese tradition, the study of philosophy is not a profession. Everyone should study philosophy just as in the West every one should go to church. The purpose of the study of philosophy is to enable a man, *as a man*, to be a man, not some particular kind of man. Other studies—not the study of philosophy—enable a man to be some special kind of man. So there were no professional philosophers; and non-professional philosophers did not have to produce formal philosophical writings. In China, there were far more philosophers who produced no formal philosophical writings than those who did. If one wishes to study the philosophy of these men, one has to go to the records of their sayings or the letters they wrote to disciples and friends. These letters did not belong to just one period in the life of the person who wrote them, nor were the records written only by a single person. Disconnectedness or even inconsistency between them is, therefore, to be expected.

The foregoing may explain why the writings and saying of some philosophers are disconnected; but it does not explain why they are brief. In some philosophic writings, such as those of Mencius and Hsün Tzu, one does find systematic reasoning and arguments. But in comparison with the philosophic writings of the West, they are still not articulate enough. The fact is that Chinese philosophers were accustomed to express themselves in the form of aphorisms, apothegms, or allusions, and illustrations. The whole book of *Lao-tzu* consists of aphorisms, and most of the chapters of the *Chuang-tzu* are full of allusions and illustrations. This is very obvious. But even in writings such as those of Mencius and Hsün Tzu, mentioned above, when compared with the philosophical writings of the West, there are still too many aphorisms, allusions, and illustrations. Aphorisms must be very brief; allusions and illustrations must be disconnected.

Aphorisms, allusions, and illustrations are thus not articulate enough. Their insufficiency in articulateness is compensated for, however, by their suggestiveness. Articulateness and suggestiveness are, of course, incompatible. The more an expression is articulate, the less it is suggestive—just as the more an expression is prosaic, the less it is poetic. The sayings and writings of the Chinese philosophers are so inarticulate that their suggestiveness is almost boundless.

Suggestiveness, not articulateness, is the ideal of all Chinese art, whether it be poetry, painting, or anything else. In poetry, what the poet intends to communicate is often not what is directly said in the poetry, but what is not said in it. According to Chinese literary tradition, in good poetry "the number of words is limited, but the ideas it suggests are limitless." So an intelligent reader of poetry reads what is outside the poem; and a good reader of books reads "what is between the lines." Such is the ideal of Chinese art, and this ideal is reflected in the way in which Chinese philosophers have expressed themselves.

The ideal of Chinese art is not without its philosophical background. In the twenty-sixth chapter of the *Chuang-tzu* it is said: "A basket-trap is for catching fish, but when one has got the fish, one need think no more about the basket. A foot-trap is for catching hares; but when one has got the hare, one need think no more about the trap. Words are for holding ideas, but when one has got the idea, one need no longer think about the words. If only I could find someone who had stopped thinking about words and could have him with me to talk to!" To talk with someone who has stopped thinking about words is not to talk with words. In the *Chuang-tzu* the statement is made that two sages met without speaking a single word, because "when their eyes met, the *Tao* was there." According to Taoism, the *Tao* (the Way) cannot be told, but only suggested. So when words are used, it is the suggestiveness of the words, and not their fixed denotations or connotations, that reveals the *Tao*. Words are something that should be forgotten when they have achieved their purpose. Why should we trouble ourselves with them any more than is necessary? This is true of the words and rhymes in poetry, and the lines and colors in painting.

During the third and fourth centuries A.D., the most influential philosophy was the Neo-Taoist School, which was known in Chinese history as the *hsüan hsüeh* (the dark or mystic learning). At that time there was a book entitled *Shih-shuo Hsin-yü*, which is a record of the clever sayings and romantic activities of the famous men of the age. Most of the sayings are very brief, some consisting of only a few words. It is stated in that book (ch. 4) that a very high official once asked a philosopher (the high official was himself a philosopher), what was the difference and similarity between Lao-Chuang (i.e., Lao Tzu and Chuang Tzu) and Confucius. The philosopher answered: "Are they not the same?" The high official was very much pleased with this answer, and instantly appointed the philosopher as his secretary. Since the answer consists of only three words in the Chinese language, this philosopher has been known as the three-word secretary. He could not say that Lao-Chuang and Confucius had nothing in common, nor could he say that they had everything in common. So he put his answer in the form of a question, which was really a good answer.

The brief sayings in the *Confucian Analects* and in the philosophy of the *Lao-tzu* are not simply conclusions from certain premises which have been lost. They are aphorisms full of suggestiveness. It is the suggestiveness that is attractive. One may gather together all the ideas one finds in the *Lao-tzu* and write them out in a new book consisting of fifty thousand or even five hundred thousand words. No matter how well this is done, however, it is just a new book. It may be read side by side with the original *Lao-tzu*, and may help people a great deal to understand the original, but it can never be a substitute for the original.

Kuo Hsiang, to whom I have already referred, was one of the great commentators on Chuang Tzu. His commentary was itself a classic of Taoist literature. He turned the allusions and metaphors of Chuang Tzu into a form of reasoning and argument, and translated his poems into prose of his own. His writing is much more articulate than that of Chuang Tzu. But between the suggestiveness of Chuang Tzu's original and the articulateness of Kuo Hsiang's commentary, people may still ask: Which is better? A monk of the Buddhist Ch'an or Zen school of a later period once said: "Everyone says that it was Kuo Hsiang who wrote a commentary on Chuang Tzu; I would say it was Chuang Tzu who wrote a commentary on Kuo Hsiang."

The Language Barrier

It is true of all philosophical writings that it is difficult for one to have a complete understanding and full appreciation of them if one cannot read them in the original. This is due to the language barrier. Because of the suggestive character of Chinese philosophical writings, the language barrier becomes even more formidable. The suggestiveness of the sayings and writings of the Chinese philosophers is something that can hardly be translated. When one reads them in translation, one misses the suggestiveness; and this means that one misses a great deal.

A translation, after all, is only an interpretation. When one translates a sentence from, say, the *Lao-tzu*, one gives one's own interpretation of its meaning. But the translation may convey only one idea, while as a matter of fact, the original may contain many other ideas besides the one given by the translator. The original is suggestive, but the translation is not, and cannot be. So it loses much of the richness inherent in the original.

There have been many translations of the *Lao-tzu* and the *Confucian Analects*. Each translator has considered the translations of others unsatisfactory. But no matter how well a translation is done, it is bound to be poorer than the original. It needs a combination of all the translations already made and many others not yet made, to reveal the richness of the *Lao-tzu* and the *Confucian Analects* in their original form.

Kumarajiva, of the fifth century A.D., one of the greatest translators of the Buddhist texts into Chinese, said that the work of translation is just like chewing food that is to be fed to others. If one cannot chew the food oneself, one has to be given food that has already been chewed. After such an operation, however, the food is bound to be poorer in taste and flavor than the original.

CHAPTER 2

THE BACKGROUND OF CHINESE
PHILOSOPHY

In the last chapter I said that philosophy is systematic reflective thinking on life. In thinking, the thinker is usually conditioned by the surroundings in which he lives. Being in certain surroundings, he feels life in a certain way, and there are therefore in his philosophy certain emphases or omissions, which constitute the characteristics of that philosophy.

This is true of an individual, as it is also true of a people. In this chapter I shall try to say something about the geographic and economic background of the Chinese people in order to show how and why Chinese civilization in general, and Chinese philosophy in particular, are what they are.

Geographic Background of the Chinese People

In the *Confucian Analects* Confucius said: "The wise man delights in water; the good man delights in mountains. The wise move; the good stay still. The wise are happy; the good endure." (VI, 21.) In reading this saying, I feel there is in it something which suggests a difference between the people of ancient China and those of ancient Greece.

China is a continental country. To the ancient Chinese their land was the world. There are two expressions in the Chinese language which can both be translated as the world. One is "all beneath the sky" and the other is "all within the four seas." To the people of a maritime country such as the Greeks, it would be inconceivable that expressions such as these could be synonymous. But that is what happens in the Chinese language, and it is not without reason.

From the time of Confucius until the end of the last century, no

Chinese thinkers had the experience of venturing out upon the high seas. Confucius and Mencius lived not far from the sea, if we think in modern terms of distance, yet in the *Analects,* Confucius mentions the sea only once. He is recorded as saying: "If my way is not to prevail, I shall get upon a raft and float out to the sea. He who will go with me will be [Chung] Yu." (V, 6.) Chung Yu was a disciple of Confucius known for his courage and bravery. It is said in the same work that when Chung Yu heard this statement, he was much pleased. Confucius, however, was not so pleased by Chung Yu's over-enthusiasm, and remarked: "Yu is more brave than myself. I do not know what to do with him." (*Ibid.*)

Mencius's reference to the sea is likewise brief. "He who has seen the sea," he says, "finds it difficult to think anything about other waters; and he who has wandered to the gate of the sage, finds it difficult to think anything about the words of others." (VIIa, 24.) Mencius is no better than Confucius, who thought only of "floating out to sea." How different were Socrates, Plato, and Aristotle, who lived in a maritime country and wandered from island to island!

Economic Background of the Chinese People

The ancient Chinese and Greek philosophers not only lived under different geographic conditions, but different economic ones as well. Since China is a continental country, the Chinese people have to make their living by agriculture. Even today the portion of the Chinese population engaged in farming is estimated at 75 to 80 percent. In an agrarian country land is the primary basis of wealth. Hence, throughout Chinese history, social and economic thinking and policy have centered around the utilization and distribution of land.

Agriculture in such an economy is equally important not only in peacetime but in wartime as well. During the period of the Warring States (480-222 B.C.), a period in many ways similar to our own, in which China was divided into many feudal kingdoms, every state devoted its greater attention to what were then called "the arts of agriculture and war." Finally the state of Ch'in, one of the seven leading states of the time, gained supremacy both in agriculture and war, and as a result succeeded in conquering the other states and thus bringing a unification to China for the first time in her history.

In the social and economic thinking of Chinese philosophers, there is a distinction between what they call "the root" and "the branch." "The root" refers to agriculture and "the branch" to commerce. The reason for this is that agriculture is concerned with production, while commerce is merely concerned with exchange. One must have production before one can have exchange. In an agrarian country, agriculture is the major form of production, and therefore throughout Chinese history, social and economic theories and policies have all attempted "to emphasize the root and slight the branch."

The people who deal with the "branch," that is, the merchants, were therefore looked down upon. They were the last and lowest of the four traditional classes of society, the other three being scholars, farmers, and artisans. The scholars were usually landlords, and the farmers were the peasants who actually cultivated the land. These were the two honorable professions in China. A family having "a tradition of studying and farming" was something of which to be proud.

Although the "scholars" did not actually cultivate the land themselves, yet since they were usually landlords, their fortunes were tied up with agriculture. A good or bad harvest meant their good or bad fortune, and therefore their reaction to the universe and their outlook on life were essentially those of the farmer. In addition their education gave them the power to express what an actual farmer felt but was incapable of expressing himself. This expression took the form of Chinese philosophy, literature, and art.

Value of Agriculture

In the *Lü-shih Ch'un-ch'iu*, a compendium of various schools of philosophy written in the third century B.C., there is a chapter titled "The Value of Agriculture." In this chapter a contrast is made between the mode of life of people who are engaged in the "root" occupation—the farmers, and that of those who are engaged in the "branch" occupation—the merchants. The farmers are primitive and simple and therefore always ready to accept commands. They are childlike and innocent and therefore unselfish. Their material properties are complex and difficult to move, and therefore they do not abandon their country when it is in danger. Merchants, on the other hand, are corrupt and therefore not obedient. They are treacherous and therefore selfish. They have simple properties which are easy to transport, and threfore they usually abandon their country when it is in danger. Hence this chapter asserts that not only is agriculture economically more important than commerce, but the mode of life of the farmers is also superior to that of the merchants. Herein lies "the value of agriculture." (XXVI, 3.) The author of this chapter found that the mode of life of people is conditioned by their economic background, and his evaluation of agriculture again shows that he was himself conditioned by the economic background of his time.

In this observation of the *Lü-shih Ch'un-ch'iu*, we find the root and source of the two main trends of Chinese thought, Taoism and Confucianism. They are poles apart from one another, yet they are also the two poles of one and the same axis. They both express, in one way or another, the aspirations and inspirations of the farmer.

"Reversal Is the Movement of Tao"

Before considering the difference between these two schools, let us first take up a theory which both of them maintained. This is that both in the sphere of nature and in that of man, when the development of anything brings it to one extreme, a reversal to the other extreme takes place; that is, to borrow an expression from Hegel, everything involves its own negation. This is one of the main theses of Lao Tzu's philosophy and also that of the *Book of Changes* as interpreted by the Confucianists. It was no doubt inspired by the movements of the sun and moon and the succession of the four seasons, to which farmers must pay particular heed in order to carry on their own work. In the Appendices of the *Book of Changes*, it is said: "When the cold goes, the warmth comes, and when the warmth comes, the cold goes." (Appendix III.) And again: "When the sun has reached its meridian, it declines, and when the moon has become full, it wanes." (Appendix I.) Such movements are referred to in the Appendices as "returning." Thus Appendix I says: "In returning we see the mind of Heaven and Earth." Similarly in the *Lao-tzu* we find the words: "Reversal is the movement of the *Tao*." (Ch. 40.)

This theory has had a great effect upon the Chinese people and has contributed much to their success in overcoming the many difficulties which they have encountered in their long history. Convinced of this theory, they remain cautious even in time of prosperity, and hopeful even in time of extreme danger. In the late war, the concept provided the Chinese people with a sort of psychological weapon, so that even in its darkest period, most people lived on the hope which was expressed in the phrase: "The dawn will soon come." It was this "will to believe" that helped the Chinese people to go through the war.

This theory has also provided the principal argument for the doctrine of the golden mean, favored by Confucianist and Taoist alike. "Never too much" has been the maxim of both. For according to them, it is better for one to be wrong by having too little, than to be wrong by having too much, and to be wrong by leaving things undone, than to be wrong by overdoing them. For by having too much and overdoing, one runs the risk of getting the opposite of what one wants.

Idealization of Nature

Taoism and Confucianism differ because they are the rationalization or theoretical expression of different aspects of the life of the farmers. The farmers are simple in their living and innocent in their thought. Seeing things from their point of view, the Taoists idealized the simplicity of primitive society and condemned civilization. They also idealized the innocence of children and despised knowledge. In the *Lao-tzu* it is said: "Let us have a small country with few inhabitants. . . . Let the people return to the use of knotted cords [for keeping records]. Let them obtain their food sweet, their clothing beautiful, their homes comfortable, their rustic tasks pleasurable. The neighbouring state might be so near at hand that one could hear the cocks crowing in it and dogs barking. But the people would grow old and die without ever having been there." (Ch. 80.) Is this not an idyllic picture of a farmer's country?

The farmers are always in contact with nature, so they admire and love nature. This admiration and love were developed by the Taoists to the fullest extent. They made a sharp distinction between what is of nature and what is of man, the natural and the artificial. According to them, what is of nature is the source of human happiness and what is of man is the root of all human suffering. They were, as the Confucianist Hsün Tzu puts it, "blinded by nature and had no knowledge of man." (*Hsün-tzu*, ch. 21.) As the final development of this trend of thinking, the Taoists maintained that the highest achievement in the spiritual cultivation of a sage lies in the identification of himself with the whole of nature, i.e., the universe.

Family System

The farmers have to live on their land, which is immovable, and the same is true of the scholar landlords. Unless one has special talent, or is especially lucky, one has to live where one's father or grandfather lived, and where one's children will continue to live. That is to say, the family in the wider sense must live together for economic reasons. Thus there developed the Chinese family system, which was no doubt one of the most complex and well-organized in the world. A great deal of Confucianism is the rational justification or theoretical expression of this social system.

The family system was the social system of China. Out of the five traditional social relationships, which are those between sovereign and subject, father and son, elder and younger brother, husband and wife, and friend and friend, three are family relationships. The remaining two, though not family relationships, can be conceived of in terms of the family. Thus the relationship between sovereign and subject can be conceived of in terms of that between father and son, and that between friend and friend in terms of the one between elder and younger brother. So, indeed, was the way in which they were usually conceived. But these are only the major family relationships, and there were many more. In the Erh Ya, which is the oldest dictionary of the Chinese language, dating from before the Christian era, there are more than one hundred terms for various family relationships, most of which have no equivalent in the English language.

For the same reason ancestor worship developed. In a family living in a particular place, the ancestor worshiped was usually the first of the family who had established himself and his descendants there on the land. He thus became the symbol of the unity of the family, and such a symbol was indispensable for a large and complex organization.

A great part of Confucianism is the rational justification of this social system, or its theoretical expression. Economic conditions prepared its basis, and Confucianism expressed its ethical significance. Since this social system was the outgrowth of certain economic conditions, and these conditions were again the product of their geographical surroundings, to the Chinese people both the system and its theoretical expression were very natural. Because of this, Confucianism naturally became the orthodox philosophy and remained so until the invasion of industrialization from modern Europe and America changed the economic basis of Chinese life.

This-worldliness and Other-worldliness

Confucianism is the philosophy of social organization, and so is also the philosophy of daily life. Confucianism emphasizes the social responsibilities of man, while Taoism emphasizes what is natural and spontaneous in him. In the *Chuang-tzu*, it is said that the Confucianists roam within the bounds of society, while the Taoists roam beyond it. In the third and fourth centuries A.D., when Taoism again became influential, people used to say that Confucius valued *ming chiao* (the teaching of names denoting the social relationships), while Lao Tzu and Chuang Tzu valued *tzu jan* (spontaneity or naturalness). These two trends of Chinese philosophy correspond roughly to the traditions of classicism and romanticism in Western thought. Read the poems of Tu Fu and Li Po, and one sees in them the difference between Confucianism and Taoism. These two great poets lived during the same period (eighth century A.D.), and concurrently expressed in their poems the two main traditions of Chinese thought.

Because it "roams within the bounds of society," Confucianism appears more this-worldly than Taoism, and because it "roams beyond the bound of society," Taoism appears more other-worldly than Confucianism. These two trends of thought rivaled one another, but also complemented each other. They exercised a sort of balance of power. This gave to the Chinese people a better sense of balance in regard to this-worldliness and other-worldliness.

There were Taoists in the third and fourth centuries who attempted to make Taoism closer to Confucianism, and there were also Confucianists in the eleventh and twelfth centuries who attempted to make Confucianism closer to Taoism. We call these Taoists the Neo-Taoists and these Confucianists the Neo-Confucianists. It was these movements that made Chinese philosophy both of this world and of the other world, as I pointed out in the last chapter.

Chinese Art and Poetry

The Confucianists took art as an instrument for moral education. The Taoists had no formal treatises on art, but their admiration of the free movement of the spirit and their idealization of nature gave profound inspiration to the great artists of China. This being the case, it is no wonder that most of the great artists of China took nature as their subject. Most of the masterpieces of Chinese painting are paintings of landscapes, animals and flowers, trees and bamboos. In a landscape painting, at the foot of a mountain or the bank of a stream, one always finds a man sitting, appreciating the beauty of nature and contemplating the *Tao* or Way that transcends both nature and man.

Likewise in Chinese poetry we find such poems as that by T'ao Ch'ien (A.D. 372-427):

> I built my hut in a zone of human habitation,
> Yet near me there sounds no noise of horse or coach,
> Would you know how that is possible?
> A heart that is distant creates a wilderness round it.
> I pluck chrysanthemums under the eastern hedge,
> Then gaze long at the distant summer hills.
> The mountain air is fresh at the dusk of day;
> The flying birds two by two return.
> In these things there lies a deep meaning;
> Yet when we would express it, words suddenly fail us.*

Here we have Taoism at its best.

The Methodology of Chinese Philosophy

In Chinese philosophy, the farmer's outlook not .only conditioned its content, such as that reversal is the movement of the *Tao*, but, what is more important, it also conditioned its methodology. Professor Northrop has said that there are two major types of concepts, that achieved by intuition and that by postulation. "A concept by intuition," he says, "is one which denotes, and the complete meaning of which is given by, something which is immediately apprehended. 'Blue' in the sense of the sensed color is a concept by intuition. . . .

* Translated by Arthur Waley.

A concept by postulation is one the complete meaning of which is designated by the postulates of the deductive theory in which it occurs. . . . 'Blue' in the sense of the number of a wave-length in electro-magnetic theory is a concept by postulation." *

Northrop also says that there are three possible types of concepts by intuition: "The concept of the differentiated aesthetic continuum. The concept of the indefinite or undifferentiated aesthetic continuum. The concept of the differentiation." (*Ibid.*, p. 187.) According to him, "Confucianism may be defined as the state of mind in which the concept of the indeterminate intuited manifold moves into the background of thought and the concrete differentiations in their relativistic, humanistic, transitory comings and goings form the content of philosophy." (*Ibid.*, p. 205.) But in Taoism, it is the concept of the indefinite or undifferentiated aesthetic continuum that forms the content of philosophy. (*Ibid.*)

I do not quite agree with all Northrop has said in this essay, but I think he has here grasped the fundamental difference betweeen Chinese and Western philosophy. When a student of Chinese philosophy begins to study Western philosophy, he is glad to see that the Greek philosophers also made the distinction between Being and Non-being, the limited and the unlimited. But he feels rather surprised to find that the Greek philosophers held that Non-being and the unlimited are inferior to Being and the limited. In Chinese philosophy the case is just the reverse. The reason for this difference is that Being and the limited are the distinct, while Non-being and the unlimited are the indistinct. Those philosophers who start with concepts by postulation have a liking for the distinct, while those who start with intuition value the indistinct.

If we link what Northrop has pointed out here with what I mentioned at the beginning of this chapter, we see that the concept of the differentiated aesthetic continuum, from which come both the concept of the undifferentiated aesthetic continuum and that of differentiation (*ibid.*, p. 187), is basically the concept of the farmers. What the farmers have to deal with, such as the farm and crops, are all things which they immediately apprehend. And in their primitivity and innocence, they value what they thus immediately appre-

* Filmer S. C. Northrop, "The Complementary Emphases of Eastern Intuition Philosophy and Western Scientific Philosophy," in *Philosophy, East and West*, C. A. Moore, ed., p. 187, Princeton University Press, 1946.

hend. It is no wonder then, that their philosophers likewise take the immediate apprehension of things as the starting point of their philosophy.

This also explains why epistemology has never developed in Chinese philosophy. Whether the table that I see before me is real or illusory, and whether it is only an idea in my mind or is occupying objective space, was never seriously considered by Chinese philosophers. No such epistemological problems are to be found in Chinese philosophy (save in Buddhism, which came from India), since epistemological problems arise only when a demarcation between the subject and the object is emphasized. And in the aesthetic continuum, there is no such demarcation. In it the knower and the known is one whole.

This also explains why the language used by Chinese philosophy is suggestive but not articulate. It is not articulate, because it does not represent concepts in any deductive reasoning. The philosopher only tells us what he sees. And because of this, what he tells is rich in content, though terse in words. This is the reason why his words are suggestive rather than precise.

Maritime Countries and Continental Countries

The Greeks lived in a maritime country and maintained their prosperity through commerce. They were primarily merchants. And what merchants have to deal with first are the abstract numbers used in their commercial accounts, and only then with concrete things that may be immediately apprehended through these numbers. Such numbers are what Northrop called concepts by postulation. Hence Greek philosophers likewise took the concept by postulation as their starting point. They developed mathematics and mathematical reasoning. That is why they had epistemological problems and why their language was so articulate.

But merchants are also townsmen. Their activities demand that they live together in towns. Hence they have a form of social organization not based on the common interest of the family so much as on that of the town. This is the reason why the Greeks organized their society around the *city* state, in contrast with the Chinese social system, which may be called that of the *family* state, because under it the state is conceived of in terms of the family. In a city state the social organization is not autocratic, because among the same class of townsmen, there is no moral reason why one should be more important than, or superior to, another. But in a family state the social organization is autocratic and hierarchic, because in a family the authority of the father is naturally superior to that of the son.

The fact that the Chinese were farmers also explains why China failed to have an industrial revolution, which is instrumental for the introduction of the modern world. In the *Lieh-tzu* there is a story which says that the Prince of the State of Sung once asked a clever artisan to carve a piece of jade into the leaf of a tree. After three years the artisan completed it, and when the artificial leaf was put upon the tree, it was made so wonderfully that no one could distinguish it from the real leaves. Thereupon the Prince was much pleased. But when Lieh Tzu heard it, he said: "If nature took three years to produce one leaf, there would be few trees with leaves on them!" (*Lieh-tzu*, ch. 8.) This is the view of one who admires the natural and condemns the artificial. The way of life of the farmers is to follow nature. They admire nature and condemn the artificial, and in their primitivity and innocence, they are easily made content. They desire no change, nor can they conceive of any change. In China there have been not a few notable inventions or discoveries, but we often find that these were discouraged rather than encouraged.

With the merchants of a maritime country conditions are otherwise. They have greater opportunity to see different people with different customs and different languages; they are accustomed to change and are not afraid of novelty. Nay, in order to have a good sale for their goods, they have to encourage novelty in the manufacture of what they are going to sell. It is no accident that in the West, the industrial revolution was first started in England, which is also a maritime country maintaining her prosperity through commerce.

What was quoted earlier in this chapter from the *Lü-shih Ch'un-ch'iu* about merchants can also be said of the people of maritime countries, provided that, instead of saying that they are corrupt and treacherous, we say that they are refined and intelligent. We can also paraphrase Confucius by saying that the people of maritime countries are the wise, while those of continental countries are the good.

And so we repeat what Confucius said: "The wise delight in water; the good delight in mountains. The wise move; the good stay still. The wise are happy; the good endure."

It is beyond the scope of this chapter to enumerate evidences to prove the relationship between the geographic and economic conditions of Greece and England on the one hand, and the development of Western scientific thought and democratic institutions on the other. But the fact that the geographic and economic conditions of Greece and England are quite different from those of China suffices to constitute a negative proof for my thesis in regard to Chinese history as mentioned in this chapter.

The Permanent and the Changeable in Chinese Philosophy

The advancement of science has conquered geography, and China is no longer isolated "within the four seas." She is having her industrialization too, and though much later than the Western world, it is better late than never. It is not correct to say that the East has been invaded by the West. Rather it is a case in which the medieval has been invaded by the modern. In order to live in a modern world, China has to be modern.

One question remains to be asked: If Chinese philosophy has been so linked with the economic conditions of the Chinese people, does what has been expressed in Chinese philosophy possess validity only for people living under those conditions?

The answer is yes and no. In the philosophy of any people or any time, there is always a part that possesses value only in relation to the economic conditions of that people or of that time, but there is always another part that is more than this. That which is not relative has lasting value. I hesitate to say that it is absolute truth, because to determine what is absolute truth is too great a task for any human being, and is reserved for God alone, if there be one.

Let us take an instance in Greek philosophy. The rational justification of the slave system by Aristotle must be considered as a theory that is relative to the economic conditions of Greek life. But to say this is not to say that there is nothing that is not relative in the social philosophy of Aristotle. The same holds true for Chinese thought. When China is industrialized, the old family system must go, and with it will go its Confucianistic rational justification. But to say this

is not to say that there is nothing that is not relative in the social
philosophy of Confucianism.

The reason for this is that the society of ancient Greece and
ancient China, though different, both belong to the general category
which we call society. Theories which are the theoretical expression
of Greek or Chinese society, are thus also in part expressions of society in general. Though there is in them something that pertains only
to Greek or Chinese societies *per se,* there must also be something
more universal that pertains to society in general. It is this latter
something that is not relative and possesses lasting value.

The same is true of Taoism. The Taoist theory is certainly wrong
which says that the utopia of mankind is the primitivity of a bygone
age. With the idea of progress, we moderns think that the ideal state
of human existence is something to be created in the future, not
something that was lost in the past. But what some moderns think
of as the ideal state of human existence, such as anarchism, is not
wholly dissimilar from that thought of by the Taoists.

Philosophy also gives us an ideal of life. A part of that ideal, as
given by the philosophy of a certain people or a certain time, must
pertain only to the kind of life resulting from the social conditions of
that people or that time. But there must also be a part that pertains
to life in general, and so is not relative but has lasting value. This
seems to be illustrated in the case of the Confucianist theory of an
ideal life. According to this theory, the ideal life is one which, though
having a very high understanding of the universe, yet remains within
the bounds of the five basic human relationships. The nature of these
human relationships may change according to circumstances. But the
ideal itself does not change. One is wrong, then, when one insists that
since some of the five human relationships have to go, therefore the
Confucianist ideal of life must go as well. And one is also wrong
when one insists that since this ideal of life is desirable, therefore all
the five human relationships must likewise be retained. One must
make a logical analysis in order to distinguish between what is permanent and what is changeable in the history of philosophy. Every philosophy has that which is permanent, and all philosophies have something in common. This is why philosophies, though different, can yet
be compared with one another and translated one in terms of the
other.

Will the methodology of Chinese philosophy change? That is to say, will the new Chinese philosophy cease to confine itself to "concept by intuition?" Certainly it will, and there is no reason why it should not. In fact, it is already changing. In regard to this change, I shall have more to say in the last chapter of this book.

CHAPTER 3

THE ORIGIN OF THE SCHOOLS

In the last chapter I said that Confucianism and Taoism are the two main streams of Chinese thought. They became so only after a long evolution, however, and from the fifth through the third centuries B.C. they were only two among many other rival schools of thought. During that period the number of schools was so great that the Chinese referred to them as the "hundred schools."

Ssu-ma T'an and the Six Schools

Later historians have attempted to make a classification of these "hundred schools." The first to do so was Ssu-ma T'an (died 110 B.C.), father of Ssu-ma Ch'ien (145-ca. 86 B.C.), and the author with him of China's first great dynastic history, the *Shih Chi* or *Historical Records*. In the last chapter of this work Ssu-ma Ch'ien quotes an essay by his father, titled "On the Essential Ideas of the Six Schools." In this essay Ssu-ma T'an classifies the philosophers of the preceding several centuries into six major schools, as follows:

The first is the *Yin-Yang chia* or *Yin-Yang* school, which is one of cosmologists. It derives its name from the *Yin* and *Yang* principles, which in Chinese thought are regarded as the two major principles of Chinese cosmology, *Yin* being the female principle, and *Yang* the male principle, the combination and interaction of which is believed by the Chinese to result in all universal phenomena.

The second school is the *Ju chia* or School of Literati. This school is known in Western literature as the Confucianist school, but the word *ju* literally means "literatus" or scholar. Thus the Western title is somewhat misleading, because it misses the implication that the followers of this school were scholars as well as thinkers; they, above all others, were the teachers of the ancient classics and thus the inheritors of the ancient cultural legacy. Confucius, to be sure, is the leading figure of this school and may rightly be considered as its founder. Nevertheless the term *ju* not only denotes "Confucian" or "Confucianist," but has a wider implication as well.

The third school is that of the *Mo chia* or Mohist school. This school had a close-knit organization and strict discipline under the leadership of Mo Tzu. Its followers actually called themselves the Mohists. Thus the title of this school is not an invention of Ssu-ma T'an, as were some of the other schools.

The fourth school is the *Ming chia* or School of Names. The followers of this school were interested in the distinction between, and relation of, what they called "names" and "actualities."

The fifth school is the *Fa chia* or Legalist school. The Chinese word *fa* means pattern or law. The school derived from a group of statesmen who maintained that good government must be one based on a fixed code of law instead of on the moral institutions which the literati stressed for government.

The sixth school is the *Tao-Te chia* or School of the Way and its Power. The followers of this school centered their metaphysics and social philosophy around the concept of Non-being, which is the *Tao* or Way, and its concentration in the individual as the natural virtue of man, which is *Te*, translated as "virtue" but better rendered as the "power" that inheres in any individual thing. This group, called by Ssu-ma T'an the *Tao-Te* school, was later known simply as the *Tao chia*, and is referred to in Western literature as the Taoist school. As pointed out in the first chapter, it should be kept carefully distinct from the Taoist religion.

Liu Hsin and His Theory of the Beginning of the Schools

The second historian who attempted to classify the "hundred schools" was Liu Hsin (ca. 46 B.C.-A.D. 23). He was one of the greatest scholars of his day, and, with his father Liu Hsiang, made a collation of the books in the Imperial Library. The resulting descriptive catalogue of the Imperial Library, known as the "Seven Summaries," was taken by Pan Ku (A.D. 32-92) as the basis for the chapter, *Yi Wen Chih* or "Treatise on Literature," contained in his dynastic history, the *History of the Former Han Dynasty*. In this "Treatise" we see that Liu Hsin classifies the "hundred schools" into ten main groups. Out of these, six are the same as those listed by Ssu-ma T'an.

The other four are the *Tsung-Heng chia* or School of Diplomatists, *Tsa chia* or School of Eclectics, *Nung chia* or School of Agrarians, and *Hsiao-shuo chia* or School of Story Tellers. In conclusion, Liu Hsin writes: "The various philosophers consist of ten schools, but there are only nine that need be noticed." By this statement he means to say that the School of Story Tellers lacks the importance of the other schools.

In this classification itself, Liu Hsin did not go very much further than Ssu-ma T'an had done. What was new, however, was his attempt for the first time in Chinese history to trace systematically the historical origins of the different schools.

Liu Hsin's theory has been greatly elaborated by later scholars, especially by Chang Hsüeh-ch'eng (1738-1801) and the late Chang Ping-lin. In essence, it maintains that in the early Chou dynasty (1122?-255 B.C.), before the social institutions of that age disintegrated, there was "no separation between officers and teachers." In other words the officers of a certain department of the government were at the same time the transmitters of the branch of learning pertaining to that department. These officers, like the feudal lords of the day, held their posts on a hereditary basis. Hence there was then only "official learning" but no "private teaching." That is to say, nobody taught any branch of learning as a private individual. Any such teaching was carried on only by officers in their capacity as members of one or another department of the government.

According to this theory, however, when the Chou ruling house lost its power during the later centuries of the Chou dynasty, the officers of the governmental departments lost their former positions and scattered throughout the country. They then turned to the teaching of their special branches of knowledge in a private capacity. Thus they were then no longer "officers," but only private "teachers." And it was out of this separation between teachers and officers that the different schools arose.

Liu Hsin's whole analysis reads as follows: "The members of the *Ju* school had their origin in the Ministry of Education. . . . This school delighted in the study of the *Liu Yi* [the Six Classics or six liberal arts] and paid attention to matters concerning human-heartedness and righteousness. They regarded Yao and Shun [two ancient sage emperors supposed to have lived in the twenty-fourth and twenty-third centuries B.C.] as the ancestors of their school, and

King Wen [1120?-1108? B.C. of the Chou dynasty] and King Wu [son of King Wen] as brilliant exemplars. To give authority to their teaching, they honored Chung-ni [Confucius] as an exalted teacher. Their teaching is the highest truth. 'That which is admired must be tested.' The glory of Yao and Shun, the prosperity of the dynasties of Yin and Chou, and the achievements of Chung-ni are the results discovered by testing their teaching.

"Those of the Taoist school had their origin in the official historians. By studying the historical examples of success and failure, preservation and destruction, and calamity and prosperity, from ancient to recent times, they learned how to hold what is essential and to grasp the fundamental. They guarded themselves with purity and emptiness, and with humbleness and meekness maintained themselves. . . . Herein lies the strong point of this school.

"Those of the Yin-Yang school had their origin in the official astronomers. They respectfully followed luminous heaven, and the successive symbols of the sun and moon, the stars and constellations, and the divisions of times and seasons. Herein lies the strong point of this school.

"Those of the Legalist school had their origin in the Ministry of Justice. They emphasized strictness in rewarding and punishing, in order to support a system of correct conduct. Herein lies the strong point of this school.

"Those of the School of Names had their origin in the Ministry of Ceremonies. For the ancients, where titles and positions differed, the ceremonies accorded to them were also different. Confucius has said: 'If names be incorrect, speech will not follow its natural sequence. If speech does not follow its natural sequence, nothing can be established.' Herein lies the strong point of this school.

"Those of the Mohist school had their origin in the Guardians of the Temple. The temple was built with plain wooden rafters and thatched roofs; hence their teaching emphasized frugality. The temple was the place where the Three Elders and Five Experienced Men were honored; hence their teaching emphasized universal love. The ceremony of selecting civil officials and that of military exercises were also held in the temple; hence their teaching emphasized the preferment of virtue and ability. The temple was the place for sacrifice to ancestors and reverence to fathers; hence their teaching was to honor the spirits. They accepted the traditional teaching of following the

four seasons in one's conduct; hence their teaching was against fatal-
ism. They accepted the traditional teaching of exhibiting filial piety
throughout the world; hence they taught the doctrine of 'agreeing
with the superior.' Herein lies the strong point of this school.

"Those of the Diplomatist school had their origin in the Ministry
of Embassies. . . . [They taught the art of] following general orders
[in diplomacy], instead of following literal instructions. Herein lies
the strength of their teaching.

"Those of the Eclectic school had their origin in the Councillors.
They drew both from the Confucianists and the Mohists, and har-
monized the School of Names and the Legalists. They knew that the
nation had need of each of these, and saw that kingly government
should not fail to unite all. Herein lies the strong point of this
school.

"Those of the Agricultural school had their origin in the Ministry
of Soil and Grain. They taught the art of sowing the various kinds
of grain and urged people to plow and to cultivate the mulberry so
that the clothing and food of the people would be sufficient. . . .
Herein lies the strong point of this school.

"Those of the School of Story Tellers had their origin in the
Petty Offices. This school was created by those who picked up the
talk of streets and alleys and repeated what they heard wherever they
went. . . . Even if in their teaching but a single word can be chosen,
still there is some contribution." ("Treatise on Literature" in the
History of the Former Han Dynasty.)

This is what Liu Hsin says about the historical origin of the ten
schools. His interpretation of the significance of the schools is inadequate, and his attribution of certain of them to certain "Minis-
tries" is in some cases arbitrary. For instance, in describing the teaching of the Taoists, he touches only on the ideas of Lao Tzu, and
omits those of Chuang Tzu altogether. Moreover, there appears to
be no similarity between the teaching of the School of Names and
the functions of the Ministry of Ceremonies, save that both emphasized the making of distinctions.

A Revision of Liu Hsin's Theory

Yet though the details of Liu Hsins's theory may be wrong, his
attempt to trace the origin of the schools to certain political and

social circumstances certainly represents a right point of view. I have quoted him at length because his description of the various schools is itself a classic in Chinese historiography.

The study of Chinese history has made great progress in China in recent times, especially during the few years just before the Japanese invasion of 1937. In the light of recent research, therefore, I have formed a theory of my own in regard to the origin of the philosophic schools. In spirit this theory agrees with that of Liu Hsin, but it must be expressed in a different way. This means that things have to be seen from a new angle.

Let us imagine what China looked like politically and socially in, say, the tenth century B.C. At the top of the political and social structure, there was the King of the Chou royal house, who was the "common lord" of all the different states. Under him were hundreds of states, each owned and governed by its Princes. Some of them were established by the founders of the Chou dynasty, who had allotted the newly conquered territory as feudal fiefs to their relatives. Others were ruled by the former rivals of the Chou house, who now, however, acknowledged the King of Chou as their "common lord."

Within each state, under the Prince, the land was again divided into many fiefs, each with its own feudal lord, who were relatives of the Prince. At that time, political power and economic control were one and the same. Those who had the land were the political and economic masters of it, and of the people who lived on it. They were the *chün tzu*, a term which literally means "sons of the Princes," but which was used as a common designation of the class of the feudal lords.

The other social class was that of the *hsiao jen*, meaning small men, or *shu min*, meaning common people or the mass. These were the serfs of the feudal lords, who cultivated the land for the *chün tzu* in time of peace, and fought for them in time of war.

The aristocrats were not only the political rulers and landlords, but also the only persons who had a chance to receive an education. Thus the houses of the feudal lords were not only centers of political and economic power, but also centers of learning. Attached to them were officers who possessed specialized knowledge along various lines. But the common people, for their part, had no chance to become educated, so that among them there were no men of learning. This is the fact behind Liu Hsin's theory that in the early Chou dynasty "there was no separation between officers and teachers."

This feudal system was formally abolished by the First Emperor of the Ch'in dynasty in 221 B.C. But hundreds of years before that, the system had already begun to disintegrate, whereas thousands of years later, economic remnants of feudalism still remained in the form of the power of the landlord class.

Historians of modern time are still not agreed as to what were the causes of the disintegration of the feudal system. Nor is it within the scope of this chapter to discuss these causes. For the present purpose, it is sufficient to say that in Chinese history the period between the seventh and third centuries B.C. was one of great social and political transformation and change.

We are not sure just when the disintegration of the feudal system began. Already as early as the seventh century there were aristocrats who through the wars of the time, or for other reasons, lost their lands and titles, and thus fell to the level of the common people. There were also common people who through skill or favoritism became high officials of the state. This illustrates the real significance of the disintegration of the Chou dynasty. It was not only the disintegration of the political power of a particular royal house, but—and this is more important—of an entire social system.

With this disintegration, the former official representatives of the various branches of learning became scattered among the common people. They had either been actual nobles themselves, or had been specialists holding hereditary offices in the service of the aristocratic ruling families. This is the significance of a quotation made by Liu Hsin from Confucius in the course of the same "Treatise" partially quoted from above: "When ceremonies become lost [at the court], it is necessary to search for them in the countryside."

Thus when these former nobles or officials scattered throughout the country, they maintained a livelihood by carrying on, in a private capacity, their specialized abilities or skills. Those of them who expressed their ideas to other private individuals became professional "teachers," and thus there arose the separation between the teacher and the officer.

The word "school" in this chapter is a translation of the Chinese word *chia*, which at the same time is used to denote a family or home. Hence it suggests something personal or private. There could be no *chia* of thought before there were persons who taught their own ideas in a private capacity.

Likewise there were different kinds of *chia* because these teachers were specialists in varying branches of learning and of the arts. Thus there were some who were specialists in the teaching of the classics and the practicing of ceremonies and music. These were known as the *ju* or literati. There were also specialists in the art of war. These were the *hsieh* or knights. There were specialists in the art of speaking, who were known as the *pien-che* or debaters. There were specialists in magic, divination, astrology, and numerology, who were known as the *fang-shih*, or practitioners of occult arts. There were also the practical politicians who could act as private advisers to the feudal rulers, and who were known as *fang-shu chih shih* or "men of methods." And finally, there were some men who possessed learning and talent, but who were so embittered by the political disorders of their time that they retired from human society into the world of nature. These were known as the *yin-che* or hermits or recluses.

According to my theory, it is from these six different kinds of people that the six schools of thought as listed by Ssu-ma T'an originated. Paraphrasing Liu Hsin, therefore, I would say:

Members of the *Ju* school had their origin in the literati.

Members of the Mohist school had their origin in the knights.

Members of the Taoist school had their origin in the hermits.

Members of the School of Names had their origin in the debators.

Members of the *Yin-Yang* school had their origin in the practitioners of occult arts.

Members of the Legalist school had their origin in the "men of methods."

The explanations of these statements will be found in the chapters that follow.

CHAPTER 4

CONFUCIUS, THE FIRST
TEACHER

CONFUCIUS is the latinized name of the person who has been known in China as K'ung Tzu or Master K'ung.* His family name was K'ung and his personal name Ch'iu. He was born in 551 B.C. in the state of Lu, in the southern part of the present Shantung province in eastern China. His ancestors had been members of the ducal house of the state of Sung, which was descended from the royal house of Shang, the dynasty that had preceded the Chou. Because of political troubles, the family, before the birth of Confucius, had lost its noble position and migrated to Lu.

The most detailed account of Confucius' life is the biography which comprises the forty-seventh chapter of the *Shih Chi* or *Historical Records* (China's first dynastic history, completed ca. 86 B.C.). From this we learn that Confucius was poor in his youth, but entered the government of Lu and by the time he was fifty had reached high official rank. As a result of political intrigue, however, he was soon forced to resign his post and go into exile. For the next thirteen years he traveled from one state to another, always hoping to find an opportunity to realize his ideal of political and social reform. Nowhere, however, did he succeed, and finally as an old man he returned to Lu, where he died three years later in 479 B. C.

Confucius and the Six Classics

In the last chapter I said that the rise of the philosophic schools began with the practice of private teaching. So far as modern scholar-

* The word "Tzu" or "Master" is a polite suffix added to names of most philosophers of the Chou Dynasty, such as Chuang Tzu, Hsün Tzu, etc., and meaning "Master Chuang," "Master Hsün," etc.

ship can determine, Confucius was the first person in Chinese history thus to teach large numbers of students in a private capacity, by whom he was accompanied during his travels in different states. According to tradition, he had several thousand students, of whom several tens became famous thinkers and scholars. The former number is undoubtedly a gross exaggeration, but there is no question that he was a very influential teacher, and what is more important and unique, China's first private teacher. His ideas are best known through the *Lun Yü* or *Confucian Analects*, a collection of his scattered sayings which was compiled by some of his disciples.

Confucius was a *ju* and the founder of the *Ju* school, which has been known in the West as the Confucian school. In the last chapter we saw how Liu Hsin wrote regarding this school that it "delighted in the study of the *Liu Yi* and emphasized matters concerning human-heartedness and righteousness." The term *Liu Yi* means the "six arts," i.e., the six liberal arts, but it is more commonly translated as the "Six Classics." These are the *Yi* or *Book of Changes*, the *Shih* or *Book of Odes* (or *Poetry*), the *Shu* or *Book of History*, the *Li* or *Rituals* or *Rites*, the *Yüeh* or *Music* (no longer preserved as a separate work), and the *Ch'un Ch'iu* or *Spring and Autumn Annals*, a chronicle history of Confucius' state of Lu extending from 722 to 479 B.C., the year of Confucius' death. The nature of these classics is clear from their titles, with the exception of the *Book of Changes*. This work was in later times interpreted by the Confucianists as a treatise on metaphysics, but originally it was a book of divination.

Concerning the relation of Confucius with the Six Classics, there are two schools of traditional scholarship. One maintains that Confucius was the author of all these works, while the other maintains that Confucius was the author of the *Spring and Autumn Annals*, the commentator of the *Book of Changes*, the reformer of the *Rituals* and *Music*, and the editor of the *Book of History* and *Book of Odes*.

As a matter of fact, however, Confucius was neither the author, commentator, nor even editor of any of the classics. In some respects, to be sure, he was a conservative who upheld tradition. Thus in the rites and music he did try to rectify any deviations from the traditional practices or standards, and instances of so doing are reported in the *Lun Yü* or *Analects*. Judging from what is said of him in the *Analects*, however, Confucius never had any intention of writing anything himself for future generations. The writing of books in a private rather than official capacity was an as yet unheard of practice which developed only after the time of Confucius. He was China's first private teacher, but not its first private writer.

The Six Classics had existed before the time of Confucius, and they constituted the cultural legacy of the past. They had been the basis of education for the aristocrats during the early centuries of feudalism of the Chou dynasty. As feudalism began to disintegrate, however, roughly from the seventh century B.C. onward, the tutors of the aristocrats, or even some of the aristocrats themselves— men who had lost their positions and titles but were well versed in the Classics—began to scatter among the people. They made their living, as we have seen in the last chapter, by teaching the Classics or by acting as skilled "assistants," well versed in the rituals, on the occasion of funeral, sacrifice, wedding, and other ceremonies. This class of men was known as the *ju* or literati.

Confucius as an Educator

Confucius, however, was more than a *ju* in the common sense of the word. It is true that in the *Analects* we find him, from one point of view, being portrayed merely as an educator. He wanted his disciples to be "rounded men" who would be useful to state and society, and therefore he taught them various branches of knowledge based upon the different classics. His primary function as a teacher, he felt, was to interpret to his disciples the ancient cultural heritage. That is why, in his own words as recorded in the *Analects*, he was "a transmitter and not an originator." (*Analects*, VII, 1.) But this is only one aspect of Confucius, and there is another one as well. This is that, while transmitting the traditional institutions and ideas, Confucius gave them interpretations derived from his own moral concepts. This is exemplified in his interpretation of the old custom that on the death of a parent, a son should mourn three years. Confucius commented on this: "The child cannot leave the arms of its parents until it is three years old. This is why the three years' mourning is universally observed throughout the world." (*Analects*, XVII, 21.) In other words, the son was utterly dependent upon his parents for at least the first three years of his life; hence upon their death he should mourn them for an equal length of time in order to express his gratitude. Likewise when teaching the Classics, Confucius gave them new interpretations. Thus in speaking of the *Book of Poetry*, he stressed its moral value by saying: "In the *Book of Poetry* there are three hundred poems. But the essence of them can be covered in one sentence: 'Have no depraved thoughts.'" (*Analects*, II, 2.) In this way Confucius was more than a mere transmitter, for in transmitting, he originated something new.

This spirit of originating through transmitting was perpetuated by the followers of Confucius, by whom, as the classical texts were handed down from generation to generation, countless commentaries and interpretations were written. A great portion of what in later times came to be known as the Thirteen Classics developed as commentaries in this way on the original texts.

This is what set Confucius apart from the ordinary literati of his time, and made him the founder of a new school. Because the followers of this school were at the same time scholars and specialists on the Six Classics, the school became known as the School of the Literati.

The Rectification of Names

Besides the new interpretations which Confucius gave to the classics, he had his own ideas about the individual and society, heaven and man.

In regard to society, he held that in order to have a well-ordered one, the most important thing is to carry out what he called the rectification of names. That is, things in actual fact should be made to accord with the implication attached to them by names. Once a disciple asked him what he would do first if he were to rule a state, whereupon Confucius replied: "The one thing needed first is the rectification of names." (*Analects*, XIII, 3.) On another occasion one of the dukes of the time asked Confucius the right principle of government, to which he answered: "Let the ruler be ruler, the minister minister, the father father, and the son son." (*Analects*, XII, 11.) In other words, every name contains certain implications which constitute the essence of that class of things to which this name applies. Such things, therefore, should agree with this ideal essence. The essence of a ruler is what the ruler ideally ought to be, or what, in

Chinese, is called "the way of the ruler." If a ruler acts according to this way of the ruler, he is then truly a ruler, in fact as well as in name. There is an agreement between name and actuality. But if he does not, he is no ruler, even though he may popularly be regarded as such. Every name in the social relationships implies certain responsibilities and duties. Ruler, minister, father, and son are all the names of such social relationships, and the individuals bearing these names must fulfill their responsibilities and duties accordingly. Such is the implication of Confucius' theory of the rectification of names.

Human-heartedness and Righteousness

With regard to the virtues of the individual, Confucius emphasized human-heartedness and righteousness, especially the former. Righteousness (yi) means the "oughtness" of a situation. It is a categorical imperative. Every one in society has certain things which he ought to do, and which must be done for their own sake, because they are the morally right things to do. If, however, he does them only because of other non-moral considerations, then even though he does what he ought to do, his action is no longer a righteous one. To use a word often disparaged by Confucius and later Confucianists, he is then acting for "profit." Yi (righteousness) and li (profit) are in Confucianism diametrically opposed terms. Confucius himself says: "The superior man comprehends yi; the small man comprehends li." (Analects, IV, 16.) Herein lies what the later Confucianists called the "distinction between yi and li," a distinction which they considered to be of the utmost importance in moral teaching.

The idea of yi is rather formal, but that of jen (human-heartedness) is much more concrete. The formal essence of the duties of man in society is their "oughtness," because all these duties are what he ought to do. But the material essence of these duties is "loving others," i.e., jen or human-heartedness. The father acts according to the way a father should act who loves his son; the son acts according to the way a son should act who loves his father. Confucius says: "Human-heartedness consists in loving others." (Analects, XII, 22.) The man who really loves others is one able to perform his duties in society. Hence in the Analects we see that Confucius sometimes uses the word jen not only to denote a special kind of virtue, but also to denote all the virtues combined, so that the term "man of jen" becomes synonymous with the man of all-round virtue. In such contexts, *jen* can be translated as "perfect virtue."

Chung *and* Shu

In the *Analects* we find the passage: "When Chung Kung asked the meaning of *jen*, the master said: '. . . Do not do to others what you do not wish yourself. . . .'" (XII, 2.) Again, Confucius is reported in the *Analects* as saying: "The man of *jen* is one who, desiring to sustain himself, sustains others, and desiring to develop himself, develops others. To be able from one's own self to draw a parallel for the treatment of others; that may be called the way to practise *jen*." (VI, 28.)

Thus the practice of *jen* consists in consideration for others. "Desiring to sustain oneself, one sustains others; desiring to develop oneself, one develops others." In other words: "Do to others what you wish yourself." This is the positive aspect of the practice, which was called by Confucius *chung* or "conscientiousness to others." And the negative aspect, which was called by Confucius *shu* or "altruism," is: "Do not do to others what you do not wish yourself." The practice as a whole is called the principle of *chung* and *shu*, which is "the way to practice *jen*."

This principle was known by some of the later Confucianists as the "principle of applying a measuring square." That is to say, it is a principle by which one uses oneself as a standard to regulate one's conduct. In the *Ta Hsüeh* or *Great Learning*, which is a chapter of the *Li Chi* (*Book of Rites*), a collection of treatises written by the Confucianists in the third and second centuries B.C., it is said: "Do not use what you dislike in your superiors in the employment of your inferiors. Do not use what you dislike in your inferiors in the service of your superiors. Do not use what you dislike in those who are before, to precede those who are behind. Do not use what you dislike in those who are behind, to follow those who are before. Do not use what you dislike on the right, to display toward the left. Do not use what you dislike on the left, to display toward the right. This is called the principle of applying a measuring square."

In the *Chung Yung* or *Doctrine of the Mean*, which is another chapter of the *Li Chi*, attributed to Tzu-ssu, the grandson of Confucius, it is said: "*Chung* and *shu* are not far from the Way. What you do not like done to yourself, do not do to others. . . . Serve your father as you would require your son to serve you. . . . Serve your ruler as you would require your subordinate to serve you. . . . Serve your elder brother as you would require your younger brother to serve you. . . . Set the example in behaving to your friends as you would require them to behave to you. . . ."

The illustration given in the *Great Learning* emphasizes the negative aspect of the principle of *chung* and *shu;* that in the *Doctrine of the Mean* emphasizes its positive aspect. In each case the "measuring square" for determining conduct is in one's self and not in other things.

The principle of *chung* and *shu* is at the same time the principle of *jen,* so that the practice of *chung* and *shu* means the practice of *jen.* And this practice leads to the carrying out of one's responsibilities and duties in society, in which is comprised the quality of *yi* or righteousness. Hence the principle of *chung* and *shu* becomes the alpha and omega of one's moral life. In the *Analects* we find the passage: "The master said: 'Shen [the personal name of Tseng Tzu, one of his disciples], all my teachings are linked together by one principle.' 'Quite so,' replied Tseng Tzu. When the master had left the room, the disciples asked: 'What did he mean?' Tseng Tzu replied: 'Our master's teaching consists of the principle of *chung* and *shu,* and that is all.' " (IV, 15.)

Everyone has within himself the "measuring square" for conduct, and can use it at any time. So simple as this is the method of practising *jen,* so that Confucius said: "Is *jen* indeed far off? I crave for *jen,* and lo! *jen* is at hand!" (*Analects,* VII, 29.)

Knowing Ming

From the idea of righteousness, the Confucianists derived the idea of "doing for nothing." One does what one ought to do, simply because it is morally right to do it, and not for any consideration external to this moral compulsion. In the *Analects,* we are told that Confucius was ridiculed by a certain recluse as "one who knows that he cannot succeed, yet keeps on trying to do it." (XIV, 41.) We also read that another recluse was told by a disciple of Confucius: "The reason why the superior man tries to go into politics, is because he holds this to be right, even though he is well aware that his principle cannot prevail." (XVIII, 7.)

As we shall see, the Taoists taught the theory of "*doing* nothing," whereas the Confucianists taught that of "doing *for* nothing." A man cannot do nothing, according to Confucianism, because for every man there is something which he ought to do. Nevertheless, what he does is "for nothing," because the value of doing what he ought to do lies in the doing itself, and not in the external result.

Confucius' own life is certainly a good example of this teaching. Living in an age of great social and political disorder, he tried his best to reform the world. He traveled everywhere and, like Socrates, talked to everybody. Although his efforts were in vain, he was never disappointed. He knew that he could not succeed, but kept on trying.

About himself Confucius said: "If my principles are to prevail in the world, it is *Ming*. If they are to fall to the ground, it is also *Ming*." (*Analects*, XIV, 38.) He tried his best, but the issue he left to *Ming*. *Ming* is often translated as Fate, Destiny or Decree. To Confucius, it meant the Decree of Heaven or Will of Heaven; in other words, it was conceived of as a purposeful force. In later Confucianism, however, *Ming* simply means the total existent conditions and forces of the whole universe. For the external success of our activity, the cooperation of these conditions is always needed. But this cooperation is wholly beyond our control. Hence the best thing for us to do is simply to try to carry out what we know we ought to carry out, without caring whether in the process we succeed or fail. To act in this way is "to know *Ming*." To know *Ming* is an important requirement for being a superior man in the Confucian sense of the term, so that Confucius said: "He who does not know *Ming* cannot be a superior man." (*Analects*, XX, 2.)

Thus to know *Ming* means to acknowledge the inevitability of the world as it exists, and so to disregard one's external success or failure. If we can act in this way, we can, in a sense, never fail. For if we do our duty, that duty through our very act is morally done, regardless of the external success or failure of our action.

As a result, we always shall be free from anxiety as to success or fear as to failure, and so shall be happy. This is why Confucius said: "The wise are free from doubts; the virtuous from anxiety; the brave from fear." (*Analects*, IX, 28.) Or again: "The superior man is always happy; the small man sad." (VII, 36.)

Confucius' Spiritual Development

In the Taoist work, the *Chuang-tzu*, we see that the Taoists often ridiculed Confucius as one who confined himself to the morality of human-heartedness and righteousness, thus being conscious only of moral values, and not super-moral value. Superficially they were right, but actually they were wrong. Thus speaking about his own spiritual development, Confucius said: "At fifteen I set my heart on learning. At thirty I could stand. At forty I had no doubts. At fifty I knew the Decree of Heaven. At sixty I was already obedient [to this Decree]. At seventy I could follow the desires of my mind without overstepping the boundaries [of what is right]." (*Analects*, II, 4.)

The "learning" which Confucius here refers to is not what we now would call learning. In the *Analects*, Confucius said: "Set your heart on the *Tao*." (VII, 6.) And again: "To hear the *Tao* in the morning and then die at night, that would be all right." (IV, 9.) Here *Tao* means the Way or Truth. It was this *Tao* which Confucius at fifteen set his heart upon learning. What we now call learning means the increase of our knowledge, but the *Tao* is that whereby we can elevate our mind.

Confucius also said: "Take your stand in the *li* [rituals, ceremonies, proper conduct]." (*Analects*, VIII, 8.) Again he said: "Not to know the *li* is to have no means of standing." (XX, 3.) Thus when Confucius says that at thirty he could "stand," he means that he then understood the *li* and so could practice proper conduct.

His statement that at forty he had no doubts means that he had then become a wise man. For, as quoted before, "The wise are free from doubts."

Up to this time of his life Confucius was perhaps conscious only of moral values. But at the age of fifty and sixty, he knew the Decree of Heaven and was obedient to it. In other words, he was then also conscious of super-moral values. Confucius in this respect was like Socrates. Socrates thought that he had been appointed by a divine order to awaken the Greeks, and Confucius had a similar consciousness of a divine mission. For example, when he was threatened with physical violence at a place called K'uang, he said: "If Heaven had wished to let civilization perish, later generations (like myself) would not have been permitted to participate in it. But since Heaven has not wished to let civilization perish, what can the people of K'uang do to me?" (*Analects*, IX, 5.) One of his contemporaries also said: "The world for long has been without order. But now Heaven is going to use the Master as an arousing tocsin." (*Analects*, III, 24.) Thus Confucius in doing what he did, was convinced that he was following the Decree of Heaven and was supported by Heaven; he was conscious of values higher than moral ones.

The super-moral value experienced by Confucius, however, was, as we shall see, not quite the same as that experienced by the Taoists. For the latter abandoned entirely the idea of an intelligent and purposeful Heaven, and sought instead for mystical union with an undifferentiated whole. The super-moral value which they knew and experienced, therefore, was freer from the ordinary concepts of the human relationships.

At seventy, as has been told above, Confucius allowed his mind to follow whatever it desired, yet everything he did was naturally right of itself. His actions no longer needed a conscious guide. He was acting without effort. This represents the last stage in the development of the sage.

Confucius' Position in Chinese History

Confucius is probably better known in the West than any other single Chinese. Yet in China itself, though always famous, his place in history has changed considerably from one period to another. Historically speaking he was primarily *a* teacher, that is, only one teacher among many. But after his death, he gradually came to be considered as *the* teacher, superior to all others. And in the second century B.C. he was elevated to an even higher plane. According to many Confucianists of that time, Confucius had actually been appointed by Heaven to begin a new dynasty that would follow that of Chou. Though in actual fact without a crown or a government, he had ideally speaking become a king who ruled the whole empire. How this apparent contradiction had happened, these Confucianists said, could be found out by studying the esoteric meaning supposedly contained in the *Spring and Autumn Annals*. This was supposed by them not to be a chronicle of Confucius' native state (as it actually was), but an important political work written by Confucius to express his ethical and political ideas. Then in the first century B.C., Confucius came to be regarded as even more than a king. According to many people of that time, he was a living god among men—a divine being who knew that after his time there would someday come the Han dynasty (206 B.C.-A.D. 220), and who therefore, in the *Spring and Autumn Annals*, set forth a political ideal which would be complete enough for the men of Han to realize. This apotheosis was the climax of Confucius' glory, and in the middle of the Han dynasty Confucianism could properly be called a religion.

The time of glorification, however, did not last very long. Already beginning in the first century A.D., Confucianists of a more rationalistic type began to get the upper hand. Hence in later times Confucius was no longer regarded as a divine being, though his position as that of *the* Teacher remained high. At the very end of the nineteenth century, to be sure, there was a brief revival of the theory that Confucius had been divinely appointed to be a king. Soon afterward, however, with the coming of the Chinese Republic, his reputation fell until he came to be regarded as something less than *the* Teacher, and at present most Chinese would say that he was primarily *a* teacher, and certainly a great one, but far from being the only teacher.

Confucius, however, was already recognized in his own day as a man of very extensive learning. For example, one of his contemporaries said: "Great indeed is the Master K'ung! His learning is so extensive that he cannot be called by a single name." (*Analects*, IX, 2.) From the quotations given earlier, we may see that he considered himself the inheritor and perpetuator of ancient civilization, and was considered by some of his contemporaries as such. By his work of originating through transmitting, he caused his school to reinterpret the civilization of the age before him. He upheld what he considered to be best in the old, and created a powerful tradition that was followed until very recent years, when, as in Confucius' own time, China again came face to face with tremendous economic and social change. In addition, he was China's first teacher. Hence, though historically speaking he was only *a* teacher, it is perhaps not unreasonable that in later ages he was regarded as *the* teacher.

❧ CHAPTER 5 ❧

MO TZU, THE FIRST OPPONENT

OF CONFUCIUS

THE next major philosopher after Confucius was Mo Tzu. His family name was Mo and his personal name was Ti. As the *Shih Chi* or *Historical Records* does not say where he came from, and in fact tells us almost nothing about his life, there has been a difference of opinion regarding his native state. Some scholars hold that he was a native of Sung (in what is today eastern Honan and western Shantung), and others that he came from Lu, the same state as Confucius. His exact dates are also uncertain, but probably he lived sometime within the years 479-381 B.C. The main source for the study of his thought is the book bearing his name, the *Mo-tzu*, which contains 53 chapters and is a collection of writings by his followers as well as by himself.

Mo Tzu was the founder of a school known after his name as the Mohist school. In ancient times his fame was as great as that of Confucius, and his teaching was no less influential. The contrast between the two men is interesting. Confucius felt a sympathetic understanding for the traditional institutions, rituals, music, and literature of the early Chou dynasty, and tried to rationalize and justify them in ethical terms; Mo Tzu, on the contrary, questioned their validity and usefulness, and tried to replace them with something that was simpler but, in his view, more useful. In short, Confucius was the rationalizer and justifier of the ancient civilization, while Mo Tzu was its critic. Confucius was a refined gentleman, while Mo Tzu was a militant preacher. A major aim of his preaching was to oppose both the traditional institutions and practices, and the theories of Confucius and the Confucianists.

49

Social Background of the Mohist School

During the feudal age of the Chou dynasty, kings, princes, and feudal lords all had their military specialists. These were the hereditary warriors who constituted the backbone of the armies of that time. With the disintegration of feudalism that took place in the latter part of the Chou dynasty, however, these warrior specialists lost their positions and titles, scattered throughout the country, and made a living by offering their services to anyone who could afford to employ them. This class of people was known as the *hsieh* or *yu hsieh*, terms which can both be translated as "knights-errant." Concerning such knights-errant, the *Shih Chi* says: "Their words were always sincere and trustworthy, and their actions always quick and decisive. They were always true to what they promised, and without regard to their own persons, they would rush into dangers threatening others." (Ch. 124.) Such was their professional ethics. A large part of Mo Tzu's teaching was an extension of this ethics.

In Chinese history both the *ju* or literati and the *hsieh* or knights-errant originated as specialists attached to the houses of the aristocrats, and were themselves members of the upper classes. In later times the *ju* continued to come mainly from the upper or middle classes, but the *hsieh*, on the contrary, more frequently were recruited from the lower classes. In ancient times, such social amenities as rituals and music were all exclusively for the aristocrats; from the point of view of the common man, therefore, they were luxuries that had no practical utility. It was from this point of view that Mo Tzu and the Mohists criticised the traditional institutions and their rationalizers, Confucius and the Confucianists. This criticism, together with the elaboration and rationalization of the professional ethics of their own social class, that of the *hsieh*, constituted the central core of the Mohist philosophy.

There is plenty of evidence for the inference that Mo Tzu and his followers came from the *hsieh*. From the *Mo-tzu*, as well as from other contemporary sources, we know that the Mohists constituted a strictly disciplined organization capable of military action. The leader of the Mohist organization was called the *Chü Tzu*, "Great Master," and had the authority of life or death over the members of the group. We are also told that Mo Tzu was the first "Great Master" of his group, and that at least once he actually led his followers to prepare for the military defense of Sung, when that state was threatened with invasion from the neighboring state of Ch'u.

The story of this episode is interesting. It is said in the *Mo-tzu* that a noted mechanical inventor, Kung-shu Pan, then employed by the state of Ch'u, had completed the construction of a new weapon for attacking city walls. Ch'u was preparing to attack Sung with this new weapon. Hearing of this, Mo Tzu went to Ch'u to persuade its king to desist. There he and Kung-shu Pan made a demonstration before the king of their weapons of attack and defense. Mo Tzu first untied his belt and laid out a city with it, using a small stick as a weapon. Kung-shu Pan thereupon set up nine different miniature machines of attack, but Mo Tzu nine times repulsed him. Finally, Kung-shu Pan had used up all his machines of attack, while Mo Tzu was far from being exhausted in the defense. Then Kung-shu Pan said: "I know how to defeat you, but I will not say it." To which Mo Tzu replied: "I know what it is, but I too will not say it."

On being asked by the king what was meant, Mo Tzu continued: "Kung-shu Pan is thinking of murdering me. But my disciples Ch'in Ku-li and others, numbering three hundred men, are already armed with my implements of defense, waiting on the city wall of Sung for the invaders from Ch'u. Though I be murdered, you cannot exterminate them." To which the King exclaimed: "Very well! Let us not attack Sung." (Ch. 50.)

If this story is true, it would give a good example for our present world in settling disputes between two countries. A war would not need to be fought in the field. All that would be necessary would be for the scientists and engineers of the two countries to demonstrate their laboratory weapons of attacking and defense, and the war would be decided without fighting!

Regardless of whether the story is true or not, it illustrates the nature of the Mohist organization, which is also confirmed from other sources. Thus in the *Huai-nan-tzu*, a work of the second century B.C., it is stated that "the disciples of Mo Tzu were one hundred and eighty in number, all of whom he could order to enter fire or tread on sword blades, and whom even death would not cause to turn on their heels." (Ch. 20.) And in the *Mo-tzu* itself, no less than nine chapters deal with the tactics of fighting a defensive war and the techniques of building instruments for defending city walls. All of this shows that the Mohists, as originally constituted, were a group of warriors.

Mo Tzu and his followers, however, differed from the ordinary knights-errant in two respects. In the first place, the latter were men ready to engage in any fighting whatever, only provided that they were paid for their efforts or favored by the feudal lords. Mo Tzu and his followers, on the contrary, were strongly opposed to aggressive war; hence they agreed to fight only in wars that were strictly for self-defense. Secondly, the ordinary *hsieh* confined themselves wholly to their code of professional ethics. Mo Tzu, however, elaborated this professional ethics and gave it a rationalistic justification. Thus though Mo Tzu's background was that of a *hsieh*, he at the same time became the founder of a new philosophic school.

Mo Tzu's Criticism of Confucianism

According to Mo Tzu, "the principles of the Confucianists ruin the whole world in four ways": (1) The Confucianists do not believe in the existence of God or of spirits, "with the result that God and the spirits are displeased." (2) The Confucianists insist on elaborate funerals and the practice of three years of mourning on the death of a parent, so that the wealth and energy of the people are thereby wasted. (3) The Confucianists lay stress on the practice of music, leading to an identical result. (4) The Confucianists believe in a predetermined fate, causing the people to be lazy and to resign themselves to this fate. (The *Mo-tzu*, ch. 48.) In another chapter entitled "Anti-Confucianism," the *Mo-tzu* also says: "Even those with long life cannot exhaust the learning required for their [Confucianist] studies. Even people with the vigor of youth cannot perform all the ceremonial duties. And even those who have amassed wealth cannot afford music. They [the Confucianists] enhance the beauty of wicked arts and lead their sovereign astray. Their doctrine cannot meet the needs of the age, nor can their learning educate the people." (Ch. 39.)

These criticisms reveal the differing social backgrounds of the Confucianists and Mohists. Already before Confucius, persons who were better educated and more sophisticated had been abandoning the belief in the existence of a personal God and of divine spirits. People of the lower classes, however, had, as always in such matters, lagged behind in this rise of skepticism, and Mo Tzu held the point of view of the lower classes. This is the significance of his first point of criticism against the Confucianists. The second and third points, too, were made from the same basis. The fourth point, however, was really irrelevant, because, though the Confucianists often spoke about *Ming* (Fate, Decree), what they meant by it was not the predetermined fate attacked by Mo Tzu. This has been pointed out in the last chapter, where we have seen that *Ming*, for the Confucianists, signified something that is beyond human control. But there are other things that remain within man's power to control if he will exert himself. Only after man has done everything he can himself, therefore, should he accept with calm and resignation what comes thereafter as inevitable. Such is what the Confucianists meant when they spoke of "knowing *Ming*."

All-embracing Love

Mo Tzu makes no criticism of the Confucianists' central idea of *jen* (human-heartedness) and *yi* (righteousness); in the *Mo-tzu*, indeed, he speaks often of these two qualities and of the man of *jen* and man of *yi*. What he means by these terms, however, differs somewhat from the concept of them held by the Confucianists. For Mo Tzu, *jen* and *yi* signify an all-embracing love, and the man of *jen* and man of *yi* are persons who practice this all-embracing love. This concept is a central one in Mo Tzu's philosophy, and represents a logical extension of the professional ethics of the class of *hsieh* (knights-errant) from which Mo Tzu sprang. This ethics was, namely, that within their group the *hsieh* "enjoy equally and suffer equally." (This was a common saying of the *hsieh* of later times.) Taking this group concept as a basis, Mo Tzu tried to broaden it by preaching the doctrine that everyone in the world should love everyone else equally and without discrimination.

In the *Mo-tzu*, there are three chapters devoted to the subject of all-embracing love. In them, Mo Tzu first makes a distinction between what he calls the principles of "discrimination" and "all-embracingness." The man who holds to the principle of discrimination says: It is absurd for me to care for friends as much as I would for myself, and to look after their parents as I would my own. As a result, such a man does not do very much for his friends. But the man who holds to the principle of all-embracingness says, on the contrary: I must care for my friends as much as I do for myself, and for their parents as I would my own. As a result, he does everything he can for his friends. Having made this distinction, Mo Tzu then asks the question: Which of these two principles is the right one?

Mo Tzu thereupon uses his "tests of judgment" to determine the right and wrong of these principles. According to him, every principle must be examined by three tests, namely: "Its basis, its verifiability, and its applicability." A sound and right principle "should be based on the Will of Heaven and of the spirits and on the deeds of the ancient sage-kings." Then "it is to be verified by the senses of hearing and sight of the common people." And finally, "it is to be applied by adopting it in government and observing whether it is beneficial to the country and the people." (*Mo-tzu*, ch. 35.) Of these three tests, the last is the most important. "Being beneficial to the country and the people" is the standard by which Mo Tzu determines all values.

This same standard is the chief one used by Mo Tzu to prove the desirability of all-embracing love. In the third of three chapters, all of which are titled "All-embracing Love," he argues:

"The task of the human-hearted man is to procure benefits for the world and to eliminate its calamities. Now among all the current calamities of the world, which are the greatest? I say that attacks on small states by large ones, disturbances of small houses by large ones, oppression of the weak by the strong, misuse of the few by the many, deception of the simple by the cunning, and disdain toward the humble by the honored: these are the misfortunes of the world. . . . When we come to think about the causes of all these calamities, how have they arisen? Have they arisen out of love of others and benefiting others? We must reply that it is not so. Rather we should say that they have arisen out of hate of others and injuring others. If we classify those in the world who hate others and injure others, shall we call them 'discriminating' or 'all-embracing'? We must say that they are 'discriminating.' So, then, is not 'mutual discrimination' the cause of the major calamities of the world? Therefore the principle of 'discrimination' is wrong.

"Whoever criticizes others must have something to substitute for what he criticizes. Therefore I say: 'Substitute all-embracingness for discrimination.' What is the reason why all-embracingness can be substituted for discrimination? The answer is that when everyone regards the states of others as he regards his own, who will attack these other states? Others will be regarded like the self. When everyone regards the cities of others as he regards his own, who will seize these other cities? Others will be regarded like the self. When everyone regards the houses of others as he regards his own, who will disturb these other houses? Others will be regarded like the self.

"Now, when states and cities do not attack and seize one another, and when clans and individuals do not disturb and harm one another, is this a calamity or a benefit to the world? We must say it is a benefit. When we come to consider the origin of the various benefits, how have they arisen? Have they arisen out of hate of others and injuring others? We must say not so. We should say that they have arisen out of love of others and benefiting others. If we classify those in the world who love others and benefit others, shall we call them 'discriminating' or 'all-embracing'? We must say that they are 'all-embracing.' Then is it not the case that 'mutual all-embracingness' is the cause of the major benefit of the world? Therefore I say that the principle of 'all-embracingness' is right." (*Mo-tzu*, ch. 16.)

Thus, using a utilitarianistic argument, Mo Tzu proves the principle of all-embracing love to be absolutely right. The human-hearted man whose task it is to procure benefits for the world and eliminate its calamities, must establish all-embracing love as the standard of action both for himself and for all others in the world. When everyone in the world acts according to this standard, "then attentive ears and keen eyes will respond to serve one another, limbs will be strengthened to work for one another, and those who know the proper principle will untiringly instruct others. Thus the aged and widowers will have support and nourishment with which to round out their old age, and the young and weak and orphans will have a place of support in which to grow up. When all-embracing love is adopted as the standard, such are the consequent benefits." (*Ibid.*) This, then, is Mo Tzu's ideal world, which can be created only through the practice of all-embracing love.

The Will of God and Existence of Spirits

There remains, however, a basic question: How to persuade people thus to love one another? One may tell them, as was said above, that the practice of all-embracing love is the only way to benefit the world and that every human-hearted man is one who practices all-embracing love. Yet people may still ask: Why should I personally act to benefit the world and why should I be a human-hearted man? One may then argue further that if the world as a whole is benefited, this means benefit for every individual in the world as well. Or as Mo Tzu says: "He who loves others, must also be loved by others. He who benefits others, must also be benefited by others. He who hates others, must also be hated by others. He who injures others, must also be injured by others." (*Mo-tzu*, ch. 17.) Thus, then, the love of others is a sort of personal insurance or investment, which "pays," as Americans would say. Most people, however, are too shortsighted to see the value of a long term investment of this sort, and there are a few instances in which such an investment does, indeed, fail to pay.

In order, therefore, to induce people to practice the principle of all-embracing love, Mo Tzu, in addition to the foregoing arguments, introduces a number of religious and political sanctions. Thus in the *Mo-tzu* there are chapters on "The Will of Heaven," and also ones titled "Proof of the Existence of Spirits." In these we read that God exists; that He loves mankind; and that His Will is that all men should love one another. He constantly supervises the activities of men, especially those of the rulers of men. He punishes with calamities persons who disobey His Will, and rewards with good fortune those who obey. Besides God, there are also numerous lesser spirits who likewise reward men who practice all-embracing love, and punish those who practice "discrimination."

In this connection there is an interesting story about Mo Tzu: "When Mo Tzu was once ill, Tieh Pi came to him and inquired: 'Sir, you hold that the spirits are intelligent and control calamities and blessings. They reward the good and punish the evil. Now you are a sage. How then can you be ill? Is it that your teaching is not entirely correct or that the spirits are after all not intelligent?' Mo Tzu replied: 'Though I am ill, why should the spirits be unintelligent? There are many ways by which a man can contract diseases. Some are contracted from cold or heat, some from fatigue. If there are a hundred doors and only one be closed, will there not be ways by which robbers can enter?'" (*Mo-tzu*, ch. 48.) In modern logical terminology, Mo Tzu would say that punishment by the spirits is a sufficient cause for the disease of a man, but not its necessary cause.

A Seeming Inconsistency

Here it is timely to point out that both the Mohists and the Confucianists seem to be inconsistent in their attitude toward the existence of spirits and the performance of rituals connected with the spirits. Certainly it seems inconsistent for the Mohists to have believed in the existence of the spirits, yet at the same time to have opposed the elaborate rituals that were conducted on the occasion of funerals and of the making of sacrifices to the ancestors. Likewise, it seems inconsistent that the Confucianists stressed those funeral and sacrificial rituals, yet did not believe in the existence of the spirits. The Mohists, for their part, were quite ready to point out this seeming inconsistency as regards the Confucianists. Thus we read in the *Mo-tzu*: "Kung-meng Tzu [a Confucianist] said: 'There are no spirits.' Again he said: 'The superior man should learn the rituals of sacrifice.' Mo Tzu said: 'To hold that there are no spirits, and yet to learn sacrificial ceremonies, is like learning the ceremonies of hospitality when there are no guests, or throwing fish nets when there are no fish.'" (Ch. 48.)

Yet the seeming inconsistencies of the Confucianists and Mohists are both unreal. According to the former, the reason for performing the sacrificial rituals is no longer a belief that the spirits actually exist, though no doubt this was the original reason. Rather, the performance springs from the sentiment of respect toward his departed forebears held by the man who offers the sacrifice. Hence the meaning of the ceremonies is poetic, not religious. This theory was later developed by Hsün Tzu and his school of Confucianism in detail, as we shall see in chapter thirteen of this book. Hence there is no real inconsistency at all.

Likewise there is no actual inconsistency in the Mohist point of view, for Mo Tzu's proof of the existence of spirits is done primarily in order that he may introduce a religious sanction for his doctrine of all-embracing love, rather than because of any real interest in supernatural matters. Thus in his chapter on "Proof of the Existence of Spirits," he attributes the existing confusion of the world to "a doubt (among men) as to the existence of spirits and a failure to understand that they can reward the good and punish the bad." He then asks: "If now all the people of the world could be made to believe that the spirits can reward the good and punish the bad, would the world then be in chaos?" (Ch. 31.) Thus his doctrine of the Will of God and the existence of spirits is only to induce people to believe that they will be rewarded if they practice all-embracing love, and punished if they do not. Such a belief among the people was something useful; hence Mo Tzu wanted it. "Economy of expenditure" in the funeral and sacrificial services was also useful; hence Mo Tzu wanted it too. From his ultra-utilitarian point of view, there was no inconsistency in wanting both things, since both were useful.

Origin of the State

Besides religious sanctions, political ones are also needed if people are to practice all-embracing love. In the *Mo-tzu*, there are three chapters titled "Agreement with the Superior," in which Mo Tzu expounds his theory of the origin of the state. According to this theory, the authority of the ruler of a state comes from two sources: the will of the people and the Will of God. Furthermore, the main task of the ruler is to supervise the activities of the people, rewarding those who practice all-embracing love and punishing those who do not. In order to do this effectively, his authority must be absolute. At this point we may ask: Why should people voluntarily choose to have such an absolute authority over them?

The answer, for Mo Tzu, is that the people accept such an authority, not because they prefer it, but because they have no alternative. According to him, before the creation of an organized state, people lived in what Thomas Hobbes has called "the state of nature." At this early time, "everyone had his own standard of right and wrong. When there was one man, there was one standard. When there were two men, there were two standards. When there were ten men, there were ten standards. The more people there were, the more were there standards. Every man considered himself as right and others as wrong." "The world was in great disorder and men were like birds and beasts. They understood that all the disorders of the world were due to the fact that there was no political ruler. Therefore, they selected the most virtuous and most able man of the world, and established him as the Son of Heaven." (*Mo-tzu*, ch. 11.) Thus the ruler of the state was first established by the will of the people, in order to save themselves from anarchy.

In another chapter bearing the same title, Mo Tzu says: "Of old when God and the spirits established the state and cities and installed rulers, it was not to make their rank high or their emolument substantial. . . . It was to procure benefits for the people and eliminate their adversities; to enrich the poor and increase the few; and to bring safety out of danger and order out of confusion." (Ch. 12.) According to this statement, therefore, the state and its ruler were established through the Will of God.

No matter what was the way in which the ruler gained his power, once he was established, he, according to Mo Tzu, issued a mandate to the people of the world, saying: "Upon hearing good or evil, one shall report it to one's superior. What the superior thinks to be right, all shall think to be right. What the superior thinks to be wrong, all shall think to be wrong." (Ch. 11.) This leads Mo Tzu to the following dictum: "Always agree with the superior; never follow the inferior." (*Ibid.*)

Thus, Mo Tzu argues, the state must be totalitarian and the authority of its ruler absolute. This is an inevitable conclusion to his theory of the origin of the state. For the state was created precisely in order to end the disorder which had existed owing to the confused standards of right and wrong. The state's primary function, therefore, is, quoting Mo Tzu, "to unify the standards." Within the state only one standard can exist, and it must be one which is fixed by the state itself. No other standards can be tolerated, because if there were such, people would speedily return to "the state of nature" in which there could be nothing but disorder and chaos. In this political theory we may see Mo Tzu's development of the professional ethics of the *hsieh*, with its emphasis upon group obedience and discipline. No doubt it also reflects the troubled political conditions of Mo Tzu's day, which caused many people to look with favor on a centralized authority, even if it were to be an autocratic one.

So, then, there can be only one standard of right and wrong. Right, for Mo Tzu, is the practice of "mutual all-embracingness," and wrong is the practice of "mutual discrimination." Through appeal to this political sanction, together with his religious one, Mo Tzu hoped to bring all people of the world to practice his principle of all-embracing love.

Such was Mo Tzu's teaching, and it is the unanimous report of all sources of his time that in his own activities he was a true example of it.

CHAPTER 6

THE FIRST PHASE OF TAOISM:
YANG CHU

In the *Confucian Analects*, we are told that Confucius, while traveling from state to state, met many men whom he called *yin che*, "those who obscure themselves," and described as persons who had "escaped from the world." (XIV, 39.) These recluses ridiculed Confucius for what they regarded as his vain efforts to save the world. By one of them he was described as "the one who knows he cannot succeed, yet keeps on trying to do so." (XIV, 41.) To these attacks, Tzu Lu, a disciple of Confucius, once replied: "It is unrighteous to refuse to serve in office. If the regulations between old and young in family life are not to be set aside, how is it then that you set aside the duty that exists between sovereign and subject? In your desire to maintain your personal purity, you subvert the great relationship of society [the relationship between sovereign and subject]." (*Ibid.,* XVIII, 7.)

The Early Taoists and the Recluses

The recluses were thus individualists who "desired to maintain their personal purity." They were also, in a sense, defeatists who thought that the world was so bad that nothing could be done for it. One of them is reported in the *Analects* to have said: "The world is a swelling torrent, and is there anyone to change it?" (XVIII, 6.) It was from men of this sort, most of them living far away from other men in the world of nature, that the Taoists were probably originally drawn.

The Taoists, however, were not ordinary recluses who "escaped the world," desiring to "maintain their personal purity," and who, once in retirement, made no attempt ideologically to justify their conduct.

60

On the contrary, they were men who, having gone into seclusion, attempted to work out a system of thought that would give meaning to their action. Among them, Yang Chu seems to have been the earliest prominent exponent.

Yang Chu's dates are not clear, but he must have lived between the time of Mo Tzu (c. 479-c. 381 B.C.) and Mencius (c. 371-c. 289 B.C.). This is indicated by the fact that though unmentioned by Mo Tzu, he, by the time of Mencius, had become as influential as were the Mohists. To quote Mencius himself: "The words of Yang Chu and Mo Ti fill the world." (*Mencius*, IIIb, 9.) In the Taoist work known as the *Lieh-tzu*, there is one chapter entitled "Yang Chu," which, according to the traditional view, represents Yang Chu's philosophy.* But the authenticity of the *Lieh-tzu* has been much questioned by modern scholarship, and the view expressed in most of the "Yang Chu" chapter is not consistent with Yang Chu's ideas as reported in other early reliable sources. Its tenets are those of extreme hedonism (hence Forke's title, *Yang Chu's Garden of Pleasure*), whereas in no other early writings do we find Yang Chu being accused as a hedonist. Yang Chu's actual ideas, unfortunately, are nowhere described very consecutively, but must be deduced from scattered references in a number of works by other writers.

Yang Chu's Fundamental Ideas

The *Mencius* says: "The principle of Yang Chu is: 'Each one for himself.' Though he might have profited the whole world by plucking out a single hair, he would not have done it." (VIIa, 26.) The *Lü-shih Ch'un-ch'iu* (third century B.C.) says: "Yang Sheng valued self." (XVII, 7.) The *Han-fei-tzu* (also third century) says: "There is a man whose policy it is not to enter a city which is in danger, nor to remain in the army. Even for the great profit of the whole world, he would not exchange one hair of his shank. . . . He is one who despises things and values life." (Ch. 50.) And the *Huai-nan-tzu* (second century B.C.) says: "Preserving life and maintaining what is genuine in it, not allowing things to entangle one's person: this is what Yang Chu established." (Ch. 13.)

* See Anton Forke, *Yang Chu's Garden of Pleasure*, and James Legge, *The Chinese Classics*, Vol II, *Prolegomena*, pp. 92-9.

In the above quotations, the Yang Sheng of the *Lü-shih Ch'un-ch'iu* has been proved by recent scholars to be Yang Chu, while the man who "for the great profit of the whole world, would not exchange one hair of his shank" must also be Yang Chu or one of his followers, because no other man of that time is known to have held such a principle. Putting these sources together, we can deduce that Yang Chu's two fundamental ideas were: "Each one for himself," and "the despising of things and valuing of life." Such ideas are precisely the opposite of those of Mo Tzu, who held the principle of an all-embracing love.

The statement of Han Fei Tzu that Yang Chu would not give up a hair from his shank even to *gain* the entire world, differs somewhat from what Mencius says, which is that Yang Chu would not sacrifice a single hair even in order to profit the whole world. Both statements, however, are consistent with Yang Chu's fundamental ideas. The latter harmonizes with his doctrine of "each one for himself"; the former with that of "despising things and valuing life." Both may be said to be but two aspects of a single theory.

Illustrations of Yang Chu's Ideas

In Taoist literature, illustrations may be found for both the above mentioned aspects of Yang Chu's ideology. In the first chapter of the *Chuang-tzu*, there is a story about a meeting between the legendary sage-ruler Yao and a hermit named Hsü Yu. Yao was anxious to hand over his rule of the world to Hsü Yu, but the latter rejected it, saying: "You govern the world and it is already at peace. Suppose I were to take your place, would I do it for the name? Name is but the shadow of real gain. Would I do it for real gain? The tit, building its nest in the mighty forest, occupies but a single twig. The tapir, slaking its thirst from the river, drinks only enough to fill its belly. You return and be quiet. I have no need of the world." Here was a hermit who would not take the world, even were it given to him for nothing. Certainly, then, he would not exchange it for even a single hair from his shank. This illustrates Han Fei Tzu's account of Yang Chu.

In the above mentioned chapter titled "Yang Chu" in the *Lieh-tzu*, there is another story which reads: "Ch'in Tzu asked Yang Chu: 'If by plucking out a single hair of your body you could save the whole world, would you do it?' Yang Chu answered: 'The whole world is surely not to be saved by a single hair.' Ch'in Tzu said: 'But supposing it possible, would you do it?' Yang Chu made no answer. Ch'in Tzu then went out and told Meng-sun Yang. The latter replied: 'You do not understand the mind of the Master. I will explain it for you. Supposing by tearing off a piece of your skin, you were to get ten thousand pieces of gold, would you do it?' Ch'in Tzu said: 'I would.' Meng-sun Yang continued: 'Supposing by cutting off one of your limbs, you were to get a whole kingdom, would you do it?' For a while Ch'in Tzu was silent. Then Meng-sun Yang said: 'A hair is unimportant compared with the skin. A piece of skin is unimportant compared with a limb. But many hairs put together are as important as a piece of skin. Many pieces of skin put together are as important as a limb. A single hair is one of the ten thousand parts of the body. How can you disregard it?' " This is an illustration of the other aspect of Yang Chu's theory.

In the same chapter of the *Lieh-tzu*, Yang Chu is reported to have said: "The men of antiquity, if by injuring a single hair they could have profited the world, would not have done it. Had the world been offered to them as their exclusive possession, they would not have taken it. If everybody would refuse to pluck out even a single hair, and everybody would refuse to take the world as a gain, then the world would be in perfect order." We cannot be sure that this is really a saying of Yang Chu, but it sums up very well the two aspects of his theory, and the political philosophy of the early Taoists.

Yang Chu's Ideas as Expressed in the Lao-tzu and Chuang-tzu

Reflections of Yang Chu's main ideas can be found in portions of the *Lao-tzu* and some chapters of the *Chuang-tzu* and the *Lü-shih Ch'un-ch'iu*. In the latter work there is a chapter titled "The Importance of Self," in which it is said: "Our life is our own possession, and its benefit to us is very great. Regarding its dignity, even the honor of being Emperor could not compare with it. Regarding its importance, even the wealth of possessing the world would not be exchanged for it. Regarding its safety, were we to lose it for one morning, we could never again bring it back. These three are points on which those who have understanding are careful." (I, 3.) This passage explains why one should despise things and value life. Even an empire, once lost, may some day be regained, but once dead, one can never live again.

The *Lao-tzu* contains passages expressing the same idea. For example: "He who in his conduct values his body more than he does the world, may be given the world. He who in his conduct loves himself more than he does the world, may be entrusted with the world." (Ch. 13.) Or: "Name or person, which is more dear? Person or fortune, which is more important?" (Ch. 44.) Here again appears the idea of despising things and valuing life.

In the third chapter of the *Chuang-tzu*, titled "Fundamentals for the Cultivation of Life," we read: "When you do something good, beware of reputation; when you do something evil, beware of punishment. Follow the middle way and take this to be your constant principle. Then you can guard your person, nourish your parents, and complete your natural term of years." This again follows Yang Chu's line of thought, and, according to the earlier Taoists, is the best way to preserve one's life against the harms that come from the human world. If a man's conduct is so bad that society punishes him, this is obviously not the way to preserve his life. But if a man is so good in his conduct that he obtains a fine reputation, this too is not the way to preserve his life. Another chapter of the *Chuang-tzu* tells us: "Mountain trees are their own enemies, and the leaping fire is the cause of its own quenching. Cinnamon is edible, therefore the cinnamon tree is cut down. *Ch'i* oil is useful, therefore the *ch'i* tree is gashed." (Ch. 4.) A man having a reputation of ability and usefulness will suffer a fate just like that of the cinnamon and *ch'i* trees.

Thus in the *Chuang-tzu* we find passages that admire the usefulness of the useless. In the chapter just quoted, there is the description of a sacred oak, which, because its wood was good for nothing, had been spared the ax, and which said to someone in a dream: "For a long time I have been learning to be useless. There were several occasions on which I was nearly destroyed, but now I have succeeded in being useless, which is of the greatest use to me. If I were useful, could I have become so great?" Again it is said that "the world knows only the usefulness of the useful, but does not know the usefulness of the useless." (Ch. 4.) To be useless is the way to preserve one's life. The man who is skillful in preserving life must not do much evil, but neither must he do much good. He must live midway between good and evil. He tries to be useless, which in the end proves of greatest usefulness to him.

Development of Taoism

In this chapter we have been seeing the first phase in the development of early Taoist philosophy. Altogether there have been three main phases. The ideas attributed to Yang Chu represent the first. Those expressed in the greater part of the *Lao-tzu* represent the second. And those expressed in the greater part of the *Chuang-tzu* represent the third and last phase. I say the greater part of the *Lao-tzu* and *Chuang-tzu*, because in the *Lao-tzu* there are also to be found ideas representing the first and third phases and in the *Chuang-tzu* ideas of the first and second phases. These two books, like many others of ancient China, are really collections of Taoist writings and sayings, made by differing persons in different times, rather than the single work of any one person.

The starting point of Taoist philosophy is the preservation of life and avoiding of injury. Yang Chu's method for so doing is "to escape." This is the method of the ordinary recluse who flees from society and hides himself in the mountains and forests. By doing this he thinks he can avoid the evils of the human world. Things in the human world, however, are so complicated that no matter how well one hides oneself, there are always evils that cannot be avoided. There are times, therefore, when the method of "escaping" does not work.

The ideas expressed in the greater part of the *Lao-tzu* represent an attempt to reveal the laws underlying the changes of things in the universe. Things change, but the laws underlying the changes remain unchanging. If one understands these laws and regulates one's actions in conformity with them, one can then turn everything to one's advantage. This is the second phase in the development of Taoism.

Even so, however, there is no absolute guarantee. In the changes of things, both in the world of nature and of man, there are always unseen elements. So despite every care, the possibility remains that one will suffer injury. This is why the *Lao-tzu* says with still deeper insight: "The reason that I have great disaster is that I have a body. If there were no body, what disaster could there be?" (Ch. 13.) These words of greater understanding are developed in much of the *Chuang-*

tzu, in which occur the concepts of the equalization of life with death, and the identity of self with others. This means to see life and death, self and others, from a higher point of view. By seeing things from this higher point of view, one can transcend the existing world. This is also a form of "escape"; not one, however, from society to mountains and forests, but rather from this world to another world. Here is the third and last phase of development in the Taoism of ancient times.

All these developments are illustrated by a story which we find in the twentieth chapter of the *Chuang-tzu*, titled "The Mountain Tree." The story runs:

"Chuang Tzu was traveling through the mountains, when he saw a great tree well covered with foliage. A tree-cutter was standing beside it, but he did not cut it down. Chuang Tzu asked him the reason and he replied: 'It is of no use.' Chuang Tzu then said: 'By virtue of having no exceptional qualities, this tree succeeds in completing its natural span.'

"When the Master (Chuang Tzu) left the mountains, he stopped at the home of a friend. The friend was glad and ordered the servant to kill a goose and cook it. The servant asked: 'One of the geese can cackle. The other cannot. Which shall I kill?' The Master said: 'Kill the one that cannot cackle.' Next day, a disciple asked Chuang Tzu the question: 'Yesterday the tree in the mountains, because it had no exceptional quality, succeeded in completing its natural span. But now the goose of our host, because it had no exceptional quality, had to die. What will be your position?'

"Chuang Tzu laughed and said: 'My position will lie between having exceptional qualities and not having them. Yet this position only seems to be right, but really is not so. Therefore those who practice this method are not able to be completely free from troubles. If one wanders about with *Tao* and *Te* (the Way and its spiritual power), it will be otherwise.'"

Then Chuang Tzu went on to say that he who links himself with *Tao* and *Te* is with the "ancestor of things, using things as things, but not being used by things as things. When that is so, what is there that can trouble him?"

In this story, the first part illustrates the theory of preserving life as practiced by Yang Chu, while the second part gives that of Chuang Tzu. "Having exceptional quality" corresponds to the doing of good things, mentioned in the earlier quotation from the third chapter of the *Chuang-tzu*. "Having no exceptional quality" corresponds to the doing of bad things in that same quotation. And a position between these two extremes corresponds to the middle way indicated in that quotation. Yet if a man cannot see things from a higher point of view, none of these methods can absolutely guarantee him from danger and harm. To see things from a higher point of view, however, means to abolish the self. We may say that the early Taoists were selfish. Yet in their later development this selfishness became reversed and destroyed itself.

❧ CHAPTER 7 ❦

THE IDEALISTIC WING OF
CONFUCIANISM: MENCIUS

ACCORDING to the *Historical Records* (ch. 74), Mencius (371 ?-289 ?
B.C.) was a native of the state of Tsou, in the present southern part
of Shantung province in East China. He was linked with Confucius
through his study under a disciple of Tzu-ssu, who in turn was Confucius' grandson. At that time, the Kings of Ch'i, a larger state also
in present Shantung, were great admirers of learning. Near the west
gate of their capital, a gate known as Chi, they had established a
center of learning which they called Chi-hsia, that is, "below Chi."
All the scholars living there "were ranked as great officers and were
honored and courted by having large houses built for them on the
main road. This was to show to all the pensioned guests of the feudal
lords that it was the state of Ch'i that could attract the most eminent scholars in the world." (*Ibid.*)

Mencius for a while was one of these eminent scholars, but he also
traveled to other states, vainly trying to get a hearing for his ideas
among their rulers. Finally, so the *Historical Records* tell us, he
retired and with his disciples composed the *Mencius* in seven books.
This work records the conversations between Mencius and the feudal
lords of his time, and between him and his disciples, and in later
times it was honored by being made one of the famous "Four Books,"
which for the past one thousand years have formed the basis of Confucian education.

Mencius represents the idealistic wing of Confucianism, and the
somewhat later Hsün Tzu the realistic wing. The meaning of this
will become clear as we go on.

The Goodness of Human Nature

We have seen that Confucius spoke very much about *jen* (human-heartedness), and made a sharp distinction between *yi* (righteousness) and *li* (profit). Every man should, without thought of personal advantage, unconditionally do what he ought to do, and be what he ought to be. In other words, he should "extend himself so as to include others," which, in essence, is the practice of *jen*. But though Confucius held these doctrines, he failed to explain *why* it is that a man should act in this way. Mencius, however, attempted to give an answer to this question, and in so doing developed the theory for which he is most famed: that of the original goodness of human nature.

Whether human nature is good or bad—that is, what, precisely, is the nature of human nature—has been one of the most controversial problems in Chinese philosophy. According to Mencius, there were, in his time, three other theories besides his own on this subject. The first was that human nature is neither good nor bad. The second was that human nature can be either good or bad (which seems to mean that in the nature of man there are both good and bad elements), and the third was that the nature of some men is good, and that of others is bad. (*Mencius*, VIa, 3-6.) The first of these theories was held by Kao Tzu, a philosopher who was contemporary with Mencius. We know more about it than the other theories through the long discussions between him and Mencius which are preserved for us in the *Mencius*.

When Mencius holds that human nature is good, he does not mean that every man is born a Confucius, that is, a sage. His theory has some similarity with one side of the second theory mentioned above, that is, that in the nature of man there are good elements. He admits, to be sure, that there are also other elements, which are neither good nor bad in themselves, but which, if not duly controlled, can lead to evil. According to Mencius, however, these are elements which man shares in common with other living creatures. They represent the "animal" aspect of man's life, and therefore, strictly speaking, should not be considered as part of the "human" nature.

To support his theory, Mencius presents numerous arguments, among them the following: "All men have a mind which cannot bear [to see the suffering of] others. . . . If now men suddenly see a child about to fall into a well, they will without exception experience a feeling of alarm and distress. . . . From this case we may perceive that he who lacks the feeling of commiseration is not a man; that he who lacks a feeling of shame and dislike is not a man; that he who lacks a feeling of modesty and yielding is not a man; and that he who lacks a sense of right and wrong is not a man. The feeling of commiseration is the beginning of human-heartedness. The feeling of shame and dislike is the beginning of righteousness. The feeling of modesty and yielding is the beginning of propriety. The sense of right and wrong is the beginning of wisdom. Man has these four beginnings, just as he has four limbs. . . . Since all men have these four beginnings in themselves, let them know how to give them full development and completion. The result will be like fire that begins to burn, or a spring which has begun to find vent. Let them have their complete development, and they will suffice to protect all within the four seas. If they are denied that development, they will not suffice even to serve one's parents." (*Mencius*, IIa, 6.)

All men in their original nature possess these "four beginnings," which, if fully developed, become the four "constant virtues," so greatly emphasized in Confucianism. These virtues, if not hindered by external conditions, develop naturally from within, just as a tree grows by itself from the seed, or a flower from the bud. This is the basis of Mencius' controversy with Kao Tzu, according to whom human nature is in itself neither good nor bad, and for whom morality is therefore something that is artificially added from without.

There remains another question, which is: Why should man allow free development to his "four beginnings," instead of to what we may call his lower instincts? Mencius answers that it is these four beginnings that differentiate man from the beasts. They should be developed, therefore, because it is only through their development that man is truly a "man." Mencius says: "That whereby man differs from birds and beasts is but slight. The mass of the people cast it away, whereas the superior man preserves it." (*Mencius*, IVb, 19.) Thus he answers a question which had not occurred to Confucius.

Fundamental Difference between Confucianism and Mohism

Here we find the fundamental difference between Confucianism and Mohism. One of Mencius' self-appointed tasks was to "oppose

Yang Chu and Mo Ti." He says: "Yang's principle of 'each one for himself' amounts to making one's sovereign of no account. Mo's principle of 'all-embracing love' amounts to making one's father of no account. To have no father and no sovereign is to be like the birds and beasts. . . . These pernicious opinions mislead the people and block the way of human-heartedness and righteousness." (*Mencius*, IIIb, 9.) It is very clear that Yang Chu's theory opposes human-heartedness and righteousness, since the essence of these two virtues is to benefit others, while Yang Chu's principle is to benefit oneself. But Mo Tzu's principle of all-embracing love also aimed to benefit others, and he was even more outspoken in this respect than the Confucianists. Why, then, does Mencius lump him together with Yang Chu in his criticism?

The traditional answer is that according to Mohist doctrine, love should have in it no gradations of greater or lesser love, whereas according to Confucianism, the reverse is true. In other words, the Mohists emphasized equality in loving others, while the Confucianists emphasized gradation. This difference is brought out in a passage in the *Mo-tzu* in which a certain Wu-ma Tzu is reported as saying to Mo Tzu: "I cannot practice all-embracing love. I love the men of Tsou [a nearby state] better than I love those of Yüeh [a distant state]. I love the men of Lu [his own state] better than I love those of Tsou. I love the men of my own district better than I love those of Lu. I love the members of my own clan better than I love those of my district. I love my parents better than I love the men of my clan. And I love myself better than I love my parents." (*Mo-tzu*, ch. 46.)

Wu-ma Tzu was a Confucianist, and the representation of him as saying, "I love myself better than I love my parents," comes from a Mohist source and is probably an exaggeration. Certainly it is not consistent with the Confucianist emphasis on filial piety. With this exception, however, Wu-ma Tzu's statement is in general agreement with the Confucianist spirit. For according to the Confucianists, there should be degrees in love.

Speaking about these degrees, Mencius says: "The superior man, in his relation to things, loves them but has no feeling of human-heartedness. In his relation to people, he has human-heartedness, but no deep feeling of family affection. One should have feelings of family affection for the members of one's family, but human-hearted-

ness for people; human-heartedness for people, but love for things."
(*Mencius*, VIIa, 45.) In a discussion with a Mohist by the name of
Yi Chih, Mencius asked him whether he really believed that men
love their neighbors' children in the same way as they love their
brothers' children; the love for a brother's child is naturally greater.
(*Mencius*, IIIa, 5.) This, according to Mencius, is quite proper; what
should be done is to extend such love until it includes the more distant members of society. "Treat the aged in your family as they
should be treated, and extend this treatment to the aged of other
people's families. Treat the young in your family as they should be
treated, and extend this treatment to the young of other people's
families." (*Mencius*, Ia, 7.) Such is what Mencius calls "extending
one's scope of activity to include others." (*Ibid.*) It is an extension
based on the principle of graded love.

To extend the love for one's family so as to include persons outside
it as well, is to practice that "principle of *chung* [conscientiousness to
others] and *shu* [altruism]" advocated by Confucius, which in turn is
equivalent to the practice of human-heartedness. There is nothing
forced in any of these practices, because the original natures of all
men have in them a feeling of commiseration, which makes it impossible for them to bear to see the suffering of others. The development
of this "beginning" of goodness causes men naturally to love others,
but it is equally natural that they should love their parents to a
greater degree than they love men in general.

Such is the Confucianist point of view. The Mohists, on the contrary, insist that the love for others should be on a par with the love
for parents. Regardless of whether this means that one should love
one's parents less, or love others more, the fact remains that the
Confucianist type of graded love should be avoided at all costs. It is
with this in mind that Mencius attacks the Mohist principle of all-
embracing love as meaning that a man treats his father as of no
account.

The above difference between the Confucianist and the Mohist
theory of love has been pointed out very clearly by Mencius and by
many others after him. Besides this, however, there is another difference of a more fundamental nature. This is, that the Confucianists
considered human-heartedness as a quality that develops naturally
from within the human nature, whereas the Mohists considered all-
embracing love as something artificially added to man from without.

Mo Tzu may also be said to have answered a question that did not occur to Confucius, namely: Why should man practice human-heartedness and righteousness? His answer, however, is based on utilitarianism, and his emphasis on supernatural and political sanctions to compel and induce people to practice all-embracing love is not consistent with the Confucianist principle that virtue should be done for its own sake. If we compare the *Mo-tzu's* chapter on "All-Embracing Love," as quoted above in the fifth chapter, with the quotations here from the *Mencius* on the four moral beginnings in man's nature, we see very clearly the fundamental difference between the two schools.

Political Philosophy

We have seen earlier that the Mohist theory of the origin of state is likewise a utilitarianistic one. Here again the Confucianist theory differs. Mencius says: "If men have satisfied their hunger, have clothes to wear, and live at ease but lack good teaching, they are close to the birds and beasts. The sage [Shun, a legendary sage-ruler] was distressed about this and appointed Hsieh as an official instructor to teach men the basic relationships of life. Father and son should love each other. Ruler and subject should be just to each other. Husband and wife should distinguish their respective spheres. Elder and younger brothers should have a sense of mutual precedence. And between friends there should be good faith." (*Mencius*, IIIa, 4.) The existence of the human relationships and the moral principles based on them is what differentiates man from birds and beasts. The state and society have their origin in the existence of these human relationships. Therefore, according to the Mohists, the state exists because it is useful. But according to the Confucianists, it exists because it ought to exist.

Men have their full realization and development only in human relationships. Like Aristotle, Mencius maintains that "man is a political animal" and can fully develop these relationships only within state and society. The state is a moral institution and the head of the state should be a moral leader. Therefore in Confucianist political philosophy only a sage can be a real king. Mencius pictures this ideal as having existed in an idealized past. According to him, there was a time when the sage Yao (supposed to have lived in the twenty-fourth century B.C.) was Emperor. When he was old, he selected a younger sage, Shun, whom he had taught how to be a ruler, so that at Yao's death, Shun became Emperor. Similarly, when Shun was old, he again selected a younger sage, Yü, to be his successor. Thus the throne was handed from sage to sage, which, according to Mencius, is as it ought to be.

If a ruler lacks the ethical qualities that make a good leader, the people have the moral right of revolution. In that case, even the killing of the ruler is no longer a crime of regicide. This is because, according to Mencius, if a sovereign does not act as he ideally ought to do, he morally ceases to be a sovereign and, following Confucius' theory of the rectification of names, is a "mere fellow," as Mencius says. (*Mencius*, IIb, 8.) Mencius also says: "The people are the most important element [in a state]; the spirits of the land and the grain are secondary; and the sovereign is the least." (*Mencius*, VIIb, 14.) These ideas of Mencius have exercised a tremendous influence in Chinese history, even as late as the revolution of 1911, which led to the establishment of the Chinese Republic. It is true that modern democratic ideas from the West played their role too in this event, but the ancient native concept of the "right of revolution" had a greater influence on the mass of the people.

If a sage becomes king, his government is called one of kingly government. According to Mencius and later Confucianists, there are two kinds of government. One is that of the *wang* or (sage) king; the other is that of the *pa* or military lord. These are completely different in kind. The government of a sage-king is carried on through moral instruction and education; that of a military lord is conducted through force and compulsion. The power of the *wang* government is moral, that of the *pa* government, physical. Mencius says in this connection: "He who uses force in the place of virtue is a *pa*. He who is virtuous and practices human-heartedness is a *wang*. When one subdues men by force, they do not submit to him in their hearts but only outwardly, because they have insufficient strength to resist. But when one gains followers by virtue, they are pleased in their hearts and will submit of themselves as did the seventy disciples to Confucius." (*Mencius*, IIa, 3.)

This distinction between *wang* and *pa* has always been maintained by later Chinese political philosophers. In terms of contemporary politics, we may say that a democratic government is a *wang* government, because it represents a free association of people, while a Fascist government is that of a *pa*, because it reigns through terror and physical force.

The sage-king in his kingly government does all he can for the welfare and benefit of the people, which means that his state must be built on a sound economic basis. Since China has always been overwhelmingly agrarian, it is natural that, according to Mencius, the most important economic basis of kingly government lies in the equal distribution of land. His ideal land system is what has been known as the "well-field system." According to this system, each square *li* (about one third of a mile) of land is to be divided into nine squares, each consisting of one hundred Chinese acres. The central square is known as the "public field," while the eight surrounding squares are the private land of eight farmers with their families, each family having one square. These farmers cultivate the public field collectively and their own fields individually. The produce of the public field goes to the government, while each family keeps for itself what it raises from its own field. The arrangement of the nine squares resembles in form the Chinese character for "well" # , which is why it is called the "well-field system." (*Mencius* IIIa, 3.)

Describing this system further, Mencius states that each family should plant mulberry trees around its five-acre homestead in its own field so that its aged members may be clothed with silk. Each family should also raise fowls and pigs, so that its aged members may be nourished with meat. If this is done, everyone under the kingly government can "nourish the living and bury the dead without the least dissatisfaction, which marks the beginning of the kingly way." (*Mencius*, Ia, 3.)

It marks, however, only the "beginning," because it is an exclusively economic basis for the higher culture of the people. Only when everyone has received some education and come to an understanding of the human relationships, does the kingly way become complete.

The practice of this kingly way is not something alien to human nature, but is rather the direct outcome of the development by the sage-king of his own "feeling of commiseration." As Mencius says: "All men have a mind which cannot bear [to see the suffering of] others. The early kings, having this unbearing mind, thereby had likewise an unbearing government." (*Mencius*, IIa, 6.) The "unbearing mind" and feeling of commiseration are one in Mencius' thought.

As we have seen, the virtue of human-heartedness, according to the Confucianists, is nothing but the development of this feeling of commiseration; this feeling in its turn cannot be developed save through the practice of love; and the practice of love is nothing more than the "extension of one's scope of activity to include others," which is the way of *chung* and *shu*. The kingly way or kingly government is nothing but the result of the king's practice of love, and his practice of *chung* and *shu*.

According to Mencius, there is nothing esoteric or difficult in the kingly way. The *Mencius* (Ib, 9) records that on one occasion, when an ox was being led to sacrifice, King Hsüan of Ch'i saw it and could not endure "its frightened appearance, as if it were an innocent person going to the place of death." He therefore ordered that it be replaced by a sheep. Mencius then told the King that this was an example of his "unbearing mind," and if he could only extend it to include human affairs, he could then govern in the kingly way. The King replied that he could not do this because he had the defect of loving wealth and feminine beauty. Whereupon Mencius told the King that these are things loved by all men. If the King, by understanding his own desires, would also come to understand the desires of all his people, and would take measures whereby the people might satisfy these desires, this would result in the kingly way and nothing else.

What Mencius told King Hsüan is nothing more than the "extension of one's own scope of activity to include others," which is precisely the practice of *chung* and *shu*. Here we see how Mencius developed the ideas of Confucius. In his exposition of this principle, Confucius had limited himself to its application to the self-cultivation of the individual, while by Mencius its application was extended to government and politics. For Confucius, it was a principle only for "sageliness within," but by Mencius it was expanded to become also a principle for "kingliness without."

Even in the former sense of "sageliness within," Mencius expresses his concept of this principle more clearly than did Confucius. He says: "He who has completely developed his mind, knows his nature. He who knows his nature, knows Heaven." (*Mencius*, VIIa, 1.) The mind here referred to is the "unbearing mind" or the "feeling of commiseration." It is the essence of our nature. Hence when we fully develop this mind, we know our nature. And according to

Mencius, our nature is "what Heaven has given to us." (*Mencius*, VIa, 15.) Therefore, when we know our nature, we also know Heaven.

Mysticism

According to Mencius and his school of Confucianism, the uni-verse is essentially a moral universe. The moral principles of man are also metaphysical principles of the universe, and the nature of man is an exemplification of these principles. It is this moral universe that Mencius and his school mean when they speak of Heaven, and an understanding of this moral universe is what Mencius calls "knowing Heaven." If a man knows Heaven, he is not only a citizen of society, but also a "citizen of Heaven," *t'ien min*, as Mencius says. (*Mencius*, VIIa, 19.) Mencius further makes a distinction between "human honors" and "heavenly honors." He says: "There are heavenly hon-ors and human honors. Human-heartedness, righteousness, loyalty, good faith, and the untiring practice of the good: these are the honors of Heaven. Princes, ministers, and officials: these are the hon-ors of man." (*Mencius*, VIa, 16.) In other words, heavenly honors are those to which a man can attain in the world of values, while human honors are purely material concepts in the human world. The citizen of Heaven, just because he is the citizen of Heaven, cares only for the honors of Heaven, but not those of man.

Mencius also remarks: "All things are complete within us. There is no greater delight than to realize this through self-cultivation. And there is no better way to human-heartedness than the practice of the principle of *shu*." (*Mencius*, VIIa, 1.) In other words, through the full development of his nature, a man can not only know Heaven, but can also become one with Heaven. Also when a man fully de-velops his unbearing mind, he has within him the virtue of human-heartedness, and the best way to human-heartedness is the practice of *chung* and *shu*. Through this practice, one's egoism and selfish-ness are gradually reduced. And when they are reduced, one comes to feel that there is no longer a distinction between oneself and others, and so of distinction between the individual and the universe. That is to say, one becomes identified with the universe as a whole. This leads to a realization that "all things are complete within us." In this phrase we see the mystical element of Mencius' philosophy.

We will understand this mysticism better, if we turn to Mencius' discussion on what he calls the *Hao Jan Chih Ch'i*, a term which I translate as the "Great Morale." In this discussion Mencius describes the development of his own spiritual cultivation.

The *Mencius* (IIa, 2) tells us that a disciple asked Mencius of what he was a specialist. Mencius replied: "I know the right and wrong in speech, and am proficient in cultivating my *Hao Jan Chih Ch'i*." The questioner then asked what this was, and Mencius replied: "It is the *Ch'i*, supremely great, supremely strong. If it be directly cultivated without handicap, then it pervades all between Heaven and Earth. It is the *Ch'i* which is achieved by the combination of righteousness and *Tao* [the way, the truth], and without these it will be weakened."

Hao Jan Chih Ch'i is a special term of Mencius. In later times, under his increasing influence, it came to be used not infrequently, but in ancient times it appears only in this one chapter. As to what it signifies, even Mencius admits that "it is hard to say." (*Ibid.*) The context of this discussion, however, includes a preliminary discussion about two warriors and their method of cultivating their valor. From this I infer that Mencius' *Ch'i* (a word which literally means vapor, gas, spiritual force) is the same *ch'i* as occurs in such terms as *yung ch'i* (courage, valor) and *shih ch'i* (morale of an army). That is why I translate *Hao Jan Chih Ch'i* as the "Great Morale." It is of the same nature as the morale of the warriors. The difference between the two, however, is that this *Ch'i* is further described as *hao jan*, which means "great to a supreme degree." The morale which warriors cultivate is a matter concerning man and man, and so is a moral value only. But the Great Morale is a matter concerning man and the universe, and therefore is a super-moral value. It is the morale of the man who identifies himself with the universe, so that Mencius says of it that "it pervades all between Heaven and Earth."

The method of cultivating the Great Morale has two aspects. One may be called the "understanding of *Tao*"; that is, of the way or principle that leads to the elevation of the mind. The other aspect is what Mencius calls the "accumulation of righteousness"; that is, the constant doing of what one ought to do in the universe as a "citizen of the universe." The combination of these two aspects is called by Mencius "the combination of righteousness and *Tao*."

After one has reached an understanding of *Tao* and the long accumulation of righteousness, the Great Morale will appear naturally of itself. The least bit of forcing will lead to failure. As Mencius says: "We should not be like the man of Sung. There was a man of Sung who was grieved that his grain did not grow fast enough. So he pulled it up. Then he returned to his home with great innocence, and said to his people: 'I am tired to-day, for I have been helping the grain to grow.' His son ran out to look at it, and found all the grain withered." (*Ibid.*)

When one grows something, one must on the one hand do something for it, but on the other never "help it to grow." The cultivation of the Great Morale is just like the growing of the grain. One must do something, which is the practice of virtue. Though Mencius here speaks of righteousness rather than human-heartedness, there is no practical difference, since human-heartedness is the inner content, of which righteousness is the outer expression. If one constantly practices righteousness, the Great Morale will naturally emerge from the very center of one's being.

Although this *Hao Jan Chih Ch'i* sounds rather mysterious, it can nevertheless, according to Mencius, be achieved by every man. This is because it is nothing more than the fullest development of the nature of man, and every man has fundamentally the same nature. His nature is the same, just as every man's bodily form is the same. As an example, Mencius remarks that when a shoemaker makes shoes, even though he does not know the exact length of the feet of his customers, he always makes shoes, but not baskets. (*Mencius*, VIa, 7.) This is so because the similarity between the feet of all men is much greater than their difference. And likewise the sage, in his original nature, is similar to everyone else. Hence every man can become a sage, if only he gives full development to his original nature. As Mencius affirms: "All men can become Yao or Shun [the two legendary sage-rulers previously mentioned]." (*Mencius*, VIb, 2.) Here is Mencius' theory of education, which has been held by all Confucianists.

CHAPTER 8

THE SCHOOL OF NAMES

THE term *Ming chia* has sometimes been translated as "sophists," and sometimes as "logicians" or "dialecticians." It is true that there is some similarity between the *Ming chia* and the sophists, logicians, and dialecticians, but it is also true that they are not quite the same. To avoid confusion, it is better to translate *Ming chia* literally as the School of Names. This translation also helps to bring to the attention of Westerners one of the important problems discussed by Chinese philosophy, namely that of the relation between *ming* (the name) and *shih* (the actuality).

The School of Names and the "Debaters"

Logically speaking, the contrast between *ming* and *shih* in ancient Chinese philosophy is something like that between subject and predicate in the West. For instance, when we say: "This is a table," or "Socrates is a man," "this" and "Socrates" are *shih* or actualities, while "table" and "man" are *ming* or names. This is obvious enough. Let us, however, try to analyze more exactly just what the *shih* or *ming* are, and what their relationship is. We are then apt to be led into some rather paradoxical problems, the solution of which brings us to the very heart of philosophy.

The members of the School of Names were known in ancient times as *pien che* (debaters, disputers, arguers). In the chapter of the *Chuang-tzu* titled "The Autumn Flood," Kung-sun Lung, one of the leaders of the School of Names, is represented as saying: "I have unified similarity and difference, and separated hardness and whiteness. I have proved the impossible as possible and affirmed what others deny. I have controverted the knowledge of all the philosophers, and refuted all the arguments brought against me." (*Chuang-tzu*, ch. 17.) These words are really applicable to the School of

Names as a whole. Its members were known as persons who made paradoxical statements, who were ready to dispute with others, and who purposely affirmed what others denied and denied what others affirmed. Ssu-ma T'an (died 110 B.C.), for example, in his essay, "On the Essential Ideas of the Six Schools," wrote: "The School of Names conducted minute examinations of trifling points in complicated and elaborate statements, which made it impossible for others to refute their ideas." (*Historical Records*, ch. 120.)

Hsün Tzu, a Confucianist of the third century B.C., describes Teng Hsi (died 501 B.C.) and Hui Shih as philosophers who "liked to deal with strange theories and indulge in curious propositions." (*Hsün-tzu*, ch. 6.) Likewise, the *Lü-shih Ch'un-ch'iu* mentions Teng Hsi and Kung-sun Lung as among those known for their paradoxical arguments. (XVIII, 4 and 5.) And the chapter titled "The World" in the *Chuang-tzu*, after listing the paradoxical arguments famous at that time, mentions the names of Hui Shih, Huan T'uan, and Kung-sun Lung. These men, therefore, would seem to have been the most important leaders of this school.

About Huan T'uan we know nothing further, but about Teng Hsi, we know that he was a famous lawyer of his time; his writings, however, no longer are preserved, and the book today bearing the title of *Teng-hsi-tzu* is not genuine. The *Lü-shih Ch'un-ch'iu* says that when Tzu-ch'an, a famous statesman, was minister of the state of Cheng, Teng Hsi, who was a native of that state, was his major opponent. He used to help the people in their lawsuits, for which services he would demand a coat as a fee for a major case, and a pair of trousers for a minor one. So skilful was he that he was patronized by numerous people; as their lawyer, he succeeded in changing right into wrong and wrong into right, until no standards of right and wrong remained, so that what was regarded as possible and impossible fluctuated from day to day. (XVIII, 4.)

Another story in the same work describes how, during a flood of the Wei River, a certain rich man of the state of Cheng was drowned. His body was picked up by a boatman, but when the family of the rich man went to ask for the body, the man who had found it demanded a huge reward. Thereupon the members of the family went to Teng Hsi for advice. He told them: "Merely wait. There is nobody else besides yourselves who wants the body." The family took his advice and waited, until the man who had found the body became much troubled and also went to Teng Hsi. To him Teng Hsi said: "Merely wait. There is nobody else but you from whom they can get the body." (*Ibid.*) We are not told what was the final end of this episode!

It would thus seem that Teng Hsi's trick was to interpret the formal letter of the law in such a way as to give varying interpretations in different cases at will. This was how he was able to "conduct minute examinations of trifling points in complicated and elaborate statements, which made it impossible for others to refute his ideas." He thus devoted himself to interpreting and analyzing the letter of the law, while disregarding its spirit and its connection with actuality. In other words, his attention was directed to "names," instead of to "actualities." Such was the spirit of the School of Names.

From this we may see that the *pien che* were originally lawyers, among whom Teng Hsi was evidently one of the first. He was, however, only a beginner in the analysis of names, and made no real contribution to philosophy as such. Hence the real founders of the School of Names were the later Hui Shih and Kung-sun Lung.

Concerning these two men the *Lü-shih Ch'un-ch'iu* tells us: "Hui Tzu [Hui Shih] prepared the law for King Hui of Wei (370-319). When it was completed and was made known to the people, the people considered it to be good." (XVIII, 5.) And again: "The states of Chao and Ch'in entered into an agreement which said: 'From this time onward, in whatever Ch'in desires to do, she is to be assisted by Chao, and in whatever Chao desires to do, she is to be assisted by Ch'in.' But soon afterward Ch'in attacked the state of Wei, and Chao made ready to go to Wei's assistance. The King of Ch'in protested to Chao that this was an infringement of the pact, and the King of Chao reported this to the Lord of P'ing-yüan, who again told it to Kung-sun Lung. Kung-sun Lung said: 'We too can send an envoy to protest to the King of Ch'in, saying: "According to the pact, each side guarantees to help the other in whatever either desires to do. Now it is our desire to save Wei, and if you do not help us to do so, we shall charge you with infringement of the pact." ' " (*Ibid.*)

Again we are told in the *Han-fei-tzu*: "When discussions on 'hardness and whiteness' and 'having no thickness' appear, the governmental laws lose their effect." (Ch. 41.) We shall see below that the doctrine of "hardness and whiteness" is one of Kung-sun Lung, while that of "having no thickness" is one of Hui Shih.

From these stories we may see that Hui Shih and Kung-sun Lung were, to some extent, connected with the legal activities of their time. Indeed, Kung-sun Lung's interpretation of the pact between Chao and Ch'in is truly in the spirit of Teng Hsi. Han Fei Tzu considered the effect of the "speeches" of these two gentlemen on law to be as bad as that of the practice of Teng Hsi. It may seem strange that Han Fei Tzu, himself a Legalist, should oppose, as destructive to law, the "discussions" of a school which had originated with lawyers. But, as we shall see in chapter 14, Han Fei Tzu and the other Legalists were really politicians, not jurists.

Hui Shih and Kung-sun Lung represented two tendencies in the School of Names, the one emphasizing the relativity of actual things, and the other the absoluteness of names. This distinction becomes evident when one comes to analyze names in their relationship to actualities. Let us take the simple statement, "This is a table." Here the word "this" refers to the concrete actuality, which is impermanent and may come and go. The word "table," however, refers to an abstract category or name which is unchanging and always remains as it is. The "name" is absolute, but the "actuality" is relative. Thus "beauty" is the name of what is absolutely beautiful, but "a beautiful thing" can only be relatively so. Hui Shih emphasized the fact that actual things are changeable and relative, while Kung-sun Lung emphasized the fact that names are permanent and absolute.

Hui Shih's Theory of Relativity

Hui Shih (fl. 350-260) was a native of the state of Sung, in the present province of Honan. We know that he once became premier of King Hui of Wei (370-319), and that he was known for his great learning. His writings, unfortunately, are lost, and what we know of his ideas may be deduced only from a series of "ten points" preserved in the chapter titled "The World" in the *Chuang-tzu*.

The first of these points is: "The greatest has nothing beyond itself, and is called the Great One. The smallest has nothing within itself, and is called the Small One." These two statements constitute what are called analytical propositions. They make no assertions in regard to the actual, for they say nothing about what, in the actual world, is the greatest thing and the smallest thing. They only touch upon the abstract concepts or names: "greatest" and "smallest." In order to understand these two propositions fully, we should compare them with a story in the chapter titled "The Autumn Flood" in the *Chuang-tzu*. From this it will become apparent that in one respect Hui Shih and Chuang Tzu had very much in common.

This story describes how in autumn, when the Yellow River was in flood, the Spirit of the River, who was very proud of his greatness, moved down the river to the sea. There he met the Spirit of the Sea, and realized for the first time that his river, great as it was, was small indeed in comparison with the sea. Yet when, full of admiration, he talked with the Spirit of the Sea, the latter replied that he himself, in his relationship to Heaven and Earth, was nothing more than a single grain lying within a great warehouse. Hence he could only be said to be "small," but not to be "great." At this the River Spirit asked the Sea Spirit: "Are we right then in saying that Heaven and Earth are supremely great and the tip of a hair is supremely small?" The Sea Spirit answered: "What men know is less than what they do not know. The time when they are alive is less than the time when they are not alive. . . . How can we know that the tip of a hair is the extreme of smallness, and Heaven and Earth are the extreme of greatness?" And he then went on to define the smallest as that which has no form, and the greatest as that which cannot be enclosed (by anything else). This definition of the supremely great and supremely small is similar to that given by Hui Shih. (*Chuang-tzu*, ch. 17.)

To say that Heaven and Earth are the greatest of things and that the tip of a hair is the smallest is to make assertions about the actual, the *shih*. It makes no analysis of the names of the actualities, the *ming*. These two propositions are what are called synthetic propositions and both may be false. They have their basis in experience; therefore their truth is only contingent, but not necessary. In experience, things that are great and things that are small are all relatively so. To quote the *Chuang-tzu* again: "If we call a thing great, because it is greater than something else, then there is nothing in the world that is not great. If we call a thing small because it is smaller than something else, then there is nothing in the world that is not small."

We cannot through actual experience decide what is the greatest and what is the smallest of actual things. But we can say independently of experience that that which has nothing beyond itself is the greatest, and that which has nothing within itself is the smallest. "Greatest" and "smallest," defined in this way, are absolute and unchanging concepts. Thus by analyzing the names, "Great One" and "Small One," Hui Shih reached the concept of what is absolute and unchanging. From the point of view of this concept, he realized that the qualities and differences of actual concrete things are all relative and liable to change.

Once we understand this position of Hui Shih, we can see that his series of "points," as reported by the *Chuang-tzu*, though usually regarded as paradoxes, are really not paradoxical at all. With the exception of the first, they are all illustrations of the relativity of things, and expressions of what may be called a theory of relativity. Let us study them one by one.

"That which has no thickness cannot be increased [in thickness], yet it is so great that it may cover one thousand miles." This states that the great and the small are so only relatively. It is impossible for that which has no thickness to be thick. In this sense it may be called small. Nevertheless, the ideal plane of geometry, though without thickness, may at the same time be very long and wide. In this sense it may be called great.

"The heavens are as low as the earth; mountains are on the same level as marshes." This, too, states that the high and the low are so only relatively. "The sun at noon is the sun declining; the creature born is the creature dying." This states that everything in the actual world is changeable and changing.

"Great similarity differs from little similarity. This is called little-similarity-and-difference. All things are in one way all similar, in another way all different. This is called great-similarity-and-difference." When we say that all men are animals, we thereby recognize that all human beings are similar in the fact that they are human beings, and are also similar in the fact that they are animals. Their similarity in being human beings, however, is greater than that in being animals, because being a human being implies being an animal, but being an animal does not necessarily imply being a human being. For there are other kinds of animals as well, which are different from human beings. It is this kind of similarity and difference, therefore, that Hui Shih calls little-similarity-and-difference. However, if we take "beings" as a universal class, we thereby recognize that all things are similar in the fact that they are beings. But if we take each thing as an individual, we thereby recognize that each individual has its own individuality and so is different from other things. This kind of similarity and difference is what Hui Shih calls great-similarity-and-difference. Thus since we can say that all things are similar to each other, and yet can also say that all things are different from each other, this shows that their similarity and difference are both relative. This argument of the School of Names was a famous one in ancient China, and was known as the "argument for the unity of similarity and difference."

"The South has no limit and yet has a limit." "The South has no limit" was a common saying of the day. At that time, the South was a little known land very much like the West of America two hundred years ago. For the early Chinese, the South was not limited by sea as was the East, nor by barren desert as were the North and West. Hence it was popularly regarded as having no limit. Hui Shih's statement may thus perhaps be merely an expression of his superior geographical knowledge, that the South is, eventually, also limited by the sea. Most probably, however, it means to say that the limited and the unlimited are both only relatively so.

"I go to the state of Yüeh today and arrived there yesterday." This states that "today" and "yesterday" are relative terms. The yesterday of today was the today of yesterday, and the today of today will be the yesterday of tomorrow. Herein lies the relativity of the present and the past.

"Connected rings can be separated." Connected rings cannot be separated unless they are destroyed. But destruction may, from another point of view, be construction. If one makes a wooden table, from the point of view of the wood, it is destruction, but from the point of view of the table, it is construction. Since destruction and construction are relative, therefore "connected rings can be separated" without destroying them.

"I know the center of the world. It is north of Yen and south of Yüeh." Among the states of the time, Yen was in the extreme north and Yüeh in the extreme south. The Chinese regarded China as being the world. Hence it was a matter of common sense that the center of the world should be south of Yen and north of Yüeh. Hui Shih's contrary assertion here is well interpreted by a commentator of the third century A.D., Ssu-ma Piao, who says: "The world has no limit, and therefore anywhere is the center, just as in drawing a circle, any point on the line can be the starting point."

"Love all things equally; Heaven and Earth are one body." In the preceding propositions, Hui Shih argues that all things are relative and in a state of flux. There is no absolute difference, or absolute separation among them. Everything is constantly changing into something else. It is a logical conclusion, therefore, that all things are one, and hence that we should love all things equally without discrimination. In the *Chuang-tzu* it is also said: "If we see things from the point of view of their difference, even my liver and gall are as far from each other as are the states of Ch'u and Yüeh. If we see things from the point of view of their similarity, all things are one." (Ch. 5.)

Kung-sun Lung's Theory of Universals

The other main leader of the School of Names was Kung-sun Lung (fl. 284-259), who was widely known in his day for his sophistic arguments. It is said that once when he was passing a frontier, the frontier guards said: "Horses are not allowed to pass." Kung-sun Lung replied: "My horse is white, and a white horse is not a horse." And so saying, he passed with his horse.

Instead of emphasizing, as did Hui Shih, that actual things are relative and changeable, Kung-sun Lung emphasized that names are absolute and permanent. In this way he arrived at the same concept of Platonic ideas or universals that has been so conspicuous in Western philosophy.

In his work titled the *Kung-sun Lung-tzu*, there is a chapter called "Discourse on the White Horse." Its main proposition is the assertion that "a white horse is not a horse." This proposition Kung-sun Lung tries to prove through three arguments. The first is: "The word 'horse' denotes a shape; the word 'white' denotes a color. That which denotes color is not that which denotes shape. Therefore I say that a white horse is not a horse." In terms of Western logic, we may say that this argument emphasizes the difference in the intension of the terms "horse," "white," and "white horse." The intension of the first term is one kind of animal, that of the second is one kind of color, and that of the third is one kind of animal plus one kind of color.

Since the intension of each of the three terms is different, therefore a white horse is not a horse.

The second argument is: "When a horse is required, a yellow horse or a black one may be brought forward, but when one requires a white horse, a yellow or a black horse cannot be brought forward. . . . Therefore a yellow horse and a black horse are both horses. They can only respond to a call for a horse but cannot respond to a call for a white horse. It is clear that a white horse is not a horse." And again: "The term 'horse' neither excludes nor includes any color; therefore yellow and black ones may respond to it. But the term 'white horse' both excludes and includes color. Yellow and black horses are all excluded because of their color. Therefore only a white horse can fit the requirements. That which is not excluded is not the same as that which is excluded. Therefore I say that a white horse is not a horse." In terms of Western logic, we may say that this argument emphasizes the difference in the extension of the terms "horse" and "white horse." The extension of the term "horse" includes all horses, with no discrimination as to their color. The extension of the term "white horse," however, includes only white horses, with a corresponding discrimination of color. Since the extension of the term "horse" and "white horse" is different, therefore a white horse is not a horse.

The third argument is: "Horses certainly have color. Therefore there are white horses. Suppose there is a horse without color, then there is only the horse as such. But how then, do we get a white horse? Therefore a white horse is not a horse. A white horse is 'horse' together with 'white.' 'Horse' with 'white' is not horse." In this argument, Kung-sun Lung seems to emphasize the distinction between the universal, "horseness," and the universal, "white-horseness." The universal, horseness, is the essential attribute of all horses. It implies no color and is just "horse as such." Such "horseness" is distinct from "white-horseness." That is to say, the horse as such is distinct from the white horse as such. Therefore a white horse is not a horse.

Besides horse as such, there is also white as such, that is, whiteness. In the same chapter it is said: "White [as such] does not specify what is white. But 'white horse' specifies what is white. Specified white is not white." Specified white is the concrete white color which is seen in this or that particular white object. The word here translated as "specified" is *ting*, which also has the meaning of "determined." The white color which is seen in this or that white object is

determined by this or that object. The universal, "whiteness," however, is not determined by any one particular white object. It is the
whiteness unspecified.

The *Kung-sun Lung-tzu* contains another chapter entitled "Discourse on Hardness and Whiteness." The main proposition in this
chapter is that "hardness and whiteness are separate." Kung-sun Lung
tries to prove this in two ways. The first is expressed in the following
dialogue: "[Supposing there is a hard and white stone], is it possible
to say hard, white, and stone are three? No. Can they be two? Yes.
How? When without hardness one finds what is white, this gives two.
When without whiteness one finds what is hard, this gives two. Seeing does not give us what is hard but only what is white, and there is
nothing hard in this. Touching does not give us what is white but
only what is hard, and there is nothing white in this." This dialogue
uses epistemological proof to show that hardness and whiteness are
separated from each other. Here we have a hard and white stone. If
we use our eyes to see it, we only get what is white, i.e., a white stone.
But if we use our hands to touch it, we only get what is hard, i.e.,
a hard stone. While we are sensing that the stone is white, we cannot
sense that it is hard, and while we are sensing that it is hard, we
cannot sense that it is white. Epistemologically speaking, therefore,
there is only a *white stone* or a *hard stone* here, but not a *hard and
white stone*. This is the meaning of the saying: "When without hardness one finds what is white, this gives two. When without whiteness
one finds what is hard, this gives two."

Kung-sun Lung's second argument is a metaphysical one. Its general idea is that both hardness and whiteness, as universals, are unspecified in regard to what particular object it is that is hard or that
is white. They can be manifested in any or all white or hard objects.
Indeed, even if in the physical world there were no hard or white
objects at all, none the less, the universal, hardness, would of necessity remain hardness, and the universal, whiteness, would remain
whiteness. Such hardness and whiteness are quite independent of
the existence of physical stones or other objects that are hard and
white. The fact that they are independent universals is shown by the
fact that in the physical world there are some objects that are hard
but not white, and other objects that are white but not hard. Thus
it is evident that hardness and whiteness are separate from each other.

With these epistemological and metaphysical arguments Kung-sun

Lung established his proposition that hardness and whiteness are separate. This was a famous proposition in ancient China, and was known as the argument for "the separateness of hardness and whiteness."
,
In the *Kung-sun Lung-tzu* there is yet another chapter entitled "Discourse on *Chih* and *Wu*." By *wu* Kung-sun Lung means concrete particular things, while by *chih* he means abstract universals. The literal meaning of *chih* is, as a noun, "finger" or "pointer," or, as a verb, "to indicate." Two explanations may be given as to why Kung-sun Lung uses the word *chih* to denote universals. A common term, that is, a name, to use the terminology of the School of Names, denotes a class of particular things and connotes the common attributes of that class. An abstract term, on the contrary, denotes the attribute or universal. Since the Chinese language has no inflection, there is no distinction in form between a common term and an abstract one. Thus, in Chinese, what Westerners would call a common term may also denote a universal. Likewise, the Chinese language has no articles. Hence, in Chinese, such terms as "horse," "the horse," and "a horse" are all designated by the one word *ma* or "horse." It would seem, therefore, that fundamentally the word *ma* denotes the universal concept, "horse," while the other terms, "a horse," "the horse," etc., are simply particularized applications of this universal concept. From this it may be said that, in the Chinese language, a universal is what a name points out, i.e., denotes. This is why Kung-sun Lung refers to universals as *chih* or "pointers."

Another explanation of why Kung-sun Lung uses *chih* to denote the universal, is that *chih* (finger, pointer, etc.) is a close equivalent of another word, also pronounced *chih* and written almost the same, which means "idea" or "concept." According to this explanation, then, when Kung-sun Lung speaks of *chih* (pointer), he really means by it "idea" or "concept." As can be seen from his arguments above, however, this "idea" is for him not the subjective idea spoken of in the philosophy of Berkeley and Hume, but rather the objective idea as found in the philosophy of Plato. It is the universal.

In the final chapter of the *Chuang-tzu* we find a series of twenty-one arguments attributed without specification to the followers of the School of Names. Among them, however, it is evident that some are based upon the ideas of Hui Shih, and others upon those of Kung-sun Lung, and they can be explained accordingly. They used to be considered as paradoxes, but they cease to be such once we understand the fundamental ideas of their authors.

Significance of the Theories of Hui Shih and Kung-sun Lung

Thus by analyzing names, and their relation with, or their distinction from, actualities, the philosophers of the School of Names discovered what in Chinese philosophy is called "that which lies beyond shapes and features." In Chinese philosophy a distinction is made between "being that lies within shapes and features," and "being that lies beyond shapes and features." "Being that lies within shapes and features" is the actual, the *shih*. For instance, the big and the small, the square and the round, the long and the short, the white and the black, are each one class of shapes and features. Anything that is the object or possible object of experience has shape and feature, and lies within the actual world. Conversely, any object in the actual world that has shape and feature is the object or possible object of experience.

When Hui Shih enunciated the first and last of his series of "points," he was talking about what lies beyond shapes and features. "The greatest," he said, "has nothing beyond itself. This is called the Great One." This defines in what manner the greatest is as it is. "Love all things equally; Heaven and Earth are one." This defines of what the greatest consists. This last statement conveys the idea that all is one and one is all. Since all is one, there can be nothing beyond the all. The all is itself the greatest one, and since there can be nothing beyond the all, the all cannot be the object of experience. This is because an object of experience always stands in apposition to the one who experiences. Hence if we say that the all can be an object of experience, we must also say that there is something that stands in apposition to the all and is its experiencer. In other words, we must say that that which has nothing beyond itself at the same time has something beyond itself, which is a manifest contradiction.

King-sun Lung, too, discovered what lies beyond shapes and features, because the universals he discussed can likewise not be objects of experience. One can see a white something, but one cannot see the universal whiteness as such. All universals that are indicated by names lie in a world beyond shapes and features, though not all universals in that world have names to indicate them. In that world, hardness is hardness and whiteness is whiteness, or as Kung-sun Lung said: "Each is alone and true" (*Kung-sun Lung-tzu*, ch. 5.)

Hui Shih spoke of "loving all things equally," and Kung-sun Lung also "wished to extend his argument in order to correct the relations between names and actualities, so as thus to transform the whole world." (*Ibid.*, ch. 1.) Both men thus apparently considered their philosophy as comprising the "*Tao* of sageliness within and kingliness without." But it was left to the Taoists fully to apply the discovery made by the School of Names of what lies beyond shapes and features. The Taoists were the opponents of this school, but they were also its true inheritors. This is illustrated by the fact that Hui Shih was a great friend of Chuang Tzu.

CHAPTER 9

THE SECOND PHASE OF TAOISM:
LAO TZU

ACCORDING to tradition, Lao Tzu (a name which literally means the "Old Master") was a native of the state of Ch'u in the southern part of the present Honan province, and was an older contemporary of Confucius, whom he is reputed to have instructed in ceremonies. The book bearing his name, the *Lao-tzu*, and in later times also known as the *Tao Te Ching* (*Classic of the Way and Power*), has therefore been traditionally regarded as the first philosophical work in Chinese history. Modern scholarship, however, has forced us drastically to change this view and to date it to a time considerably after Confucius.

Lao Tzu the Man and Lao-tzu the Book

Two questions arise in this connection. One is about the date of the man, Lao Tzu (whose family name is said to have been Li, and personal name, Tan), and another about the date of the book itself. There is no necessary connection between the two, for it is quite possible that there actually lived a man known as Lao Tan who was senior to Confucius, but that the book titled the *Lao-tzu* is a later production. This is the view I take, and it does not necessarily contradict the traditional accounts of Lao Tzu the man, because in these accounts there is no statement that the man, Lao Tzu, actually wrote the book by that name. Hence I am willing to accept the traditional stories about Lao Tzu the man, while at the same time placing the book, *Lao-tzu*, in a later period. In fact, I now believe the date of the book to be later than I assumed when I wrote my *History of Chinese Philosophy*. I now believe it was written or composed after

Hui Shih and Kung-sun Lung, and not before, as I there indicated. This is because the *Lao-tzu* contains considerable discussion about the Nameless, and in order to do this it would seem that men should first have become conscious of the existence of names themselves.

My position does not require me to insist that there is absolutely no connection between Lao Tzu the man and *Lao-tzu* the book, for the book may indeed contain a few sayings of the original Lao Tzu. What I maintain, however, is that the system of thought in the book as a whole cannot be the product of a time either before or contemporary with that of Confucius. In the pages following, however, to avoid pedantry, I shall refer to Lao Tzu as having said so and so, instead of stating that the book *Lao-tzu* says so and so, just as we today still speak of sunrise and sunset, even though we know very well that the sun itself actually neither rises nor sets.

Tao, *the Unnamable*

In the last chapter, we have seen that the philosophers of the School of Names, through the study of names, succeeded in discovering "that which lies beyond shapes and features." Most people, however, think only in terms of "what lies within shapes and features," that is, the actual world. Seeing the actual, they have no difficulty in expressing it, and though they use names for it, they are not conscious that they are names. So when the philosophers of the School of Names started to think about the names themselves, this thought represented a great advance. To think about names is to think about thinking. It is thought about thought and therefore is thought on a higher level.

All things that "lie within shapes and features" have names, or, at least, possess the possibility of having names. They are namable. But in contrast with what is namable, Lao Tzu speaks about the unnamable. Not everything that lies beyond shapes and features is unnamable. Universals, for instance, lie beyond shapes and features, yet they are not unnamable. But on the other hand, what is unnamable most certainly does lie beyond shapes and features. The *Tao* or Way of the Taoists is a concept of this sort.

In the first chapter of the *Lao-tzu* we find the statement: "The *Tao* that can be comprised in words is not the eternal *Tao*; the name that can be named is not the abiding name. The Unnamable is the *yu* (being) *wu* (non-being) — Could there be some common ground w/ Being & Nothingness w/ Taoism & Existentialism ?

must read Being & Nothingness

beginning of Heaven and Earth; the namable is the mother of all things." And in chapter thirty-two: "The *Tao* is eternal, nameless, the Uncarved Block. . . . Once the block is carved, there are names." Or in chapter forty-one: "The *Tao*, lying hid, is nameless." In the Taoist system, there is a distinction between *yu* (being) and *wu* (non-being), and between *yu-ming* (having-name, namable) and *wu-ming* (having-no-name, unnamable). These two distinctions are in reality only one, for *yu* and *wu* are actually simply abbreviated terms for *yu-ming* and *wu-ming*. Heaven and Earth and all things are namables. Thus Heaven has the name of Heaven, Earth the name Earth, and each kind of thing has the name of that kind. There being Heaven, Earth and all things, it follows that there are the names of Heaven, Earth, and all things. Or as Lao Tzu says: "Once the Block is carved, there are names." The *Tao*, however, is unnamable; at the same time it is that by which all namables come to be. This is why Lao Tzu says: "The Unnamable is the beginning of Heaven and Earth; the namable is the mother of all things."

Since the *Tao* is unnamable, it therefore cannot be comprised in words. But since we wish to speak about it, we are forced to give it some kind of designation. We therefore call it *Tao*, which is really not a name at all. That is to say, to call the *Tao Tao*, is not the same as to call a table table. When we call a table table, we mean that it has some attributes by which it can be named. But when we call the *Tao Tao*, we do not mean that it has any such namable attributes. It is simply a designation, or to use an expression common in Chinese philosophy, *Tao* is a name which is not a name. In Chapter twenty-one of the *Lao-tzu* it is said: "From the past to the present, its [*Tao's*] name has not ceased to be, and has seen the beginning [of all things]." The *Tao* is that by which anything and everything comes to be. Since there are always things, *Tao* never ceases to be and the name of *Tao* also never ceases to be. It is the beginning of all beginnings, and therefore it has seen the beginning of all things. A name that never ceases to be is an abiding name, and such a name is in reality not a name at all. Therefore it is said: "The name that can be named is not the abiding name."

"The Unnamable is the beginning of Heaven and Earth." This proposition is only a formal and not a positive one. That is to say, it fails to give any information about matters of fact. The Taoists thought that since there are things, there must be that by which all these things come to be. This "that" is designated by them as *Tao*, which, however, is really not a name. The concept of *Tao*, too, is a formal and not a positive one. That is to say, it does not describe anything about what it is through which all things come to be. All we can say is that *Tao*, since it is that through which all things come to be, is necessarily not a mere thing among these other things. For if it were such a thing, it could not at the same time be that through which *all* things whatsoever come to be. Every kind of thing has a name, but *Tao* is not itself a thing. Therefore it is "nameless, the Uncarved Block."

Anything that comes to be is a being, and there are many beings. The coming to be of beings implies that first of all there is Being. These words, "first of all," here do not mean first in point of time, but first in a logical sense. For instance, if we say there was first a certain kind of animal, then man, the word "first" in this case means first in point of time. But if we say that first there must be animals before there are men, the word "first" in this case means first in a logical sense. The statement about "the origin of the species" makes an assertion about matters of fact, and required many years' observation and study by Charles Darwin before it could be made. But the second of our sayings makes no assertion about matters of fact. It simply says that the existence of men logically implies the existence of animals. In the same way, the being of all things implies the being of Being. This is the meaning of Lao Tzu's saying: "All things in the world come into being from Being (*Yu*); and Being comes into being from Non-being (*Wu*)." (Ch. 40.)

This saying of Lao Tzu does not mean that there was a time when there was only Non-being, and that then there came a time when Being came into being from Non-being. It simply means that if we analyze the existence of things, we see there must first be Being before there can be any things. *Tao* is the unnamable, is Non-being, and is that by which all things come to be. Therefore, before the being of Being, there must be Non-being, from which Being comes into being. What is here said belongs to ontology, not to cosmology. It has nothing to do with time and actuality. For in time and actuality, there is no Being; there are only beings.

There are many beings, but there is only one Being. In the *Lao-tzu* it is said: "From *Tao* there comes one. From one there comes two. From two there comes three. From three there comes all things."

(Ch. 42.) The "one" here spoken of refers to Being. To say that "from *Tao* comes one," is the same as that from Non-being comes Being. As for "two" and "three," there are many interpretations. But this saying, that "from one there comes two. From two there comes three. From three there comes all things," may simply be the same as saying that from Being come all things. Being is one, and two and three are the beginning of the many.

The Invariable Law of Nature

In the final chapter of the *Chuang-tzu*, "The World," it is said that the leading ideas of Lao Tzu are those of the *T'ai Yi* or "Super One," and of Being, Non-being, and the invariable. The "Super One" is the *Tao*. From the *Tao* comes one, and therefore *Tao* itself is the "Super One." The "invariable" is a translation of the Chinese word *ch'ang*, which may also be translated as eternal or abiding. Though things are ever changeable and changing, the laws that govern this change of things are not themselves changeable. Hence in the *Lao-tzu* the word *ch'ang* is used to show what is always so, or in other words, what can be considered as a rule. For instance, Lao Tzu tells us: "The conquest of the world comes invariably from doing nothing." (Ch. 48.) Or again: "The way of Heaven has no favorites, it is invariably on the side of the good man." (Ch. 79.)

Among the laws that govern the changes of things, the most fundamental is that "when a thing reaches one extreme, it reverts from it." These are not the actual words of Lao Tzu, but a common Chinese saying, the idea of which no doubt comes from Lao Tzu. Lao Tzu's actual words are: "Reversing is the movement of the *Tao*" (ch. 40), and: "To go further and further means to revert again." (Ch. 25.) The idea is that if anything develops certain extreme qualities, those qualities invariably revert to become their opposites.

This constitutes a law of nature. Therefore: "It is upon calamity that blessing leans, upon blessing that calamity rests." (Ch. 58.) "Those with little will acquire, those with much will be led astray." (Ch. 22.) "A hurricane never lasts the whole morning, nor a rainstorm the whole day." (Ch. 23.) "The most yielding things in the world master the most unyielding." (Ch. 43.) "Diminish a thing and it will increase. Increase a thing and it will diminish." (Ch. 42.) All these paradoxical theories are no longer paradoxical, if one understands the fundamental law of nature. But to the ordinary people who have no idea of this law, they seem paradoxical indeed. Therefore Lao Tzu says: "The gentleman of the low type, on hearing the Truth, laughs loudly at it. If he had not laughed, it would not suffice to be the Truth." (Ch. 41.)

It may be asked: Granted that a thing, on reaching an extreme, then reverts, what is meant by the word "extreme"? Is there any absolute limit for the development of anything, going beyond which would mean going to the extreme? In the *Lao-tzu* no such question is asked and therefore no answer is given. But if there had been such a question, I think Lao Tzu would have answered that no absolute limit can be prescribed for all things under all circumstances. So far as human activities are concerned, the limit for the advancement of a man remains relative to his subjective feelings and objective circumstances. Isaac Newton, for example, felt that compared with the total universe, his knowledge of it was no more than the knowledge of the sea possessed by a boy who is playing at the seashore. With such a feeling as this, Newton, despite his already great achievements in physics, was still far from reaching the limits of advancement in his learning. If, however, a student, having just finished his textbook on physics, thinks that he then knows all there is to know about science, he certainly cannot make further advancement in his learning, and will as certainly "revert back." Lao Tzu tells us: "If people of wealth and exalted position are arrogant, they abandon themselves to unavoidable ruin." (Ch. 9.) Arrogance is the sign that one's advancement has reached its extreme limit. It is the first thing that one should avoid.

The limit of advancement for a given activity is also relative to objective circumstances. When a man eats too much, he suffers. In overeating, what is ordinarily good for the body becomes something harmful. One should eat only the right amount of food. But this right amount depends on one's age, health, and the quality of food one eats.

These are the laws that govern the changes of things. By Lao Tzu they are called the invariables. He says: "To know the invariables is called enlightenment." (Ch. 16.) Again: "He who knows the invariable is liberal. Being liberal, he is without prejudice. Being without prejudice, he is comprehensive. Being comprehensive, he is vast. Being vast, he is with the Truth. Being with the Truth, he lasts forever and will not fail throughout his lifetime." (*Ibid.*)

Human Conduct

Lao Tzu warns us: "Not to know the invariable and to act blindly is to go to disaster." (*Ibid.*) One should know the laws of nature and conduct one's activities in accordance with them. This, by Lao Tzu, is called "practicing enlightenment." The general rule for the man "practicing enlightenment" is that if he wants to achieve anything, he starts with its opposite, and if he wants to retain anything, he admits in it something of its opposite. If one wants to be strong, one must start with a feeling that one is weak, and if one wants to preserve capitalism, one must admit in it some elements of socialism.

Therefore Lao Tzu tells us: "The sage, putting himself in the background, is always to the fore. Remaining outside, he is always there. Is it not just because he does not strive for any personal end, that all his personal ends are fulfilled?" (Ch. 7.) Again: "He does not show himself; therefore he is seen everywhere. He does not define himself; therefore he is distinct. He does not assert himself; therefore he succeeds. He does not boast of his work; therefore he endures. He does not contend, and for that very reason no one in the world can contend with him." (Ch. 22.) These sayings illustrate the first point of the general rule.

In the *Lao-tzu* we also find: "What is most perfect seems to have something missing, yet its use is unimpaired. What is most full seems empty, yet its use is inexhaustible. What is most straight seems like crookedness. The greatest skill seems like clumsiness. The greatest eloquence seems like stuttering." (Ch. 45.) Again: "Be twisted and one shall be whole. Be crooked and one shall be straight. Be hollow and one shall be filled. Be tattered and one shall be renewed. Have little and one shall obtain. But have much and one shall be perplexed." (Ch. 22.) This illustrates the second point of the general rule.

Such is the way in which a prudent man can live safely in the world and achieve his aims. This is Lao Tzu's answer and solution to the original problem of the Taoists, which was, how to preserve life and avoid harm and danger in the human world. (See end of Ch. 6 above.) The man who lives prudently must be meek, humble, and easily content. To be meek is the way to preserve your strength and so be strong. Humility is the direct opposite of arrogance, so that if arrogance is a sign that a man's advancement has reached its extreme limit, humility is a contrary sign that that limit is far from reached. And to be content safeguards one from going too far, and therefore from reaching the extreme. Lao Tzu says: "To know how to be content is to avoid humiliation; to know where to stop is to avoid injury." (Ch. 45.) Again: "The sage, therefore, discards the excessive, the extravagant, the extreme." (Ch. 29.)

All these theories are deducible from the general theory that "reversing is the movement of the *Tao*." The well-known Taoist theory of *wu-wei* is also deducible from this general theory. *Wu-wei* can be translated literally as "having-no-activity" or "non-action." But using this translation, one should remember that the term does not actually mean complete absence of activity, or doing nothing. What it does mean is lesser activity or doing less. It also means acting without artificiality and arbitrariness.

Activities are like many other things. If one has too much of them, they become harmful rather than good. Furthermore, the purpose of doing something is to have something done. But if there is over-doing, this results in something being over-done, which may be worse than not having the thing done at all. A well-known Chinese story describes how two men were once competing in drawing a snake; the one who would finish his drawing first would win. One of them, having indeed finished his drawing, saw that the other man was still far behind, so decided to improve it by adding feet to his snake. Thereupon the other man said: "You have lost the competition, for a snake has no feet." This is an illustration of over-doing which defeats its own purpose. In the *Lao-tzu* we read: "Conquering the world is invariably due to doing nothing; by doing something one cannot conquer the world." (Ch. 48.) The term "doing nothing" here really means "not over-doing."

Artificiality and arbitrariness are the opposite of naturalness and spontaneity. According to Lao Tzu, *Tao* is that by which all things come to be. In this process of coming to be, each individual thing obtains something from the universal *Tao*, and this something is called *Te*. *Te* is a word that means "power" or "virtue," both in the moral and non-moral sense of the latter term. The *Te* of a thing is what it naturally is. Lao Tzu says: "All things respect *Tao* and value *Te*." (Ch. 51.) This is because *Tao* is that by which they come to be, and *Te* is that by which they are what they are.

According to the theory of "having-no-activity," a man should restrict his activities to what is necessary and what is natural. "Necessary" means necessary to the achievement of a certain purpose, and never over-doing. "Natural" means following one's *Te* with no arbitrary effort. In doing this one should take simplicity as the guiding principle of life. Simplicity (*p'u*) is an important idea of Lao Tzu and the Taoists. *Tao* is the "Uncarved Block" (*p'u*), which is simplicity itself. There is nothing that can be simpler than the unnamable *Tao*. *Te* is the next simplest, and the man who follows *Te* must lead as simple a life as possible.

The life that follows *Te* lies beyond the distinctions of good and evil. Lao Tzu tells us: "If all people of the world know that beauty is beauty, there is then already ugliness. If all people of the world know that good is good, there is then already evil." (Ch. 2.) Lao Tzu, therefore, despised such Confucian virtues as human-heartedness and righteousness, for according to him these virtues represent a degeneration from *Tao* and *Te*. Therefore he says: "When the *Tao* is lost, there is the *Te*. When the *Te* is lost, there is [the virtue of] human-heartedness. When human-heartedness is lost, there is [the virtue of] righteousness. When righteousness is lost, there are the ceremonials. Ceremonials are the degeneration of loyalty and good faith, and are the beginning of disorder in the world." (Ch. 38.) Here we find the direct conflict between Taoism and Confucianism.

People have lost their original *Te* because they have too many desires and too much knowledge. In satisfying their desires, people are seeking for happiness. But when they try to satisfy too many desires, they obtain an opposite result. Lao Tzu says: "The five colors blind the eye. The five notes dull the ear. The five tastes fatigue the mouth. Riding and hunting madden the mind. Rare treasures hinder right conduct." (Ch. 5.) Therefore, "there is no disaster greater than not knowing contentment with what one has; no greater sin than having desire for acquisition." (Ch. 46.) This is why Lao Tzu emphasizes that people should have few desires.

Likewise Lao Tzu emphasizes that people should have little knowledge. Knowledge is itself an object of desire. It also enables people to know more about the objects of desire and serves as a means to gain these objects. It is both the master and servant of desire. With increasing knowledge people are no longer in a position to know how to be content and where to stop. Therefore, it is said in the *Lao-Tzu*:

"When knowledge and intelligence appeared, Gross Artifice began." (Ch. 18.)

Political Theory

From these theories Lao Tzu deduces his political theory. The Taoists agree with the Confucianists that the ideal state is one which has a sage as its head. It is only the sage who can and should rule. The difference between the two schools, however, is that according to the Confucianists, when a sage becomes the ruler, he should do many things for the people, whereas according to the Taoists, the duty of the sage ruler is not to do things, but rather to undo or not to do at all. The reason for this, according to Lao Tzu, is that the troubles of the world come, not because there are many things not yet done, but because too many things are done. In the *Lao-tzu* we read: "The more restrictions and prohibitions there are in the world, the poorer the people will be. The more sharp weapons the people have, the more troubled will be the country. The more cunning craftsmen there are, the more pernicious contrivances will appear. The more laws are promulgated, the more thieves and bandits there will be." (Ch. 27.)

The first act of a sage ruler, then, is to undo all these. Lao Tzu says: "Banish wisdom, discard knowledge, and the people will be benefited a hundredfold. Banish human-heartedness, discard righteousness, and the people will be dutiful and compassionate. Banish skill, discard profit, and thieves and robbers will disappear." (Ch. 19.) Again: "Do not exalt the worthies, and the people will no longer be contentious. Do not value treasures that are hard to get, and there will be no more thieves. If the people never see such things as excite desire, their mind will not be confused. Therefore the sage rules the people by emptying their minds, filling their bellies, weakening their wills, and toughening their sinews, ever making the people without knowledge and without desire." (Ch. 3.)

The sage ruler would undo all the causes of trouble in the world. After that, he would govern with non-action. With non-action, he does nothing, yet everything is accomplished. The *Lao-tzu* says: "I act not and the people of themselves are transformed. I love quiescence and the people of themselves go straight. I concern myself with nothing, and the people of themselves are prosperous. I am without desire, and the people of themselves are simple." (Ch. 57.)

"Do nothing, and there is nothing that is not done." This is another of the seemingly paradoxical ideas of the Taoists. In the *Lao-tzu* we read: "*Tao* invariably does nothing and yet there is nothing that is not done." (Ch. 37.) *Tao* is that by which all things come to be. It is not itself a thing and therefore it cannot act as do such things. Yet all things come to be. Thus *Tao* does nothing, yet there is nothing that is not done. It allows each thing to do what it itself can do According to the Taoists, the ruler of a state should model himself on *Tao*. He, too, should do nothing and should let the people do what they can do themselves. Here is another meaning of *wu-wei* (non-action), which later, with certain modifications, become one of the important theories of the Legalists (*Fa chia*).

Children have limited knowledge and few desires. They are not far away from the original *Te*. Their simplicity and innocence are characteristics that every man should if possible retain. Lao Tzu says: "Not to part from the invariable *Te* is to return to the state of infancy." (Ch. 28.) Again: "He who holds the *Te* in all its solidity may be likened to an infant." (Ch. 55.) Since the life of the child is nearer to the ideal life, the sage ruler would like all of his people to be like small children. Lao Tzu says: "The sage treats all as children." (Ch. 49.) He "does not make them enlightened, but keeps them ignorant." (Ch. 65.)

"Ignorant" here is a translation of the Chinese *yu*, which means ignorance in the sense of simplicity and innocence. The sage not only wants his people to be *yu*, but wants himself to be so too. Lao Tzu says: "Mine is the mind of the very ignorant." (Ch. 20.) In Taoism *yu* is not a vice, but a great virtue.

But is the *yu* of the sage really the same as the *yu* of the child and the common people? Certainly not. The *yu* of the sage is the result of a conscious process of cultivation. It is something higher than knowledge, something more, not less. There is a common Chinese saying: "Great wisdom is like ignorance." The *yu* of the sage is great wisdom, and not the *yu* of the child or of ordinary people. The latter kind of *yu* is a gift of nature, while that of the sage is an achievement of the spirit. There is a great difference between the two. But in many cases the Taoists seemed to have confused them. We shall see this point more clearly when we discuss the philosophy of Chuang Tzu.

CHAPTER 10

THE THIRD PHASE OF TAOISM:
CHUANG TZU

Cʜᴜᴀɴɢ Cʜᴏᴜ, better known as Chuang Tzu (c. 369-c. 286), is perhaps the greatest of the early Taoists. We know little of his life save that he was a native of the little state of Meng on the border between the present Shantung and Honan provinces, where he lived a hermit's life, but was nevertheless famous for his ideas and writings. It is said that King Wei of Ch'u, having heard his name, once sent messengers with gifts to invite him to his state, promising to make him chief minister. Chuang Tzu, however, merely laughed and said to them: ". . . Go away, do not defile me. . . . I prefer the enjoyment of my own free will." (*Historical Records*, ch. 63.)

Chuang Tzu the Man and Chuang-tzu the Book

Though Chuang Tzu was a contemporary of Mencius and a friend of Hui Shih, the book titled the *Chuang-tzu*, as we know it today, was probably compiled by Kuo Hsiang, Chuang Tzu's great commentator of the third century A.D. We are thus not sure which of the chapters of *Chuang-tzu* the book were really written by Chuang Tzu himself. It is, in fact, a collection of various Taoist writings, some of which represent Taoism in its first phase of development, some in its second, and some in its third. It is only those chapters representing the thought of this third climactic phase that can properly be called Chuang Tzu's own philosophy, yet even they may not all have been written by Chuang Tzu himself. For though the name of Chuang Tzu can be taken as representative of the last phase of early Taoism, it is probable that his system of thought was brought to full completion only by his followers. Certain chapters of the *Chuang-tzu*, for example, contain statements about Kung-sun Lung, who certainly lived later than Chuang Tzu.

Way of Achieving Relative Happiness

The first chapter of the *Chuang-tzu*, titled "The Happy Excursion," is a simple text, full of amusing stories. Their underlying idea is that there are varying degrees in the achievement of happiness. A free development of our natures may lead us to a relative kind of happiness; absolute happiness is achieved through higher understanding of the nature of things.

To carry out the first of these requirements, the free development of our nature, we should have a full and free exercise of our natural ability. That ability is our *Te*, which comes directly from the *Tao*. Regarding the *Tao* and *Te*, Chuang Tzu has the same idea as Lao Tzu. For example, he says: "At the great beginning there was Nonbeing. It had neither being nor name and was that from which came the One. When the One came into existence, there was the One but still no form. When things obtained that by which they came into existence, it was called the *Te*." (Ch. 12.) Thus our *Te* is what makes us what we are. We are happy when this *Te* or natural ability of ours is fully and freely exercised, that is, when our nature is fully and freely developed.

In connection with this idea of free development, Chuang Tzu makes a contrast between what is of nature and what is of man. "What is of nature," he says, "is internal. What is of man is external. . . . That oxen and horses should have four feet is what is of nature. That a halter should be put on a horse's head, or a string through an ox's nose, is what is of man." (Ch. 17.) Following what is of nature, he maintains, is the source of all happiness and goodness, while following what is of man is the source of all pain and evil.

Things are different in their nature and their natural ability is also not the same. What they share in common, however, is that they are all equally happy when they have a full and free exercise of their natural ability. In "The Happy Excursion" a story is told of a very large and a small bird. The abilities of the two are entirely different. The one can fly thousands of miles, while the other can hardly reach from one tree to the next. Yet they are both happy when they each do what they are able and like to do. Thus there is no absolute uniformity in the natures of things, nor is there any need for such uniformity. Another chapter of the *Chuang-tzu* tells us: "The duck's legs are short, but if we try to lengthen them, the duck will feel pain.

The crane's legs are long, but if we try to shorten them, the crane will feel grief. Therefore we are not to amputate what is by nature long, nor to lengthen what is by nature short." (Ch. 8.)

Political and Social Philosophy

Such, however, is just what artificiality tries to do. The purpose of all laws, morals, institutions, and governments, is to establish uniformity and suppress difference. The motivation of the people who try to enforce this uniformity may be wholly admirable. When they find something that is good for them, they may be anxious to see that others have it also. This good intention of theirs, however, only makes the situation more tragic. In the *Chuang-tzu* there is a story which says: "Of old, when a seabird alighted outside the capital of Lu, the Marquis went out to receive it, gave it wine in the temple, and had the *Chiu-shao* music played to amuse it, and a bullock slaughtered to feed it. But the bird was dazed and too timid to eat or drink anything. In three days it was dead. This was treating the bird as one would treat oneself, not the bird as a bird. . . . Water is life to fish but is death to man. Being differently constituted, their likes and dislikes must necessarily differ. Therefore the early sages did not make abilities and occupations uniform." (Ch. 18.) When the Marquis treated the bird in a way which he considered the most honorable, he certainly had good intentions. Yet the result was just opposite to what he expected. This is what happens when uniform codes of laws and morals are enforced by government and society upon the individual.

This is why Chuang Tzu violently opposes the idea of governing through the formal machinery of government, and maintains instead that the best way of governing is through non-government. He says: "I have heard of letting mankind alone, but not of governing mankind. Letting alone springs from the fear that people will pollute their innate nature and set aside their *Te*. When people do not pollute their innate nature and set aside their *Te*, then is there need for the government of mankind?" (Ch. 11.)

If one fails to leave people alone, and tries instead to rule them with laws and institutions, the process is like putting a halter around a horse's neck or a string through an ox's nose. It is also like lengthening the legs of the duck or shortening those of the crane. What is natural and spontaneous is changed into something artificial, which is called by Chuang Tzu "overcoming what is of nature by what is of man." (Ch. 17.) Its result can only be misery and unhappiness.

Thus Chuang Tzu and Lao Tzu both advocate government through non-government, but for somewhat different reasons. Lao Tzu emphasizes his general principle that "reversing is the movement of the *Tao*." The more one governs, he argues, the less one achieves the desired result. And Chuang Tzu emphasizes the distinction between what is of nature and what is of man. The more the former is overcome by the latter, the more there will be misery and unhappiness.

Thus far we have only seen Chuang Tzu's way of achieving relative happiness. Such relative happiness is achieved when one simply follows what is natural in oneself. This every man can do. The political and social philosophy of Chuang Tzu aims at achieving precisely such relative happiness for every man. This and nothing more is the most that any political and social philosophy can hope to do.

Emotion and Reason

Relative happiness is relative because it has to depend upon something. It is true that one is happy when one has a full and free exercise of one's natural ability. But there are many ways in which this exercise is obstructed. For instance, there is death which is the end of all human activities. There are diseases which handicap human activities. There is old age which gives man the same trouble. So it is not without reason that the Buddhists consider these as three of the four human miseries, the fourth, according to them, being life itself. Hence, happiness which depends upon the full and free exercise of one's natural ability is a limited and therefore relative happiness.

In the *Chuang-tzu* there are many discussions about the greatest of all disasters that can befall man, death. Fear of death and anxiety about its coming are among the principal sources of human unhappiness. Such fear and anxiety, however, may be diminished if we have a proper understanding of the nature of things. In the *Chuang-tzu* there is a story about the death of Lao Tzu. When Lao Tzu died, his friend Chin Shih, who had come after the death, criticized the violent lamentations of the other mourners, saying: "This is to violate the principle of nature and to increase the emotion of man, forgetting what we have received [from nature]. These were called by the ancients the penalty of violating the principle of nature. When the Master came, it was because he had the occasion to be born. When he went, he simply followed the natural course. Those who are quiet at the proper occasion and follow the natural course, cannot be affected by sorrow or joy. They were considered by the ancients as the men of the gods, who were released from bondage." (Ch. 3.)

To the extent that the other mourners felt sorrow, to that extent they suffered. Their suffering was the "penalty of violating the principle of nature." The mental torture inflicted upon man by his emotions is sometimes just as severe as any physical punishment. But by the use of understanding, man can reduce his emotions. For example, a man of understanding will not be angry when rain prevents him from going out, but a child often will. The reason is that the man possesses greater understanding, with the result that he suffers less disappointment or exasperation than the child who does get angry. As Spinoza has said: "In so far as the mind understands all things are necessary, so far has it greater power over the effects, or suffers less from them." (*Ethics*, Pt. 5, Prop. VI.) Such, in the words of the Taoists, is "to disperse emotion with reason."

A story about Chuang Tzu himself well illustrates this point. It is said that when Chuang Tzu's wife died, his friend Hui Shih went to condole. To his amazement he found Chuang Tzu sitting on the ground, singing, and on asking him how he could be so unkind to his wife, was told by Chuang Tzu: "When she had just died, I could not help being affected. Soon, however, I examined the matter from the very beginning. At the very beginning, she was not living, having no form, nor even substance. But somehow or other there was then her substance, then her form, and then her life. Now by a further change, she has died. The whole process is like the sequence of the four seasons, spring, summer, autumn, and winter. While she is thus lying in the great mansion of the universe, for me to go about weeping and wailing would be to proclaim myself ignorant of the natural laws. Therefore I stop." (*Chuang-tzu*, ch. 18.) On this passage the great commentator Kuo Hsiang comments: "When ignorant, he felt sorry. When he understood, he was no longer affected. This teaches man to disperse emotion with reason." Emotion can be counteracted with reason and understanding. Such was the view of Spinoza and also of the Taoists.

The Taoists maintained that the sage who has a complete understanding of the nature of things, thereby has no emotions. This, however, does not mean that he lacks sensibility. Rather it means that he is not disturbed by the emotions, and enjoys what may be called "the peace of the soul." As Spinoza says: "The ignorant man is not only agitated by external causes in many ways, and never enjoys true peace in the soul, but lives also ignorant, as it were, both of God and of things, and as soon as he ceases to suffer, ceases also to be. On the other hand, the wise man, in so far as he is considered as such, is scarcely moved in his mind, but, being conscious by a certain eternal necessity of himself, of God, and things, never ceases to be, and always enjoys the peace of the soul." (*Ethics*, Pt. 5, Prop. XLII.)

Thus by his understanding of the nature of things, the sage is no longer affected by the changes of the world. In this way he is not dependent upon external things, and hence his happiness is not limited by them. He may be said to have achieved absolute happiness. Such is one line of Taoist thought, in which there is not a little atmosphere of pessimism and resignation. It is a line which emphasizes the inevitability of natural processes and the fatalistic acquiescence in them by man.

Way of Achieving Absolute Happiness

There is another line of Taoist thought, however, which emphasizes the relativity of the nature of things and the identification of man with the universe. To achieve this identification, man needs knowledge and understanding of still a higher level, and the happiness resulting from this identification is really absolute happiness, as expounded in Chuang Tzu's chapter on "The Happy Excursion."

In this chapter, after describing the happiness of large and small birds, Chuang Tzu adds that among human beings there was a man named Lieh Tzu who could even ride on the wind. "Among those who have attained happiness," he says, "such a man is rare. Yet although he was able to dispense with walking, he still had to depend upon something." This something was the wind, and since he had to depend upon the wind, his happiness was to that extent relative. Then Chuang Tzu asks: "But suppose there is one who chariots on the normality of the universe, rides on the transformation of the six elements, and thus makes excursion into the infinite, what has he to depend upon? Therefore it is said that the perfect man has no self; the spiritual man has no achievement; and the true sage has no name." (Ch. 1.)

What is here said by Chuang Tzu describes the man who has achieved absolute happiness. He is the perfect man, the spiritual man, and the true sage. He is absolutely happy, because he transcends the ordinary distinctions of things. He also transcends the distinction between the self and the world, the "me" and the "non-me." Therefore he has no self. He is one with the Tao. The Tao does nothing and yet there is nothing that is not done. The Tao does nothing, and therefore has no achievements. The sage is one with the Tao and therefore also has no achievements. He may rule the whole world, but his rule consists of just leaving mankind alone, and letting everyone exercise his own natural ability fully and freely. The Tao is nameless and so the sage who is one with the Tao is also nameless.

The Finite Point of View

The question that remains is this: How can a person become such a perfect man? To answer it, we must make an analysis of the second chapter of the Chuang-tzu, the Ch'i Wu Lun, or "On the Equality of Things." In the "Happy Excursion" Chuang Tzu discusses two levels of happiness, and in "On the Equality of Things" he discusses two levels of knowledge. Let us start our analysis with the first or lower level. In our chapter on the School of Names, we have said that there is some similarity between Hui Shih and Chuang Tzu. Thus in the Ch'i Wu Lun, Chuang Tzu discusses knowledge of a lower level which is similar to that found in Hui Shih's ten so-called paradoxes.

The chapter Ch'i Wu Lun begins with a description of the wind. When the wind blows, there are different kinds of sound, each with its own peculiarity. These this chapter calls "the sounds of earth." But in addition there are other sounds that are known as "the sounds of man." The sounds of earth and the sounds of man together constitute "the sounds of Heaven."

The sounds of man consist of the words (yen) that are spoken in the human world. They differ from such "sounds of earth" as those caused by the wind, inasmuch as when words are said, they represent human ideas. They represent affirmations and denials, and the opinions that are made by each individual from his own particular finite point of view. Being thus finite, these opinions are necessarily one-sided. Yet most men, not knowing that their opinions are based on finite points of view, invariably consider their own opinions as right and those of others as wrong. "The result," as the *Ch'i Wu Lun* says, "is the affirmations and denials of the Confucianists and Mohists, the one regarding as right what the other regards as wrong, and re-garding as wrong what the other regards as right."

When people thus argue each according to his own one-sided view, there is no way either to reach a final conclusion, or to determine which side is really right or really wrong. The *Ch'i Wu Lun* says: "Suppose that you argue with me. If you beat me, instead of my beating you, are you necessarily right and am I necessarily wrong? Or, if I beat you, and not you me, am I necessarily right and are you necessarily wrong? Is one of us right and the other wrong? Or are both of us right or both of us wrong? Neither you nor I can know, and others are all the more in the dark. Whom shall we ask to pro-duce the right decision? We may ask someone who agrees with you; but since he agrees with you, how can he make the decision? We may ask someone who agrees with me; but since he agrees with me, how can he make the decision? We may ask someone who agrees with both you and me; but since he agrees with both you and me, how can he make the decision? We may ask some one who differs from both you and me; but since he differs from both you and me, how can he make the decision?"

This passage is reminiscent of the manner of argument followed by the School of Names. But whereas the members of that school argue thus in order to contradict the common sense of ordinary peo-ple, the *Ch'i Wu Lun's* purpose is to contradict the followers of the School of Names. For this school did actually believe that argument could decide what is really right and really wrong.

Chuang Tzu, on the other hand, maintains that concepts of right and wrong are built up by each man on the basis of his own finite point of view. All these views are relative. As the *Ch'i Wu Lun* says: "When there is life, there is death, and when there is death, there is life. When there is possibility, there is impossibility, and when there is impossibility, there is possibility. Because there is right, there is wrong. Because there is wrong, there is right." Things are ever subject to change and have many aspects. Therefore many views can be held about one and the same thing. Once we say this, we assume that a higher standpoint exists. If we accept this assumption, there is no need to make a decision ourselves about what is right and what is wrong. The argument explains itself.

The Higher Point of View

To accept this premise is to see things from a higher point of view, or, as the *Ch'i Wu Lun* calls it, to see things "in the light of Heaven." "To see things in the light of Heaven" means to see things from the point of view of that which transcends the finite, which is the *Tao*. It is said in the *Ch'i Wu Lun*: "The 'this' is also 'that.' The 'that' is also 'this.' The 'that' has a system of right and wrong. The 'this' also has a system of right and wrong. Is there really a distinction between 'that' and 'this'? Or is there really no distinction between 'that' and 'this'? That the 'that' and the 'this' cease to be opposites is the very essence of *Tao*. Only the essence, an axis as it were, is the center of the circle responding to the endless changes. The right is an endless change. The wrong is also an endless change. Therefore it is said that there is nothing better than to use the 'light.' " In other words, the 'that' and the 'this,' in their mutual opposition of right and wrong, are like an endlessly revolving circle. But the man who sees things from the point of view of the *Tao* stands, as it were, at the center of the circle. He understands all that is going on in the movements of the circle, but does not himself take part in these movements. This is not owing to his inactivity or resignation, but because he has transcended the finite and sees things from a higher point of view. In the *Chuang-tzu*, the finite point of view is compared with the view of the well-frog. The frog in the well can see only a little sky, and so thinks that the sky is only so big.

From the point of view of the *Tao*, everything is just what it is. It is said in the *Ch'i Wu Lun*: "The possible is possible. The impossible is impossible. The *Tao* makes things and they are what they are. What are they? They are what they are. What are they not? They are not what they are not. Everything is something and is good for something. There is nothing which is not something or is not good for something. Thus it is that there are roof-slats and pillars, ugliness and beauty, the peculiar and the extraordinary. All these by means of the *Tao* are united and become one." Although all things differ, they are alike in that they all constitute something and are good for something. They all equally come from the *Tao*. Therefore from the viewpoint of the *Tao*, things, though different, yet are united and become one.

The *Ch'i Wu Lun* says again: "To make a distinction is to make some construction. But construction is the same as destruction. For things as a whole there is neither construction nor destruction, but they turn to unity and become one." For example, when a table is made out of wood, from the viewpoint of that table, this is an act of construction. But from the viewpoint of the wood or the tree, it is one of destruction. Such construction or destruction are so, however, only from a finite point of view. From the viewpoint of the *Tao*, there is neither construction nor destruction. These distinctions are all relative.

The distinction between the "me" and the "non-me" is also relative. From the viewpoint of the *Tao*, the "me" and the "non-me" are also united and become one. The *Ch'i Wu Lun* says: "There is nothing larger in the world than the point of a hair, yet Mount T'ai is small. There is nothing older than a dead child, yet Peng Tsu [a legendary Chinese Methuselah] had an untimely death. Heaven and Earth and I came into existence together, and all things with me are one." Here we again have Hui Shih's dictum: "Love all things equally, Heaven and Earth are one body."

Knowledge of the Higher Level

This passage in the *Ch'i Wu Lun*, however, is immediately followed by another statement: "Since all things are one, what room is there for speech? But since I have already spoken of the one, is this not already speech? One plus speech make two. Two plus one make three. Going on from this, even the most skillful reckoner will not be able to reach the end, and how much less able to do so are ordinary people! If proceeding from nothing to something we can reach three, how much further shall we reach, if we proceed from something to something! Let us not proceed. Let us stop here." It is in this statement that the *Ch'i Wu Lun* goes a step further than Hui

Shih, and begins to discuss a higher kind of knowledge. This higher knowledge is "knowledge which is not knowledge."

What is really "one" can neither be discussed nor even conceived. For as soon as it is thought of and discussed, it becomes something that exists externally to the person who is doing the thinking and speaking. So since its all-embracing unity is thus lost, it is actually not the real "one" at all. Hui Shih said: "The greatest has nothing beyond itself and is called the Great One." By these words he described the Great One very well indeed, yet he remained unaware of the fact that since the Great One has nothing beyond itself, it is impossible either to think or speak of it. For anything that can be thought or spoken of has something beyond itself, namely, the thought and the speaking. The Taoists, on the contrary, realized that the "one" is unthinkable and inexpressible. Thereby, they had a true understanding of the "one" and advanced a step further than did the School of Names.

In the *Ch'i Wu Lun* it is also said: "Referring to the right and the wrong, the 'being so' and 'not being so': if the right is really right, we need not dispute about how it is different from the wrong; if the 'being so' is really being so, we need not dispute about how it is different from 'not being so.' . . . Let us forget life. Let us forget the distinction between right and wrong. Let us take our joy in the realm of the infinite and remain there." The realm of the infinite is the realm wherein lives the man who has attained to the *Tao*. Such a man not only has knowledge of the "one," but also has actually experienced it. This experience is the experience of living in the realm of the infinite. He has forgotten all the distinctions of things, even those involved in his own life. In his experience there remains only the undifferentiable one, in the midst of which he lives.

Described in poetical language, such a man is he "who chariots on the normality of the universe, rides on the transformations of the six elements, and thus makes excursion into the infinite." He is really the independent man, so his happiness is absolute.

Here we see how Chuang Tzu reached a final resolution of the original problem of the early Taoists. That problem is how to preserve life and avoid harm and danger. But, to the real sage, it ceases to be a problem. As is said in the *Chuang-tzu*: "The universe is the unity of all things. If we attain this unity and identify ourselves with it, then the members of our body are but so much dust and dirt, while life and death, end and beginning, are but as the succession of day and night, which cannot disturb our inner peace. How much less shall we be troubled by worldly gain and loss, good-luck and bad-luck!" (Ch. 20.) Thus Chuang Tzu solved the original problem of the early Taoists simply by abolishing it. This is really the philosophical way of solving problems. Philosophy gives no information about matters of fact, and so cannot solve any problem in a concrete and physical way. It cannot, for example, help man either to gain longevity or defy death, nor can it help him to gain riches and avoid poverty. What it can do, however, is to give man a point of view, from which he can see that life is no more than death and loss is equal to gain. From the "practical" point of view, philosophy is useless, yet it can give us a point of view which is very useful. To use an expression of the *Chuang-tzu*, this is the "usefulness of the useless." (Ch. 4.)

Spinoza has said that in a certain sense, the wise man "never ceases to be." This is also what Chuang Tzu means. The sage or perfect man is one with the Great One, that is, the universe. Since the universe never ceases to be, therefore the sage also never ceases to be. In the sixth chapter of the *Chuang-tzu*, we read: "A boat may be stored in a creek; a net may be stored in a lake; these may be said to be safe enough. But at midnight a strong man may come and carry them away on his back. The ignorant do not see that no matter how well you store things, smaller ones in larger ones, there will always be a chance for them to be lost. But if you store the universe in the universe, there will be no room left for it to be lost. This is the great truth of things. Therefore the sage makes excursions into that which cannot be lost, and together with it he remains." It is in this sense that the sage never ceases to be.

Methodology of Mysticism

In order to be one with the Great One, the sage has to transcend and forget the distinctions between things. The way to do this is to discard knowledge, and is the method used by the Taoists for achieving "sageliness within." The task of knowledge in the ordinary sense is to make distinctions; to know a thing is to know the difference between it and other things. Therefore to discard knowledge means to forget these distinctions. Once all distinctions are forgotten, there remains only the undifferentiable one, which is the great whole. By achieving this condition, the sage may be said to have knowledge of another and higher level, which is called by the Taoists "knowledge which is not knowledge."

In the *Chuang-tzu* there are many passages about the method of forgetting distinctions. In the sixth chapter, for example, a report is given of an imaginary conversation between Confucius and his favorite disciple, Yen Hui. The story reads: "Yen Hui said: 'I have made some progress.' 'What do you mean?' asked Confucius. 'I have forgotten human-heartedness and righteousness,' replied Yen Hui. 'Very well, but that is not enough,' said Confucius. Another day Yen Hui again saw Confucius and said: 'I have made some progress.' 'What do you mean?' asked Confucius. 'I have forgotten rituals and music,' replied Yen Hui. 'Very well, but that is not enough,' said Confucius. Another day Yen Hui again saw Confucius and said: 'I have made some progress.' 'What do you mean?' asked Confucius. 'I sit in forgetfulness,' replied Yen Hui.

"At this Confucius changed countenance and asked: 'What do you mean by sitting in forgetfulness?' To which Yen Hui replied: 'My limbs are nerveless and my intelligence is dimmed. I have abandoned my body and discarded my knowledge. Thus I become one with the Infinite. This is what I mean by sitting in forgetfulness.' Then Confucius said: 'If you have become one with the Infinite, you have no personal likes and dislikes. If you have become one with the Great Evolution [of the universe], you are one who merely follow its changes. If you really have achieved this, I should like to follow your steps.'"

Thus Yen Hui achieved "sageliness within" by discarding knowledge. The result of discarding knowledge is to have no knowledge. But there is a difference between "*having-no* knowledge" and "*having no-knowledge*." The state of "*having-no* knowledge" is one of original ignorance, whereas that of "*having no-knowledge*" comes only after one has passed through a prior stage of having knowledge. The former is a gift of nature, while the latter is an achievement of the spirit.

Some of the Taoists saw this distinction very clearly. It is significant that they used the word "forget" to express the essential idea of their method. Sages are not persons who remain in a state of original ignorance. They at one time possessed ordinary knowledge and made the usual distinctions, but they since forgot them. The difference between them and the man of original ignorance is as great as that between the courageous man and the man who does not fear simply because he is insensible to fear.

But there were also Taoists, such as the authors of some chapters of the *Chuang-tzu*, who failed to see this difference. They admired the primitive state of society and mind, and compared sages with children and the ignorant. Children and the ignorant have no knowledge and do not make distinctions, so that they both seem to belong to the undifferentiable one. Their belonging to it, however, is entirely unconsciousness. They remain in the undifferentiable one, but they are not conscious of the fact. They are ones who *have-no* knowledge, but not who have *no-knowledge*. It is the latter acquired state of *no-knowledge* that the Taoists call that of the "knowledge which is not knowledge."

CHAPTER 11

THE LATER MOHISTS

In the *Mo-tzu*, there are six chapters (chs. 40-45) which differ in character from the other chapters and possess a special logical interest. Of these, chapters forty to forty-one are titled "Canons" and consist of definitions of logical, moral, mathematical, and scientific ideas. Chapters forty-two to forty-three are titled "Expositions of the Canons," and consist of explanations of the definitions contained in the preceding two chapters. And chapters forty-four and forty-five are titled "Major Illustrations" and "Minor Illustrations" respectively. In them, several topics of logical interest are discussed. The general purpose of all six chapters is to uphold the Mohist point of view and refute, in a logical way, the arguments of the School of Names. The chapters as a whole are usually known as the "Mohist Canons."

In the last chapter we have seen that in the *Ch'i Wu Lun*, Chuang Tzu discussed two levels of knowledge. On the first level, he proved the relativity of things and reached the same conclusion as that of Hui Shih. But on the second level, he went beyond him. On the first level, he agreed with the School of Names and criticized common sense from a higher point of view. On the second level, however, he in turn criticized the School of Names from a still higher point of view. Thus the Taoists refuted the arguments of the School of Names as well, but the arguments they used are, logically speaking, on a higher level than those of the School of Names. Both their arguments and those of the School of Names require an effort of reflective thinking to be understood. Both run counter to the ordinary canons of common sense.

The Mohists as well as some of the Confucianists, on the other hand, were philosophers of common sense. Though the two groups differed in many ways, they agreed with one another in being practical. In opposition to the arguments of the School of Names, they developed, almost along similar lines of thought, epistemological and logical theories to defend common sense. These theories appear in the "Mohist Canons" and in the chapter titled "On The Rectification of Names" in the *Hsün-tzu*, the author of which, as we shall see in chapter thirteen, was one of the greatest Confucianists of the early period.

Discussions on Knowledge and Names

The epistemological theory set forth in the "Mohist Canons" is a kind of naïve realism. There is, it maintains, a knowing faculty which "is that by means of which one knows, but which itself does not necessarily know." (Ch. 42.) The reason for this is that, in order to have knowledge, the knowing faculty must be confronted with an object of knowledge. "Knowledge is that in which the knowing [faculty] meets the object and is able to apprehend its form and shape." (Ch. 42.) Besides the sensory organs for knowing, such as those of seeing and hearing, there also exists the mind, which is "that by means of which one understands the object of knowledge." (*Ibid.*) In other words, the mind interprets the impressions of external objects which are brought to it by the senses.

The "Mohist Canons" also provide various logical classifications of knowledge. From the point of view of its source, knowledge is to be classified into three types: that derived through the personal experience of the knower; that transmitted to him by authority (i.e., obtained by him either through hearsay or written records); and knowledge by inference (i.e., obtained through making deductions on the basis of what is known about what is unknown). Also from the point of view of the various objects of knowledge, it is to be classified into four kinds: knowledge of names, that of actualities, that of correspondence, and that of action. (Ch. 40.)

It will be remembered that names, actualities, and their relationships to one another, were the particular interest of the School of Names. According to the "Mohist Canons," "a name is that with which one speaks about a thing," while "an actuality is that about which one speaks." (Ch. 42.) When one says: "This is a table," "table" is a name, and is that with which one speaks about "this," while "this" is the actuality about which one is speaking. Expressed in terms of Western logic, a name is the predicate of a proposition, and an actuality is the subject of it.

In the "Mohist Canons," names are classified into three kinds: general, classifying, and private. " 'Thing' is a general name. All actualities must bear this name. 'Horse' is a classifying name. All actualities of that sort must have that name. 'Tsang' [the name of a person] is a private name. This name is restricted to this actuality." (Ch. 42.)

The knowledge of correspondence is that which knows which name corresponds to which actuality. Such kind of knowledge is required for the statement of such a proposition as: "This is a table." When one has this kind of knowledge, one knows that "names and actualities pair with each other." (Ch. 42.)

The knowledge of action is the knowledge of how to do a certain thing. This is what Americans call "know-how."

Discussions on Dialectic

Of the chapter titled "Minor Illustrations," a large part is devoted to the discussions of dialectic. This chapter says: "Dialectic serves to make clear the distinction between right and wrong, to discriminate between order and disorder, to make evident points of similarity and difference, to examine the principles of names and actualities, to differentiate what is beneficial and what is harmful, and to remove doubts and uncertainties. It observes the happenings of all things, and investigates the order and relation between the various judgments. It uses names to designate actualities, propositions to express ideas, statements to set forth causes, and taking and giving according to classes." (Ch. 45.)

The first part of this passage deals with the purpose and function of dialectic; the second part with its methodology. In another part of the same chapter, it is said that there are seven methods of dialectic: "A particular judgment indicates what is not all so. A hypothetical judgment indicates what is at present not so. Imitation consists in taking a model. What is imitated is what is taken as a model. If the cause is in agreement with the imitation, it is correct. If it is not in agreement with the imitation, it is not correct. This is the method of imitation. The method of comparison consists in using one thing to explain another. The method of parallel consists in comparing two series of propositions consistently throughout. The method of analogy says: 'You are so. Why should I alone not be so?' The method of extension consists in attributing the same to what is not known as to what is known. When the other is said to be the same [as this], how can I say that it is different?" (Ch. 45.)

The method of imitation in this passage is the same as that of "using statements to set forth causes" of the preceding quotation. And the method of extension is the same as the "taking and giving according to classes" of the preceding passage. These are the two most important of the methods, and correspond roughly to the deductive and inductive methods of Western logic.

Before giving further explanation of these two methods, something may be said regarding what in the "Mohist Canons" is called a cause. A cause is defined as "that with which something becomes," and is also classified into two kinds, the major and minor. (Ch. 40.) "A minor cause is one with which something may not necessarily be so, but without which it will never be so." "A major cause is one with which something will necessarily be so, and without which it will never be so." (Ch. 42.) It is evident that what the "Mohist Canons" call a minor cause is what in modern logic would be called a necessary cause, while what the "Mohist Canons" call a major cause is what modern logic would describe as a necessary and sufficient cause. In modern logic there is the distinction of yet another kind of cause, the sufficient cause, which is one with which something will necessarily be so, but without which it may or may not be so. This distinction the Mohists failed to make.

In modern logical reasoning, if we want to know whether a general proposition is true or not, we verify it with facts or experiment. If, for example, we want to make sure that certain bacteria are the cause of a certain disease, the way to verify the matter is to take as a formula the general proposition that the bacteria A are the cause of the disease B, and then make an experiment to see whether the supposed cause really produces the expected result or not. If it does, it really is the cause; if not, it is not. This is deductive reasoning and is also what the "Mohist Canons" call the method of imitation. For to take a general proposition as a formula is to take it as a model, and to make an experiment with it is to make an imitation of it. That the supposed cause produces the expected result, means that "the cause is in agreement with the imitation." And that it does not, means that "the cause is not in agreement with the imitation." It is in this way that we can distinguish a true from a false cause, and determine whether a cause is a major or minor one.

As regards the other form of reasoning through extension, it may be illustrated through the dictum that all men are mortal. We are able to make this dictum, because we know that all men of the past were mortal, and that men of today and of the future are the same in kind as those of the past. Hence we draw the general conclusion that all men are mortal. In this inductive reasoning, we use "the method of extension." That men of the past were mortal is what is known. And that men of today and of the future are and will be mortal is what is not known. To say that all men are mortal, therefore, is "to attribute the same to what is not known as to what is known." We can do this because "the other is said to be the same [as this]." We are "taking and giving according to class."

Clarification of All-embracing Love

Versed in the method of dialectic, the later Mohists did much in clarifying and defending the philosophical position of their school.

Following the tradition of Mo Tzu's utilitarianistic philosophy, the later Mohists maintain that all human activities aim at obtaining benefit and avoiding harm. Thus in the "Major Illustrations" we are told: "When one cuts a finger in order to preserve a hand, this is to choose the greater benefit and the lesser harm. To choose the lesser harm is not to choose harm, but to choose benefit. . . . If on meeting a robber one loses a finger so as to save one's life, this is benefit. The meeting with the robber is harm. Choice of the greater benefit is not a thing done under compulsion. Choice of the lesser harm is a thing done under compulsion. The former means choosing from what has not yet been obtained. The latter means discarding from what one has already been burdened with." (Ch. 44.) Thus for all human activities the rule is: "Of the benefits, choose the greatest; of the harms, choose the slightest." (Ibid.)

Both Mo Tzu and the later Mohists identified the good with the beneficial. Beneficialness is the essence of the good. But what is the essence of beneficialness? Mo Tzu did not raise this question, but the later Mohists did and gave an answer. In the first "Canon," it is said: "The beneficial is that with the obtaining of which one is pleased. The harmful is that with the obtaining of which one is displeased." (Ch. 40.) Thus the later Mohists provided a hedonistic justification for the utilitarianistic philosophy of the Mohist school.

This position reminds us of the "principle of utility" of Jeremy Bentham. In his *Introduction to the Principles of Morals and Legislation,* Bentham says: "Nature has placed mankind under the governance of two sovereign masters, pain and pleasure. It is for them alone to point out what we ought to do. . . . The principle of utility recognizes this subjection, and assumes it for the foundation of that system, the object of which is to rear the fabric of felicity by the hands of reason and law." (P. 1.) Thus Bentham reduces good and bad to a question of pleasure and pain. According to him the aim of morality is "the greatest happiness of the greatest number." (*Ibid.*)

This is also what the later Mohists do. Having defined "the beneficial," they go on to define the virtues in the light of this concept. Thus in the first "Canon" we find: "Righteousness consists in doing the beneficial." "Loyalty consists in benefiting one's ruler." "Filial piety consists in benefiting one's parents." "Meritorious accomplishment consists in benefiting the people." (Ch. 40.) "Benefiting the people" means "the greatest happiness of the greatest number."

Regarding the theory of all-embracing love, the later Mohists maintain that its major attribute is its all-embracing character. In the "Minor Illustrations" we read: "In loving men one needs to love *all* men before one can regard oneself as loving men. In not loving men one does not need not to love any man [before one can regard oneself as not loving men]. Not to have all-embracing love is not to love men. When riding horses, one need not ride all horses in order to regard oneself as riding a horse. For if one rides only a few horses, one is still riding horses. But when not riding horses, one must ride no horse at all in order to regard oneself as not riding horses. This is the difference between all-inclusiveness [in the case of loving men] and the absence of all-inclusiveness [in the case of riding horses]." (Ch. 44.)

Every man, as a matter of fact, has someone whom he loves. Every man, for example, loves his own children. Hence the mere fact that a man loves someone does not mean that he loves men in general. But on the negative side, the fact that he does wrong to someone, even his own children, does mean that he does not love men. Such is the reasoning of the Mohists.

Defense of All-embracing Love

Against this view of the later Mohists, there were at that time two main objections. The first was that the number of men in the world is infinite; how, then, is it possible for one to love them all? This objection was referred to under the title: "Infinity is incompatible with all-embracing love." And the second objection was that if failure to love a single man means failure to love men in general, there should then be no such punishment as "killing a robber." This objection was known under the title: "To kill a robber is to kill a man." The later Mohists used their dialectic to try to refute these objections.

In the second "Canon" there is the statement: "Infinity is not incompatible with all-embracingness. The reason is given under 'full or not.' " (Ch. 40.) The second "Exposition of the Canons" develops this statement as follows: "Infinity: (Objection:) 'If the South has a limit, it can be included *in toto*. [There was a common belief in ancient China that the South had no limit.] If it has no limit, it cannot be included *in toto*. It is impossible to know whether it has a limit or not and hence it is impossible to know whether it can all be included or not. It is impossible to know whether people fill this [space] or not, and hence it is impossible to know whether they can be included *in toto* or not. This being so, it is perverse to hold that all people can be included in our love.' (Answer:) 'If people do not fill what is unlimited, then [the number of] people has a limit, and there is no difficulty in including anything that is limited [in number]. But if people do fill what is unlimited, then what is [supposed to be] unlimited is limited, and then there is no difficulty in including what is limited.' " (Ch. 43.)

"To kill a robber is to kill a man" is the other major objection to the Mohists, because killing a man is not consistent with loving all men equally and universally. To this objection the "Minor Illustrations" answers as follows:

"A white horse is a horse. To ride a white horse is to ride a horse. A black horse is a horse. To ride a black horse is to ride a horse. Huo [name of a person] is a man. To love Huo is to love a man. Tsang [name of a person] is a man. To love Tsang is to love a man. This is to affirm what is right.

"But Huo's parents are men. Yet when Huo serves his parents, he is not serving men. His younger brother is a handsome man. Yet when he loves his younger brother, he is not loving handsome men. A cart is wood, but to ride a cart is not to ride wood. A boat is wood, but to ride a boat is not to ride wood. A robber is a man, but that there are many robbers does not mean that there are many men; and that there are no robbers does not mean that there are no men.

"How is this explained? To hate the existence of many robbers is not to hate the existence of many men. To wish that there were no robbers is not to wish that there were no men. The world generally agrees on this. And this being the case, although a robber-man is a man, yet to love robbers is not to love men, and not to love robbers is not to love men. Likewise to kill a robber-man is not to kill a man. There is no difficulty in this proposition." (Ch. 45.)

With such dialectic as this the later Mohists refuted the objection that the killing of a robber is inconsistent with their principle of all-embracing love.

Criticism of Other Schools

Using their dialectic, the later Mohists not only refute the objections of other schools against them, but also make criticisms of their own against these schools. For example, the "Mohist Canons" contain a number of objections against the arguments of the School of Names. Hui Shih, it will be remembered, had argued for the "unity of similarity and difference." In his ten paradoxes he passed from the premise that "all things are similar to each other," to the conclusion: "Love all things equally. Heaven and Earth are one body." This, for the later Mohists, is a fallacy arising from the ambiguity of the Chinese word t'ung. T'ung may be variously used to mean "identity," "agreement," or "similarity." In the first "Canon" there is a statement which reads: "T'ung: There is that of identity, that of part-and-whole relationship, that of co-existence, and that of generic relation." (Ch. 40.) And the "Exposition" explains further: "T'ung: That there are two names for one actuality is identity. Inclusion in one whole is part-and-whole relationship. Both being in the same room is co-existence. Having some points of similarity is generic relation." (Ch. 42.) The same "Canon" and "Exposition" also have a discussion on "difference," which is just the reverse of t'ung.

The "Mohist Canons" fail actually to mention Hui Shih by name.

As a matter of fact, no name is ever mentioned in these chapters. But from this analysis of the word *t'ung*, Hui Shih's fallacy becomes clear. That all things are similar to each other means that they have generic relationship, that they are of the same class, the class of "things." But that Heaven and Earth are one body means that they have a part-and-whole relationship. The truth of the one proposition as applied to a particular situation cannot be inferred from the truth of the other, even though the same word, *t'ung*, is used in both cases.

As regards Kung-sun Lung's argument for "the separation of hardness and whiteness," the later Mohists thought only in terms of concrete hard and white stones as they actually exist in the physical universe. Hence they maintained that the qualities of hardness and whiteness both simultaneously inhere in the stone. As a result, they "are not mutually exclusive," but "must pervade each other." (Chaps. 40, 42.)

The later Mohists also criticized the Taoists. In the second "Canon" we read: "Learning is useful. The reason is given by those who oppose it." (Ch. 41.) The second "Exposition" comments on this: "Learning: By maintaining that people do not know that learning is useless, one is thereby informing them of this fact. This informing that learning is useless, is itself a teaching. Thus by holding that learning is useless, one teaches. This is perverse." (Ch. 43.)

This is a criticism of a statement in the *Lao-tzu*: "Banish learning and there will be no grieving." (Ch. 20.) According to the later Mohists, learning and teaching are related terms. If learning is to be banished, so is teaching. For once there is teaching, there is also learning, and if teaching is useful, learning cannot be useless. The very teaching that learning is useless proves in itself that it is useful.

In the second "Canon" we read: "To say that in argument there is no winner is necessarily incorrect. The reason is given under 'argument'." The second "Exposition" comments on this: "In speaking, what people say either agrees or disagrees. There is agreement when one person says something is a puppy, and another says it is a dog. There is disagreement when one says it is an ox, and another says it is a horse. [That is to say, when there is disagreement, there is argument.] When neither of them wins, there is no argument. Argument is that in which one person says the thing is so, and another says it is not so. The one who is right will win." (Ch. 43.)

In the second "Canon" we also read: "To hold that all speech is

perverse is perverse. The reason is given under 'speech.' " (Ch. 41.)
The second "Exposition" comments on this: "[To hold that all
speech] is perverse, is not permissible. If the speech of this man
[who holds this doctrine] is permissible, then at least this speech is
not perverse, and there is some speech that is permissible. It the
speech of this man is not permissible, then it is wrong to take it as
being correct." (Ch. 43.)

The second "Canon" also says: "That knowing it and not knowing
it are the same, is perverse. The reason is given under 'no means.' "
(Ch. 41.) And the second "Exposition" comments: "When there is
knowledge, there is discussion about it. Unless there is knowledge,
there is no means [of discussion]." (Ch. 43.)

Yet again the second "Canon" states: "To condemn criticism is
perverse. The reason is given under 'not to condemn.' " (Ch. 41.) On
which the second "Exposition" comments: "To condemn criticism
is to condemn one's own condemnation. If one does not condemn it,
there is nothing to be condemned. When one cannot condemn
it, this means not to condemn criticism." (Ch. 43.)

These are all criticisms against Chuang Tzu. Chuang Tzu maintained that nothing can be decided in argument. Even if someone
wins, he said, the winner is not necessarily right or the loser necessarily wrong. But according to the later Mohists, Chuang Tzu, by
expressing this very doctrine, showed himself in disagreement with
others and was himself arguing. If he won the argument, did not this
very fact prove him to be wrong? Chuang Tzu also said: "Great argument does not require words." And again: "Speech that argues falls
short of its aim." (Chuang-tzu, ch. 2.) Hence "all speech is perverse." Furthermore, he held that everything is right in its own way
and in its own opinion, and one should not criticize the other. (Ibid.)
But according to the later Mohists, what Chuang Tzu said itself consists of speech and itself constitutes a criticism against others. So if
all speech is perverse, is not this saying of Chuang Tzu also perverse?
And if all criticism against others is to be condemned, then Chuang
Tzu's criticism should be condemned first of all. Chuang Tzu also
talked much about the importance of having no knowledge. But
such discussion is itself a form of knowledge. When there is no
knowledge, there can be no discussion about it.

In criticizing the Taoists, the later Mohists pointed out certain
logical paradoxes that have also appeared in Western philosophy. It

is only with the development of a new logic in recent times that these paradoxes have been solved. Thus in contemporary logic, the criticisms made by the later Mohists are no longer valid. Yet it is interesting to note that the later Mohists were so logically minded. More than any other school of ancient China, they attempted to create a pure system of epistemology and logic.

CHAPTER 12

THE *YIN-YANG* SCHOOL AND
EARLY CHINESE COSMOGONY

In the second chapter of this book I said that the *Yin-Yang* School had its origin in the occultists. These occultists were anciently known as the *fang shih*, that is, practitioner of occult arts. In the "Treatise on Literature" (ch. 30) in the *History of the Former Han Dynasty*, which is based on the *Seven Summaries* by Liu Hsin, these occult arts are grouped into six classes.

The Six Classes of Occult Arts

The first is astrology. "Astrology," says this chapter in the *Han History*, "serves to arrange in order the twenty-eight constellations, and note the progressions of the five planets and of the sun and the moon, so as to record thereby the manifestations of fortune and misfortune."

The second deals with almanacs. "Almanacs," says the same treatise, "serve to arrange the four seasons in proper order, to adjust the times of the equinoxes and solstices, and to note the concordance of the periods of the sun, moon, and five planets, so as thereby to examine into the actualities of cold and heat, life and death. . . . Through this art, the miseries of calamities and the happiness of prosperity all appear manifest."

The third is connected with the Five Elements. "This art," says the "Treatise on Literature," "arises from the revolutions of the Five Powers [Five Elements], and if it is extended to its farthest limits, there is nothing to which it will not reach."

The fourth is divination by means of the stalks of the milfoil plant and that done with the tortoise shell or shoulder bones of the ox. These were the two main methods of divination in ancient China.

In the latter method, the diviner bored a hole in a tortoise shell or a flat piece of bone, and then applied heat to it by a metal rod in such a way as to cause cracks to radiate from the hole. These cracks were interpreted by the diviner according to their configuration as an answer to the question asked. In the former method, the diviner manipulated the stalks of the milfoil in such a way as to produce certain numerical combinations which could be interpreted by means of the *Book of Changes*. Such interpretation was the primary purpose of the original corpus of this work.

The fifth group is that of miscellaneous divinations and the sixth is the system of forms. The latter included physiognomy together with what in later times has been known as *feng-shui*, literally, "wind and water." *Feng-shui* is based on the concept that man is the product of the universe. Hence his house or burial place must be so arranged as to be in harmony with the natural forces, i.e., with "wind and water."

In the days when feudalism was in its prime during the early centuries of the Chou dynasty, every aristocratic house had attached to it hereditary experts in these various occult arts, who had to be consulted when any act of importance was contemplated. But with the gradual disintegration of feudalism, many of these experts lost their hereditary positions and scattered throughout the country, where they continued to practice their arts among the people. They then came to be known as the *fang shih* or practitioners of occult arts.

Occultism or magic is itself, of course, based on superstition, but it has often been the origin of science. The occult arts share with science the desire to interpret nature in a positive manner, and to acquire the services of nature through its conquest by man. Occultism becomes science when it gives up its belief in supernatural forces, and tries to interpret the universe solely in terms of forces that are natural. The concepts of what these natural forces are may in themselves initially look rather simple and crude, yet in them we find the beginnings of science.

Such has been the contribution of the *Yin-Yang* school to Chinese thought. This school represents a scientific tendency in the sense that it tried to give a positive interpretation to natural events in terms solely of natural forces. By the word positive I mean that which has to do with matters of fact.

In ancient China there were two lines of thought that thus tried to interpret the structure and origin of the universe. One is found in the writings of the *Yin-Yang* school, while the other is found in some of the "Appendices" added by anonymous Confucianists to the original text of the *Book of Changes*. These two lines of thought seem to have developed independently. In the "Grand Norm" and "Monthly Commands," which we will examine below, there is stress on the Five Elements but no mention of the *Yin* and *Yang*; in the "Appendices" of the *Book of Changes*, on the contrary, much is said about the *Yin* and *Yang*, but nothing about the Five Elements. Later, however, these two lines of thought became intermingled. This was already the case by the time of Ssu-ma T'an (died 110 B.C.), so that in the *Historical Records* he lumps them together as the *Yin-Yang* school.

The Five Elements as Described in the "Grand Norm"

The term *Wu Hsing* is usually translated as the Five Elements. We should not think of them as static, however, but rather as five dynamic and interacting forces. The Chinese word *hsing* means "to act" or "to do," so that the term *Wu Hsing*, literally translated, would mean the Five Activities, or Five Agents. They are also known as the *Wu Te*, which means Five Powers.

The term *Wu Hsing* appears in a text traditionally said to antedate the twentieth century B.C. (See the *Book of History*, Part III, Book II, ch. I, 3.) The authenticity of this text cannot be proved, however, and even if it were proved, we cannot be sure whether the term *Wu Hsing* means the same thing in it as it does in other texts whose date is better fixed. The first really authentic account of the *Wu Hsing*, therefore, is to be found in another section of the *Book of History* (Part V, Book 4), known as the *Hung Fan* or "Great Plan" or "Grand Norm." Traditionally, the "Grand Norm" is said to be the record of a speech delivered to King Wu of the Chou dynasty by the Viscount of Chi, a prince of the Shang dynasty which King Wu conquered at the end of the twelfth century B.C. In this speech, the Viscount of Chi in turn attributes his ideas to Yü, traditional founder of the Hsia Dynasty who is said to have lived in the twenty-second century B.C. These traditions are mentioned as examples of the way the writer of this treatise tried to give importance to the *Wu Hsing* theory. As to the actual date of the "Grand Norm," modern scholarship inclines to place it within the fourth or third centuries B.C.

In the "Grand Norm" we are given a list of "Nine Categories." "First [among the categories]," we read, "is that of the *Wu Hsing*. The first [of these] is named Water; the second, Fire; the third, Wood; the fourth, Metal; the fifth, Soil. [The nature of] Water is to moisten and descend; of Fire, to flame and ascend; of Wood, to be crooked and straighten; of Metal, to yield and to be modified; of Soil, to provide for sowing and reaping."

Next comes the category of the Five Functions. "Second," we read, "is that of the Five Functions. The first [of these] is personal appearance; the second, speech; the third, vision; the fourth, hearing; the fifth, thought. Personal appearance should be decorous; speech should follow order; vision should be clear; hearing, distinct; thought, profound. Decorum produces solemnity; following order, regularity; clearness, intelligence; distinctness, deliberation; profundity, wisdom."

Skipping now to the eighth of the Nine Categories, we come to what the "Grand Norm" calls the various indications: "The eighth is that of various indications. These are rain, sunshine, heat, cold, wind, and seasonableness. When these five come fully and in their regular order, the various plants will be rich and luxuriant. If there is extreme excess in any of them, disaster follows. The following are the favorable indications: the solemnity of the sovereign will be followed by seasonable rain; his regularity, by seasonable sunshine; his intelligence, by seasonable heat; his deliberation, by seasonable cold; his wisdom, by seasonable wind. The following are the unfavorable indications: the madness of the sovereign will be followed by steady rain; his insolence, by steady sunshine; his idleness, by steady heat; his haste, by steady cold; his ignorance, by steady wind."

In the "Grand Norm" we find that the idea of the *Wu Hsing* is still crude. In speaking of them, its author is still thinking in terms of the actual substances, water, fire, etc., instead of abstract forces bearing these names, as the *Wu Hsing* came to be regarded later on. The author also tells us that the human and natural worlds are interlinked; bad conduct on the part of the sovereign results in the appearance of abnormal phenomena in the world of nature. This theory, which was greatly developed by the *Yin-Yang* school in later times, is known as that of "the mutual influence between nature and man."

Two theories have been advanced to explain the reasons for this interaction. One is teleological. It maintains that wrong conduct on the part of the sovereign causes Heaven to become angry. That anger results in abnormal natural phenomena, which represent warnings given by Heaven to the sovereign. The other theory is mechanistic. It maintains that the sovereign's bad conduct automatically results in a disturbance of nature and thus mechanically produces abnormal phenomena. The whole universe is a mechanism. When one part of it becomes out of order, the other part must be mechanically affected. This theory represents the scientific spirit of the Yin-Yang school, while the other reflects its occult origin.

The "Monthly Commands"

The next important document of the Yin-Yang school is the Yüeh Ling or "Monthly Commands," which is first found in the Lü-shih Ch'un-ch'iu, a work of the late third century B.C., and later was also embodied in the Li Chi (Book of Rites). The "Monthly Commands" gains its name from the fact that it is a small almanac which tells the ruler and men generally what they should do month by month in order to retain harmony with the forces of nature. In it, the structure of the universe is described in terms of the Yin-Yang school. This structure is spacio-temporal, that is, it relates both to space and to time. The ancient Chinese, being situated in the northern hemisphere, quite naturally regarded the south as the direction of heat and the north as that of cold. Hence the Yin-Yang school correlated the four seasons with the four compass points. Summer was correlated with the south; winter with the north; spring with the east, because it is the direction of sunrise; and autumn with the west, because this is the direction of sunset. The school also regarded the changes of day and night as representing, on a miniature scale, the changes of the four seasons of the year. Thus morning is a miniature representation of spring; noon, of summer; evening, of autumn; and night, of winter.

South and summer are hot, because south is the direction and summer the time in which the Power or Element of Fire is dominant. North and winter are cold, because north is the direction and winter the time in which the Power of Water is dominant, and water is associated with ice and snow, which are cold. Likewise, the Power of Wood is dominant in the east and in spring, because spring is the time when plants (symbolized by "wood") begin to grow and the east is correlated with spring. The Power of Metal is dominant in the west and in autumn, because metal was regarded as something hard and harsh, and autumn is the bleak time when growing plants reach their end, while the west is correlated with autumn. Thus four of the five Powers are accounted for, leaving only the Power of Soil without a fixed place and season. According to the "Monthly Commands," however, Soil is the central of the Five Powers, and so occupies a place at the center of the four compass points. Its time of domination is said to be a brief interim period coming between summer and autumn.

With such a cosmological theory, the Yin-Yang school tried to explain natural phenomena both in terms of time and space, and furthermore maintained that these phenomena are closely interrelated with human conduct. Hence, as stated above, the "Monthly Commands" sets forth regulations as to what the sovereign should do month by month, which is the reason for its name.

Thus we are told: "In the first month of spring the east wind resolves the cold. Creatures that have been torpid during the winter begin to move. . . . It is in this month that the vapors of heaven descend and those of earth ascend. Heaven and earth are in harmonious co-operation. All plants bud and grow." (Book of Rites, ch. 4.)

Because man's conduct should be in harmony with the way of nature, we are told that in this month, "He [the sovereign] charges his assistants to disseminate [lessons of] virtue and harmonize governmental orders, so as to give effect to the expressions of his satisfaction and to bestow his favors to the millions of the people. . . . Prohibitions are issued against cutting down trees. Nests should not be thrown down. . . . In this month no warlike operations should be undertaken; the undertaking of such is sure to be followed by calamities from Heaven. This avoidance of warlike operations means that they are not to be commenced on our side."

If, in each month, the sovereign fails to act in the manner befitting that month, but instead follows the conduct appropriate to another month, abnormal natural phenomena will result. "If in the first month of spring, the governmental proceedings proper to summer are carried out, rain will fall unseasonably, plants and trees will decay prematurely, and the state will be kept in continual fear. If the proceedings proper to autumn are carried out, there will be great pestilence among the people, boisterous winds will work their violence, and rain will descend in torrents. . . . If the proceedings proper to winter are carried out, pools of water will produce destructive effects, and snow and frost will prove very injurious. . . ."

Tsou Yen

A major figure of the *Yin-Yang* school in the third century B.C. was Tsou Yen. According to Ssu-ma Ch'ien's *Shih Chi* or *Historical Records,* Tsou Yen was a native of the State of Ch'i in the central part of present Shantung province, and lived shortly after Mencius. He "wrote essays totaling more than a hundred thousand words," but all have since been lost. In the *Historical Records* itself, however, Ssu-ma Ch'ien gives a fairly detailed account of Tsou Yen's theories.

According to this work (ch. 74), Tsou Yen's method was "first to examine small objects, and to extend this to large ones until he reached what was without limit." His interests seem to have been centered on geography and history.

As regards geography, Ssu-ma Ch'ien writes: "He began by classifying China's notable mountains, great rivers and connecting valleys; its birds and beasts; the productions of its waters and soils, and its rare products; and from this he extended his survey to what is beyond the seas, and which men are unable to see. . . . He maintained that what scholars call the Middle Kingdom [i.e., China] holds a place in the whole world of but one part in eighty-one. He named China the Spiritual Continent of the Red Region. . . . Besides China [there are other continents] similar to the Spiritual Continent of the Red Region, making [with China] a total of nine continents. . . . Around each of these is a small encircling sea, so that men and beasts cannot pass from one to another. These [nine continents] form one division. There are nine divisions like this. Around their outer edge is a vast ocean which encompasses them at the point where heaven and earth meet."

As regards Tsou Yen's historical concepts, Ssu-ma Ch'ien writes: "He first spoke about modern times, and from this went back to the time of Huang Ti [the legendary Yellow Emperor], all of which has been recorded by scholars. Moreover, he followed the great events in the rise and fall of ages, recorded their omens and institutions, and extended his survey backward to the time when heaven and earth had not yet been born, to what was profound and abstruse and not to be examined. . . . Starting from the time of the separation of heaven and earth and coming down, he made citations of the revolutions and transformations of the Five Powers, and the [different ways of] government and different omens appropriate to each of the Powers."

A Philosophy of History

The last few lines of the quotation show that Tsou Yen developed a new philosophy of history, according to which historical changes are interpreted in accordance with the revolutions and transformations of the Five Powers. The details of this theory are not reported by Ssu-ma Ch'ien, but it is treated in one section of the *Lü-shih Ch'un-ch'iu*, even though in this section Tsou Yen's name is not explicitly mentioned. Thus this work states (XIII, 2):

"Whenever an Emperor or King is about to arise, Heaven must first manifest some favorable omen to the common people. In the time of the Yellow Emperor, Heaven first made huge earthworms and mole crickets appear. The Yellow Emperor said: 'The force of Soil is in ascendancy.' Therefore he assumed yellow as his color, and took Soil as the pattern for his affairs.

"In the time of Yü [founder of the Hsia dynasty] Heaven first made grass and trees appear which did not die in the autumn and winter. Yü said: 'The force of Wood is in ascendancy.' Therefore he assumed green as his color and took Wood as the pattern for his affairs.

"In the time of T'ang [founder of the Shang dynasty] Heaven made some knife blades appear in the water. T'ang said: 'The force of Metal is in ascendancy.' He therefore assumed white as his color and took Metal as the pattern for his affairs.

"In the time of King Wen [founder of the Chou dynasty] Heaven made a flame appear, while a red bird, holding a red book in its mouth, alighted on the altar of soil of the House of Chou. King Wen said: 'The force of Fire is in ascendancy.' Therefore he assumed red as his color, and took Fire as the pattern of his affairs.

"Water will inevitably be the next force that will succeed Fire. Heaven will first make the ascendancy of Water manifest. The force of Water being in ascendancy, black will be assumed as its color, and

Water will be taken as the pattern for affairs. . . . When the cycle is complete, the operation will revert once more to Soil."

The *Yin-Yang* school maintained that the Five Elements produce one another and also overcome one another in a fixed sequence. It also maintained that the sequence of the four seasons accords with this process of the mutual production of the Elements. Thus Wood, which dominates spring, produces Fire, which dominates summer. Fire in its turn produces Soil, which dominates the "center"; Soil again produces Metal, which dominates autumn; Metal produces Water, which dominates winter; and Water again produces Wood, which dominates spring.

According to the above quotation, the succession of dynasties like wise accords with the natural succession of the Elements. Thus Earth, under whose Power the Yellow Emperor ruled, was overcome by the Wood of the Hsia dynasty. The Wood of this dynasty was overcome by the Metal of the Shang dynasty, Metal was overcome by the Fire of the Chou dynasty, and Fire would in its turn be overcome by the Water of whatever dynasty was to follow the Chou. The Water of this dynasty would then again be overcome by the Soil of the dynasty following, thus completing the cycle.

As described in the *Lü-shih Ch'un-ch'iu*, this is but a theory, but soon afterward it had its effect in practical politics. Thus in the year 221 B.C., the First Emperor of the Ch'in dynasty, known as Ch'in Shih-Huang-Ti (246-210 B.C.), conquered all the rival feudal states and thus created a unified Chinese empire under the Ch'in. As the successor to the Chou dynasty, he actually believed that "the force of Water is in ascendancy," and so, according to Ssu-ma Ch'ien's *Historical Records*, "assumed black as his color" and "took Water as the pattern for affairs." "The name of the Yellow River," says the *Historical Records*, "was changed to that of Power Water, because it was supposed to mark the beginning of the Power of Water. With harshness and violence, and an extreme severity, everything was decided by the law. For by punishing and oppressing, by having neither human-heartedness nor kindness, but only conforming to strict justice, there would come an accord with [the transformations of] the Five Powers." (Ch. 6.)

Because of its very harshness, the Ch'in dynasty did not last long, and was soon succeeded by that of Han (206 B.C.-A.D. 220). The Han Emperors also believed that they had become Emperors "by virtue of" one of the Five Powers, but there was considerable dispute as to which of the Powers it was. This was because some people maintained that the Han was the successor of the Ch'in, and therefore ruled through Soil, whereas others maintained that the Ch'in had been too harsh and short to be counted as a legitimate dynasty, so that the Han dynasty was actually the successor of the Chou. Support for both sides was found from many omens which were subject to varying interpretations. Finally, in 104 B.C., the Emperor Wu decided and formally announced that Soil was the Power for the Han. Even afterward, however, there were still differences of opinion.

Following the Han dynasty, people no longer paid very much attention to this question. Yet as late as 1911, when the last dynasty was brought to an end by the Chinese Republic, the official title of the Emperor was still "Emperor through [the Mandate of] Heaven and in accordance with the Movements [of the Five Powers]."

The Yin and Yang Principles As Described in the "Appendices" of the Book of Changes

The theory of the Five Elements interpreted the structure of the universe, but did not explain the origin of the world. This was provided by the theory of the Yin and Yang.

The word yang originally meant sunshine, or what pertains to sunshine and light; that of yin meant the absence of sunshine, i.e., shadow or darkness. In later development, the Yang and Yin came to be regarded as two cosmic principles or forces, respectively representing masculinity, activity, heat, brightness, dryness, hardness, etc., for the Yang, and femininity, passivity, cold, darkness, wetness, softness, etc., for the Yin. Through the interaction of these two primary principles, all phenomena of the universe are produced. This concept has remained dominant in Chinese cosmological speculation down to recent times. An early reference to it appears already in the Kuo Yü or Discussions of the States (which was itself compiled, however, probably only in the fourth or third century B.C.) This historical work records that when an earthquake occurred in the year 780 B.C., a savant of the time explained: "When the Yang is concealed and cannot come forth, and when the Yin is repressed and cannot issue forth, then there are earthquakes." (Chou Yü, I, 10.)

Later, the theory of the *Yin* and *Yang* came to be connected primarily with the *Book of Changes*. The original corpus of this book consists of what are known as the eight trigrams, each made up of combinations of three divided or undivided lines, as follows: ☰, ☴, ☵, ☶, ☳, ☲, ☱, ☷ . By combining any two of these trigrams with one another into diagrams of six lines each, ䷀, ䷁, ䷂, etc., a total of sixty-four combinations is obtained which are known as the sixty-four hexagrams. The original text of the *Book of Changes* consists of these hexagrams, and of descriptions of their supposed symbolic meaning.

According to tradition, the eight trigrams were invented by Fu Hsi, China's first legendary ruler, antedating even the Yellow Emperor. According to some scholars, Fu Hsi himself combined the eight trigrams so as to obtain the sixty-four hexagrams; according to others, this was done by King Wen of the twelfth century B.C. The textual comments on the hexagrams as a whole and on their *hsiao* (the individual lines in each hexagram) were, according to some scholars, written by King Wen; according to others, the comments on the hexagrams were written by King Wen, while those on the *hsiao* were by the Duke of Chou, the illustrious son of King Wen. Whether right or wrong, these attributions attest the importance which the Chinese attached to the eight trigrams and sixty-four hexagrams.

Modern scholarship has advanced the theory that the trigrams and hexagrams were invented early in the Chou dynasty as imitations of the cracks formed on a piece of tortoise shell or bone through the method of divination that was practiced under the Shang dynasty (1766?-1123? B.C.), the dynasty that preceded the Chou. This method has already been mentioned at the beginning of this chapter. It consisted of applying heat to a shell or bone, and then, according to the cracks that resulted, determining the answer to the subject of divination. Such cracks, however, might assume an indefinite number of varying configurations, and so it was difficult to interpret them according to any fixed formula. Hence during the early part of the Chou dynasty this kind of divination seems to have been supplemented by another method, in which the stalks of a certain plant, known as the milfoil, were shuffled together so as to get varying combinations yielding odd and even numbers. These combinations were limited in number and so could be interpreted according to fixed formulas. It is now believed that the undivided and divided (i.e., odd and even) lines of the trigrams and hexagrams were graphic representations of these combinations. Thus the diviners, by shuffling the stalks of the milfoil, could obtain a given line or set of lines, and then, by reading the comments on it contained in the *Book of Changes*, could give an answer to the question on which divination was made.

This, then, was the probable origin of the *Book of Changes*, and explains its title, which refers to the changing combinations of lines. Later, however, many supplementary interpretations were added to the *Book of Changes*, some moral, some metaphysical, and some cosmological. These were not composed until the latter part of the Chou dynasty, or even the earlier portion of the following Han dynasty, and are contained in a series of appendices known as the "Ten Wings." In this chapter we shall discuss only the cosmological interpretations, leaving the remainder for chapter fifteen.

Besides the concept of *Yin* and *Yang*, another important idea in the "Appendices" is that of number. Since divination was usually regarded by the ancients as a method for revealing the mystery of the universe, and since divination through the use of stalks of the milfoil plant was based on the combination of varying numbers, it is not surprising that the anonymous writers of the "Appendices" tended to believe that the mystery of the universe is to be found in numbers. According to them, therefore, the numbers of the *Yang* are always odd, and those of the *Yin* are always even. Thus in "Appendix III" we read: "The number for Heaven [i.e., *Yang*] is one; that for Earth [i.e. *Yin*] is two; that for Heaven is three; that for Earth is four; that for Heaven is five; that for Earth is six; that for Heaven is seven; that for Earth is eight; that for Heaven is nine; that for Earth is ten. The numbers for Heaven and the numbers for Earth correspond with and complement one another. The numbers of Heaven [put together] are twenty-five; the numbers of Earth [put together] are thirty; the numbers of both Heaven and Earth [put together] are fifty-five. It is by these numbers that the evolutions and mystery of the universe are performed."

Later the *Yin-Yang* school tried to connect the Five Elements with the *Yin* and *Yang* by means of numbers. Thus it maintained that one, the number for Heaven, produces Water, and six, the number for Earth, completes it. Two, the number for Earth, produces Fire, and seven, the number for Heaven, completes it. Three, the number for Heaven, produces Wood, and eight, the number for Earth, completes it. Four, the number for Earth, produces Metal, and nine, the number for Heaven, completes it. Five, the number for Heaven, produces Soil, and ten, the number for Earth, completes it. Thus one, two, three, four and five are the numbers that produce the Five Elements; six, seven, eight, nine and ten are the numbers that complete them.* This is the theory, therefore, that was used to explain the statement just quoted above: "The numbers for Heaven and the numbers for Earth correspond with and complement one another." It is remarkably similar to the theory of the Pythagoreans in ancient Greece, as reported by Diogenes Laertius, according to which the four elements of Greek philosophy, namely Fire, Water, Earth and Air, are derived, though indirectly, from numbers.†

This, however, is in China a comparatively late theory, and in the "Appendices" themselves there is no mention of the Five Elements. In these "Appendices" each of the eight trigrams is regarded as symbolizing certain things in the universe. Thus we read in "Appendix V": "(The trigram) *Ch'ien* ☰ is Heaven, round, and is the father. . . . (The trigram) *K'un* ☷ is Earth and is the mother. . . . (The trigram) *Chen* ☳ is thunder. . . . (The trigram) *Sun* ☴ is wood and wind. . . . (The trigram) *K'an* ☵ is water . . . and is the moon. . . . (The trigram) *Li* ☲ is fire and the sun. . . . (The trigram) *Ken* ☶ is mountain. . . . (The trigram) *Tui* ☱ is marsh."

In the trigrams, the undivided lines symbolize the Yang principle, and the divided lines the Yin principle. The trigrams *Ch'ien* and *K'un*, being made up entirely of undivided and divided lines respectively, are the symbols *par excellence* of the Yang and Yin, while the remaining six trigrams are supposedly produced through the intercourse of these primary two. Thus *Ch'ien* and *K'un* are father and mother, while the other trigrams are usually spoken of in the "Appendices" as their "sons and daughters."

Thus the first line (from the bottom) of *Ch'ien* ☰, combined with the second and third lines of *K'un* ☷, results in *Chen* ☳, which is called the eldest son. The first line of *K'un*, similarly com-

---

* See Cheng Hsüan's (A.D. 127-200) commentary to the "Monthly Commands" in the *Book of Rites*, ch. 4.
† See *Lives and Opinions of Eminent Philosophers*, Book VIII, ch. 19.

bined with *Ch'ien*, results in *Sun* ☴, which is called the eldest daughter. The second line of *Ch'ien*, combined with the first and third lines of *K'un*, results in *K'an* ☵, which is called the second son. The second line of *K'un*, similarly combined with *Ch'ien*, results in *Li* ☲, which is called the second daughter. The third line of *Ch'ien*, combined with the first and second lines of *K'un*, results in *Ken* ☶, which is called the youngest son. And the third line of *K'un*, similarly combined with *Ch'ien*, results in *Tui* ☱, which is called the youngest daughter.

This process of combination or intercourse between *Ch'ien* and *K'un*, which results in the production of the remaining six trigrams, is a graphic symbolization of the process of intercourse between the *Yin* and the *Yang*, whereby all things in the world are produced. That the world of things is produced through such intercourse of the *Yin* and *Yang*, is similar to the fact that living beings are produced through the intercourse of the male and female. It will be remembered that the *Yang* is the male principle, and the *Yin*, the female principle.

In "Appendix III" of the *Book of Changes* we read: "There is an intermingling of the genial influences of heaven and earth, and the transformation of all things proceeds abundantly. There is a communication of seed between male and female, and all things are produced." Heaven and earth are the physical representations of the *Yin* and *Yang*, while *Ch'ien* and *K'un* are their symbolic representations. The *Yang* is the principle that "gives beginning" to things; the *Yin* is that which "completes" them. Thus the process of the production of things by the *Yang* and *Yin* is completely analogous to that of the production of living beings by the male and female.

In the religion of the primitive Chinese, it was possible to conceive of a father god and mother goddess who actually gave birth to the world of things. In the *Yin-Yang* philosophy, however, such anthropomorphic concepts were replaced by, or interpreted in terms of, the *Yin* and *Yang* principles, which, though analogous to the female and male of living beings, were nevertheless conceived of as completely impersonal natural forces.

CHAPTER 13

THE REALISTIC WING
OF CONFUCIANISM: HSÜN TZU

The three greatest figures of the School of Literati in the Chou dynasty were Confucius (551-479), Mencius (371?-289?) and Hsün Tzu. The latter's dates are not definitely known, but probably lay within the years 298 and 238 B.C.

Hsün Tzu's personal name is K'uang, but he was also known under the alternative name of Hsün Ch'ing. He was a native of the state of Chao in the southern part of the present Hopei and Shansi provinces. The *Shih Chi* or *Historical Records* says in its biography of him (ch. 74) that when he was fifty he went to the state of Ch'i, where he was probably the last great thinker of the academy of Chi-hsia, the great center of learning of that time. The book bearing his name contains thirty-two chapters, many of them detailed and logically developed essays which probably come directly from his pen.

Among the literati, Hsün Tzu's thought is the antithesis of that of Mencius. Some people say that Mencius represents the left wing of the school, while Hsün Tzu represents its right wing. This saying, while suggestive, is too much of a simplified generalization. Mencius was left in that he emphasized individual freedom, but he was right in that he valued super-moral values and therefore was nearer to religion. Hsün Tzu was right in that he emphasized social control, but left in that he expounded naturalism and therefore was in direct opposition to any religious ideas.

Position of Man

Hsün Tzu is best known because of his theory that human nature is originally evil. This is directly opposed to that of Mencius according to which human nature is originally good. Superficially, it may seem that Hsün Tzu had a very low opinion of man, yet the truth is quite the contrary. Hsün Tzu's philosophy may be called a philosophy of culture. His general thesis is that everything that is good and valuable is the product of human effort. Value comes from culture and culture is the achievement of man. It is in this that man has the same importance in the universe as Heaven and Earth. As Hsün Tzu says: "Heaven has its seasons, Earth has its resources, man has his culture. This is what is meant [when it is said that man] is able to form a trinity [with Heaven and Earth]." (*Hsün-tzu*, ch. 17.)

Mencius said that by developing one's mind to the utmost, one knows one's nature, and by knowing one's nature, one knows Heaven. (*Mencius*, VIIa, 1.) Thus, according to Mencius, a sage, in order to become a sage, must "know Heaven." But Hsün Tzu maintains, on the contrary: "It is only the sage who does not seek to know Heaven." (*Hsün-tzu*, ch. 17.)

According to Hsün Tzu, the three powers of the universe, Heaven, Earth and man, each has its own particular vocation: "The stars make their rounds; the sun and moon alternately shine; the four seasons succeed one another; the *Yin* and *Yang* go through their great mutations; wind and rain are widely distributed; all things acquire their harmony and have their lives." (*Ibid.*) Such is the vocation of Heaven and Earth. But the vocation of man is to utilize what is offered by Heaven and Earth and thus create his own culture. Hsün Tzu asks: "Is it not much better to heap up wealth and use it advantageously than to exalt Heaven and think about it?" (*Ibid.*) And then he continues: "If we neglect what man can do and think about Heaven, we fail to understand the nature of things." (*Ibid.*) For in so doing, according to Hsün Tzu, man forgets his own vocation; by daring to "think" about Heaven, he arrogates the vocation of Heaven. This is "to give up that wherewith man can form a trinity with Heaven and Earth, and yet still desire such a trinity. This is a great illusion." (*Ibid.*)

Theory of Human Nature

Human nature, too, should be cultured, for, from Hsün Tzu's view, the very fact that it is uncultured means that it cannot be

good. Hsün Tzu's thesis is that "the nature of man is evil; his goodness is acquired training." (*Hsün-tzu*, ch. 23.) According to him,
"nature is the unwrought material of the original; what are acquired
are the accomplishments and refinements brought about by culture.
Without nature there would be nothing upon which to add the
acquired. Without the acquired, nature could not become beautiful
of itself." (*Ibid.*)

Although Hsün Tzu's view of human nature is the exact opposite
of that of Mencius, he agrees with him that it is possible for every
man to become a sage, if he choose. Mencius had said that any man
can become a Yao or Shun (two traditional sages). And Hsün Tzu
says likewise that "any man in the street can become a Yü [another
traditional sage]." (*Ibid.*) This agreement has led some people to
say that there is no real difference between the two Confucianists
after all. Yet as a matter of fact, despite this seeming agreement, the
difference is very real.

According to Mencius, man is born with the "four beginnings"
of the four constant virtues. By fully developing these beginnings, he
becomes a sage. But according to Hsün Tzu, man is not only born
without any beginnings of goodness, but, on the contrary, has actual
"beginnings" of evilness. In the chapter titled "On the Evilness of
Human Nature," Hsün Tzu tries to prove that man is born with
inherent desire for profit and sensual pleasure. But, despite these
beginnings of evilness, he asserts that man at the same time possesses
intelligence, and that this intelligence makes it possible for him to
become good. In his own words: "Every man on the street has the
capacity of knowing human-heartedness, righteousness, obedience to
law and uprightness, and the means to carry out these principles.
Thus it is evident that he can become a Yü." (*Ibid.*) Thus whereas
Mencius says that any man can become a Yao or Shun, because he
is originally good, Hsün Tzu argues that any man can become a Yü,
because he is originally intelligent.

Origin of Morality

This leads to the question: How, then, can man become morally
good? For if every man is born evil, what is the origin of good? To
answer this question, Hsün Tzu offers two lines of argument.

In the first place, Hsün Tzu maintains that men cannot live without some kind of a social organization. The reason for this is that, in order to enjoy better living, men have need of co-operation and mutual support. Hsün Tzu says: "A single individual needs the support of the accomplishments of hundreds of workmen. Yet an able man cannot be skilled in more than one line, and one man cannot hold two offices simultaneously. If people all live alone and do not serve one another, there will be poverty." (Ch. 10.) Likewise, men need to be united in order to conquer other creatures: "Man's strength is not equal to that of the ox; his running is not equal to that of the horse; and yet ox and horse are used by him. How is this? I say that it is because men are able to form social organizations, whereas the others are unable. . . . When united, men have greater strength; having greater strength, they become powerful; being powerful, they can overcome other creatures." (*Ibid.*)

For these two reasons, men must have a social organization. And in order to have a social organization, they need rules of conduct. These are the *li* (rites, ceremonies, customary rules of living) which hold an important place in Confucianism generally, and are especially emphasized by Hsün Tzu. Speaking about the origin of the *li*, he says: "Whence do the *li* arise? The answer is that man is born with desires. When these desires are not satisfied, he cannot remain without seeking their satisfaction. When this seeking for satisfaction is without measure or limit, there can only be contention. When there is contention, there will be disorder. When there is disorder, everything will be finished. The early kings hated this disorder, and so they established the *li* [rules of conduct] and *yi* [righteousness, morality], to set an end to this confusion." (Ch. 19.)

In another chapter, Hsün Tzu writes: "People desire and hate the same things. Their desires are many, but things are few. Since they are few there will inevitably be strife." (Ch. 10.) Hsün Tzu here points to one of the fundamental troubles in human life. If people did not all desire and hate the same things—for instance, if one liked to conquer and the other enjoyed being conquered—there would be no trouble between them and they would live together quite harmoniously. Or, if all the things that everyone desired were very plentiful, like the free air, then too there would be no trouble. Or yet again if people could live quite apart from one another, the problem would be much simpler. But the world is not so ideal. People must live together, and in order to do so without contention, a limit must be imposed on everyone in the satisfaction of his desires. The function of the *li* is to set this limit. When there are the *li*, there is morality. He who acts according to the *li* acts morally. He who acts against them acts immorally.

This is one line of Hsün Tzu's argument to explain the origin of moral goodness. It is quite utilitarianistic, and resembles that of Mo Tzu.

Hsün Tzu also employs another line of argument. He writes: "Man is not truly man in the fact that he, uniquely, has two feet and no hair [over his body], but rather in the fact that he makes social distinctions. Birds and beasts have fathers and offspring, but not the affection between father and son. They are male and female, but do not have the proper separation between males and females. Hence in the Way of Humanity there must be distinctions. No distinctions are greater than those of society. No social distinctions are greater than the *li*." (Ch. 5.)

Here Hsün Tzu points out the difference between what is of nature and what is of culture, or, as Chuang Tzu puts it, what is of nature and what is of man. The fact that birds and beasts have fathers and offspring and that they are either male or female, is a fact of nature. The social relationships between father and son, husband and wife, on the contrary, are products of culture and civilization. They are not gifts of nature, but achievements of spirit. Man should have social relations and the *li*, because it is these that distinguish him from birds and beasts. According to this line of argument, man must have morality, not because he cannot help it, but because he ought to have it. This line of argument is more akin to that of Mencius.

In Confucianism, *li* is a very comprehensive idea. It can be translated as ceremonies, rituals, or rules of social conduct. It is all these, but in the above arguments, it is taken more or less in the third sense. In this sense, the function of the *li* is to regulate. The *li* provide regulation for the satisfaction of man's desires. But in the sense of ceremonies and rituals, the *li* have another function, that of refining. In this sense, the *li* give refinement and purification to man's emotions. In this latter interpretation, Hsün Tzu also made a great contribution.

Theory of Rites and Music

For the Confucianists, the most important of the ceremonies are those of mourning and sacrifice (especially to the ancestors). These ceremonies were universal at that time, and as popularly practiced they contained not a little of superstition and mythology. In justifying them, however, the Confucianists gave them new interpretations and read into them new ideas. These we find in the *Hsün-tzu* and the *Li Chi* or *Book of Rites*.

Among the Confucian classics, there are two devoted to the rites. One is the *Yi Li* or *Book of Etiquette and Ceremonial*, which is a factual record of the procedures of ceremonies as practiced at that time. The other is the *Li Chi*, which consists of the interpretations on the ceremonies given by the Confucianists. I believe that most of the chapters of the *Li Chi* were written by the followers of Hsün Tzu.

Our mind has two aspects, the intellectual and the emotional. When our loved ones die, we know, through our intellect, that the dead are dead and that there is no rational ground for believing in the immortality of the soul. If we were to act solely under the direction of our intellect, therefore, we would need no mourning rites. But since our mind also has its emotional aspect, this causes us, when our loved ones die, to hope that the dead may live again and that there may be a soul that will continue existing in the other world. When we thus give way to our fancy, we take superstition as truth, and deny the judgment of our intellect.

Thus there is a difference between what we know and what we hope. Knowledge is important, but we cannot live with knowledge only. We need emotional satisfaction as well. In determining our attitude towards the dead, we have to take both aspects into consideration. As interpreted by the Confucianists, the mourning and sacrificial rites did precisely this. I have said that these rites were originally not without superstition and mythology. But with the interpretations of the Confucianists, these aspects were purged. The religious elements in them were transformed into poetry, so that they were no longer religious, but simply poetic.

Religion and poetry are both expressions of the fancy of man. They both mingle imagination with reality. The difference between them is that religion takes what it itself says as true, while poetry takes what it itself says as false. What poetry presents is not reality, and it knows that it is not. Therefore it deceives itself, yet it is a conscious self-deception. It is very unscientific, yet it does not contradict science. In poetry we obtain emotional satisfaction without obstructing the progress of the intellect.

According to the Confucianist, when we perform the mourning and sacrificial rites, we are deceiving ourselves without being really deceived. In the *Li Chi*, Confucius is reported to have said: "In dealing with the dead, if we treat them as if they were really dead, that would mean a want of affection, and should not be done. If we treat them as if they were really alive, that would mean a want of wisdom, and should not be done." (Ch. 2.) That is to say, we cannot treat the dead simply as we know, or hope, them to be. The middle way is to treat them both as we know and as we hope them to be. This way consists in treating the dead as if they were living.

In his "Treatise on Rites," Hsün Tzu says: "The rites are careful about the treatment of man's life and death. Life is the beginning of man, death is his end. If the beginning and end of man are both well treated, the Way of Humanity is complete. . . . If we render adequate service to our parents when they are living but not when they are dead, that means that we respect our parents when they have knowledge, but neglect them when they do not. One's death means that one is gone forever. That is the last chance for a subject to serve his sovereign, and a son his parents. . . . The mourning rites serve to decorate the dead by the living, to send off the dead as if they were still living, and to render the same service to the dead as that to the living, a service uniform from the beginning to the end. . . . Therefore the function of the mourning rites is to make clear the meaning of life and death, to send off the dead with sorrow and respect, and thus to complete the end of man." (Ch. 19.)

In the same chapter, Hsün Tzu says: "The sacrificial rites are the expression of man's affectionate longing. They represent the height of piety and faithfulness, of love and respect. They represent also the completion of propriety and refinement. Their meaning cannot be fully understood except by the sages. The sages understand their meaning. Superior men enjoy their practice. They become the routine of the officer. They become the custom of the people. Superior men consider them to be the activity of man, while ordinary people consider them as something that has to do with spirits and ghosts. . . .

They exist to render the same service to the dead as to the living, to render the same service to the lost as to the existing. What they serve has neither shape nor even a shadow, yet they are the completion of culture and refinement." With this interpretation, the meaning of the mourning and sacrificial rites becomes completely poetic, not religious.

There are other kinds of sacrifice besides those offered to ancestors. These Hsün Tzu interprets from the same point of view. In his chapter titled "Treatise on Nature," one passage reads: "Why is it that it rains after people have offered sacrifice for rain? Hsün Tzu said: 'There is no reason for that. It is the same as if there had been rain without praying for it. When there is an eclipse of the sun and the moon, we make demonstrations to save them. When rain is deficient, we pray for it. And when there are important affairs, we divine before we reach any decision. We do these things not because we can thereby get what we want. They are simply a sort of decorum. The superior man considers them as a sort of decorum, while ordinary people consider them as having supernatural force. One will be happy if one considers them as a sort of decorum; one will not, if one considers them as having supernatural force.' " (Ch. 17.)

We pray for rain, and divine before we make any important decision, because we want to express our anxiety. That is all. If we were to take prayer as really being able to move the gods, or divination as really being able to make predictions about the future, this would result in superstition with all its consequences.

Hsün Tzu is also the author of a "Treatise on Music," in which he writes: "Man cannot be without joy, and when there is joy, it must have a physical embodiment. When this embodiment does not conform to the right principle, there will be disorder. The early kings hated this disorder, and so they established the music of the *Ya* and *Sung* [two of the divisions of the *Book of Odes*] to guide it. They caused its music to be joyful and not degenerate, and its beauty to be distinct and not limited. They caused it in its indirect and direct appeals, its complexity and simplicity, its frugality and richness, its rests and notes, to stir up the goodness in men's minds and to prevent evil feelings from gaining any foothold. This is the manner in which the early kings established music." (Ch. 20.) Thus music, for Hsün Tzu, functions as an instrument for moral education. This has been the prevailing Confucianist view of music.

Logical Theories

In the *Hsün-tzu* there is a chapter titled "On the Rectification of Names." This subject is an old one in Confucianism. The term itself was originated by Confucius, as we have seen in chapter four. He said: "Let the ruler be ruler, the subject be subject; let the father be father and the son be son." (*Analects*, XII, 11.) Likewise Mencius said: "To be without the relationship of ruler and of father is to be like the beasts." (*Mencius*, IVb, 9.) Because the interests of these two thinkers were purely ethical, their application of the rectification of names was likewise confined primarily to the sphere of ethics. Hsün Tzu, however, lived in an age when the School of Names was flourishing. Hence his theory of the rectification of names possesses logical as well as ethical interest.

In his chapter, "On the Rectification of Names," Hsün Tzu first describes his epistemological theory, which is similar to that of the later Mohists. He writes: "That in man by which he knows is [called the faculty of] knowing. That in [the faculty of] knowing which corresponds [to external things] is called knowledge." (Ch. 22.) The faculty of knowing consists of two parts. One is what he calls "the natural senses," such as those of the ears and eyes. The other is the mind itself. The natural senses receive impressions, and the mind interprets and gives meaning to them. Hsün Tzu writes: "The mind gives meaning to impressions. It gives meaning to impressions, and only then, by means of the ear, can sound be known; by means of the eye, can forms be known. . . . When the five senses note something but cannot classify it, and the mind tries to identify it but fails to give it meaning, then one can only say that there is no knowledge." (*Ibid.*)

As to the origin and use of names, Hsün Tzu says: "Names were made in order to denote actualities, on the one hand so as to make evident the distinctions between superior and inferior [in society], and on the other hand to distinguish similarities and differences." (*Ibid.*) That is to say, names were originated partly for ethical and partly for logical reasons.

As to the logical use of names, he says: "Names are given to things. When things are alike, they are named alike; when different, they are named differently. . . . The one who knows that different actualities have different names, and who therefore never refers to different actualities otherwise than by different names, will not experience any confusion. Likewise he who refers to the same actualities should never use any other but the same names." (*Ibid.*)

Regarding the logical classification of names, he writes further: "Although things are innumerable, there are times when we wish to speak of them all in general, so we call them 'things.' 'Things' is the most general term. We press on and generalize; we generalize and generalize still more, until there is nothing more general. Then only we stop. There are times when we wish to speak of one aspect, so we say 'birds and beasts.' 'Birds and beasts' is the great classifying term. We press on and classify. We classify and classify still more, until there is no more classification to be made, and then we stop." (*Ibid.*) Thus Hsün Tzu distinguishes two kinds of names, the general and the classifying. The general name is the product of the synthetic process of our reasoning, while the classifying name is that of its analytic process.

All names are man-made. When they were in the process of invention, there was no reason why an actuality should be designated by one particular name rather than another. The animal that came to be known as "dog," for example, might equally well have been called "cat" instead. Once, however, certain names came through convention to be applied to certain actualities, they could be attached to these and none other. As Hsün Tzu explains: "There are no names necessarily appropriate themselves. Names were named by convention. But when the convention having been established, it has become customary, this is called an appropriate name." (*Ibid.*)

He also writes: "Should a true King arise, he must certainly follow the ancient terms and make the new ones." (*Ibid.*) Thus the invention of new names and determination of their meanings is a function of the ruler and his government. Hsün Tzu says: "When the kings had regulated names, the names were fixed and actualities distinguished. Their principles were thus able to be carried out, and their will could be known. They thus carefully led the people to unity. Therefore, the making of unauthorized distinctions between words, and the making of new words, so as thus to confuse the correct nomenclature, cause the people to be in doubt, and bring much litigation, was called great wickedness. It was a crime like that of using false credentials or false measures." (*Ibid.*)

Fallacies of Other Schools

Hsün Tzu considered most of the arguments of the School of Names and the later Mohists to be based upon logical sophistries and so fallacious. He grouped them into three classes of fallacies.

The first is what he calls "the fallacy of corrupting names with names." (*Ibid.*) In this class, he includes the Mohist argument that "to kill a robber is not to kill a man." This is because, according to Hsün Tzu, the very fact of being a robber implies being a man, since by extension the category which bears the name "man" includes the category which has the name "robber." When one speaks of a robber, therefore, one means by this a being who is at the same time a man.

The second class Hsün Tzu calls "the fallacy of corrupting names with actualities." (*Ibid.*) In this group he includes the argument that "mountains and abysses are on the same level," which is a rephrasing by Hsün Tzu of Hui Shih's argument that "mountains and marshes are on the same level." Actualities, being concrete, are individual cases, while names, being abstract, represent general categories or rules. When one tries to disprove general rules by individual exceptions, the result is a corruption of the name by the actuality. Thus a particular abyss that happens to be located on a high mountain may indeed be on the same level as a particular mountain that happens to be on low land. But one cannot infer from this exceptional instance that all abysses are on the same level with all mountains.

The third class is what Hsün Tzu calls "the fallacy of corrupting actualities with names." (*Ibid.*) Here he includes the Mohist argument that "ox-and-horse are not horse," an argument which is the same in kind as Kung-sun Lung's statement that "a white horse is not a horse." If one examines the name of ox-and-horse, one sees that it is indeed not equivalent to that of the name horse. Yet as a matter of fact some of the creatures belonging to the group known as "ox-and-horse" are, as actualities, indeed horses.

Hsün Tzu then concludes that the rise of all these fallacies is due to the fact that no sage-king exists. Were there to be such a sage-king, he would use his political authority to unify the minds of the people, and lead them to the true way of life in which there is no place or need for disputation and argument.

Hsün Tzu here reflects the spirit of the troubled age of his time. It was an age in which men longed desperately for a political unification which would bring these troubles to an end. Such a unification, though in actual fact one of China only, was regarded, by these people, as equivalent to a unification of the whole world.

Among Hsün Tzu's disciples, the two most famous were Li Ssu and Han Fei Tzu, both of whom were to have a great influence on Chinese history. Li Ssu later became Prime Minister of the First Emperor of the Ch'in dynasty, the man who finally forcibly unified China in 221 B.C. Together with his master, he labored not only for a political but an ideological unification as well, a movement which culminated in the Burning of the Books in 213 B.C. The other disciple, Han Fei Tzu, became a leading figure in the Legalist school which supplied the theoretical justification for this political and ideological unification. The ideas of this school will be described in the next chapter.

HAN FEI TZU AND THE
LEGALIST SCHOOL

THE feudalistic society of the early Chou dynasty operated according to two principles: one was that of the *li* (rituals, ceremonies.
rules of conduct, mores); the other was that of the *hsing* (penalties,
punishments). The *li* formed the unwritten code of honor governing the conduct of the aristocrats, who were known as *chün tzu* (a
term literally meaning son of a prince, princely man, or gentleman);
the *hsing*, on the contrary, applied only to the people of ordinary
birth who were known as *shu jen* (common men) or *hsiao jen* (small
men). This is the meaning of the saying in the *Li Chi* (*Book of
Rites*): "The *li* do not go down to the common people; the *hsing* do
not go up to the ministers." (Ch. 10.)

Social Background of the Legalists

This was possible because the structure of Chinese feudalistic society was comparatively simple. Kings, princes, and feudal lords were
all related to each other either by blood or by marriage. In theory
the princes of each state were subordinate to the king, and the feudal
lords within these states were in turn subordinate to their prince.
But in actual fact, these nobles, having long inherited their rights
from their ancestors, came in the course of time to regard these
rights as existing independently of their theoretical allegiance to
their superiors. Thus the many states that belonged to the hegemony
theoretically controlled by the central Chou King were in actual fact
semi-independent, and within each of these states there were likewise
many semi-independent "houses" of lesser nobles. Being relatives,
these various feudatories maintained social and diplomatic contacts,
and transacted business, if any, according to their unwritten code of

"gentleman's agreements." That is to say, their conduct was governed by *li*.

The kings and princes at the top had no direct dealings with the common people. They left such matters to the lesser feudal lords, each of whom ruled the common people living within his own fief. Since such fiefs were usually not large, their populations were limited. Hence the nobles were able in considerable measure to rule the people under them on a personal basis. Punishments were applied to keep their subjects obedient. Thus we find that in early Chinese feudalistic society, relationships, both high and low were maintained on a basis of personal influence and personal contact.

The distintegration of this type of society in the later centuries of the Chou dynasty brought with it far-reaching social and political changes. The social distinctions between the class of princely men on the one hand and small men on the other were no longer so absolutely demarcated. Already in the time of Confucius, we see how aristocrats sometimes lost their land and titles, and how members of the common people, either by talent or good luck, succeeded in becoming socially and politically prominent. The old fixity of social classes was breaking down. Likewise, as time wore on, the territories of the larger states became ever larger through aggression and conquest. In order to carry on warfare or prepare for war, these states needed a strong government, that is, a government with a high concentration of power. As a consequence, the structure as well as the functions of government became ever more complex than formerly.

New situations brought with them new problems. Such were the conditions faced by all the rulers of the feudal states of the time, and it was the common endeavor of all the schools of thought since Confucius to solve these problems. Most of their proposed solutions, however, were not realistic enough to be practical. What the rulers needed were not idealistic programs for doing good to their people, but realistic methods for dealing with the new situations faced by their government.

There were certain men who had a keen understanding of real and practical politics. The rulers of the time used to seek the advice of these men, and if their suggestions proved effective, they often became trusted advisers of the rulers, and in some cases became Prime Ministers. Such advisers were known as *fang shu chih shih* or "men of method."

They were so called because they developed methods for governing large areas; methods which left a high concentration of power in the person of the ruler, and 'which they boasted were foolproof. According to them, it was quite unnecessary that a ruler be a sage or superman. By faithfully applying their methods, a person of even merely average intelligence could govern, and govern well. There were also some "men of method" who went further and supplied a rational justification or theoretical expression for their techniques. It was this that constituted the thought of the Legalist school.

Thus it is wrong to associate the thought of the Legalist school with jurisprudence. In modern terms, what this school taught was the theory and method of organization and leadership. If one wants to organize people and be their leader, one will find that the Legalist theory and practice are still instructive and useful, but only if one is willing to follow totalitarian lines.

Han Fei Tzu, the Synthesizer of the Legalist School

In this chapter, I take Han Fei Tzu as the culminating representative of the Legalist school. He was a descendant of the royal house of the state of Han, in present Western Honan province. The *Shih Chi* or *Historical Records* says of him: "Together with Li Ssu, he studied under Hsün Tzu. Li Ssu considered himself not equal to Han Fei." (Ch. 63.) He was an able writer and composed a lengthy work bearing his name in fifty-five chapters. Ironically enough, it was in Ch'in, the state which more than any other applied his principles and thus conquered the other states, that he died in prison in 233 B.C. The cause was a political intrigue on the part of his former fellow student, Li Ssu, who was an official in Ch'in, and who may have been jealous of the growing favor accorded to Han Fei Tzu.

Before Han Fei Tzu, who was the last and greatest theorizer of the Legalist school, there had been three groups, each with its own line of thought. One was headed by Shen Tao, a contemporary of Mencius, who held that *shih* was the most important factor in politics and government. Another was headed by Shen Pu-hai (died 337 B.C.), who stressed that *shu* was the most important factor. Still another was headed by Shang Yang, also known as Lord Shang (died 338 B.C.), who, for his part, emphasized *fa*. *Shih* means power or authority; *fa* means law or regulation; *shu* means the method or art of conducting affairs and handling men, i.e., "statecraft."

Han Fei Tzu considered all three alike as indispensable. He said: "The intelligent ruler carries out his regulations as would Heaven, and handles men as if he were a divine being. Being like Heaven, he commits no wrong, and being like a divine being, he falls into no difficulties. His *shih* [power] enforces his strict orders, and nothing that he encounters resists him. . . . Only when this is so can his laws [*fa*] be carried out in concert." (*Han-fei-tzu*, ch. 48.) The intelligent ruler is like Heaven because he acts in accordance with law fairly and impartially. This is the function of *fa*. He is like a divine being, because he has the art of handling men, so that men are handled without knowing how they are handled. This is the function of the *shu*. And he has the authority or power to enforce his orders. This is the function of *shih*. These three together are "the implements of emperors and kings" (ch. 43), no one of which can be neglected.

Legalist Philosophy of History

Perhaps the Chinese traditional respect for past experience stems from the ways of thought of their overwhelmingly agrarian population. Farmers are rooted to the soil and travel but rarely. They cultivate their land in accordance with seasonal changes which repeat themselves year after year. Past experience is a sufficient guide for their work, so that whenever they want to try something new, they first look back to past experience for precedent.

This mentality has influenced Chinese philosophy a great deal, so that since the time of Confucius, most philosophers have appealed to ancient authority as justification for their own teaching. Thus Confucius' ancient authorities were King Wen and the Duke of Chou, of the beginning of the Chou dynasty. In order to improve upon Confucius, Mo Tzu appealed to the authority of the legendary Yü, who supposedly lived a thousand years earlier than King Wen and the Duke of Chou. Mencius, to get the better of the Mohists, went still further back to Yao and Shun, who were supposed to have antedated Yü. And finally the Taoists, in order to gain a hearing for their ideas against those of both the Confucianists and Mohists, appealed to the authority of Fu Hsi and Shen Nung, who were reputed to have lived several centuries earlier than either Yao or Shun.

By thus looking to the past, these philosophers created a regressive view of history. Although belonging to different schools, they all agreed that the golden age of man lies in the past rather than the future. The movement of history since then has been one of progressive degeneration. Hence man's salvation consists not in the creation of something new, but in a return to what has already existed.

To this view of history the Legalists, the last major school of the Chou period, took sharp exception. They fully understood the changing needs of the time and viewed them realistically. Although admitting that the people of ancient times were more innocent and in this sense perhaps more virtuous, they maintained that this was due to material circumstances rather than to any inherent superior goodness. Thus according to Han Fei Tzu, anciently "there were few people but plenty of supplies, and therefore the people did not quarrel. But nowadays people do not consider a family of five children as large, and each child having again five children, before the death of the grandfather there may be twenty-five grandchildren. The result is that there are many people but few supplies, and that one has to work hard for a meager return. So the people fall to quarreling." (*Han-fei-tzu*, ch. 49.)

Because of these completely new circumstances, according to Han Fei Tzu, new problems can only be solved by new measures. Only a fool can fail to realize this obvious fact. Han Fei Tzu illustrates this kind of folly with a story: "There was once a man of Sung who tilled his field. In the midst of the field stood a stem of a tree, and one day a hare in full course rushed against that stem, broke its neck, and died. Thereupon the man left his plough and stood waiting at that tree in the hope that he would catch another hare. But he never caught another hare and was ridiculed by the people of Sung. If, however, you wish to rule the people of today by the methods of government of the early kings, you do exactly the same thing as the man who waited by the tree. . . . Therefore affairs go according to their time, and preparations are made in accordance with affairs." (*Ibid.*)

Before Han Fei Tzu, Lord Shang already said similarly: "When the guiding principles of the people become unsuited to the circumstances, their standards of value must change. As conditions in the world change, different principles are practised." (*Book of Lord Shang*, II, 7.)

This conception of history as a process of change is a commonplace to our modern mind, but it was revolutionary viewed against the prevailing theories of the other schools of ancient China.

Way of Government

To meet new political circumstances, the Legalists proposed new ways of government, which, as stated above, they claimed to be infallible. The first necessary step, according to them, was to set up laws. Han Fei Tzu writes: "A law is that which is recorded on the registers, set up in the government offices, and promulgated among the people." (*Han-fei-tzu*, ch. 38.) Through these laws the people are told what they should and should not do. Once the laws are promulgated, the ruler must keep a sharp watch on the conduct of the people. Because he possesses *shih* or authority, he can punish those who violate his laws, and reward those who obey them. By so doing he can successfully rule the people, no matter how numerous they may be.

Han Fei Tzu writes on this point: "In his rule of a state, the sage does not depend upon men doing good themselves, but brings it about that they can do no wrong. Within the frontiers of a state, there are no more than ten people who will do good of themselves; nevertheless, if one brings it about that the people can do no wrong, the entire state can be kept peaceful. He who rules a country makes use of the majority and neglects the few, and so does not concern himself with virtue but with law." (Ch. 50.)

Thus with law and authority, the ruler rules his people. He need have no special ability or high virtue, nor need he, as the Confucianists maintained, set a personal example of good conduct, or rule through personal influence.

It may be argued that this procedure is not really foolproof, because the ruler needs ability and knowledge to make laws and keep a watch on the conduct of the people, who may be large in number. The Legalists answer this objection by saying that the ruler need not do all these things himself. If he merely possesses *shu*, the art of handling men, he can then get the right men to do everything for him.

The concept of *shu* is of philosophical interest. It is also one aspect of the old doctrine of the rectification of names. The term used by the Legalists for this doctrine is "holding the actualities responsible for their names." (*Han-fei-tzu*, ch. 43.)

By "actualities," the Legalists mean the individuals who hold government office, while by "names," they mean the titles of the offices thus held. These titles are indicative of what the individuals who hold the office in question should ideally accomplish. Hence "holding the actualities responsible for their names," means holding the individuals who occupy certain offices responsible for carrying out what should be ideally accomplished in these offices. The ruler's duty is to attach a particular name to a particular individual, that is to say, confer a given office upon a given person. The functions pertaining to this office have already been defined by law and are indicated by the name given to it. Hence the ruler need not, and should not, bother about the methods used to carry out his work, so long as the work itself is done and well done. If it is well done, the ruler rewards him; if not, he punishes him. That is all.

It may yet be asked how the ruler is to know which man is the best for a certain office. The Legalists answer that this too can be known by the same *shu* or method of statecraft. Han Fei Tzu says: "When a minister makes claims, the ruler gives him work according to what he has claimed, but holds him wholly responsible for accomplishment corresponding to this work. When the accomplishment corresponds to this work, and the work corresponds to what the man has claimed he could do, he is rewarded. If the accomplishment does not correspond to the work, nor the work correspond to what the man has claimed for himself, he is punished." (Ch. 7.) After this procedure has been followed in several instances, if the ruler is strict in his rewards and punishments, incompetent people will no longer dare to take office even if it is offered to them. Thus all incompetents are eliminated, leaving government positions only to those who can successfully fill them.

Yet the problem still remains: How is the ruler to know whether an "actuality" does in fact correspond to its "name"? The Legalist reply is that it is up to the ruler himself, if he is uncertain, to test the result. If he is not sure that his cook is really a good cook, he can settle the matter simply by tasting his cooking. He need not always judge results for himself, however. He can appoint others to judge for him, and these judges will then, in their turn, be held strictly responsible for their names.

Thus, according to the Legalists, their way of government is really foolproof. The ruler need only retain the authority of rewards and punishments in his own hands. He will then rule by "doing nothing, yet there is nothing that is not done."

Such rewards and punishments are what Han Fei Tzu calls "the two handles of the ruler." (Ch. 7.) Their effectiveness derives from the fact that it is the nature of man to seek profit and to avoid harm. Han Fei Tzu says: "In ruling the world, one must act in accordance with human nature. In human nature there are the feelings of liking and disliking, and hence rewards and punishments are effective. When rewards and punishments are effective, interdicts and commands can be established, and the way of government is complete." (Ch. 48.)

Han Fei Tzu, as a student of Hsün Tzu, was convinced that human nature is evil. But he differed from Hsün Tzu in that he was not interested in the latter's stress on culture as a means of changing human nature so as to make it something good. According to him and the other Legalists, it is precisely because human nature is what it is, that the Legalist way of government is practical. The Legalists proposed this way of government on the assumption that man is what he is, i.e., naturally evil, and not on the assumption that he is to be converted into what he ought to be.

Legalism and Taoism

"Doing nothing, yet there is nothing that is not done." This is the Taoist idea of *wu wei*, having-no-activity or non-action, but it is also a Legalist idea. According to Han Fei Tzu and the Legalists, the one great virtue required of a ruler is that he follow the course of non-action. He should do nothing himself but should merely let others do everything for him. Han Fei Tzu says: "Just as the sun and moon shine forth, the four seasons progress, the clouds spread, and the wind blows, so does the ruler not encumber his mind with knowledge, or himself with selfishness. He relies for good government or disorder upon laws and methods [*shu*]; leaves right and wrong to be dealt with through rewards and punishments; and refers lightness and heaviness to the balance of the scale." (Ch. 29.) In other words, the ruler possesses the implements and mechanism through which government is conducted, and having these, does nothing, yet there is nothing that is not done.

Taoism and Legalism represent the two extremes of Chinese

thought. The Taoists maintained that man originally is completely innocent; the Legalists, on the other hand, that he is completely evil. The Taoists stood for absolute individual freedom; the Legalists for absolute social control. Yet in the idea of non-action, the two extremes meet. That is to say, they had here some common ground.

Under somewhat different wording, the Legalist way of government was also maintained by the later Taoists. In the *Chuang-tzu* we find a passage that speaks about "the way of employing human society." In this passage distinctions are made between having-activity and having-no-activity, and between "being employed by the world" and "employing the world." Having-no-activity is the way of employing the world; having-activity is the way of being employed by the world. The ruler's reason for existence is to rule the whole world. Hence his function and duty is not to do things himself, but to tell others to do them for him. In other words, his method of rule is to employ the world by having-no-activity. The duty and function of subordinates, on the other hand, is to take orders and do things accordingly. In other words, the function of the subordinate is to be employed by the world by having activity. The same passage says: "The superior must have no activity, so as thus to employ the world; but the subordinates must have activity, so as thus to be employed by the world. This is the invariable way." (*Chuang-tzu*, ch. 13.)

The *Chuang-tzu* continues: "Therefore, the rulers of old, although their knowledge spread throughout the whole universe, did not themselves think. Although their eloquence beautified all things, they did not themselves speak. Although their abilities exhausted all things within the four seas, they did not themselves act." (*Ibid.*) A ruler should be so, because if he once thinks about something, this means that there is something else about which he does not think; yet his whole duty and function is to think about *all* things under his rule. The solution, therefore, is for him not to try to think, speak, and act himself, but merely to tell others to think, speak, and act in his place. In this way he does nothing, and yet there is nothing that is not done.

As to the detailed procedure by which the ruler is thus to "employ the world," the same passage says: "Those of old who made manifest the great *Tao*, first made manifest Heaven, and *Tao* and *Te* came next. *Tao* and *Te* being manifested, the virtues of human-heartedness and righteousness came next. These being manifested, the division of offices came next. These being manifested, actualities and names came next. These being manifested, employment without interference came next. This being manifested, examinations and discriminations came next. These being manifested, judgement of right and wrong came next. This being manifested, rewards and punishments came next. With the manifestation of rewards and punishments, the foolish and the wise assumed their proper positions, the noble and the humble occupied their proper places, and the virtuous and the worthless were employed according to their nature. . . . This is perfect peace, the acme of good government." (*Ibid.*)

It is clear that the latter part of this program is the same as that of the Legalists. Yet the passage goes on by saying: "Those of antiquity who spoke about the great *Tao*, mentioned actualities and names only at the fifth step, and rewards and punishments only at the ninth step. He who speaks immediately about actualities and names, does not know the fundamentals [that underlie them]. He who speaks immediately about rewards and punishments, does not know their beginning. . . . Such a one knows the implements of government, but not its principles. He can be employed by the world, but is not sufficient to employ the world. He is a one-sided man and only knows how to talk." (*Ibid.*)

Here we have the criticism of the Taoists against the Legalists. The Legalist way of government requires unselfishness and impartiality on the part of the ruler. He must punish those who ought to be punished, even though they be his friends and relatives, and he must reward those who ought to be rewarded, even though they be his enemies. If he fails only a few times to do this, the whole mechanism breaks down. Such requirements are too much for a man of only average intelligence. He who can really fulfill them is nothing less than a sage.

Legalism and Confucianism

The Confucianists maintained that the people should be governed by *li* and morality, not by law and punishment. They upheld the traditional way of government, but did not realize that the circumstances that had once rendered this way practical had already changed. In this respect, they were conservative. In another respect, however, they were at the same time revolutionary, and reflected in their ideas the changes of the time. Thus they no longer upheld the traditional class distinctions that were based merely on the accident of birth or fortune. Confucius and Mencius, to be sure, continued to speak about the difference between the princely man and the small man. Yet for them, this distinction depended upon the moral worth of the individual, and was not necessarily based upon inherited class differences.

I pointed out at the beginning of this chapter that in early Chinese feudalistic society, the nobles were governed according to the *li*, but the common people only according to the punishments. Hence the Confucian insistence that not only the nobles, but the mass of the people as well, should be governed by *li* rather than by punishment, was in fact a demand for a higher standard of conduct to be applied to the people. In this sense the Confucianists were revolutionary.

In Legalist thought, too, there were no class distinctions. Everyone was equal before law and the ruler. Instead of elevating the common people to a higher standard of conduct, however, the Legalists lowered the nobles to a lower standard by discarding *li* and putting sole reliance on rewards and punishments for all alike.

The Confucianist ideas are idealistic, while those of the Legalists are realistic. That is the reason why, in Chinese history, the Confucianists have always accused the Legalists of being mean and vulgar, while the Legalists have accused the Confucianists of being bookish and impractical.

CHAPTER 15

CONFUCIANIST METAPHYSICS

In chapter twelve we have seen that the *Yi Ching* or *Book of Changes* (also known simply as the *Yi*) was originally a book of divination. Later the Confucianists gave it cosmological, metaphysical, and ethical interpretations, which constitute the "Appendices" now found in the *Book of Changes*.

The cosmological theory contained in the "Appendices" has already been considered in chapter twelve, and we shall revert to it again in chapter twenty-three. In the present chapter we shall confine ourselves to the metaphysical and ethical theories found in the "Appendices" and in the *Chung Yung*.

The *Chung Yung* or *Doctrine of the Mean* is one of the chapters in the *Li Chi* (*Book of Rites*). According to tradition, it was written by Tzu-ssu, the grandson of Confucius, but in actual fact a large part of it seems to have been written at a somewhat later date. The "Appendices" and the *Chung Yung* represent the last phase in the metaphysical development of ancient Confucianism. So great is their metaphysical interest, indeed, that the Neo-Taoists of the third and fourth centuries A.D. considered the *Yi* as one of the three major classics of speculative philosophy, the others being the *Lao-tzu* and *Chuang-tzu*. Similarly, Emperor Wu (502-549) of the Liang dynasty, himself a Buddhist, wrote commentaries on the *Chung Yung*, and in the tenth and eleventh centuries, monks of the Ch'an sect of Buddhism also wrote such commentaries, which marked the beginning of Neo-Confucianism.

The Principles of Things

The most important metaphysical idea in the "Appendices," as in Taoism, is that of *Tao*. Yet it is quite different from the concept of *Tao* of the Taoists. For the latter, *Tao* is nameless, unnamable.

166

But for the authors of the "Appendices," not only is *Tao* namable, but, strictly speaking, it is *Tao* and *Tao* only that is thus namable.

We may distinguish between the two concepts by referring to the *Tao* of Taoism as the *Tao*, and to that of the "Appendices" as *tao*. The *Tao* of Taoism is the unitary "that" from which springs the production and change of all things in the universe. The *tao* of the "Appendices," on the contrary, are multiple, and are the principles which govern each separate category of things in the universe. As such, they are somewhat analogous to the concept of the "universal" in Western philosophy. Kung-sun Lung, as we have seen, regarded hardness as a universal of this kind, since it is this hardness that enables concrete objects in our physical universe to be hard. Likewise, in the terminology of the "Appendices," that by which hard things are hard would be called the *tao* of hardness. This *tao* of hardness is separable from the hardness of individual physical objects, and constitutes a namable metaphysical principle.

There are many such *tao*, such as the *tao* of sovereignship and of ministership, or of fatherhood and sonhood. They are what a sovereign, a minister, a father, and a son *ought* to be. Each of them is represented by a name, and an individual should ideally act according to these various names. Here we find the old theory of the rectification of names of Confucius. In him, however, this was only an ethical theory, whereas in the "Appendices" it becomes metaphysical as well.

The *Yi*, as we have seen, was originally a book of divination. By the manipulation of the stalks of the milfoil plant, one is led to a certain line of a certain hexagram, the comments on which in the *Yi* are supposed to provide the information one is seeking. Hence these comments are to be applied to the various specific cases in actual life. This procedure led the authors of the "Appendices" to the concept of the formula. Seeing the *Yi* from this point of view, they considered the comments on the hexagrams and the individual lines of these hexagrams as formulas, each representing one or more *tao* or universal principles. The comments on the entire sixty-four hexagrams and their 384 individual lines are thus supposed to represent all the *tao* in the universe.

The hexagrams and their individual lines are looked upon as graphic symbols of these universal *tao*. "Appendix III" says: "The

Yi consists of symbols." Such symbols are similar to what in symbolic logic are called variables. A variable functions as a substitute for a class or a number of classes of concrete objects. An object belonging to a certain class and satisfying certain conditions can fit into a certain formula with a certain variable; that is, it can fit into the comment made on a certain hexagram or a certain line within a hexagram, these hexagrams or lines being taken as symbols. This formula represents the *tao* which the objects of this class ought to obey. From the point of view of divination, if they obey it, they will enjoy good luck, but if not, they will suffer bad fortune. From the point of view of moral teaching, if they obey it, they are right, but if not, they are wrong.

The first of the sixty-four hexagrams, *Ch'ien*, for example, is supposed to be the symbol of virility, while the second hexagram, *K'un*, is that of docility. Everything that satisfies the condition of being virile can fit into a formula in which the symbol of *Ch'ien* occurs, and everything that satisfies the condition of being docile can fit into one in which the symbol of *K'un* occurs. Hence the comments on the hexagram *Ch'ien* and its individual lines are supposed to represent the *tao* for all things in the universe that are virile; those on the hexagram *K'un* and its individual lines represent the *tao* for all things that are docile.

Thus in "Appendix I," the section dealing with the hexagram *K'un* says: "If it takes the initiative, it will become confused and lose the way. If it follows, it will docilely gain the regular [way]." And in "Appendix IV": "Although the *Yin* has its beauties, it keeps them under restraint in its service of the king, and does not dare to claim success for itself. This is the *tao* of Earth, of a wife, of a subject. The *tao* of Earth is, not to claim the merit of achievement, but on another's behalf to bring things to their proper issue."

Quite the opposite is the hexagram of *Ch'ien*, the symbol of Heaven, of a husband, of a sovereign. The judgements made on this hexagram and its individual lines represent the *tao* of Heaven, of a husband, of a sovereign.

Hence if one wants to know how to be a ruler or a husband, one should look up what is said in the *Yi* under the hexagram *Ch'ien*, but if one wants to know how to be a subject or a wife, one should look under the hexagram *K'un*. Thus in "Appendix III" it is said: "With the expansion of the use of the hexagrams, and the application of them to new classes, everything that man can do in the world is there." Again: "What does the *Yi* accomplish? The *Yi* opens the door to the myriad things in nature and brings man's task to completion. It embraces all the governing principles of the world. This, and no more or less, is what the *Yi* accomplishes."

It is said that the name of the *Yi* has three meanings: (1) easiness and simpleness, (2) transformation and change, and (3) invariability.* Transformation and change refers to the individual things of the universe. Simpleness and invariability refers to their *tao* or underlying principles. Things ever change, but *tao* are invariable. Things are complex, but *tao* are easy and simple.

The Tao of the Production of Things

Besides the *tao* of every class of things, there is another *Tao* for all things as a whole. In other words, besides the specific multiple *tao*, there is a general unitary *Tao* which governs the production and transformation of all things. "Appendix III" says: "One *Yang* and one *Yin*: this is called the *Tao*. That which ensues from this is goodness, and that which is completed thereby is the nature [of man and things]." This is the *Tao* of the production of things, and such production is the major achievement of the universe. In "Appendix III" it is said: "The supreme virtue of Heaven is to produce."

When a thing is produced, there must be that which is able to produce it, and there must also be that which constitutes the material from which this production is made. The former is the active element and the latter the passive one. The active element is virile and is the *Yang*; the passive element is docile and is the *Yin*. The production of things needs the cooperation of these two elements. Hence the words: "One *Yang* and one *Yin*: this is the *Tao*."

Everything can in one sense be *Yang* and in another sense *Yin*, according to its relation with other things. For instance, a man is *Yang* in relation to his wife, but *Yin* in relation to his father. The metaphysical *Yang* which produces all things, however, can only be *Yang*, and the metaphysical *Yin* out of which everything is produced can only be *Yin*. Hence in the metaphysical statement: "One *Yang*

---

* See Cheng Hsüan (A.D. 127-200), *Discussion of the Yi*, quoted by K'ung Ying-ta (574-648), in the Preface to his sub-commentary on Wang Pi's (226-49) *Commentary on the Yi*.

and one *Yin*: this is called the *Tao*," the *Yin* and *Yang* thus spoken of are *Yin* and *Yang* in the absolute sense.

It is to be noticed that two kinds of statement occur in the "Appendices." The first consists of statements about the universe and the concrete things in it; the other consists of statements about the system of abstract symbols of the *Yi* itself. In "Appendix III" it is said: "In the *Yi* there is the Supreme Ultimate which produces the Two Forms. The Two Forms produce the Four Emblems, and these Four Emblems produce the eight trigrams." Although this saying later became the foundation of the metaphysics and cosmology of the Neo-Confucianists, it does not refer to the actual universe, but rather to the system of symbols in the *Yi*. According to the "Appendices," however, these symbols and formulas have their exact counterparts in the universe itself. Hence the two kinds of statement are really interchangeable. Thus the saying, "one *Yang* and one *Yin*: this is called *Tao*," is a statement about the universe. Yet it is interchangeable with the other saying that "in the *Yi* there is the Supreme Ultimate which produces the Two Forms." The *Tao* is equivalent to the Supreme Ultimate, while the *Yin* and *Yang* correspond to the Two Forms.

"Appendix III" also states: "The supreme virtue of Heaven is to produce." Again: "To produce and to reproduce is the function of the *Yi*." Here again are two kinds of statement. The former relates to the universe, and the latter to the *Yi*. Yet they are at the same time interchangeable.

The Tao of the Transformation of Things

One meaning of the name *Yi*, as we have seen, is transformation and change. The "Appendices" emphasize that all things in the universe are ever in a process of change. The comment on the third line of the eleventh hexagram states: "There is no level place without a bank, and no departure without a return." This saying is considered by the "Appendices" as the formula according to which things undergo change. This is the *Tao* of the transformation of all things.

If a thing is to reach its completion and the state of completion is to be maintained, its operation must occur at the right place, in the right way, and at the right time. In the comments of the *Yi*, this rightness is usually indicated by the words *cheng* (correct, proper) and *chung* (the mean, center, middle). As to *cheng*, "Appendix I" states: "The woman has her correct place within, and the man has his correct place without. The correctness of position of man and woman is the great principle of Heaven and Earth. . . . When the father is father, and the son son; when the elder brother is elder brother, and the younger brother younger brother; when husband is husband, and wife wife: then the way of the family is correct. When it is correct, all under Heaven will be established."

Chung means neither too much nor too little. The natural inclination of man is to take too much. Hence both the "Appendices" and the *Lao-tzu* consider excess a great evil. The *Lao-tzu* speaks about *fan* (reversal, ch. 40) and *fu* (returning, ch. 16), and the "Appendices" also speak about *fu*. Among the hexagrams, indeed, there is one titled *Fu* (the 24th hexagram). "Appendix I" says about this hexagram: "In *Fu* we see the mind of Heaven and Earth."

Using this concept of *fu*, "Appendix VI" interprets the order of arrangement of the sixty-four hexagrams. The *Yi* was originally divided into two books. This "Appendix" considers the first of these as dealing with the world of nature, and the second as dealing with that of man. Concerning the first book, it says: "Following the existence of Heaven and Earth, there is the production of all things. The space between Heaven and Earth is full of all these things. Hence [the hexagram] *Ch'ien* [Heaven] and [the hexagram] *K'un* [Earth] are followed by the hexagram *Tun*, which means fullness." Then the "Appendix" tries to show how each hexagram is usually followed by another which is opposite in character.

About the second book, this same "Appendix" says: "Following the existence of Heaven and Earth, there is the existence of all things. Following the existence of all things, there is the distinction of male and female. Following this distinction, there is the distinction between husband and wife. Following this distinction, there is the distinction between father and son. Following this distinction, there is the distinction between sovereign and subject. Following this distinction, there is the distinction between superiority and inferiority. Following this distinction, there are social order and justice." Then, as in the case of the first part of the *Yi*, the "Appendix" tries to show how one hexagram is usually followed by another which is opposite in character.

The sixty-third hexagram is *Chi-chi*, which means something accomplished. At this point this "Appendix" says: "But there can never be an end of things. Hence *Chi-chi* is followed by *Wei-chi* [the sixty-fourth hexagram, meaning something not yet accomplished]. With this hexagram, [the *Yi*] comes to a close."

According to this interpretation, the arrangement of the hexagrams implies at least three ideas: (1) that all that happens in the universe, natural and human alike, forms a continuous chain of natural sequence; (2) that in the process of evolution, everything involves its own negation; and (3) that in the process of evolution, "there can never be an end of things."

The "Appendices" agree with the *Lao-tzu* that in order to do something with success, one must be careful not to be too successful; and that in order to avoid losing something, one must complement it with something of its opposite. Thus "Appendix III" says: "The man who keeps danger in mind is one who retains his position. The man who keeps ruin in mind is one who survives. The man who has disorder in mind is one who has peace. Therefore, the superior man, when all is peaceful, does not forget danger. When he is acting, he does not forget about ruin. When he has society under control, he does not forget disorder. Hence it is possible, with his own person secure, for him to protect the state."

The "Appendices" also agree with the *Lao-tzu* that modesty and humbleness are the great virtues. "Appendix I" remarks: "It is the way of Heaven to diminish the swollen and augment the modest. It is the way of Earth to subvert the swollen and give free course to the modest. . . . It is the way of man to hate the swollen and love the modest. Modesty, in a high position, sheds luster on it; in a low position it cannot be passed by unobserved. This is the final goal of the superior man."

The Mean and Harmony

The idea of *chung* is fully developed in the *Chung Yung* or *Doctrine of the Mean*. *Chung* is like the Aristotelian idea of the "golden mean." Some would understand it as simply doing things no more than halfway, but this is quite wrong. The real meaning of *chung* is neither too much nor too little, that is, just right. Suppose that one is going from Washington to New York. It will then be just right to stop at New York, but to go right through to Boston, will be to do too much, and to stop at Philadelphia, will be to do too little. In a prose poem by Sung Yü of the third century B.C., he describes a beautiful girl with the words: "If she were one inch taller, she would be too tall. If she were one inch shorter, she would be too short. If she used powder, her face would be too white. If she used rouge, her face would be too red." (*Wen Hsüan, chüan* 19.) The description means that her figure and complexion were just right. "Just right" is what the Confucianists call *chung*.

Time is an important factor in the idea of being just right. It is just right to wear a fur coat in winter, but it is not just right to wear it in summer. Hence the Confucianists often use the word *shih* (time or timely) in conjunction with the word *chung*, as in the term *shih chung* or "timely mean." Mencius, for example, says of Confucius: "When it was proper to go into office, then to go into it; when it was proper to remain out of office, then to remain out of it; when it was proper to continue in it long, then to continue in it long; when it was proper to withdraw from it quickly, then to withdraw from it quickly: such was Confucius." (*Mencius*, IIa, 22.) Hence "among the sages, Confucius was the timely one." (*Ibid.*, Vb, 1.)

The *Chung Yung* says: "To have no emotions of pleasure or anger, sorrow or joy, welling up: this is to be described as the state of *chung*. To have these emotions welling up but in due proportion: this is to be described as the state of *ho* [harmony]. *Chung* is the chief foundation of the world. *Ho* is the great highway for the world. Once *chung* and *ho* are established, Heaven and Earth maintain their proper position, and all creatures are nourished." (Ch. 1.) When the emotions do not come forth at all, the mind neither goes too far nor falls short. It is just right. This is an illustration of the state of *chung*. And when the emotions do come forth, but in due proportion, this is also the state of *chung*, for harmony results from *chung*, and *chung* serves to harmonize what might otherwise be discordant.

What is said about the emotions also applies to the desires. In personal conduct as well as in social relations, there are medium points which serve as right limits for the satisfaction of the desires and the expression of the emotions. When all desires and emotions of a person are satisfied and expressed to the right degree, the person achieves a harmony within his person which results in good mental health. Likewise, when all the desires and feelings of the various types of people who comprise a society are satisfied and expressed to the right degree, the society achieves harmony within itself which results in peace and order.

Harmony is the reconciling of differences into a harmonious unity. The *Tso Chuan* reports a speech by the statesman Yen Tzu (died 493 B.C.), in which he makes a distinction between harmony and uniformity or identity. Harmony, he says, may be illustrated by cooking. Water, vinegar, pickles, salt, and plums are used to cook fish. From these ingredients there results a new taste which is neither that of the vinegar nor of the pickles. Uniformity or identity, on the other hand, may be likened to the attempt to flavor water with water, or to confine a piece of music to one note. In both cases there is nothing new.* Herein lies the distinction between the Chinese words *t'ung* and *ho*. *T'ung* means uniformity or identity, which is incompatible with difference. *Ho* means harmony, which is not incompatible with difference; on the contrary, it results when differences are brought together to form a unity. But in order to achieve harmony, the differences must each be present in precisely their proper proportion, which is *chung*. Thus the function of *chung* is to achieve harmony.

A well-organized society is a harmonious unity in which people of differing talents and professions occupy their proper places, perform their proper functions, and are all equally satisfied and not in conflict with one another. An ideal world is also a harmonious unity. The *Chung Yung* says: "All things are nurtured together without injuring one another. All courses are pursued without collision. This is what makes Heaven and Earth great." (Ch. 30.)

Harmony of this sort, which includes not only human society, but permeates the entire universe, is called the Supreme Harmony. In "Appendix I" of the *Yi*, it is said: "How vast is the originating power of [the hexagram] *Ch'ien*. . . . Unitedly to protect the Supreme Harmony: this is indeed profitable and auspicious."

The Common and the Ordinary

The *Chung Yung* says: "What Heaven confers is called the nature. The following of this nature is called the Way [*Tao*]. The cultivation

* See the *Tso Chuan*, twentieth year of Duke Chao, 522 B.C.

of this Way is called spiritual culture. The Way is that which no man for a moment can do without. What a man can do without is not the Way." (Ch. 1.) Here we touch upon the idea of the importance of the common and the ordinary, which is another important concept in the *Chung Yung*. This concept is expressed by the word *yung*, in the title of this work, which means common or ordinary.

Everyone finds it necessary to eat and drink every day. Hence eating and drinking are the common and ordinary activities of mankind. They are common and ordinary just because they are so important that no man can possibly do without them. The same is true of human relations and moral virtues. They appear to some people as so common and ordinary as to be of little value. Yet they are so simply because they are so important that no man can do without them. To eat and drink, and to maintain human relations and moral virtues, is to follow the nature of man. It is nothing else but the Way or *Tao*. What is called spiritual culture or moral instruction is nothing more than the cultivation of this Way.

Since the Way is that which no man in actual fact can do without, what is the need of spiritual culture? The answer is that although all men are, to some extent, really following the Way, not all men are sufficiently enlightened to be conscious of this fact. The *Chung Yung* says: "Amongst men there are none who do not eat and drink, but there are few who really appreciate the taste." (Ch. 4.) The function of spiritual culture is to give people an understanding that they are all, more or less, actually following the Way, so as to cause them to be conscious of what they are doing.

Furthermore, although all men are, as a matter of necessity, compelled to follow the Way to some extent, not all can follow it to perfection. Thus no one can live in a society utterly devoid of human relationships; at the same time there are few who can meet with perfection all the requirements made by these human relationships. The function of spiritual culture is to perfect what man is, as a matter of fact, already doing to a greater or lesser degree.

Thus the *Chung Yung* says: "The Way of the superior man is obvious and yet obscure. The ordinary man and ordinary woman in all their ignorance can yet have knowledge of it, yet in its perfection even a sage finds in it something which he does not know. The ordinary man and ordinary woman with all their stupidity can yet practice it, yet in its perfection even a sage finds in it something which he cannot practice. . . . Thus the Way of the superior man begins with the relationship between husband and wife, but in its fullest extent reaches to all that is in Heaven and Earth." (Ch. 12.) Thus though all men, even in their ignorance and stupidity, are following the Way to some extent, spiritual cultivation is nevertheless required to bring them to enlightenment and perfection.

Enlightenment and Perfection

In the *Chung Yung*, this perfection is described as *ch'eng* (sincerity, realness) and goes together with enlightenment. The *Chung Yung* says: "Progress from perfection to enlightenment is called the nature. From enlightenment to perfection it is called spiritual culture. When there is perfection, there is enlightenment. When there is enlightenment, there is perfection." (Ch. 21.) That is to say, once one understands all the significance of the ordinary and common acts of daily life, such as eating, drinking, and the human relationships, one is already a sage. The same is true when one practices to perfection what one understands. One cannot fully understand the significance of these things unless one practices them. Nor can one practice them to perfection, unless one fully understands their significance.

The *Chung Yung* says again: "The quality of *ch'eng* does not simply consist in perfecting oneself. It is that whereby one perfects all other things. The perfection of the self lies in the quality of *jen* [human-heartedness]. The perfection of other things lies in wisdom. In this is the virtue of the nature. It is the way through which comes the union between inner and outer." (Ch. 25.) The meaning of this passage seems clear, yet I wonder whether the words, human-heartedness and wisdom, should not be interchanged.

The *Chung Yung* says also: "It is only he who has the most *ch'eng* who can develop his nature to the utmost. Able to do this, he is able to do the same to the nature of other men. Able to do this, he is able to do the same to the nature of things. Able to do this, he can assist the transforming and nourishing operations of Heaven and Earth. Being able to do this, he can form a trinity with Heaven and Earth." (Ch. 22.)

While perfecting oneself, one must also see that others are likewise perfected. One cannot perfect oneself while disregarding the perfection of others. The reason is that one can develop one's nature to the utmost only through the human relationships, that is, within the sphere of society. This goes back to the tradition of Confucius and Mencius, that for self-perfection one must practice *chung, shu,* and human-heartedness; that is, it consists in helping others. To perfect oneself is to develop to the utmost what one has received from Heaven. And to help others is to assist the transforming and nourishing operations of Heaven and Earth. By fully understanding the significance of these things, one is enabled to form a trinity with Heaven and Earth. Such understanding is what the *Chung Yung* calls enlightenment, and forming a trinity in this way is what it calls perfection.

Is anything extraordinary needed in order to achieve this trinity? No, nothing more is needed than to do the common and ordinary things and to do them "just right," with understanding of their full significance. By so doing, one can gain the union of inner and outer, which is not only a trinity of Heaven, Earth, and man, but means a unity of man *with* Heaven and Earth. In this way one can achieve other-worldliness, yet at the same time not lose this-worldliness. It is with the development of this idea that the later Neo-Confucianists attacked the other-worldly philosophy of Buddhism.

Such is the Confucianist way of elevating the mind to a state in which the individual becomes one with the universe. It differs from the Taoist method, which is, through the negation of knowledge, to elevate the mind above the mundane distinctions between the "this" and the "other." The Confucianist method, on the other hand, is, through the extension of love, to elevate the mind above the usual distinctions between the self and other things.

WORLD POLITICS AND
WORLD PHILOSOPHY

It is said that "history never repeats itself," yet also that "there is nothing new under the sun." Perhaps the whole truth lies in a combination of these two sayings. From a Chinese point of view, so far as international politics is concerned, the history of our world in the present and immediately preceding centuries looks like a repetition of the Chinese history of the Ch'un Ch'iu and Chan Kuo periods.

Political Conditions Preceding the Unification by Ch'in

The Ch'un Ch'iu period (722-481 B.C.) is so named because it is the period covered by the *Ch'un Ch'iu* or *Spring and Autumn Annals*. And the Chan Kuo period (480-222 B.C.) derives its name, which means Warring States, from the fact that it was a period of intensified warfare between the feudal states. As we have seen, men's conduct during the feudal age was governed by *li* (ceremonies, rituals, rules of proper conduct). Not only were there *li* governing the conduct of the individual, but also those for the state as well. Some of these were to be practiced in time of peace, but others were designed for use in war. These peacetime and wartime *li*, as observed by one state in its relations to another, were equivalent to what we now would call international law.

We see that in recent times international law has become more and more ineffective. In late years there have been many instances in which one nation has attacked another without first sending an ultimatum and declaring war, or the airplanes of one nation have bombed the hospitals of another, while pretending that they did not see the red cross. And in the periods of Chinese history mentioned above, we see a similar decline in the effectiveness of the *li*.

In the Ch'un Ch'iu period, there were still people who respected the international *li*. The *Tso Chuan* reports a famous battle of Hung that took place in 638 B.C. between the states of Ch'u and Sung. The old-fashioned Duke Hsiang of Sung personally directed the Sung forces. At a certain moment, the Ch'u army was crossing a river to form its lines, whereupon the commander under Duke Hsiang immediately asked for permission to attack the army during its crossing. To this the Duke replied, however, that he would not attack an army before it had formed its lines. The result was a disastrous defeat of the Sung army, in which the Duke himself was wounded. In spite of this, however, he defended his original decision, saying: "A superior man does not inflict a second wound on one who has already been wounded, nor does he take prisoner any one who has gray hair." This infuriated one of his commanders, who told the Duke: "If it is good to refrain from inflicting a second wound, why not refrain from inflicting any wound at all? If it is good to refrain from taking prisoner any one who has gray hair, why not surrender to your enemy?" (*Tso Chuan*, twenty-second year of Duke Hsi.) What the Duke said accorded with the traditional *li*, which represented the chivalrous spirit of the feudal knights. What the commander said represented the practice of a changing age.

It is interesting though discouraging to note that all the known methods which statesmen of today use in an effort to keep peace among nations are much the same as those which the statesmen of these early periods of Chinese history attempted without success. For example, a conference for the limitation of armaments was held in 551 B.C. (*Tso Chuan*, twenty-seventh year of Duke Hsiang.) Some time later a proposal was made to divide the "world" of that time into two "spheres of influence"; one in the east, to be controlled by the King of Ch'i with the title of Eastern Emperor; the other in the west, to be controlled by the King of Ch'in with the title of Western Emperor. (*Historical Records*, ch. 46.) There were also various alliances of states with one another. During the Chan Kuo period these fell into two general patterns: the "vertical," which ran from north to south, and the "horizontal," which ran from west to east. At that time there were seven major states, of which Ch'in was the most aggressive. The vertical type of alliance was one directed against Ch'in by the other six states, and was so called because Ch'in lay in the extreme west, while the other six states were scattered to the east of it, ranging from north to south. The horizontal type of alliance, on the other hand, was one in which Ch'in combined with one or more of the other six states in order to attack the remainder, and therefore was extended from the west toward the east.

Ch'in's policy was "to make alliance with distant states, but attack the ones that were near." In this way it always eventually succeeded in breaking up the vertical alliances that opposed it. By its superiority in "agriculture and war" and extensive use of "fifth column" techniques among the other states, Ch'in, after a series of bloody campaigns, succeeded in conquering the other six states one by one, and finally unified the whole of China in 221 B.C. Thereupon the King of Ch'in gave to himself the grandiose title of First Emperor of Ch'in (Ch'in Shih-huang-ti) by which he is known to history. At the same time he abolished feudalism and thus for the first time in history created a centralized Chinese empire under the Ch'in dynasty.

The Unification of China

Though the First Emperor was thus the first to achieve actual unity, the desire for such unity had been cherished by all people for a long time previous. In the *Mencius* we are told that King Hui of Liang asked: "How may the world be at peace?" To which Mencius replied: "When there is unity, there will be peace." "But who can unify the world?" asked the King. "He who does not delight in killing men can unify it," answered Mencius. (Ia, 6.) This statement clearly expresses the aspiration of the time.

The word "world" used here is a translation of the Chinese term *t'ien-hsia*, which literally means "all beneath the sky." Some translators render it as "empire," because, so they maintain, what the Chinese in ancient times called the *t'ien-hsia* was confined to the limits of the Chinese feudal states. This is quite true. But we should not confuse the intension of a term with its extension as it was understood by the people of a particular time. The latter usage is limited by the knowledge of facts possessed by these people, but the former is a matter of definition. For instance, we cannot say that the word *jen* (persons) should be translated as "Chinese," simply because in ancient times what the Chinese meant by the word was confined to people of Chinese blood. When the ancient Chinese spoke about *jen*, what they meant was really human beings, even though at that time their knowledge of human beings was limited to those of China. In the same way, when they spoke about the *t'ien-hsia*, they meant the world, even though in early times their knowledge of the world did not extend beyond the Chinese states.

From the age of Confucius onward, the Chinese people in general and their political thinkers in particular began to think about political matters in terms of the world. Hence the unification of China by Ch'in seemed, to the people of that time, very much as the unification of the whole world would seem to us today. Since the unification of 221 B.C., for more than two thousand years, with the exception of certain periods which the Chinese have considered as abnormal, they have lived under one government in one world. They have thus been accustomed to a centralized organization that would operate for world peace. But in recent times they have been plunged into a world with international political conditions similar to those of the remote periods of the Ch'un Ch'iu and Chan Kuo. In the process they have been compelled to change their habits of thinking and acting. In this respect, in the eyes of the Chinese, there has been a repetition of history, which has contributed much to their present suffering. (See note at the end of the chapter.)

The Great Learning

To illustrate the internationalistic character of Chinese philosophy, let us turn now to some of the ideas of the *Ta Hsüeh*, or *Great Learning*. The *Ta Hsüeh*, like the *Chung Yung*, is a chapter in the *Li Chi* (*Book of Rites*), and like the *Chung Yung*, it was, during the Sung dynasty (960-1279), grouped by the Neo-Confucianists with the *Confucian Analects* and the *Mencius*, to form the "Four Books" which comprised the primary texts for Neo-Confucian philosophy.

The *Great Learning* was attributed by the Neo-Confucianists, though with no real proof, to Tseng Tzu, one of the chief disciples of Confucius. It was considered by them to be an important manual for the learning of *Tao*. Its opening section reads:

"The teaching of the *Great Learning* is to manifest one's illustrious virtue, love the people, and rest in the highest good. . . . The ancients who wished to manifest illustrious virtue throughout the world, first ordered well their own states. Wishing to order well their own states, they first regulated their own families. Wishing to regulate their own families, they first cultivated their own selves. Wishing to cultivate their own selves, they first rectified their own minds. Wishing to rectify their own minds, they first sought for absolute sincerity in their thoughts. Wishing for absolute sincerity in their thoughts, they first extended their knowledge. This extension of knowledge consists in the investigation of things.

"Things being investigated, only then did their knowledge become extended. Their knowledge being extended, only then did their thought become sincere. Their thought being sincere, only then did their mind become rectified. Their mind being rectified, only then did their selves become cultivated. Their selves being cultivated, only then did their families become regulated. Their families being regulated, only then did their states become rightly governed. Their states being rightly governed, only then could the world be at peace."

These statements have been known as the three "main cords" and eight "minor wires" of the *Ta Hsüeh*. According to later Confucianists, the three cords really comprise only one cord, which is "to manifest one's illustrious virtue." "To love the people" is the way "to manifest one's illustrious virtue," while "to rest in the highest good" is "to manifest one's illustrious virtue" in the highest perfection.

The "eight wires" are likewise really only one wire, which is the cultivation of one's own self. In the above quotation, the steps preceding the cultivation of the self, such as the investigation of things, extension of knowledge, etc., are the ways and means for cultivating the self. And the steps following the cultivation of the self, such as the regulation of the family, etc., are the ways and means for cultivating the self to its highest perfection, or as the text says, for "resting in the highest good." Man cannot develop his nature to perfection unless he tries his best to do his duties in society. He cannot perfect himself without at the same time perfecting others.

"To manifest one's illustrious virtue" is the same as "to cultivate one's self." The former is merely the content of the latter. Thus several ideas are reduced to a single idea, which is central in Confucianism.

It is unnecessary that one should be head of a state or of some world organization, before one can do something to bring good order to the state and peace to the world. One should merely do one's best to do good for the state as a member of the state, and do good for the world as a member of the world. One is then doing one's full share of bringing good order to the state and peace to the world. By thus sincerely trying to do one's best, one is resting in the highest good.

For the purpose of the present chapter, it is enough to point out that the author of the *Ta Hsüeh* was thinking in terms of world politics and world peace. He was not the first to think in this way, but it is significant that he did it so systematically. For him, the good order of one's own state is neither the final goal in terms of politics nor in terms of the spiritual cultivation of the self.

Here we need not discuss the problem of how the investigation of things can be the ways and means for the spiritual cultivation of the self. This problem will return to us when we take up Neo-Confucianism later.

Eclectic Tendency in the Hsün-tzu

In the world of Chinese philosophy, the latter part of the third century B.C. saw a strong tendency towards syncretism and eclecticism. The major work of the School of Eclectics, the *Lü-shih Ch'un-ch'iu,* was composed at that time. But, although this work devoted chapters to most of the schools of its time, it failed to give a theoretical justification for the idea of eclecticism as such. Both Confucianist and Taoist writers, however, did present such a theory, which shows how, despite their other differences, they both reflected the eclectic spirit of the time.

These writers agreed that there is a single absolute Truth which they called the *Tao.* Most of the different schools have seen some one particular aspect of the *Tao,* and in this sense have made some contribution to its manifestation. The Confucianist writers, however, maintained that it was Confucius who had seen the whole Truth, and so the other schools were subordinate to the Confucian school, though in a sense complementary to it. The Taoist writers, on the contrary, maintained that it was Lao Tzu and Chuang Tzu who had seen the whole Truth, and therefore that Taoism was superior to all other schools.

In the *Hsün-tzu* there is a chapter titled "On Freedom from Blindness," in which we read:

"In the past, the traveling scholars were blinded, so they had different schools of thought. Mo Tzu was blinded by utility and did not know the value of culture. Sung Tzu [a contemporary of Mencius, who maintained that the desires of men are really very few] was blinded by desire, but did not know [that men seek for] gain. Shen Tzu [Shen Tao, a member of the Legalist school] was blinded by law but did not know [the value of] talent. Shen Tzu [Shen Puhai, another member of the Legalist school] was blinded by authority but did not know wisdom. Hui Tzu [Hui Shih of the School of Names] was blinded by words but did not know facts. Chuang Tzu was blinded by what is of nature but did not know what is of man.

"From the point of view of utility, the *Tao* is nothing more than seeking for profit. From the point of view of [fewness of] desires, the *Tao* is nothing more than satisfaction. From the point of view of law, the *Tao* is nothing more than regulations. From the point of view of authority, the *Tao* is nothing more than caprice. From the point of view of what is of nature, the *Tao* is nothing more than *laissez-faire*. From the point of view of words, the *Tao* is nothing more than argumentation.

"These different views are single aspects of the *Tao*. The essence of the *Tao* is constant and includes all changes. It cannot be grasped by a single corner. Those with perverted knowledge who see only a single aspect of the *Tao* will not be able to comprehend its totality. . . . Confucius was human-hearted and wise and was not blinded. Therefore he comprehended the *Tao* and was sufficient to be ranked with the early rulers." (Ch. 21.)

In another chapter Hsün Tzu says: "Lao Tzu had vision regarding acquiescence, but did not see exertion. Mo Tzu had vision regarding uniformity, but did not see individuality. Sung Tzu had vision regarding [the fact that the desires of some men are] few, but did not see [the fact that those of other men are] many." (Ch. 17.) According to Hsün Tzu, the vision and blindness of a philosopher go together. He has vision, yet usually at the same time is blinded by his vision. Hence the excellence of his philosophy is at the same time its shortcoming.

Eclectic Tendency in the Chuang-tzu

The author of the last chapter of the *Chuang-tzu, T'ien Hsia* or "The World," gives the Taoist view of syncretism. This chapter is really a summarized account of ancient Chinese philosophy. We are not sure who the author was, but he was certainly one of the best historians and critics of early Chinese philosophy.

This chapter first makes a distinction between the whole Truth and partial truth. The whole Truth is the *Tao* of "sageliness within and kingliness without," the study of which is called "the *Tao* method." Partial truth is a particular aspect of the whole Truth, the study of which is called "the art method." This chapter says: "In the world there are many who use the art method. Each one considers his own [thought] as perfect without need of any addition. Where is there then what the ancients called the *Tao* method? . . . There is that by which the sage flourishes; there is that through which the king completes his achievement. Both originate in the One."

The One is the "*Tao* of sageliness within and kingliness without." The chapter goes on to make a distinction between the fundamental and the branch, the fine and the coarse, in the *Tao.* It says: "How perfect were the men of old. . . . They understood the fundamental principles and connected them with minute regulations reaching to all points of the compass, embracing the great and the small, the fine and the coarse; their influence was everywhere.

"Some of their teachings which were correctly embodied in measures and institutions are still preserved in ancient laws and the records of historians. Those teachings that were recorded in the books of *Poetry, History, Rites,* and *Music* were known to most of the gentlemen and teachers of [the states of] Tsou and Lu [i.e., the Confucianists]. The *Book of Poetry* describes aims; the *Book of History* describes events; the *Rites* direct conduct; *Music* secures harmony. The *Yi* [*Book of Changes*] shows the principles of the *Yin* and *Yang*. The *Ch'un Ch'iu* [*Spring and Autumn Annals*] shows names and duties."

Thus the *T'ien Hsia* chapter maintains that the Confucianists had some connection with the *Tao.* But what they knew is confined to "measures and institutions." They knew nothing about the underlying principle. That is to say, they knew only the coarser aspects and lesser branches of the *Tao*, but not what is fine and fundamental in it.

The *T'ien Hsia* chapter continues by saying: "Now the world is in great disorder. The virtuous and the sage are obscured. *Tao* and virtue lose their unity and many in the world get hold of some one aspect of the whole to enjoy for themselves. The case is like the senses of hearing, sight, smell, and taste, which have specific functions, but cannot be interchanged. Or like the skill of the various artisans, which are each excellent in its kind and useful in its turn, yet are not comprehensive. Each is a student of some one aspect. . . . Thus the *Tao* of sageliness within and kingliness without becomes obscured and loses its clearness; it becomes repressed and loses its development."

Then the same treatise makes a classification of the different schools, granting to each that it has "heard" of some one aspect of the *Tao*, but at the same making sharp criticisms of the school's shortcomings. Lao Tzu and Chuang Tzu are greatly admired. Yet, remarkably enough, these two leaders of Taoism, like the other schools, are by implication criticized by the remark that they, too, have merely "heard some one aspect of the *Tao*."

It thus seems to be the implication of the *T'ien Hsia* chapter that the Confucianists knew the concrete "measures and institutions" but not their underlying principle, whereas the Taoists knew the principle but not the measures and institutions. In other words, the Confucianists knew the "branches" of the *Tao*, but not its fundamental aspect, while the Taoists knew its fundamental aspect, but not its branches. Only a combination of the two constitutes the whole Truth.

Eclecticism of Ssu-Ma T'an and Liu Hsin

This eclectic tendency was continued in the Han dynasty. The *Huai-nan-tzu* or *Book of the Prince of Huai-nan* is a book of the same nature as the *Lü-shih Ch'un-ch'iu*, though with a stronger tendency towards Taoism. In addition to this book, the two historians, Ssu-ma T'an (died 110 B.C.) and Liu Hsin (ca. 46 B.C.-A.D. 23), who have been quoted in chapter three, also display eclectic tendencies. Of them, Ssu-ma T'an was a Taoist. In the essay quoted in chapter three, "On the Essentials of the Six Schools," he says: "In the 'Great Appendix' ['Appendix III'] of the *Yi*, there is the statement: 'In the world there is one purpose, but there are a hundred ideas about it; there is a single goal, but the paths toward it differ.' This is just the case with the different schools of thought, . . . all of which seek social order but follow widely different paths in their words of explanation, some of which are clear and others not." (*Historical Records*, ch. 130.) He then goes on to mention the excellencies and shortcomings of the six philosophic schools, but concludes by considering Taoism as combining all the best points of the other schools, and therefore as being superior to all.

Liu Hsin, on the other hand, was a Confucianist. In his *Seven Summaries*, as quoted in the chapter on literature contained in the *History of the Former Han Dynasty*, he lists ten schools of thought, and quotes the same passage from "Appendix III" of the *Book of Changes* as does Ssu-ma T'an. Then he concludes: "Each of the schools developed its strong points; and each developed knowledge and investigation to the utmost in order to set forth clearly its main purposes. Although they had prejudices and shortcomings, still a summary of their teachings shows that they were branches and descendants of the *Liu Yi* (Six Classics). . . . If one were able to cultivate the *Liu Yi* and observe the sayings of the nine schools [omitting that of the Story Tellers as of no philosophical importance], discarding their errors and gathering their good points, it would be possible to master the manifold aspects of thought." (*History of the Former Han Dynasty*, ch. 30.)

All these statements reflect the strong desire for unity that existed even in the world of thought. The people of the third century B.C., discouraged by centuries of inter-state warfare, longed for a political unification; their philosophers, consequently, also tried to bring about a unification in thought. Eclecticism was the first attempt. Eclecticism in itself, however, cannot build a unified system. The eclectics believed in the whole Truth, and hoped by selecting from the various schools their "strong points," to attain to this Truth or *Tao*. What they called the *Tao*, however, was, it is to be feared, simply a patch-work of many disparate elements, unconnected by any underlying organic principle, and hence unworthy of the high title they attached to it.

Note on the Chinese concept of Nationalism (see p. 181).

Dr. Derk Bodde writes: "I would question this statement. The Six Dynasties (third through sixth century), Yüan (1280-1367) and Ch'ing (1644-1911) periods, for example, were in actual fact of so long duration as to accustom the Chinese to the idea of disunity or foreign domination, even though such a situation was in theory regarded as 'abnormal.' Moreover, even in the 'normal' periods of unity, there was often extensive political maneuvering and military action against a succession of outside peoples, such as the Hsiung-nu, as well as against occasional rebels within the empire. I would hardly regard the present conditions as presenting an unfamiliar situation to the Chinese, therefore, even though their effects are accentuated by the fact that they operate on a truly worldwide scale."

The historical facts which Dr. Bodde mention are no doubt correct, but what concerns me in this paragraph is not these historical facts themselves, but what the Chinese people up to the end of the last century, or even the beginning of this century, have felt about them. The emphasis upon the foreign domination of the Yüan and Ch'ing dynasties is one made from the point of view of modern nationalism. It is true that from early times the Chinese have made a sharp distinction between *Chung Kuo* or *hua hsia* (Chinese) and *yi ti* (barbarian), but the emphasis of this distinction is more cultural than racial. The Chinese have traditionally considered that there are three kinds of living beings: Chinese, barbarians, and beasts. Of these, the Chinese are most cultured, the barbarians come next, and the beasts are completely uncultured.

When the Mongols and Manchus conquered China, they had already to a considerable extent adopted the culture of the Chinese. They dominated the Chinese politically, but the Chinese dominated them culturally. They therefore did not create a marked break or change in the continuity and unity of Chinese culture and civilization, with which the Chinese were most concerned. Hence traditionally the Chinese have considered the Yüan and Ch'ing as simply two of the many dynasties that have followed each other in Chinese history. This can be seen from the official arrangement of the dynastic histories. The Ming dynasty, for instance, in one sense represented a nationalistic revolution against the Yüan; nevertheless, the official *History of the Yüan Dynasty*, compiled under the Ming, treated the Yüan as the normal successor of the purely Chinese Sung dynasty. Likewise Huang Tsung-hsi (1610-1695), one of the nationalistic scholars who opposed the Manchus, in his *Sung Yüan Hsüeh-an* or *Biographical History of Confucianist Philosophers of the Sung and Yüan Dynasties*, found no moral fault in such scholars as Hsü

Heng (1209-1281) and Wu Ch'eng (1249-1333), who though Chinese had served under the Yüan with high official rank.

The Chinese Republic has similarly compiled an official *History of the Ch'ing Dynasty*, in which this dynasty is treated as the normal successor of the Ming. This history was later banned by the present government, because the treatment of certain events connected with the revolution of 1911 was regarded as unsatisfactory. Hence it is possible that the new official *History of the Ch'ing Dynasty* will eventually be written in a quite different way. What I am here concerned with, however, is the traditional view. So far as tradition is concerned, the Yüan and Ch'ing were just as "normal" as other dynasties. One may say that the Chinese lack nationalism, but that is precisely my point. They lack nationalism because they have been accustomed to think in terms of *t'ien hsia*, the world.

As to the fact that the Chinese have had to fight such non-Chinese groups as the Hsiung-nu, etc., traditionally what the Chinese have felt is that sometimes it was necessary for them to fight the barbarians, just as sometimes it was necessary to fight the beasts. They did not feel that such people as the Hsiung-nu were in a position to divide the world with China, just as the American people do not feel that the red Indians are in a position to divide America with them.

Because the Chinese did not greatly emphasize racial distinctions, it resulted that during the third and fourth centuries A.D. various non-Chinese peoples were allowed to move freely into China. This movement constituted what is called the "inner colonization," and was a primary cause for the political troubles of the Six Dynasties period. Such "inner colonization" is precisely what Hitler, in his *Mein Kampf*, criticized from a super-nationalistic point of view.

The introduction of Buddhism seems to have given many Chinese the realization that civilized people other than the Chinese existed, but traditionally there have been two kinds of opinion regarding India. Those Chinese who opposed Buddhism believed that the Indians were simply another tribe of barbarians. Those who believed in Buddhism, on the other hand, regarded India as the "pure land of the West." Their praise of India was that of a realm transcending this world. Hence even the introduction of Buddhism, despite its enormous effect upon Chinese life, did not change the belief of the Chinese that they were the only civilized people in the *human* world.

As a result of these concepts, when the Chinese first came in contact with Europeans in the sixteenth and seventeenth centuries, they thought that they were simply barbarians like preceding barbarians, and so they spoke of them as barbarians. As a consequence they did not feel greatly disturbed, even though they suffered many defeats in fighting with them.

They began to be disturbed, however, when they found that the Europeans possessed a civilization equal to, though different from, that of the Chinese. What was novel in the situation was not that peoples other than the Chinese existed, but that their civilization was one of equal power and importance. In Chinese history one can find a parallel for such a situation only in the Ch'un Ch'iu and Chan Kuo periods, when different but equally civilized states existed that fought with one another. That is why the Chinese now feel that there is a repetition in history.

If one reads the writings of the great statesmen of the last century, such as Tseng Kuo-fan (1811-1872) and Li Hung-chang (1823-1901), there is much evidence that they felt about the impact of the West precisely in this way. This note attempts to describe the reasons for their feeling.

CHAPTER 17

THEORIZER OF THE HAN EMPIRE:
TUNG CHUNG-SHU

Mᴇɴᴄɪᴜs once said that those who do not delight in killing men would unify the world. (*Mencius*, Ia, 6.) It would seem that he was wrong, because, some hundred years later, it was the state of Ch'in that unified the whole of China. Ch'in was superior to the other states in the arts of both "agriculture and war," that is, it was superior both economically and militarily. It was known at the time as "the state of tigers and wolves." By sheer force of arms, coupled with the ruthless ideology of the Legalists, it succeeded in conquering all its rivals.

The Amalgamation of the Yin-Yang and Confucianist Schools

Yet Mencius was not wholly wrong, for the Ch'in dynasty, which was established after the unification of 221 B.C., lasted only about fifteen years. Soon after the death of the First Emperor his empire disintegrated in a series of rebellions against the harsh Ch'in rule, and was succeeded by the Han dynasty (206 B.C.-A.D. 220). The Han inherited the concept of political unity of the Ch'in, and continued its unfinished work, that is, the building up of a new political and social order.

Tung Chung-shu (c. 179-c. 104 B.C.) was the great theorizer in such an attempt. A native of the southern part of the present Hopei province, he was largely instrumental in making Confucianism the orthodox belief of the Han dynasty, at the expense of the other schools of thought. He was also prominent in the creation of the institutional basis for this Confucian orthodoxy: the famed Chinese examination system, which began to take form during his time. Under this system, entry into the ranks of the government officials who ruled the country was not dependent upon noble birth or wealth, but rather upon success in a series of periodic examinations which were conducted by the government simultaneously throughout the country, and were open to all members of society with but trifling exceptions. These examinations, to be sure, were still embryonic in the Han dynasty and did not become really universal until several centuries later. It is to Tung Chung-shu's credit, however, that he was one of the first to propose them, and it is also significant that in so doing he insisted upon the Confucian classics as the ideological basis for their operation.

It is said of Tung Chung-shu that he was so devoted to his literary studies that once for three years he did not even look out into his garden. As a result, he wrote a lengthy work known as the *Ch'un-ch'iu Fan-lu*, or *Luxuriant Dew from the Spring and Autumn Annals*. It is also said that he used to expound his teachings from behind a curtain, and that these were transmitted by his disciples, one to another, to a remote distance, so that there were some who never had the privilege of seeing his countenance. (See his biography in the *History of the Former Han Dynasty*, ch. 56.)

What Tung Chung-shu tried to do was to give a sort of theoretical justification to the new political and social order of his time. According to him, since man is a part of Heaven, the justification of the behavior of the former must be found in the behavior of the latter. He thought with the *Yin-Yang* school that a close interconnection exists between Heaven and man. Starting with this premise, he combined a metaphysical justification, which derives chiefly from the *Yin-Yang* school, with a political and social philosophy which is chiefly Confucianist.

The word Heaven is a translation of the Chinese word *T'ien*, which is sometimes rendered as "Heaven" and sometimes as "nature." Neither translation is quite adequate, however, especially in Tung Chung-shu's philosophy. My colleague Professor Y. L. Chin has said: "Perhaps if we mean by *T'ien* both nature and the divinity which presides over nature, with emphasis sometimes on the one and sometimes on the other, we have something approaching the Chinese term." (Unpublished manuscript.) This statement is not true in certain cases, for instance, in those of Lao Tzu and Chuang Tzu, but it is certainly so in the case of Tung Chung-shu. In this chapter, when the word Heaven occurs, I ask the reader to recall this statement of Professor Chin as the definition of the word *T'ien* in Tung Chung-shu's philosophy.

In chapter twelve it was pointed out that there were two distinct lines of thought in ancient China, those of the *Yin* and *Yang* and of the Five Elements, each of which provided a positive interpretation for the structure and origin of the universe. Later, however, these two lines became amalgamated, and in Tung Chung-shu this amalgamation is particularly conspicuous. Thus in his philosophy we find both the theory of the *Yin* and *Yang* and that of the Five Elements.

Cosmological Theory

According to Tung Chung-shu, the universe has ten constituents: Heaven, Earth, the *Yin* and *Yang*, the Five Elements of Wood, Fire, Soil, Metal, and Water, and finally man.* His idea of the *Yin* and *Yang* is very concrete. He says: "Within the universe there exist the ethers of the *Yin* and *Yang*. Men are constantly immersed in them, just as fish are constantly immersed in water. The difference between the *Yin* and *Yang* ethers and water is that water is visible, whereas the ethers are invisible." (Ch. 81.)

The order of the Five Elements given by Tung Chung-shu differs from that given by the "Grand Norm." (See ch. 12 of this book.) According to him, the first is Wood, the second, Fire, the third Soil, the fourth Metal, and the fifth Water. These Five Elements "each in turn produces the next and is overcome by the next but one in turn." (Ch. 42.) Thus Wood produces Fire, Fire produces Soil, Soil produces Metal, Metal produces Water, and Water produces Wood. This is the process of their mutual production. But Wood overcomes Soil, Soil overcomes Water, Water overcomes Fire, Fire overcomes Metal, and Metal overcomes Wood. This is the process of their mutual overcoming.

For Tung Chung-shu, as for the *Yin-Yang* school, Wood, Fire, Metal, and Water each presides over one of the four seasons as well as one of the four directions of the compass. Wood presides over the east and spring, Fire over the south and summer, Metal over the west and autumn, and Water over the north and winter. Soil

---

* See the *Ch'un-ch'iu Fan-lu*, ch. 81. All quotations in the present chapter, unless otherwise stated, are from this work.

presides over the center and gives assistance to all the other elements. The alternation of the four seasons is explained by the operations of the *Yin* and *Yang*. (Ch. 42.)

The *Yin* and *Yang* wax and wane and follow fixed circuits which take them through all the four directions. When the *Yang* first waxes, it moves to assist Wood in the east, and then there comes spring. As it grows in strength, it moves to the south where it assists Fire, and then there comes summer. But according to the universal law of "reversal" as maintained by the *Lao-tzu* and the *Yi* "Appendices," growth must be followed by decay. Hence the *Yang*, having reached its extreme height, begins to wane, while at the same time the *Yin* begins to wax in turn. The *Yin*, as it does this, moves east to assist Metal,* and then there comes autumn. As it gains more strength, it moves north to assist Water, and then there comes winter. But having there reached its climax, it begins to wane, while at the same time the *Yang* starts a new cycle of growth.

Thus the changes of the four seasons result from the waxing and waning movements of the *Yin* and *Yang*, and their succession is really a succession of the *Yin* and *Yang*. Tung Chung-shu says: "The constant principle of the universe is the succession of the *Yin* and *Yang*. The *Yang* is Heaven's beneficent force, while the *Yin* is its chastising force. . . . In the course of Heaven, there are three seasons [spring, summer, and autumn] of formation and growth, and one season [winter] of mourning and death." (Ch. 49.)

This shows, according to Tung, that "Heaven has trust in the *Yang* but not in the *Yin*; it likes beneficence but not chastisement." (Ch. 47.) It also shows that "Heaven has its own feelings of joy and anger, and a mind which experiences sadness and pleasure, analogous to those of man. Thus if a grouping is made according to kind, Heaven and man are one." (Ch. 49.)

Man, therefore, both in his physiological and mental aspects, is a replica or duplicate of Heaven. (Ch. 41.) As such, he is far superior to all other things of the world. Man, Heaven, and Earth are "the origins of all things." "Heaven gives them birth, Earth gives them nourishment, and man gives them perfection." (Ch. 19.) As to how man accomplishes this perfection, Tung says that it is done

* Not west, though west is the direction for autumn. The reason for this is, according to Tung, that "Heaven has trust in the *Yang*, but not in the *Yin*."

through *li* (ritual) and *yüeh* (music), that is to say, through civilization and culture. If there were no civilization and culture, the world
would be like an unfinished work, and the universe itself would
suffer imperfection. Thus of Heaven, Earth, and man, he says:
"These three are related to each other like the hands and feet;
united they give the finished physical form, so that no one of them
may be dispensed with." (Ch. 19.)

Theory of Human Nature

Since Heaven has its *Yin* and *Yang*, and man is a replica of
Heaven, the human mind consequently also contains two elements:
hsing (man's nature) and *ch'ing* (the emotions or feelings). The
word *hsing* is used by Tung Chung-shu sometimes in a broader and
sometimes a narrower sense. In the narrow sense, it is something that
exists separate from and in opposition to *ch'ing*, whereas in the
broader sense it embraces *ch'ing*. In this latter meaning, Tung sometimes refers to *hsing* as the "basic stuff." (Ch. 35.) This basic stuff
of man, therefore, consists both of *hsing* (used in the narrow sense)
and *ch'ing*. From *hsing* comes the virtue of human-heartedness,
whereas from *ch'ing* comes the vice of covetousness. This *hsing*, in
the narrow sense, is equivalent to Heaven's *Yang*, and *ch'ing* to its
Yin. (Ch. 35.)

In this connection Tung Chung-shu takes up the old controversy
as to whether human nature, that is, the basic stuff of man, is good
or bad. He cannot agree with Mencius that the nature is good, for
he says: "Goodness is like a kernel of grain, and the nature is like
the growing plant of the grain. Though the plant produces the kernel, it cannot itself be called a kernel. [Similarly] though the *hsing*
[here used in its broader sense, i.e., the basic stuff] produces goodness, it cannot itself be called goodness. The kernel and goodness
are both brought to completion through man's continuation of
Heaven's work, and are external [to the latter]. They do not lie
within [the scope of] what Heaven itself does. What Heaven does
extends to a certain point and then stops. What lies within this
stopping point pertains to Heaven. What lies outside of it pertains
to the *chiao* [teaching, culture] of the [sage-] kings. The *chiao* of the
[sage-] kings lies outside the *hsing* [basic stuff], yet without it the
hsing cannot be fully developed." (Ch. 36.)

Thus Tung Chung-shu emphasizes the value of culture, which is indeed that which makes man equal to Heaven and Earth. In this respect he approaches Hsün Tzu. He differs from him, however, in that he does not consider the basic stuff of man to be actually evil. Goodness is a continuation of nature, not a reversal of it.

Inasmuch as culture, for Tung, is a continuation of nature, he also approaches Mencius. Thus he writes: "It is said by some that since the nature [of man] contains the beginning of goodness and the mind contains the basic stuff of goodness, how, then, can it be that [the nature itself] is not good? But I reply that this is not so. For the silk cocoon contains silk fibers and yet is not itself silk, and the egg contains the chicken, yet is not itself a chicken. If we follow these analogies, what doubt can there be?" (Ch. 5.) The question raised here represents the view of Mencius. In answering it, Tung Chung-shu makes clear the difference between Mencius and himself.

But the difference between these two philosophers is really not much more than verbal. Tung Chung-shu himself says: "Mencius evaluates [the basic stuff of man] in comparison with the doings of the birds and beasts below, and therefore says that human nature is itself already good. I evaluate it in comparison with the sages above, and therefore say that human nature is not yet good." (Ch. 25.) Thus the difference between Mencius and Tung Chung-shu is reduced to that between two phrases: "already good" and "not yet good."

Social Ethics

According to Tung Chung-shu, the theory of the Yin and Yang is also a metaphysical justification of the social order. He writes: "In all things there must be correlates. Thus if there is the upper, there must be the lower. If there is the left, there must be the right. . . . If there is cold, there must be heat. If there is day, there must be night. These are all correlates. The Yin is the correlate of the Yang, the wife of the husband, the subject of the sovereign. There is nothing that does not have a correlate, and in each correlation there is the Yin and Yang. Thus the relationships between sovereign and subject, father and son, and husband and wife, are all derived from the principles of the Yin and Yang. The sovereign is *Yang*, the subject is *Yin*; the father is *Yang*, the son is *Yin*; the husband is *Yang*, the wife is *Yin*. . . . The three cords [*kang*]of the Way of the [true] King may be sought in Heaven." (Ch. 53.)

According to the Confucianists before this period, there are in society five major human relationships, namely, those between sovereign and subject, father and son, husband and wife, elder and younger brother, and friend and friend. Out of these, Tung selects three and calls them the three *kang*. The literal meaning of *kang* is a major cord in a net, to which all the other strings are attached. Thus the sovereign is the *kang* of his subjects, that is, he is their master. Likewise the husband is the *kang* of the wife, and the father is the *kang* of the son.

Besides the three *kang* there exist the five *ch'ang*, which were upheld by all Confucianists. *Ch'ang* means a norm or constant, and the five *ch'ang* are the five constant virtues of Confucianism, namely, *jen* (human-heartedness), *yi* (righteousness), *li* (propriety, rituals, rules of proper conduct), *chih* (wisdom) and *hsin* (good faith). Although Tung Chung-shu did not especially emphasize this point himself, it was commonly held by all the Han scholars that the five virtues have their correlations in the Five Elements. Thus human-heartedness is correlated with Wood in the east; righteousness with Metal in the west; propriety with Fire in the south; wisdom with Water in the north; and good faith with Soil in the center.*

The five *ch'ang* are the virtues of an individual, and the three *kang* are the ethics of society. The compound word *kang-ch'ang* meant, in olden times, morality or moral laws in general. Man must develop his nature in the direction of the moral laws, which are the essentials of culture and civilization.

Political Philosophy

Not all men, however, can do this by themselves. Hence it is the function of government to help them in their development. Tung Chung-shu writes: "Heaven has produced men with natures that contain the basic stuff' of goodness but are not able to be good in themselves. Therefore Heaven has established for them [the insti-

---

* See the *Pai Hu T'ung Yi* or *General Principles from the White Tiger* [*Lodge*], a work compiled in A.D. 79, *chüan* 8.

tution of] the king to make them good. This is the purpose of
Heaven." (Ch. 35.)

The king governs with beneficence, rewards, punishments, and
executions. These "four ways of government" are modeled on the
four seasons. Tung says: "Beneficence, rewards, punishments, and
executions, match spring, summer, autumn, and winter respectively,
like the fitting together of [the two parts of] a tally. Therefore I say
that the king is co-equal with Heaven, meaning that Heaven has four
seasons, while the king has four ways of government. Such are what
Heaven and man share in common." (Ch. 55.)

The organization of government is also modeled on the pattern of
the four seasons. According to Tung, the fact that government officials are graded into four ranks is modeled on the fact that a year
has four seasons. Likewise, the fact that each official in each rank
has three assistants under him, is modeled on the fact that each
season has three months. The officials are thus graded, because men
naturally fall into four grades in regard to their ability and virtue.
Hence the government selects all men who deserve to be selected,
and employs them according to these natural grades of virtue and
ability. "Thus Heaven selects the four seasons, and brings them to
completion with the twelve [months]; in this way the transformations of Heaven are completely expressed. And it is only the sage who
can similarly give complete expression to the changes of man and
harmonize them with those of Heaven." (Ch. 24.)

Since the relation between Heaven and man is so close and intimate, hence, Tung maintains, all wrongdoings in human government
must result in the manifestation of abnormal phenomena in the
world of nature. As had already been done by the *Yin-Yang* school,
he supplies both a teleological and a mechanistic explanation for this
theory.

Teleologically speaking, when there is something wrong in human
government, this necessarily causes displeasure and anger on the part
of Heaven. Such displeasure or anger is expressed through natural
visitations or prodigies, such as earthquakes, eclipses of the sun or
moon, droughts or floods. These are Heaven's way of warning the
ruler to correct his mistakes.

Mechanistically speaking, however, according to Tung Chung-shu,
"all things avoid that from which they differ and cleave to that to
which they are similar," and "things definitely call to themselves

their own kind." Hence abnormalities on the part of man necessarily call forth abnormalities on the part of nature. Tung Chung-shu, contradicting his teleological theory expressed elsewhere, maintains that this is the law of nature and that in it there is nothing supernatural. (Ch. 57.)

Philosophy of History

In chapter twelve we saw how Tsou Yen maintained the theory that the changes of dynasties in history are influenced by the movements of the Five Powers. A certain dynasty, because it is associated with a certain Power, must conduct its government in a manner appropriate to that Power. Tung Chung-shu modifies this theory by maintaining that the succession of dynasties does not accord with the movement of the Five Powers, but with a sequence of what he calls the "Three Reigns." These are the Black, White, and Red Reigns. Each has its own system of government and each dynasty represents one Reign. (Ch. 23.)

In actual history, according to Tung, the Hsia dynasty (traditionally 2205-1766 B.C.) represented the Black Reign; the Shang dynasty (1766?-1122? B.C.) the White Reign; and the Chou dynasty (1122?-255 B.C.) the Red Reign. This constituted one cycle in the evolution of history. After the Chou dynasty, the new dynasty would again represent the Black Reign, and the same sequence would recur.

It is interesting to note that in modern times, colors have also been used to denote varying systems of social organization, and that they are the same three as those of Tung Chung-shu. Thus, following his theory, we might say that Fascism represents the Black Reign, Capitalism the White Reign, and Communism the Red Reign.

Of course, this is only coincidence. According to Tung Chung-shu, the three Reigns do not differ fundamentally. He maintains that when a new king founds a dynasty, he does so because he has received a special Mandate from Heaven. Hence he must effect certain external changes to make apparent that he has received the new Mandate. These include the shifting of his capital to a new place, assumption of a new title, changing the beginning of the year, and altering the color of clothing worn on official occasions. "As to the great bonds of human relationships," says Tung, "and as to morality, government, moral instruction, customs and the meaning of words, these remain wholly as they were before. For why, indeed, should they be changed? Therefore, the king of a new dynasty has the reputation of changing his institutions, but does not as a matter of fact alter the basic principles." (Ch. 1.)

These basic principles are what Tung calls the *Tao*. His biography in the *History of the Former Han Dynasty* (ch. 56) quotes him as saying: "The great source of *Tao* derives from Heaven; Heaven does not change, nor does the *Tao*."

The theory that the ruler rules through the Mandate of Heaven is not a new one. In the *Book of History* we find sayings implying this theory, and Mencius made it already sufficiently clear. But Tung Chung-shu made it the more articulate by incorporating it into his whole philosophy of nature and man.

In the feudal age, all rulers inherited their authority from their ancestors. Even the First Emperor of the Ch'in dynasty was no exception. But the founder of the Han dynasty was different. Rising from the common people, he succeeded in becoming Emperor of the (to the Chinese) entire civilized world. This needed some justification, and Tung Chung-shu provided that justification.

His theory that a ruler rules through the Mandate of Heaven justified the exercise of imperial authority and at the same time set certain limits on it. The Emperor had to be watchful for manifestations of Heaven's pleasure or displeasure, and to act accordingly. It was the practice of the Han Emperors, and, to a greater or lesser extent, of the Emperors of later dynasties, to examine themselves and the policies of their government, and to try to reform them when abnormal natural phenomena gave them cause to be uneasy.

Tung's theory of the succession of the Reigns also set a certain limit to the tenure of a given dynasty. No matter how good an imperial house may be, the length of its rule is limited. When the end comes, it must give way to another dynasty, the founder of which has received a new Mandate. Such are the measures through which the Confucianists tried to lay restraints upon the power of an absolute monarchy.

Interpretation of the Ch'un Ch'iu

According to Tung Chung-shu, neither the Ch'in nor the Han was the direct successor of the Chou dynasty. In actual fact, he asserted, it was Confucius who received the Mandate of Heaven to succeed the Chou and to represent the Black Reign. He was not a king *de facto,* but one *de jure.*

This is a strange theory, but it was actually maintained and believed by Tung Chung-shu and his school. The *Ch'un Ch'iu,* or *Spring and Autumn Annals,* which was originally a chronicle of Confucius' native state of Lu, was supposed by them (incorrectly) to be a very important political work of Confucius in which he exercised his right as the new king. He represented the Black Reign and instituted all the changes that go with this Reign. Tung Chung-shu was famous for his interpretation of the *Ch'un Ch'iu,* and could justify all aspects of his philosophy by quotations from it. As a matter of fact, he commonly quoted the *Ch'un Ch'iu* as the main source of his authority. That is why his work is titled the *Ch'un-ch'iu Fan-lu* or *Luxuriant Dew from the Ch'un Ch'iu.*

Tung divides the centuries covered by the *Ch'un Ch'iu* (722-481 B.C.) into three periods, which he calls the "three ages." These are: (1) the age that was personally witnessed by Confucius; (2) that which he heard of through the oral testimony of elder living contemporaries; (3) that which he heard of through transmitted records. According to Tung Chung-shu, Confucius, when writing the *Ch'un Ch'iu,* used differing words or phrases to record the events occurring in these three periods. It is by studying the way in which these words or phrases are used that one may discover the esoteric meaning of the *Ch'un Ch'iu.*

Three Stages of Social Progress

There have been three important commentaries written on the *Ch'un Ch'iu,* and since the Han dynasty these have become classics themselves. They are the Tso Commentary, known as the *Tso Chuan* (which probably was originally not written *in toto* as a commentary on the *Ch'un Ch'iu,* but was later attached to that work), and the Kung Yang and Ku Liang Commentaries. All three are supposedly named after the authors who composed them. Among the three, the Kung Yang Commentary, in particular, interprets the *Ch'un Ch'iu* in agreement with the theories of Tung Chung-shu. Thus in this Commentary we find the same theory of the "three ages." During the latter part of the Han dynasty, Ho Hsiu (129-182) wrote a commentary on the Kung Yang Commentary, in which he still further elaborated this theory.

According to Ho Hsiu, the *Ch'un Ch'iu* is a record of the process through which Confucius ideally transformed the age of decay and disorder into that of "approaching peace," and finally into that of "universal peace." He identifies the earliest of the three ages, "the age of which Confucius heard through transmitted records," as one of "decay and disorder." In this period Confucius devoted his whole attention to his own state of Lu, and took Lu as the center of his reforms. The next period, "the age of which Confucius heard through oral testimony," is identified by Ho Hsiu as that of "approaching peace." It was an age in which Confucius, having given good government to his own state, next brought peace and order to all the other Chinese states lying within the "Middle Kingdom." Finally, the last of the three periods, "the age which Confucius personally witnessed," is identified by Ho Hsiu as that of "universal peace." It was an age in which Confucius, having brought all the Chinese states to peace and order, also civilized all the surrounding barbarian tribes. In this period, Ho Hsiu said: "The whole world, far and near, great and small, was like one." * Of course Ho Hsiu did not mean that these things were actually accomplished by Confucius. He meant that they were what Confucius would have accomplished if he had actually had the power and authority. Even so, however, the theory remains fantastic, since Confucius himself was alive only during the latter part of the three supposed ages of the *Ch'un Ch'iu*.

Ho Hsiu's account of the way in which Confucius, working out from his own state, ideally brought the entire world to peace and order, is similar to the stages in acquiring world peace that are expounded in the *Great Learning*. In this respect, therefore, the *Ch'un Ch'iu* becomes an exemplification of the *Great Learning*.

This theory of the three stages of social progress is also found in the *Li Yün* or "Evolution of Rites," one of the chapters in the *Li Chi*. According to this treatise, the first stage was a world of disorder, the second was that of "small tranquility," and the third that of "great unity." The *Li Yün* describes this final age as follows: "When the great *Tao* was in practice, the world was common to all; men of talents, virtue and ability were selected; sincerity was emphasized

* See Ho Hsiu's *Commentary on the Kung Yang Commentary to the Ch'un Ch'iu*, 1st year of Duke Yin, 722 B.C.

and friendship was cultivated. Therefore, men did not love only their own parents, nor did they treat as children only their own sons. A competent provision was secured for the aged till their death, employment was given to the able-bodied, and a means was provided for the upbringing of the young. Kindness and compassion were shown to widows, orphans, childless men, and those who were disabled by disease, so that they all had the wherewithal for support. Men had their proper work and women had their homes. They hated to see the wealth of natural resources undeveloped, [so they developed it, but this development] was not for their own use. They hated not to exert themselves, [so they worked, but their work] was not for their own profit. . . . This was called the great unity." (*Li Chi*, ch. 7.)

Though the author of the *Li Yün* put this great unity into a golden age of the past, it certainly represented a current dream of the Han people, who would surely have liked to see something more than simply the political unity of the empire.

CHAPTER 18

THE ASCENDANCY OF
CONFUCIANISM AND REVIVAL
OF TAOISM

THE Han dynasty was not only the chronological successor of the Ch'in, but in many ways was its continuator as well. It stabilized the unification which the Ch'in had first achieved.

The Unification of Thought

Among the many policies adopted by Ch'in for this purpose, one of the most important had been that for the unification of thought. After it had conquered all the rival states, Li Ssu, its Prime Minister, submitted a memorial to the Ch'in First Emperor (Ch'in Shih-huang-ti) which said: "Of old, the world was scattered and in confusion. . . . Men valued what they had themselves privately studied, thus casting into disrepute what their superiors had established. At present, Your Majesty has united the world. . . . Yet there are those who with their private teachings mutually abet each other, and discredit the institutions of laws and instructions. . . . If such conditions are not prohibited, the imperial power will decline above and partizanships will form below." (*Historical Records,* ch. 87.)

Then he made a most drastic recommendation: All historical records, save those of Ch'in, all writings of the "hundred schools" of thought, and all other literature, save that kept in custody of the official Erudites, and save works on medicine, pharmacy, divination, agriculture, and arboriculture, should be delivered to the government and burned. As for any individuals who might want to study, they should "take the officials as their teachers." (*Ibid.,* ch. 6.)

The First Emperor approved this recommendation and ordered it carried out in 213 B.C. Actually, sweeping though it was, it was nothing more than the logical application of an idea that had long existed in Legalist circles. Thus Han Fei Tzu had already said: "In the state of the intelligent ruler, there is no literature of books and records, but the laws serve as teachings. There are no sayings of the former kings, but the officials act as teachers." (*Han-fei-tzu*, ch. 49.)

The purpose of Li Ssu's recommendation is apparent. He wanted to be sure that there should be but one world, one government, one history, and one way of thought. Books on medicine and other practical subjects were therefore exempted from the general destruction because, as we should say now, they were technical works and so had nothing to do with "ideology."

The very violence of the Ch'in dynasty, however, led to its speedy downfall, and following the rise of the Han dynasty, a good deal of the ancient literature and the writings of the "hundred schools" came to light again. Yet though they disapproved of the extreme measures of their predecessors, the Han rulers came to feel that a second attempt along different lines should be made to unify the thought of the empire, if political unity were to be long maintained. This new attempt was made by Emperor Wu (140-87 B.C.), who in so doing was following a recommendation made by Tung Chung-shu.

In a memorial presented to the Emperor around the year 136 B.C., Tung wrote: "The principle of Great Unification in the *Ch'un Ch'iu* is a permanent warp passing through the universe, and an expression of what is proper extending from the past to the present. But the teachers of today have diverse Ways, men have diverse doctrines, and each of the philosophic schools has its own particular position and differs in the ideas which it teaches. Hence it is that the rulers possess nothing whereby they may effect general unification." And he concluded his memorial by recommending: "All not within the field of the *Liu Yi* [Six Classics] should be cut short and not allowed to progress further." (*History of the Former Han Dynasty*, ch. 56.)

Emperor Wu approved this recommendation and formally announced that Confucianism, in which these Six Classics held a dominant place, was to be the official state teaching. A considerable time was needed, to be sure, before the Confucianists consolidated their newly gained position, and in the process they adopted many ideas from the other rival schools, thus making of Confucianism something very different from the early Confucianism of the Chou dynasty. We have seen in the last chapter how this process of eclectic amalgamation operated. Nevertheless, from the time of Emperor Wu onward, the Confucianists were given a better chance by the government to expound their teachings than were the other schools.

The principle of Great Unification referred to by Tung Chung-shu is also discussed in the *Kung Yang Commentary* on the *Ch'un Ch'iu*. Thus the opening sentence of the *Ch'un Ch'iu* is: "First year [of Duke Yin], spring, the King's first month." And on this the *Commentary* remarks: "Why does [the *Ch'un Ch'iu*] speak of 'the King's first month'? It has reference to the Great Unification." According to Tung Chung-shu and the Kung Yang school, this Great Unification was one of the programs that Confucius set up for his ideally established new dynasty when he wrote the *Ch'un Ch'iu*.

The measure carried out by Emperor Wu at Tung Chung-shu's recommendation was more positive and yet more moderate than that suggested by Li Ssu to the First Emperor of Ch'in, even though both equally aimed at an intellectual unification of the entire empire. Instead of rejecting all schools of philosophy indiscriminately, as did the Ch'in measure, thus leaving a vacuum in the world of thought, the Han measure selected one of them, Confucianism, from among the "hundred schools," and gave it pre-eminence as the state teaching. Another difference is that the Han measure decreed no punishment for the private teaching of the ideas of the other schools. It only provided that persons who wished to be candidates for official positions should study the Six Classics and Confucianism. By thus making Confucianism the basis of government education, it laid the foundation for China's famed examination system used to recruit government officials. In this way the Han measure was in fact a compromise between the Ch'in measure and the previous practice of private teaching, which had become general after the time of Confucius. It is interesting to see that China's first private teacher now became her first state teacher.

The Position of Confucius in Han Thought

As a result, the position of Confucius became very high by the middle of the first century B.C. About this time, a new type of literature came into existence known as the *wei shu* or apocrypha.

Shu means book or writing, and *wei* literally means the woof of a fabric, and is used in apposition to *ching*, a word which is usually translated as classic, but literally means warp. It was believed by many people of the Han period that Confucius, after writing the Six Classics, that is, the six warps of his teaching, had still left something unexpressed. Hence, they thought, he then wrote the six woofs, corresponding to the six warps, by way of supplement. Thus the combination of the six warps and six woofs would constitute the entire teaching of Confucius. Actually, of course, the apocrypha are Han forgeries.

In the apocrypha the position of Confucius reached the highest level it has ever had in China. In one of them, for example, the *Ch'un Ch'iu Wei: Han Han Tzu*, or *Apocryphal Treatise on the Spring and Autumn Annals: Guarded Shoots of the Han Dynasty*, it is written: "Confucius said: 'I have examined the historical records, drawn upon ancient charts, and investigated and collected cases of anomalies, so as to institute laws for the emperors of the Han dynasty.'" And another apocryphal treatise on the *Spring and Autumn Annals*, known as the *Expository Charts on Confucius*, states that Confucius was actually the son of a god, the Black Emperor, and recounts many supposed miracles in his life. Thus in these apocrypha we find Confucius being regarded as a super-human being, a god among men who could foretell the future. If these views had prevailed, Confucius would have held in China a position similar to that of Jesus Christ, and Confucianism would have become a religion in the proper sense of the term.

Soon afterwards, however, Confucianists of a more realistic or rationalistic way of thinking protested against these "extraordinary and strange views" about Confucius and Confucianism. According to them, Confucius was neither a god nor a king, but simply a sage. He neither foresaw the coming of the Han Dynasty, nor did he institute laws for any dynasty. He simply inherited the cultural legacy of the great tradition of the past, to which he gave a new spirit and transmitted for all ages.

The Controversy of the Old and New Text Schools

These Confucianists formed a group known as the Old Text school. This school was so called, because it claimed to possess texts of the Classics which went back before the "fires of Ch'in," that is, the burning of the books of 213 B.C., and hence were written in a form of script that had already become archaic by the time of their recovery. In opposition to this group, Tung Chung-shu and others belonged to the New Text school, so called because its versions of the Classics were written in the form of script that was generally current during the Han dynasty.

The controversy between these two schools has been one of the greatest in the history of Chinese scholarship. It is not necessary here to go into its details. All that need be said is that the Old Text school arose as a reaction or revolution against the New Text school. At the end of the Former Han dynasty, it received backing from Liu Hsin (ca. 46 B.C.-A.D. 23), one of the greatest scholars of the time. Indeed, so great was his enthusiasm that at a much later time he was accused, quite falsely, by followers of the New Text school, of having singlehandedly forged all the classics written in the old script.

In recent years it has occurred to me that the origin of these two schools may perhaps go back to the two "wings" of Confucianism that existed before the Ch'in dynasty. The New Text school would thus be a continuation of the idealistic wing in early Confucianism, and the Old Text of the realistic wing. In other words, the one would derive from the group headed by Mencius and the other from that headed by Hsün Tzu.

In the *Hsün-tzu*, there is a chapter titled "Against the Twelve Philosophers," one passage of which says: "There were some who in a general way followed the former kings but did not know their fundamentals. . . . Basing themselves on ancient traditions, they developed theories which were called those of the Five Elements. Their views were peculiar, contradictory, and without standards; dark and without illustrations; confined and without explanations. Tzu-ssu [grandson of Confucius] began these and Meng K'o [Mencius] followed." (Ch. 4.)

This passage has long puzzled modern scholars, because both in the *Chung Yung*, supposedly the work of Tzu-ssu, and in the *Mencius*, there is no mention of the Five Elements. Nevertheless, we do find in the *Chung Yung* one passage which reads: "When a nation is about to flourish, there are sure to be happy omens; when it is about to perish, there are sure to be unlucky omens." Likewise the *Mencius* states at one point: "In the course of five hundred years, it is inevitable that a [true] king will arise." (VIIb, 13.) These passages would seem to indicate that both Mencius and the author of the *Chung Yung* (who, if not Tzu-ssu himself, must have been one of his followers) did believe to some extent that an interaction exists between Heaven and man and that history operates in cycles. These doctrines, it will be remembered, were prominent in the *Yin-Yang* or Five Elements school.

If, then, we consider Tung Chung-shu as being in some way connected with Mencius' wing of Confucianism, Hsün Tzu's accusations against this wing assume added significance. For if Tung Chung-shu's views actually go back in embryonic form to those of the followers of Mencius, then the latter, judging from their later development by Tung Chung-shu, could indeed be characterized as "peculiar" and "dark."

This hypothesis is further strengthened by the fact that Mencius, like Tung Chung-shu, attached particular value to the *Ch'un Ch'iu* as the work of Confucius. Thus he said: "Confucius was alarmed [by the disorder of the world] and made the *Ch'un Ch'iu*. The *Ch'un Ch'iu* should be the work of the Son of Heaven. Therefore Confucius said: 'Those who understand me, will do so because of the *Ch'un Ch'iu*, and those who blame me, will do so also because of the *Ch'un Ch'iu*.'" (*Mencius*, IIIb, 9.) Mencius' theory that Confucius, in composing the *Ch'un Ch'iu*, was doing work that pertains to the Son of Heaven, could, if further developed, easily lead to Tung Chung-shu's theory that Confucius had actually received a Mandate from Heaven to become the Son of Heaven.

Tung Chung-shu, furthermore, in expounding his theory of human nature, explicitly compared it with that of Mencius. As we have seen in the last chapter, the differences between the two theories are actually only nominal.

If we accept the hypothesis that the New Text school is the continuation of the idealistic wing of Confucianism headed by Mencius, it is only reasonable to suppose that the Old Text school likewise stems from the realistic wing of Hsün Tzu. Thus it is noticeable that the thinkers of the first century A.D., who were followers of the Old Text school, all took a naturalistic view of the universe similar to that of Hsün Tzu and the Taoists. (Hsün Tzu himself, as we have seen earlier, was influenced by the Taoists in this respect.)

Yang Hsiung and Wang Ch'ung

An example of this point of view is provided by Yang Hsiung (53 B.C.-A.D. 18), one of the members of the Old Text school. His *T'ai Hsüan* or *Supreme Mystery* is to a considerable extent permeated with the concept that "reversal is the movement of the *Tao*"—a concept basic both in the *Lao-tzu* and *Book of Changes*.

He also wrote a treatise known as the *Fa Yen* or *Model Speeches*, in which he attacked the *Yin-Yang* school. In this same work, to be sure, he expresses praise for Mencius. This in itself, however, does not invalidate my theory, because even though Mencius may have had some inclination toward the *Yin-Yang* school, he certainly never reached the extremes that characterized the New Text school in the Han Dynasty.

The greatest thinker of the Old Text school is undoubtedly Wang Ch'ung (A.D. 27-ca. 100), an iconoclast with a remarkable spirit of scientific skepticism, whose chief work is the *Lun Heng* or *Critical Essays*. Writing of the spirit which characterizes this work, he says: "Though the *Shih* [*Book of Odes*] numbered three hundred, one phrase can cover them all, namely, 'With undepraved thoughts' [a saying of Confucius in the *Analects*]. And though the chapters of my *Lun Heng* may be numbered in the tens, one phrase covers them all, namely, 'Hatred of fictions and falsehoods.'" (*Lun Heng*, ch. 61.) Again he says: "In things there is nothing more manifest than having results, and in argument there is nothing more decisive than having evidence." (Ch. 67.)

Using this spirit, he vigorously attacks the theories of the *Yin-Yang* school, and especially its doctrine that an interaction exists between Heaven and man, either teleologically or mechanistically. As to its teleological aspect, he writes: "The Way of Heaven is that of spontaneity, which consists of non-activity. But if Heaven were to reprimand men, that would constitute action and would not be spontaneous. The school of Huang [the legendary Yellow Emperor] and Lao [Lao Tzu], in its discussion on the Way of Heaven, has found the truth." (Ch. 42.)

As to the mechanistic aspect of the theory, Wang Ch'ung says: "Man holds a place in the universe like that of a flea or louse under a jacket or robe. . . . Can the flea or louse, by conducting themselves either properly or improperly, affect the changes or movements in the ether under the jacket? . . . They are not capable of this, and to suppose that man alone is thus capable is to misconceive of the principle of things and of the ether." (Ch. 43.)

Taoism and Buddhism

Thus Wang Ch'ung prepared the way for the revival of Taoism that came one century later. In speaking about Taoism, I must emphasize again the distinction between *Tao chia* and *Tao chiao*, that is, between Taoism as a philosophy and Taoism as a religion. By the revival of Taoism, I here mean that of Taoist philosophy. This revived Taoist philosophy I will call Neo-Taoism.

It is interesting to note that Taoism as a religion also had its beginnings toward the end of the Han dynasty, and there are some who refer to this popular form of Taoism as new Taoism. The Old Text school purged Confucianism of its *Yin-Yang* elements, and the latter later mingled with Taoism to form a new kind of eclecticism known as the Taoist religion. In this way, while the position of Confucius was being reduced from that of a divinity to one of a teacher, Lao Tzu was becoming the founder of a religion which ultimately, in imitation of Buddhism, developed temples, a priesthood, and a liturgy. In this way it became an organized religion almost totally unrecognizable to early Taoist philosophy, which is why it is known as the Taoist religion.

In the first century A.D., already before this was happening, Buddhism was introduced into China from India via Central Asia. In the case of Buddhism as of Taoism, I must emphasize the distinction between *Fo chiao* and *Fo hsüeh*, that is, between Buddhism as a religion and Buddhism as a philosophy. As just stated, Buddhism as a religion did much to inspire the institutional organization of religious Taoism. The latter, as an indigenous faith, was greatly stimulated in its development by the nationalistic sentiments of people who watched with resentment the successful invasion of China by the foreign religion of Buddhism. By some, indeed, Buddhism was considered as a religion of the barbarians. Religious Taoism, to some extent, thus grew as an indigenous substitute for Buddhism, and in the process it borrowed a great deal, including institutions, rituals, and even the form of much of its scriptures, from its foreign rival.

But besides Buddhism as an institutionalized religion, there also existed Buddhism as a philosophy. And whereas the Taoist religion was almost invariably opposed to the Buddhist religion, Taoist philosophy took Buddhist philosophy as its ally. Taoism, to be sure, is less other-worldly than Buddhism. Nevertheless, some similarity exists between their forms of mysticism. Thus the *Tao* of the Taoists is described as unnamable, and the "real suchness" or ultimate reality of the Buddhists is also described as something that cannot be spoken of. It is neither one, nor is it many; it is neither not-one, nor is it not not-many. Such terminology represents what is called in Chinese "thinking into the not-not."

In the third and fourth centuries A.D., famous scholars, who were usually Taoists, were often intimate friends of famous Buddhist monks. The scholars were usually well-versed in Buddhist *sutras,* and the monks in Taoist texts, especially the *Chuang-tzu.* When they met together, they talked in what was known at that time as *ch'ing t'an,* or "pure conversation." When they reached the subject of the not-not, they stopped talking and just silently understood each other with a smile.

In this kind of situation, one finds the spirit of Ch'an (commonly known in the West under its Japanese name of Zen). The Ch'an school is a branch of Chinese Buddhism which is really a combination of the most subtle and delicate aspects of both the Buddhist and Taoist philosophies. It exercised a great influence later on in Chinese philosophy, poetry and painting, as we shall see in chapter twenty-two, where it will be discussed in detail.

Political and Social Background

For the moment, let us turn back to the political and social background that lay behind the ascendancy of Confucianism in the Han dynasty and the subsequent revival of Taoism. The triumph of the former was not due to mere good luck or the fancy of certain people of the time. There were certain circumstances which made it almost inevitable.

The Ch'in conquered the other states by a spirit of severity and ruthlessness which was shown both in its domestic control and foreign relations, and was based on the Legalist philosophy. After the fall of Ch'in, therefore, everyone blamed the Legalist school for its harshness and complete disregard of the Confucian virtues of human-heartedness and righteousness. It is significant that Emperor Wu, besides issuing his decree making Confucianism the state teaching, also decreed in 141 B.C. that all persons who had become experts in the philosophies of Shen Pu-hai, Shang Yang and Han Fei (leaders of the Legalist school), as well as Su Ch'in and Chang Yi (leaders of the Diplomatist school), should be rejected from government posts.*

Thus the Legalist school became the scapegoat for all the blunders of the Ch'in rulers. And among the various schools, those farthest removed from the Legalist were the Confucianist and Taoist. Hence it is natural that there should be a reaction in their favor. During the early part of the Han dynasty, in fact, Taoism, then known as the "learning of Huang [the Yellow Emperor] and Lao [Lao Tzu]," became quite influential for some time. This can be illustrated by the fact that Emperor Wen (179-157 B.C., grandfather of Emperor Wu) was a great admirer of the "Huang-Lao school"; also that, as pointed out in the last chapter, the historian Ssu-ma T'an, in his "Essay On the Essential Ideas of the Six Schools," gave highest rank to the Taoist school.

According to the political philosophy of Taoism, a good government is not one that does many things, but on the contrary that does as little as possible. Therefore if a sage-king rules, he should try to undo the bad effects caused by the over-government of his predecessor. This was precisely what the people of the early part of the Han dynasty needed, for one of the troubles with the Ch'in had been that it had had too much government. Hence when the founder of the Han dynasty, Emperor Kao-tsu, led his victorious revolutionary army toward Ch'ang-an, the Ch'in capital in present Shensi province, he announced to the people his "three-item contract": Persons committing homicide were to receive capital punishment; those injuring or stealing were to be punished accordingly; but aside from these simple provisions, all other laws and regulations of the Ch'in government were to be abolished. (*Historical Records*, ch. 8.) In this way the founder of the Han dynasty was practicing the "learning of Huang and Lao," even though, no doubt, he was quite unconscious of the fact.

Thus the Taoist philosophy accorded well with the needs of the rulers of the earlier part of the Han dynasty, whose policy it was to

* See the *History of the Former Han Dynasty*, ch. 6.

undo what the Ch'in government had done, and to give the country
a chance to recuperate from its long and exhausting wars. When this
end had been accomplished, however, the Taoist philosophy became
no longer practical, and a more constructive program was called for.
This the rulers found in Confucianism.

The social and political philosophy of Confucianism is both conservative yet at the same time revolutionary. It is conservative in that
it is essentially a philosophy of aristocracy, yet it is revolutionary in
that it gave a new interpretation of this aristocracy. It maintained
the distinction between superior man and small man, which had
been generally accepted in the feudal China of Confucius' time. But
at the same time it insisted that this distinction should not be based,
as originally, upon birth, but rather upon individual talent and virtue. Therefore, it considered it quite right that the virtuous and
talented among the people should be the ones to occupy noble and
high positions in society.

It has been pointed out in chapter two that Confucianism gave
a theoretical justification for the family system which has been the
backbone of Chinese society. With the disintegration of the feudal
system, the common people gained emancipation from their feudal
lords, but the old family system remained. Hence Confucianism
likewise remained the underlying philosophy of the existing social
system.

The main result of the abolition of the feudal system was the
formal separation of political power from economic power. It is
true that the new landlords retained great influence, even politically,
in their local communities. At least, however, they were no longer
the actual political rulers of these communities, even though through
their wealth and prestige they could often influence the government-
appointed officials. This represented a step forward.

The new aristocrats, such as officials and landlords, though many
of them were far from being the virtuous and talented persons demanded by Confucianism, nevertheless all had need for something
that Confucianism was particularly qualified to supply. This was a
knowledge of the complicated ceremonies and rituals needed to maintain the social distinctions. Thus one of the early acts of the founder
of the Han dynasty, having conquered all his rivals, was to order
Shu-sun Tung, a Confucianist, together with his followers, to draw
up a court ceremonial. After the first audience was held at court

with the new ceremonies, the founder of the dynasty exclaimed with satisfaction: "Now I realize the nobility of being the Son of Heaven!" (*Historical Records*, ch. 8.)

Shu-sun Tung's action was disapproved of by some of his fellow Confucianists, but its success suggests one reason why the new aristocrats liked Confucianism, even though they might be opposed to or be ignorant of its true spirit.

Most important of all, however, is the fact pointed out by me in chapter three, that what is known in the West as the Confucianist school is really the School of Literati. The Literati were not only thinkers but also scholars versed in the ancient cultural legacy, and this was a combination that the other schools failed to offer. They taught the literature of the past and carried on the great cultural traditions, giving them the best interpretation they could find. In an agrarian country in which people were unusually respectful of the past, these Literati could not fail to become the most influential group.

As for the Legalist school, though it became the scapegoat for the blunders of the Ch'in rulers, it was never wholly discarded. In chapter thirteen, I have pointed out that the Legalists were realistic politicians. They were the ones who could present new methods of government to meet new political conditions. Hence, as the Chinese empire expanded, its rulers could not but rely on the principles and techniques of the Legalists. Consequently, ever since the Han dynasty, orthodox Confucianists have commonly accused the rulers of dynasties of being "Confucianists in appearance but Legalists in reality." As a mater of fact, both Confucianism and Legalism have had their proper sphere of application. The proper sphere for Confucianism is that of social organization, spiritual and moral culture, and learned scholarship. And the proper sphere for Legalism is that of the principles and techniques of practical government.

Taoism, too, has had its opportunities. In Chinese history there have been many periods of political and social confusion and disorder, when people have had little time or interest for classical scholarship, and have been inclined to criticize the existing political and social system. At such times, therefore, Confucianism has naturally tended to weaken and Taoism to become strong. Taoism has then supplied a sharp criticism against the existing political and social system, as well as an escapist system of thought for avoiding harm and danger. These are exactly what meet the desires of a people living in an age of disorder and confusion.

The collapse of the Han dynasty in A.D. 220 was followed by a prolonged period of disunity and confusion which was brought to a close only when the country was finally reunited under the Sui dynasty in A.D. 589. These four centuries were marked by frequent warfare and political cleavage between a series of dynasties that ruled in Central and South China, and another series that had control in the North. It was also marked by the rise to prominence of various nomadic non-Chinese groups, some of whom forcibly broke their way through the Great Wall and settled in North China, and others of whom entered through peaceful colonization. A number of the dynasties of the north were ruled by these alien groups, who, however, failed to extend their power as far south as the Yangtze river. Because of these political characteristics, this period of four centuries from the Han to the Sui dynasties is commonly known as that of the Six Dynasties, or again, as that of the Northern and Southern Dynasties.

This, then, was politically and socially a dark age, in which pessimism was rife. In some respects it somewhat resembled the roughly contemporary period of the Middle Ages in Europe, and just as in Europe Christianity was the dominant force, so in China the new religion of Buddhism made great strides. It is quite wrong to say, however, as some people do, that it was an age of inferior culture. On the contrary, if we take the word culture in a narrower sense, we may say that it was an age in which, in several respects, we reach one of the peaks of Chinese culture. Painting, calligraphy, poetry, and philosophy were at this time all at their best.

In the next two chapters I shall present the leading indigenous philosophy of the age, a philosophy which I call Neo-Taoism.

CHAPTER 19

NEO-TAOISM:

THE RATIONALISTS

Neo-Taoism is a new term for the thought which in the third and fourth centuries A.D. was known as the *hsüan hsüeh*, or literally, "dark learning." The word *hsüan*, meaning dark, abstruse, or mysterious, occurs in the first chapter of the *Lao-tzu*, for example, in which the *Tao* is described as "*hsüan* of the *hsüan*," i.e., "mystery of mysteries." Hence the term *hsüan hsüeh* indicates that this school is a continuation of Taoism.

The Revival of Interest in the School of Names

In chapters eight, nine, and ten, we have seen how the School of Names contributed to Taoism the idea of "transcending shapes and features." In the third and the fourth centuries, with the Taoist revival, there came a revival of interest in the School of Names. The Neo-Taoists studied Hui Shih and Kung-sun Lung, and linked their *hsüan hsüeh* with what they called *ming-li*, i.e., the "distinguishing of terms [*ming*] and analysis of principles [*li*]." (This phrase is used by Kuo Hsiang in his commentary to the last chapter of the *Chuang-tzu*). As we have seen in chapter eight, this is what Kung-sun Lung also did.

In the *Shih-shuo Hsin-yü*, a book about which we shall read more in the next chapter, it is said: "A visitor asked Yüeh Kuang for the meaning of the statement: 'A *chih* does not reach.' Yüeh Kuang made no comment on the statement, but immediately touched the table with the handle of a fly whisk, saying: 'Does it reach or does it not?' The visitor answered: 'It does.' Yüeh then lifted the fly whisk and asked: 'If it reaches, how can it be taken away?' " (Ch. 4.) This statement that a *chih* does not reach is one of the arguments used by the followers of Kung-sun Lung, as reported in the last chapter of the *Chuang-tzu*. The word *chih* literally means a finger, but in chapter eight I translated it as "universal." Here, however, Yüeh Kuang evidently takes it in its literal sense as finger. The fly whisk cannot reach the table, just as the finger cannot reach the table.

To touch a table with a finger or something else is ordinarily considered as reaching the table. According to Yüeh Kuang, however, if the reaching is really reaching, then it cannot be taken away. Since the handle of the fly whisk could be taken away, its apparent reaching was not a real reaching. Thus by examining the term "reaching," Yüeh Kuang analyzed the principle of reaching. This is an illustration of what was known at that time as "conversation on the *ming-li*."

A Reinterpretation of Confucius

It is to be noticed that the Neo-Taoists, or at least a large part of them, still considered Confucius to be the greatest sage. This was partly because the place of Confucius as the state teacher was by now firmly established, and partly because some of the important Confucian Classics were accepted by the Neo-Taoists, though in the process they were reinterpreted according to the spirit of Lao Tzu and Chuang Tzu.

For instance, the *Analects* contains a saying of Confucius: "Yen Hui was nearly perfect, yet he was often empty." (XI, 18.) By this Confucius probably meant that although Yen Hui, his favorite disciple, was very poor, i.e., "empty," that is, devoid of worldly goods, he was nevertheless very happy, which showed that his virtue was nearly perfect. In the *Chuang-tzu*, however, as we have seen in chapter ten, there is an apocryphal story about Yen Hui's "sitting in forgetfulness," i.e., engaging in mystic meditation. Hence with this story in mind one commentator on the *Analects*, T'ai-shih Shu-ming (474-546), said:

"Yen Hui disregarded human-heartedness and righteousness, and forgot ceremonies and music. He gave up his body and discarded his knowledge. He forgot everything and became one with the infinite. This is the principle of forgetting things. When all things were forgotten, he was thus empty. And yet, compared with the sages, he was still not perfect. The sages forget that they forget, whereas even the great worthies cannot forget that they forget. If Yen Hui could not forget that he forgot, it would seem that something still remained in his mind. That is why he is said to have been *often* empty." *

Another commentator, Ku Huan (died 453), commenting on the same passage, remarks: "The difference between the sages and the worthies is that the latter retain a desire to be without desire, while the former do not have that desire for no desire. Therefore the mind of the sages is perfectly empty, while that of the worthies is only partially so. From the point of view of the world, the worthies lack any desire. But from the point of view of what is not of this world, the worthies do desire to be without desire. The emptiness of Yen Hui's mind was not yet complete. That is why he is said to have been *often* empty." (*Ibid.*)

The Neo-Taoists, despite their Taoism, considered Confucius to be even greater than Lao Tzu and Chuang Tzu. Confucius, they maintained, did not speak about forgetfulness, because he had already forgotten that he had learned to forget. Nor did he speak about absence of desire, because he had already reached the stage of lacking any desire to be without desire. Thus the *Shih-shuo Hsin-yü* records a "pure conversation" between P'ei Hui and Wang Pi. The latter was one of the great figures of the school of "dark learning," whose *Commentaries* on the *Lao-tzu* and *Book of Changes* have become classics in themselves. The conversation reads:

"Wang Pi [226-249], when young, once went to see P'ei Hui. [P'ei] Hui asked him why, since W*u* [Non-being] is fundamental for all things, Confucius did not speak about it, whereas Lao Tzu expounded this idea without stopping. To this Wang Pi answered: 'The sage [Confucius] identified himself with W*u* [Non-being] and realized that it could not be made the subject of instruction, with the result that he felt compelled to deal only with Y*u* [Being]. But Lao Tzu and Chuang Tzu had not yet completely left the sphere of Y*u* [Being], with the result that they constantly spoke of their own deficiencies.'" (Ch. 4.) This explanation reflects the idea expressed by Lao Tzu that "he who knows does not speak; he who speaks does not know." (*Lao-tzu*, ch. 56.)

* Quoted by Huang Kan (488-545), in his *Sub-Commentary on the Analects*, *chüan* 6.

Hsiang Hsiu and Kuo Hsiang

One of the greatest, if not the greatest, philosophical works of this period is the *Commentary on the Chuang-tzu* by Kuo Hsiang (died ca. 312). There has been a historical problem as to whether this work was really his, for he was accused of being a plagiarist by his contemporaries, who asserted that his *Commentary* was really the work of another slightly earlier scholar, Hsiang Hsiu (ca. 221-ca. 300). It would seem that both men wrote *Commentaries* on the *Chuang-tzu*, and that their ideas were very much the same, so that in the course of time their *Commentaries* probably became combined to form a single work. The *Shih-shuo Hsin-yü* (ch. 4), for example, speaks of a Hsiang-Kuo interpretation (i.e., an interpretation by Hsiang Hsiu and Kuo Hsiang) made on the "Happy Excursion" (the first chapter of the *Chuang-tzu*), as existing in apposition to one by Chih-tun (314-366), a famous Buddhist monk of the time. Hence the present *Commentary on the Chuang-tzu*, though it bears the name of Kuo Hsiang, seems to represent the joint Hsiang-Kuo interpretation of the *Chuang-tzu*, and probably was the work of both men. The *Chin Shu* or *History of the Chin Dynasty* is probably right, therefore, when in its biography of Hsiang Hsiu it says that he wrote a *Commentary on the Chuang-tzu*, and that then Kuo Hsiang "extended it." (Ch. 49.)

According to this same *History of the Chin Dynasty*, both Hsiang Hsiu and Kuo Hsiang were natives of the present Honan province, and were great figures in the school of "dark learning," as well as being "fine or pure conversationalists." In this chapter I shall take these two philosophers as representative of the exponents of the rationalistic group in Neo-Taoism, and refer to their *Commentary on the Chuang-tzu* as the Hsiang-Kuo interpretation, following the usage of the *Shih-shuo Hsin-yü*.

The Tao is "Nothing"

The Hsiang-Kuo interpretation made several most important revisions in the original Taoism of Lao Tzu and Chuang Tzu. The first is that the *Tao* is really *wu*, i.e., "nothing" or "nothingness." Lao Tzu and Chuang Tzu also had maintained that the *Tao* is Wu, but by Wu they meant having no name. That is, according to them, the

Tao is not a thing; hence it is unnamable. But according to the Hsiang-Kuo interpretation, the *Tao* is really literally nothing. "The *Tao* is everywhere, but everywhere it is nothing." (*Commentary on the Chuang-tzu*, ch. 6.)

The same text says: "In existence, what is prior to things? We say that the *Yin* and *Yang* are prior to things. But the *Yin* and *Yang* are themselves things; what then, is prior to the *Yin* and *Yang*? We may say that *Tzu Jan* [nature or naturalness] is prior to things. But *Tzu Jan* is simply the naturalness of things. Or we may say that the *Tao* is prior to things. But the *Tao* is nothing. Since it is nothing, how can it be prior to things? We do not know what is prior to things, yet things are continuously produced. This shows that things are spontaneously what they are; there is no Creator of things." (Ch. 22.)

In another passage, it is also stated: "Some people say that the penumbra is produced by the shadow, the shadow by the bodily form, and the bodily form by the Creator. I would like to ask whether the Creator is or is not. If He is not, how can He create things? But if He is, He is simply one of these things, and how can one thing produce another? . . . Therefore there is no Creator, and everything produces itself. Everything produces itself and is not produced by others. This is the normal way of the universe." (Ch. 2.)

Lao Tzu and Chuang Tzu denied the existence of a personal Creator by substituting in His place an impersonal *Tao*, which is that by which all things come to be. Hsiang-Kuo went a step further by insisting that the *Tao* is really *nothing*. According to them, the statement of the earlier Taoists that all things come into being from the *Tao* simply means that all things come to be by themselves. Hence they write: "The *Tao* is capable of nothing. To say that anything is derived from the *Tao* means that it comes of itself." (Ch. 6.)

Likewise, the statement of the earlier Taoists that all things come into being from Being, and Being comes into being from Non-being, simply means that Being comes into being by itself. In one passage of the *Commentary* it is said: "Not only is it the case that Non-being cannot become Being, but Being also cannot become Non-being. Though Being may change in thousands of ways, it cannot change itself into Non-being. Therefore there is no time when there is no Being. Being eternally exists." (Ch. 22.)

The "Self-transformation" of Things

That everything spontaneously produces itself is what Hsiang-Kuo call the theory of *tu hua* or self-transformation. According to this theory, things are not created by any Creator, but these things are nevertheless not lacking in relations, one with another. Relations exist and these relations are necessary. Thus the *Commentary* states: "When a man is born, insignificant though he be, he has the properties that he necessarily has. However trivial his life may be, he needs the whole universe as a condition for his existence. All things in the universe, all that exist, cannot cease to exist without some effect on him. If one factor is lacking, he might not exist. If one principle is violated, he might not be living." (Ch. 6.)

Everything needs every other thing, but everything nevertheless exists for its own sake and not for the sake of any other thing. The *Commentary* says: "In the world, everything considers itself as 'this' and other things as 'other.' The 'this' and the 'other' each works for itself. [They seem to be far away from each other like] the mutual opposition of east and west. Yet the 'this' and the 'other' have a relation to each other like that between the lips and the teeth. The lips do not exist for the teeth, but when the lips are lost, the teeth feel cold. Therefore the work of the 'other' for itself has contributed a great deal to help the 'this'." (Ch. 17.) According to Hsiang-Kuo, the interrelationship of things is like that between the armies of two allied forces. Each army fights for its own country, but each at the same time helps the other, and the defeat or victory of the one cannot but have an effect on the other.

Everything that exists in the universe needs the universe as a whole as a necessary condition for its existence, yet its existence is not directly produced by any other particular thing. When certain conditions or circumstances are present, certain things are necessarily produced. But this does not mean that they are produced by any single Creator or by any individual. In other words, things are produced by conditions in general, and not by any other specific thing in particular. Socialism, for instance, is a product of certain general economic conditions, and was not manufactured by Marx or Engels, still less by the former's *Communist Manifesto*. In this sense, we can say that everything produces itself and is not produced by others.

Hence everything cannot but be what it is. The *Commentary*

states: "It is not by accident that we have our life. It is not by chance
that our life is what it is. The universe is very extended; things are
very numerous. Yet, in it and among them, we are just what we are.
. . . What we are not, we cannot be. What we are, we cannot but
be. What we do not do, we cannot do. What we can do, we cannot
but do. Let everything be what it is, then there will be peace."
(Ch. 5.)

This is also true of social phenomena. The *Commentary* says
again: "There is nothing which is not natural. . . . Peace or disorder, success or failure, . . . are all the product of nature, not of
man." (Ch. 7.) By "the product of nature," Hsiang-Kuo mean that
they are the necessary result of certain conditions or circumstances.
In chapter 14 of the *Chuang-tzu*, the text states that sages disturb
the peace of the world; to which the *Commentary* says: "The current
of history, combined with present circumstances, is responsible for
the present crisis. It is not due to any certain individuals. It is due
to the world at large. The activity of the sages does not disturb the
world, but the world itself becomes disorderly."

Institutions and Morals

Hsiang-Kuo consider the universe as being in a continuous state of
flux. They write in their *Commentary*: "Change is a force, unobserv-
able yet most strong. It transports heaven and earth toward the new,
and carries mountains and hills away from the old. The old does not
stop for a moment, but immediately becomes the new. All things
ever change. . . . All that we meet secretly passes away. We ourselves in the past are not we ourselves now. We still have to go forward with the present. We cannot keep ourselves still." (Ch. 6.)

Society, too, is always in a state of flux. Human needs are constantly changing. Institutions and morals that are good for one time
may not be good for another. The *Commentary* says: "The institutions of the former kings served to meet the needs of their own time.
But if they continue to exist when time has changed, they become
a bogey to the people, and begin to be artificial." (Ch. 14.)

Again: "Those who imitate the sages imitate what they have done.
But what they have done has already passed away, and therefore it
cannot meet the present situation. It is worthless and should not be
imitated. The past is dead while the present is living. If one attempts

Commentary on Chuang-Tzu (Chap. 9)

Similar to Zen though.

to handle the living with the dead, one will certainly fail." (Ch. 9.)

Society changes with circumstances. When the circumstances change, institutions and morals should change with them. If they do not, they become artificial and are "a bogey to the people." It is natural that new institutions and new morals should spontaneously produce themselves. The new and the old differ from each other because their times are different. Both of them serve to meet the needs of their time, so neither is superior nor inferior to the other. Hsiang-Kuo do not oppose institutions and morals as such, as did Lao Tzu and Chuang Tzu. They simply oppose those institutions and morals that are out-of-date and therefore unnatural for the present world.

Yu-wei *and* Wu-wei

Thus Hsiang-Kuo give a new interpretation to the earlier Taoist ideas about the natural and the artificial and about *yu-wei* or having activity, and *wu-wei* or having no activity (also translated as non-action). When there is a change of social circumstances, new institutions and morals spontaneously produce themselves. To let them go means to follow the natural and be *wu-wei*, i.e., without action. To oppose them and to keep the old ones that are already out-of-date is to be artificial and *yu-wei*, i.e., with action. In one passage of the *Commentary* it is said: "When water runs down from a high to a low place, the current is irresistible. When small things group with what is small, and large things with what is large, their tendency cannot be opposed. When a man is empty and without bias, everyone will contribute his wisdom to him. What does he do, who is the leader of men, when facing these currents and tendencies? He simply trusts the wisdom of the time, relies on the necessity of circumstances, and lets the world take care of itself. That is all." (Ch. 6.)

If an individual, in his activities, allows his natural abilities to exercise themselves fully and freely, he is *wu-wei*. Otherwise he is *yu-wei*. In one passage of the *Commentary* it is said: "A good driver must let his horse exercise itself to the full of its ability. The way to do so is to give it freedom. . . . If he allows his horses to do what they can do, compelling neither the slow ones to run fast nor the fast ones to walk slowly, though he may travel through the whole world with them, they rather enjoy it. Hearing that horses should be set free,

some people think that they should be left wild. Hearing the theory
of non-action, some people think that lying down is better than
walking. These people are far wrong in understanding the ideas of
Chuang Tzu." (Ch. 9.) Despite this criticism, it would seem that in
their understanding of Chuang Tzu such people were not far wrong.
Yet Hsiang-Kuo, in their own interpretation of him, were certainly
highly original.

Hsiang-Kuo also give a new interpretation to the ideas of simplicity
and primitivity of the earlier Taoists. In their *Commentary* they
write: "If by primitivity we mean the undistorted, the man whose
character is not distorted is the most primitive, though he may be
capable of doing many things. If by simplicity we mean the unmixed,
the form of the dragon and the features of the phoenix are the most
simple, though their beauty is all surpassing. On the other hand, even
the skin of a dog or a goat cannot be primitive and simple, if its
natural qualities are distorted by, or mixed with, foreign elements."
(Ch. 15.)

Knowledge and Imitation

Lao Tzu and Chuang Tzu both opposed sages of the sort ordinarily regarded as such by the world. In the earlier Taoist literature,
the word "sage" has two meanings. By it, the Taoists either mean the
perfect man (in the Taoist sense) or the man with all sorts of knowledge. Lao Tzu and Chuang Tzu attacked knowledge, and hence the
sage of the latter kind, the man who has knowledge. But from the
preceding pages we can see that Hsiang-Kuo had no objection to
some men's being sages. What they did object to is the attempt of
some people to imitate the sages. Plato was born a Plato, and Chuang
Tzu a Chuang Tzu. Their genius was as natural as the form of a
dragon or the features of a phoenix. They were as "simple" and
"primitive" as anything can be. They were not wrong in writing their
Republic and "Happy Excursion," for in so doing they were merely
following their own natures.

This view is exemplified in the following passage from the *Commentary*: "By knowledge we mean [the activity that attempts] what
is beyond [one's natural ability]. That which is within the proper
sphere [of one's natural ability] is not called knowledge. By being
within the proper sphere we mean acting according to one's natural

ability, attempting nothing that is beyond. If carrying ten thousand *ch'un* [thirty catties] is in accordance with one's ability, one will not feel the burden as weighty. If discharging ten thousand functions [is in accordance with one's ability], one will not feel the task as taxing." (Ch. 3.) Thus if we understand knowledge in this sense, neither Plato nor Chuang Tzu should be considered as having any knowledge.

It is only the imitators that have knowledge. Hsiang-Kuo seem to have regarded imitation as wrong for three reasons. First, it is useless. They write in the *Commentary*: "Events in ancient times have ceased to exist. Though they may be recorded, it is not possible for them to happen again in the present. The ancient is not the present, and the present is even now changing. Therefore we should give up imitation, act according to our nature, and change with the times. This is the way to perfection." (Ch. 13.) Everything is in a flux. Every day we have new problems, new needs, and meet new situations. We should have new methods to deal with these new situations, problems, and needs. Even at a single given moment, the situations, problems, and needs of different individuals differ from one another. So must their methods. What, then, is the use of imitation?

Second, imitation is fruitless. One passage of the *Commentary* tells us: "With conscious effort, some people have tried to be a Li Chu [a great artisan] or a Shih K'uang [a great musician], but have not succeeded. Yet without knowing how, Li Chu and Shih K'uang were especially talented in their eye and ear. With conscious effort, some people have tried to be sages, but have not succeeded. Yet without knowing how, the sages became sages. Not only is it the sages and Li Chu and Shih K'uang who are difficult to imitate. We cannot even be fools, or dogs, by simply wishing or trying to be so." (Ch. 5.) Everything must be what it is. One thing simply cannot be the other.

Third, imitation is harmful. The *Commentary* states again: "There are some people who are not satisfied with their own nature and always attempt what is beyond it. This is to attempt what is impossible, and is like a circle imitating a square, or a fish imitating a bird. . . . They go ever further, the more remote their goal seems to be. The more knowledge they gain, the more nature they lose." (Ch. 2.)

Again: "The nature of everything has its limit. If one is led on by what is beyond it, one's nature will be lost. One should disregard the inducement, and live according to oneself, not according to others.

In this way the integrity of one's nature will be preserved." (Ch. 10.) Not only is there no possibility for one to succeed by imitating others, but by that very act, there is a great probability that one will lose one's self. This is the harm of imitation.

Thus imitation is useless, fruitless, and harmful. The only sensible mode of life is "to live according to oneself," which is also to practice the theory of non-action.

The Equality of Things

But if one can really live according to oneself, disregarding the inducements offered by others, that means that one is already able to get rid of what Hsiang-Kuo call the "trouble of preferring one thing to another." (Ch. 2.) In other words, one is already able to understand the principle of the equality of things and to see things from a higher point of view. One is already on the royal road to the state of non-distinction of the undifferentiable whole.

In the second chapter of the *Chuang-tzu*, Chuang Tzu emphasized the theory of non-distinction, especially the non-distinction of right and wrong. In their *Commentary*, Hsiang-Kuo expound this theory with more eloquence. Thus to the saying of Chuang Tzu that "the universe is a finger, all things are a horse," the *Commentary* observes: "In order to show that there is no distinction between right and wrong, there is nothing better than illustrating one thing with another. In so doing we see that all things agree in that they all consider themselves to be right and others to be wrong. Since they all agree that all others are wrong, hence in the world there can be no right; and since they all agree that they themselves are right, hence in the world there can be no wrong.

"How can it be shown that this is so? If the right is really absolutely right, in the world there should be none that considers it to be wrong. If the wrong is really absolutely wrong, in the world there should be none that considers it to be right. The fact that there are uncertainty between right and wrong, and a confusion in distinctions, shows that the distinctions between right and wrong are due to a partiality of view, and that all things are really in agreement." In our observation, we see this truth everywhere. Therefore, the perfect man, knowing that the universe is a finger and all things are a horse, thus rests in great peace. All things function according to their nature, and enjoy themselves. [Between them] there is no distinction between right and wrong." (Ch. 2.)

Absolute Freedom and Absolute Happiness

If one can transcend the distinctions between things, one can enjoy the absolute freedom and have the absolute happiness that are described in the first chapter of the *Chuang-tzu*. In the many stories contained in this chapter, Chuang Tzu mentions the great roc bird, the small bird, the cicada, the "small knowledge" of the morning mushroom, whose life extends only to the same evening, the "great knowledge" of the old trees whose experience covers thousands of years, small officers of limited talents, and the philosopher Lieh Tzu who could ride on the wind. Regarding these stories, the Hsiang-Kuo *Commentary* says: "If there is satisfaction for their natures, the roc has nothing to be proud of in comparison with the small bird, and the small bird has no desire for the Celestial Lake [the dwelling place of the roc]. Therefore, though there is a difference between the great and the small, their happiness is the same." (Ch. 1.)

Their happiness, however, is only relative happiness. If things only enjoy themselves in their finite spheres, their enjoyment must also be finite. Thus in his first chapter, Chuang Tzu concludes his stories with one about the really independent man who transcends the finite and becomes one with the infinite, so that he enjoys infinite and absolute happiness. Because he transcends the finite and identifies himself with the infinite, he has "no self." Because he follows the nature of things and lets everything enjoy itself, he has "no achievement." And because he is one with the *Tao*, which is unnamable, he has "no name."

This idea is developed by the Hsiang-Kuo *Commentary* with clarity and eloquence: "Everything has its proper nature, and that nature has its proper limitation. The differences between things are like those between small and great knowledge, short and long life. . . . All believe in their own sphere and none is intrinsically superior to others." After giving different illustrations, Chuang Tzu concludes with the independent man who forgets his own self and its opposite, and who ignores all the differences. "All things enjoy themselves in their own sphere, but the independent man has neither achievement nor name. Therefore, he who unites the great and the small is one who ignores the distinction between the great and the small. If one insists on the distinctions, the roc, the cicada, the small officer, and Lieh Tzu riding on the wind, are all troublesome things. He who equalizes life and death is one who ignores the distinction of life and death. If one insists on the distinction, the *ta ch'un* [an old tree] and the chrysalis, P'eng Tsu [a Chinese Methuselah] and the morning mushroom, all suffer early death. Therefore, he who makes excursion into the realm of non-distinction between great and small has no limitation. He who ignores the distinction of life and death has no terminal. But those whose happiness lies within the finite sphere will certainly suffer limitation. Though they are allowed to make excursions, they are not able to be independent." (Ch. 1.)

In the first chapter, Chuang Tzu describes the independent man as "one who chariots on the normality of the universe, rides upon the transformation of the six elements, and makes excursion into the infinite." On this the Hsiang-Kuo *Commentary* remarks: "The universe is the general name of all things. The universe has all things as its contents, and all things must take *Tzu Jan* [the natural] as their norm. What is spontaneously so, and not made to be so, is the natural. The roc can fly in high places, the quail in low ones. The *ta-ch'un* tree can live for a long time, the mushroom for a short one. All these capacities are natural, and are not caused or learned. They are not caused to be so, but are naturally so; that is the reason why they are normal. Therefore to chariot on the normality of the universe is to follow the nature of things. To ride upon the transformation of the six elements is to make excursion along the road of change and evolution. If one proceeds in this way, where can one reach the end? If one chariots on whatever one meets, what will one be required to depend upon? This is the happiness and freedom of the perfect man who unites his own self with its opposite.

"If one has to depend upon something, one cannot be happy, unless one gets hold of the thing upon which one depends. Although Lieh Tzu could pursue his way in such a fine manner, he still had to depend upon the wind, and the roc was even more dependent. Only he who makes no distinction between himself and other things and follows the great evolution, can really be independent and always free. He not only sets himself free, but also follows the nature of those who have to depend upon something, allowing them to have that something upon which they depend. When they have that upon

Commentary on Chuang-Tzu Chap.1

which they depend, they all enjoy the Great Freedom." (Ch. 1.)

In the Hsiang-Kuo system, the *Tao* is really nothing. In this system, *T'ien* or *T'ien Ti* (literally "Heaven" or "Heaven and Earth," but here translated as the universe) becomes the most important idea. *T'ien* is the general name of things, and is thus the totality of all that is. To see things from the point of view of *T'ien* and to identify oneself with *T'ien*, is to transcend things and their differences, or, as the Neo-Taoists said, "to transcend shapes and features."

Thus the Hsiang-Kuo *Commentary*, besides making important revisions in original Taoism, also expressed more articulately what in the *Chuang-tzu* is only suggestive. Those, however, who prefer suggestiveness to articulateness, would no doubt agree with a certain Ch'an monk who remarked: "People say that it was Kuo Hsiang who wrote a commentary on Chuang Tzu. I would say that it was Chuang Tzu who wrote a commentary on Kuo Hsiang." (See chapter one, page 15.)

CHAPTER 20

NEO-TAOISM:

THE SENTIMENTALISTS

In their *Commentary* to the *Chuang-tzu*, Hsiang Hsiu and Kuo Hsiang gave a theoretical exposition of the man who has a mind or spirit transcending the distinctions of things and who lives "according to himself but not according to others." This quality of such a man is the essence of what the Chinese call *feng liu*.

Feng Liu *and the Romantic Spirit*

In order to understand *feng liu*, we must turn to the *Shih-shuo Hsin-yü* or *Contemporary Records of New Discourses* (abbreviated as *Shih-shuo*), a work by Liu Yi-ch'ing (403-444), supplemented by a commentary by Liu Hsün (463-521). The Neo-Taoists and their Buddhist friends of the Chin dynasty were famous for what was known at the time as *ch'ing t'an*, that is, pure or fine conversation. The art of such conversation consisted in expressing the best thought, which was usually Taoistic, in the best language and tersest phraseology. Because of its rather precious nature, it could be held only between friends of a comparable and rather high intellectual level, and hence it was regarded as one of the most refined of intellectual activities. The *Shih-shuo* is a record of many such "pure conversations" and their famous participants. Through them, it gives a vivid picture of those people of the third and fourth centuries who were followers of the *feng liu* ideas. Ever since its compilation, therefore, it has been a major source for studying the *feng liu* tradition.

What, then, is the meaning of *feng liu*? It is one of those elusive terms which to the initiated conveys a wealth of ideas, but is most difficult to translate exactly. Literally, the two words that form it mean "wind and stream," which does not seem to help us very much.

Nevertheless, they do, perhaps, suggest something of the freedom and ease which are some of the characteristics of the quality of *feng liu*.

I confess that I have not yet understood the full significance of the words romanticism or romantic in English, but I suspect that they are a fairly rough equivalent of *feng liu*. *Feng liu* is chiefly connected with Taoism. This is one of the reasons why I have said in chapter two that the Confucianist and Taoist traditions in Chinese history are in some degree equivalent to the classical and romantic traditions in the West.

The Han (206 B.C.-A.D. 220) and Chin (265-420) are not only the names of two different dynasties in Chinese history, but also, because of their very different social, political, and cultural characteristics, are designations of two different styles of literature and art, and of two different manners of living. The Han style and manner are ones of dignity and grandeur; those of the Chin are ones of elegance and freedom. Elegance is also one of the characteristics of *feng liu*.

"Yang Chu's Garden of Pleasure"

Something must first be said here about the seventh chapter in the Taoist work known as the *Lieh-tzu*, a chapter titled "Yang Chu" (translated by Anton Forke as *Yang Chu's Garden of Pleasure*). As we have already seen in our chapter six, what is said in this "Yang Chu" chapter cannot represent the view of the genuine Yang Chu of ancient times. The *Lieh-tzu* itself, indeed, is now considered by Chinese scholars as a work of the third century A.D. Hence its "Yang Chu" chapter must also be a production of this period. It accords well with the general trend of thought of that time, and is in fact an expression of one aspect of *feng liu*.

In the "Yang Chu" chapter, a distinction is made between the external and the internal. Thus the spurious "Yang Chu" is reported as saying: "There are four things which do not allow people to have peace. The first is long life, the second is reputation, the third is rank, and the fourth is riches. Those who have these things fear ghosts, fear men, fear power, and fear punishment. They are called fugitives. . . . Their lives are controlled by externals. But those who follow their destiny do not desire long life. Those who are not fond of honor do not desire reputation. Those who do not want power desire no rank. And those who are not avaricious have no desire for riches. Of this sort of men it may be said that they live in accordance with their nature. . . . They regulate their lives by internal things."

In another passage an imaginary conversation is recorded between Tzu-ch'an, a famous statesman of the state of Cheng who lived in the sixth century B.C., and his two brothers. Tzu-ch'an governed the state for three years and governed well. But his two brothers were out of his control; one of them was fond of feasting and the other of gallantry.

One day, Tzu-ch'an spoke to his brothers, saying: "Those things in which man is superior to beasts and birds are his mental faculties. Through them he gets righteousness and propriety, and so glory and rank fall to his share. You are only moved by what excites your senses, and indulge only in licentious desires, endangering your lives and natures. . . ."

To this the brothers answered: "If one tries to set external things in order, these external things do not necessarily become well-ordered, and one's person is already given toil and trouble. But if one tries to set the internal in order, the external things do not necessarily fall into disorder, and one's nature becomes free and at ease. Your system of regulating external things will do temporarily and for a single kingdom, but it is not in harmony with the human heart. Our method of regulating what is internal, on the contrary, can be extended to the whole world, and [when it is extended] there is no need for princes and ministers."

What this chapter calls regulating the internal corresponds to what Hsiang-Kuo call living according to oneself; what it calls regulating external things corresponds to what Hsiang-Kuo call living according to others. One should live according to oneself, and not according to others. That is to say, one should live in accord with one's own reason or impulse, and not according to the customs and morals of the time. To use a common expression of the third and fourth centuries, one should live according to *tzu-jan* (the spontaneous, the natural), and not according to *ming-chiao* (institutions and morals). All the Neo-Taoists agree on this. But there is still a difference among them between the rationalists and sentimentalists. The former, as represented by Hsiang-Kuo, emphasize living according to reason, while the latter, as represented by the men who will be mentioned below, emphasize living according to impulse.

The idea of living according to impulse is expressed in extreme form in the "Yang Chu" chapter. In one passage we read that Yen P'ing-chung asked Kuan Yi-wu (both famous statesmen of the state of Ch'i in ancient times, though historically they were not contemporaries) about cultivating life. "Kuan Yi-wu replied: 'The only way is to give it its free course, neither checking nor obstructing it.' Yen P'ing-chung asked: 'And as to details?'

"Kuan Yi-wu replied: 'Allow the ear to hear anything that it likes to hear. Allow the eye to see whatever it likes to see. Allow the nose to smell whatever it likes to smell. Allow the mouth to say whatever it likes to say. Allow the body to enjoy whatever it likes to enjoy. Allow the mind to do whatever it likes to do.

" 'What the ear likes to hear is music, and prohibition of the hearing of music is called obstruction to the ear. What the eye likes to see is beauty, and prohibition of the seeing of beauty is called obstruction to sight. What the nose likes to smell is perfume, and prohibition of the smelling of perfume is called obstruction to smell. What the mouth likes to talk about is right and wrong, and prohibition of the talking about right and wrong is called obstruction to understanding. What the body likes to enjoy is rich food and fine clothing, and prohibition of the enjoying of these is called obstruction to the sensations of the body. What the mind likes is to be free, and prohibition of this freedom is called obstruction to the nature.

" 'All these obstructions are the main causes of the vexations of life. To get rid of these causes and enjoy oneself until death, for a day, a month, a year, or ten years—this is what I call cultivating life. To cling to these causes and be unable to rid oneself of them, so as thus to have a long but sad life, extending a hundred, a thousand, or even ten thousand years—this is not what I call cultivating life.'

"Kuan Yi-wu then went on: 'Now that I have told you about cultivating life, what about the way of taking care of the dead?' Yen P'ing-chung replied: 'Taking care of the dead is a very simple matter. . . . For once I am dead, what does it matter to me? They may burn my body, or cast it into deep water, or inter it, or leave it uninterred, or throw it wrapped up in a mat into some ditch, or cover it with princely apparel and embroidered garments and rest it in a stone sarcophagus. All depends on chance.'

"Turning to Pao-shu Huang-tzu, Kuan Yi-wu then said to him: 'We two have by this made some progress in the way of life and death.' "

Living According to Impulse

What the "Yang Chu" chapter here describes represents the spirit of the age of Chin, but not the whole or best of that spirit. For in this chapter, as exemplified by the above, what "Yang Chu" seems to be interested in is mostly the search for pleasure of a rather coarse sort. To be sure, the pursuit of such pleasure is not, according to Neo-Taoism, necessarily to be despised. Nevertheless, if this is made our sole aim, without any understanding of what "transcends shapes and features," to use the Neo-Taoist expression, this can hardly be called *feng liu* in the best sense of the term.

In the *Shih-shuo* we have a story about Liu Ling (c. 221-c. 300), one of the Seven Worthies of the Bamboo Grove (seven "famous scholars" who gathered for frequent convivial conversations in a certain bamboo grove). This story tells us that Liu evoked criticism through his habit of remaining completely naked when in his room. To his critics he rejoined: "I take the whole universe as my house and my own room as my clothing. Why, then, do you enter here into my trousers?" (Ch. 23.) Thus Liu Ling, though he sought for pleasure, had a feeling of what lies beyond the world, i.e., the universe. This feeling is essential for the quality of *feng liu*.

Those who have this feeling and who cultivate their mind in Taoism, must have a more subtle sensitivity for pleasure and more refined needs than sheerly sensual ones. The *Shih-shuo* records many unconventional activities among the "famous scholars" of the time. They acted according to pure impulse, but not with any thought of sensuous pleasure. Thus one of the stories in the *Shih-shuo* says: "Wang Hui-chih [died c. 388, son of China's greatest calligrapher, Wang Hsi-chih] was living at Shan-yin [near present Hangchow]. One night he was awakened by a heavy snowfall. Opening the window, he saw a gleaming whiteness all about him. . . . Suddenly he thought of his friend Tai K'uei. Immediately he took a boat and went to see Tai. It required the whole night for him to reach Tai's house, but when he was just about to knock at the door, he stopped and returned home. When asked the reason for this act, he replied:

'I came on the impulse of my pleasure, and now it is ended, so I go back. Why should I see Tai?' " (Ch. 23.)

The *Shih-shuo* records another story which says that Chung Hui (225-264, a statesman, general, and writer) regretted that he had not yet enjoyed the opportunity of meeting Chi K'ang (223-262, a philosopher and writer). Therefore he one day went with several other notables to visit him. Chi K'ang's hobby was that of forging metal, and when Chung Hui arrived there, he found Chi K'ang at his forge under a great tree. Hsiang Hsiu (author of the *Commentary on Chuang-tzu* described in the last chapter) was assisting Chi K'ang to blow the fire with a bellows, and Chi K'ang himself continued his hammering just as if no one else were there. For a while the host and guests did not exchange a single word. But when Chung Hui started to go, Chi K'ang asked him: "What did you hear that caused you to come, and what have you seen that causes you to go?" To this Chung Hui answered: "I heard what I heard, so I came, and I have seen what I have seen, so I go." (Ch. 24.)

The men of the Chin dynasty greatly admired the physical and spiritual beauty of a great personality. Chi K'ang was famous for his personality, which was compared by some people to a jade mountain and by others to a pine tree. (*Shih-shuo*, ch. 14.) Perhaps it was these things that Chung heard of and saw.

Another story in the *Shih-shuo* tells us: "When Wang Hui-chih was traveling by boat, he met Huan Yi traveling by land along the bank. Wang Hui-chih had heard of Huan Yi's fame as a flute player but he was not acquainted with him. When someone told him that the man traveling on the bank was Huan Yi, he sent a messenger to ask him to play the flute. Huan Yi had also heard of the fame of Wang Hui-chih, so he descended from his chariot, sat on a chair, and played the flute three times. After that, he ascended his chariot and went away. The two men did not exchange even a single word." (Ch. 23.)

They did not do this because what they wished to enjoy was only the pure beauty of the music. Wang Hui-chih asked Huan Yi to play the flute for him, because he knew he could play it well, and Huan Yi played for him, because he knew Wang could appreciate his playing. When this had been done, what else was there to talk about?

The *Shih-shuo* contains another story which says that Chih-tun (314-366, famous Buddhist monk) was fond of cranes. Once a friend gave him two young ones. When they grew up, Chih-tun was forced to clip their wings so that they would not fly away. When this was done, the cranes looked despondent, and Chih-tun too was depressed, and said: "Since they have wings that can reach the sky, how can they be content to be a pet of man?" Hence when their feathers had grown again, he let the cranes fly away. (Ch. 2.)

Another story tells us about Juan Chi (210-263, a philosopher and poet), and his nephew Juan Hsien, who were two of the Seven Worthies of the Bamboo Grove. All members of the Juan family were great drinkers, and when they met, they did not bother to drink out of cups, but simply sat around a large wine jar and drank from that. Sometimes the pigs also came, wanting a drink, and then the Juans drank together with the pigs. (Ch. 23.)

The sympathy of Chih-tun for the cranes and the indiscriminate generosity of the Juans to the pigs show that they had a feeling of equality and non-differentiation between themselves and other things of nature. This feeling is essential in order to have the quality of *feng liu* and to be artistic. For a true artist must be able to project his own sentiment to the object he depicts, and then express it through his medium. Chih-tun himself would not have liked to be a pet of man, and he projected this sentiment to the cranes. Though he is not known to have been an artist, he was, in this sense, a very real one.

The Emotional Factor

As we have seen in chapter ten, the sage, according to Chuang Tzu, has no emotions. He has a high understanding of the nature of things, and so is not affected by their changes and transformations. He "disperses emotion with reason." The *Shih-shuo* records many people who had no emotions. The most famous case is that of Hsieh An (320-385). When he was Prime Minister at the Chin court, the northern state of Ch'in started a large-scale offensive against Chin. Its army was led by the Ch'in Emperor in person, and so great was it that the Emperor boasted that his soldiers, by throwing their whips into the Yangtze River, could block its course. The people of Chin were greatly alarmed, but Hsieh An calmly and quietly appointed one of his nephews, Hsieh Hsün, to lead an army against the invaders. At a battle famous in history as the Battle of the Fei

River, in the year 383, Hsieh Hsün won a decisive victory and the men of Ch'in were driven back. When the news of the final victory reached Hsieh An, he was playing chess with a friend. He opened the letter, read it, and then put it aside and continued to play as before. When the friend asked what was the news from the front, Hsieh An, as calmly as ever, replied: "Our boys have decisively defeated the enemy." (Ch. 6.)

The *San Kuo Chih* or *History of the Three Kingdoms*, however, records a discussion between Ho Yen (died 249) and Wang Pi (226-249, greatest commentator on the *Lao-tzu*) on the subject of the emotions. Ho Yen, following the original theory of Chuang Tzu, maintained that "the sage has neither pleasure nor anger, sorrow nor gladness." In this he was seconded by Chung Hui (the man who went to visit Chi K'ang in the story given above). Wang Pi, however, held a different opinion. According to him, "that in which the sage is superior to ordinary people is the spirit. But what the sage has in common with ordinary people are the emotions. The sage has a superior spirit, and therefore is able to be in harmony with the universe and to hold communion with *Wu* [i.e., the *Tao*]. But the sage has ordinary emotions, and therefore cannot respond to things without joy or sorrow. He responds to things, yet is not ensnared by them. It is wrong to say that because the sage has no ensnarement, he therefore has no emotions." (Ch. 28, *Commentary*.)

The theory of Wang Pi can be summarized by the statement that the sage "has emotions but no ensnarement." What this statement exactly means, Wang Pi does not make clear. Its implications were developed much later by Neo-Confucianism, and we shall have a chance to analyze them in chapter 24. At present we need merely point out that though many of the Neo-Taoists were very rational, there were also many who were very sentimental.

As stated earlier, the Neo-Taoists stressed subtle sensitivity. Having this sensitivity, coupled with the afore-mentioned theory of self-expression, it is not surprising that many of them gave free vent to their emotions anywhere and at any time these emotions arose.

An example is the *Shih-shuo's* story about Wang Jung (234-305), one of the Seven Worthies of the Bamboo Grove. When Wang lost a child, his friend Shan Chien went to condole him. Wang could not restrain himself from weeping, whereupon Shan said to him: "It was only a baby, so why do you behave like this?" Wang Jung replied: "The sage forgets emotions, and lowly people [who are insensitive] do not reach emotions. It is people like ourselves who have the most emotions." To this Shan Chien agreed and wept also. (Ch. 17.)

This saying of Wang Jung explains very well why many of the Neo-Taoists were sentimentalists. In most cases, however, they were sentimental, not about some personal loss or gain, but about some general aspect of life or of the universe. The *Shih-shuo* says that Wei Chieh (286-312, known as the most beautiful personality of his time), when about to cross the Yangtze River, felt much depressed, and said: "When I see this vast [river], I cannot help but feel that all kinds of sentiments are gathering in my mind. Being not without feeling, how can one endure these emotions?" (Ch. 2.)

The *Shih-shuo* says also that every time Huan Yi, the flute player mentioned earlier, heard people singing, he would exclaim: "What can I do!" Hsieh An heard of this and remarked: "Huan Yi can indeed be said to have deep feelings." (Ch. 23.)

Because of this subtle sensitivity, these men of *feng liu* spirit were often impressed by things that would not ordinarily impress others. They had sentiments about life and the universe as a whole, and also about their own sensitivity and sentiments. The *Shih-shuo* tells us that when Wang Ch'in ascended the Mao Mountain (in present Shantung province), he wept and said: "Wang Po-yu of Lang-ya [i.e., myself] must at last die for his emotions." (Ch. 23.)

The Factor of Sex

In the West, romanticism often has in it an element of sex. The Chinese term *feng liu* also has that implication, especially in its later usage. The attitude of the Chin Neo-Taoists towards sex, however, seems to be purely aesthetic rather than sensuous. As illustration, the *Shih-shuo* tells us that the neighbor of Juan Chi had a beautiful wife. The neighbor was a wine merchant, and Juan Chi used to go to his house to drink with the merchant's wife. When Juan became drunk, he would sleep beside her. The husband at first was naturally suspicious, but after paying careful attention, he found that Juan Chi did nothing more than sleep there. (Ch. 23.)

The *Shih-shuo* says again that Shan T'ao (205-283, statesman and general), Chi K'ang, and Juan Chi were great friends. Shan T'ao's wife, Han, noticed the close friendship of the three and asked her husband about it. Shan T'ao said: "At present they are the only men who can be my friends." It was the custom in China then that a lady was not allowed to be introduced to the friends of her husband. Hence Han told her husband that, when next his two friends came, she would like to have a secret peep at them. So on the next visit, she asked her husband to have them stay overnight. She prepared a feast for them, and, during the night, peeped in at the guests through a hole in the wall. So absorbed was she in looking at them that she stood there the whole night. In the morning the husband came to her room and asked: "What do you think of them?" She replied: "In talent you are not equal to them, but with your knowledge, you can make friends with them." To this Shan T'ao said: "They, also, consider my knowledge to be superior." (Ch. 19.)

Thus both Juan Chi and the Lady Han seemed to enjoy the beauty of the opposite sex without any sensuous inclinations. Or, it may be said, they enjoyed the beauty, forgetting the sex element.

Such are the characteristics of the *feng liu* spirit of the Chin Neo-Taoists. According to them, *feng liu* derives from *tzu-jan* (spontaneity, naturalness), and *tzu-jan* stands in opposition to *ming chiao* (morals and institutions), which form the classical tradition of Confucianism. Even in this period, however, when Confucianism was in eclipse, one famous scholar and writer named Yüeh Kuang (died 304) said: "In the *ming-chiao*, too, there is fundamentally room for happiness." (*Shih-shuo*, ch. 1.) As we shall see in chapter twenty-four, Neo-Confucianism was an attempt to find such happiness in *ming-chiao*.

CHAPTER 21

THE FOUNDATION OF
CHINESE BUDDHISM

THE introduction of Buddhism into China has been one of the greatest events in Chinese history, and since its coming, it has been a major factor in Chinese civilization, exercising particular influence on religion, philosophy, art, and literature.

Introduction and Development of Buddhism in China

The exact date of the introduction of Buddhism is a disputed problem not yet settled by historians, but it took place probably in the first half of the first century A.D. Traditionally, it is said to have entered during the reign of Emperor Ming (58-75), but there is now evidence that it had already been heard of in China before this time. Its subsequent spread was a long and gradual process. From Chinese literary sources we know that in the first and second centuries A.D., Buddhism was considered as a religion of the occult arts, not greatly differing from the occultism of the *Yin-Yang* school or of the later Taoist religion.

In the second century the theory was actually developed in certain circles that Buddha had been nothing more than a disciple of Lao Tzu. This theory gained its inspiration from a statement in the biography of Lao Tzu in the *Shih Chi* or *Historical Records* (ch. 63), where it is said that Lao Tzu, late in life, disappeared and nobody knew where he went. Elaborating this statement, ardent Taoists created the story that when Lao Tzu went to the West, he finally reached India, where he taught the Buddha and other Indians, and had a total of twenty-nine disciples. The implication was that the teaching of the Buddhist *Sutras* (sacred texts) was simply a foreign variant of that of the *Tao Te Ching*, that is, of the *Lao-tzu*.

In the third and fourth centuries an increasing number of Buddhist texts of a more metaphysical nature was translated, so that Buddhism became better understood. At this time Buddhism was regarded as similar to philosophical Taoism, especially the philosophy of Chuang Tzu, rather than to Taoism as a religion. Often the Buddhist writings were interpreted with ideas taken from philosophical Taoism. This method was called that of *ko yi*, that is, interpretation by analogy.

Such a method naturally led to inaccuracy and distortion. Hence in the fifth century, by which time the flood of translations was rapidly increasing, the use of analogy was definitely abandoned. Yet the fact remains that the great Buddhist writers of the fifth century, even including the Indian teacher, Kumarajiva, continued to use Taoist terminology, such as *Yu* (Being, existent), *Wu* (Non-being, non-existent), *yu-wei* (action) and *wu-wei* (non-action), to express Buddhist ideas. The difference between this practice and the method of analogy, however, is that in the latter one sees only the superficial similarity of words, while in the former one sees the inner connections of the ideas expressed by them. Hence, judging from the nature of the works of these writers, this practice, as we shall see later, did not indicate any misunderstanding or distortion of Buddhism, but rather a synthesis of Indian Buddhism with Taoism, leading to the foundation of a Chinese form of Buddhism.

Here it should be pointed out that the terms, "Chinese Buddhism" and "Buddhism in China," are not necessarily synonymous. Thus there were certain schools of Buddhism which confined themselves to the religious and philosophical tradition of India, and made no contact with those of China. An example is the school known by the Chinese as the *Hsiang tsung* or *Wei-shih tsung* (School of Subjective Idealism), which was introduced by the famous Chinese pilgrim to India, Hsüan-tsang (596-664). Schools like this may be called "Buddhism in China." Their influence was confined to restricted groups of people and limited periods. They did not and could not reach the thought of every intellectual, and therefore played little or no part in the development of what may be called the Chinese mind.

On the other hand, "Chinese Buddhism" is the form of Buddhism that has made contact with Chinese thought and thus has developed in conjunction with Chinese philosophical tradition. In later pages we will see that the Middle Path school of Buddhism bears some similarity to philosophical Taoism. Its interaction with the latter resulted in the Ch'an or Zen school, which though Buddhist, is at the same time Chinese. Although a school of Buddhism, its influence on Chinese philosophy, literature, and art has been far reaching.

General Concepts of Buddhism

Following the introduction of Buddhism into China, tremendous efforts were made to translate the Buddhist texts into Chinese. Texts of both the Hinayana (Small Vehicle) and Mahayana (Great Vehicle) divisions of Buddhism were translated, but only the latter gained a permanent place in Chinese Buddhism.

On the whole, the way in which Mahayana Buddhism most influenced the Chinese has been in its concept of the Universal Mind, and in what may be called its negative method of metaphysics. Before going into a discussion of these, we must first survey some of the general concepts of Buddhism.

Although there are many schools of Buddhism, each with something different to offer, all generally agree in their belief in the theory of *Karma* (translated in Chinese as *Yeh*). *Karma* or *Yeh* is usually rendered in English as deed or action, but its actual meaning is much wider than that, for what it covers is not merely confined to overt action, but also includes what an individual sentient being speaks and thinks. According to Buddhism, all the phenomena of the universe, or, to be more exact, of the universe of an individual sentient being, are the manifestations of his mind. Whenever he acts, speaks, or even thinks, his mind is doing something, and that something must produce its results, no matter how far in the future. This result is the retribution of the *Karma*. The *Karma* is the cause and its retribution is the effect. The being of an individual is made up of a chain of causes and effects.

The present life of a sentient being is only one aspect in this whole process. Death is not the end of his being, but is only another aspect of the process. What an individual is in this life, comes as a result of what he did in the past, and what he does in the present will determine what he will be in the future. Hence what he does now will bear its fruits in a future life, and what he will do then will again bear its fruits in yet another future life, and so on *ad infinitum*. This chain of causation is what is called *Samsara*, the Wheel of Birth and Death. It is the main source from which come the sufferings of individual sentient beings.

According to Buddhism, all these sufferings arise from the individual's fundamental Ignorance of the nature of things. All things in the universe are the manifestations of the mind and therefore are illusory and impermanent, yet the individual ignorantly craves for and cleaves to them. This fundamental Ignorance is called *Avidya*, which in Chinese is translated as *Wu-ming*, non-enlightenment. From Ignorance come the craving for and cleaving to life, because of which the individual is bound to the eternal Wheel of Birth and Death, from which he can never escape.

The only hope for escape lies in replacing Ignorance with Enlightenment, which in Sanskrit is called *Bodhi*. All the teachings and practices of the various Buddhist schools are attempts to contribute something to the *Bodhi*. From them the individual, in the course of many rebirths, may accumulate *Karma* which does not crave for and cleave to things, but avoids craving and cleaving. The result is an emancipation of the individual possessing this *Karma* from the Wheel of Birth and Death. And this emancipation is called *Nirvana*.

What, exactly, does the state of *Nirvana* signify? It may be said to be the identification of the individual with the Universal Mind, or with what is called the Buddha-nature; or it is the realization or self-consciousness of the individual's original identification with the Universal Mind. He *is* the Universal Mind, but formerly he did not realize it, or was not self-conscious of it. The school of Mahayana Buddhism known by the Chinese as the *Hsing tsung* or School of Universal Mind expounded this theory. (For this school, *hsing* or nature and *hsin* or mind are the same.) In expounding it, the school introduced the idea of Universal Mind into Chinese thought.

There were other schools of Mahayana Buddhism, however, such as that known by the Chinese as the *K'ung tsung* or School of Emptiness, also known as the School of the Middle Path, which would not describe *Nirvana* in this way. Their method of approach is what I call the negative method.

The Theory of Double Truth

This School of the Middle Path proposed what it called the theory of double truth: truth in the common sense and truth in the higher sense. Furthermore, it maintained, not only are there these two kinds of truth, but they both exist on varying levels. Thus what, on the lower level, is truth in the higher sense, becomes, on the higher level, merely truth in the common sense. One of the great Chinese Masters of this school, Chi-tsang (549-623), describes this theory as including the three following levels of double truth:

(1) The common people take all things as really *yu* (having being, existent) and know nothing about *wu* (having no being, non-existent). Therefore the Buddhas have told them that actually all things are *wu* and empty. On this level, to say that all things are *yu* is the common sense truth, and to say that all things are *wu* is the higher sense truth.

(2) To say that all things are *yu* is one-sided, but to say that all things are *wu* is also one-sided. They are both one-sided, because they give people the wrong impression that *wu* or non-existence only results from the absence or removal of *yu* or existence. Yet in actual fact, what is *yu* is simultaneously what is *wu*. For instance, the table standing before us need not be destroyed in order to show that it is ceasing to exist. In actual fact it is ceasing to exist all the time. The reason for this is that when one starts to destroy the table, the table which one thus intends to destroy has already ceased to exist. The table of this actual moment is no longer the table of the preceding moment. It only *looks* like that of the preceding moment. Therefore on the second level of double truth, to say that all things are *yu* and to say that all things are *wu* are both equally common sense truth. What one ought to say is that the "not-one-sided middle path" consists in understanding that things are neither *yu* nor *wu*. This is the higher sense truth.

(3) But to say that the middle truth consists in what is not one-sided (i.e., what is neither *yu* nor *wu*), means to make distinctions. And all distinctions are themselves one-sided. Therefore on the third level, to say that things are neither *yu* nor *wu*, and that herein lies the not-one-sided middle path, is merely common sense truth. The higher truth consists in saying that things are neither *yu* nor *wu*, neither not-*yu* nor not-*wu*, and that the middle path is neither one-

sided nor not-one-sided. (*Erh-ti Chang* or *Chapter on the Double Truth*, sec. 1.)

In this passage I have retained the Chinese words *yu* and *wu*, because in their use the Chinese thinkers of the time saw or felt a similarity between the central problem discussed by Buddhism and that discussed by Taoism, in which the same words are prominent. Though deeper analysis shows that the similarity is in some respects superficial, nevertheless, when the Taoists spoke of *Wu* as transcending shapes and features, and the Buddhists spoke of *Wu* as "not-not," there is a real similarity.

Still another real similarity between the Buddhists of this particular school and the Taoists is their method of approach and the final results achieved by this method. The method is to make use of different levels of discourse. What is said in one level is to be immediately denied by a saying on a higher level. As we have seen in chapter ten, this is also the method used in the *Ch'i Wu Lun* or "Equality of Things" in the *Chuang-tzu*, and it is the method that has just been discussed above.

When all is denied, including the denial of the denial of all, one arrives at the same situation as found in the philosophy of Chuang Tzu, in which all is forgotten, including the fact that one has forgotten all. This state is described by Chuang Tzu as "sitting in forgetfulness," and by the Buddhists as *Nirvana*. One cannot ask this school of Buddhism what, exactly, the state of *Nirvana* is, because, according to it, when one reaches the third level of truth, one cannot affirm anything.

Philosophy of Seng-chao

One of the great teachers of this same school in China in the fifth century was Kumarajiva, who was an Indian but was born in a state in the present Chinese Turkistan. He came to Ch'ang-an (the present Sian in Shensi province) in 401, and lived there until his death in 413. During these thirteen years, he translated many Buddhist texts into Chinese and taught many disciples, among them some who became very famous and influential. In this chapter I shall mention two of them, Seng-chao and Tao-sheng.

Seng-chao (384-414) came from the vicinity of the above-mentioned city of Ch'ang-an. He first studied Lao Tzu and Chuang

Tzu, but later became a disciple of Kumarajiva. He wrote several essays which have been collected as the *Chao Lun* or *Essays of Seng-chao*. One of them, titled "There Is No Real Unreality," says: "All things have that in them which makes them not be *yu* [having being, existent] and also have that in them which makes them not be *wu* [having no being, non-existent]. Because of the former, they are *yu* and yet not *yu*. Because of the latter, they are *wu* and yet not *wu*. . . . Why is this so? Suppose the *yu* is really *yu*, then it should be *yu* for all time and should not owe its *yu* to the convergence of causes. [According to Buddhism, the existence of anything is due to the convergence of a number of causes.] Suppose the *wu* is really *wu*, then it should be *wu* for all time and should not owe its *wu* to the dissolution of causes. If the *yu* owes its *yu* to causation, then the *yu* is not really *yu*. . . . But if all things are *wu*, then nothing would come about. If something comes about, it cannot be altogether nothing. . . . If we want to affirm that things are *yu*, yet there is no real existence of this *yu*. If we want to affirm that they are *wu*, yet they have their shapes and features. To have shapes and features is not the same as *wu*, and to be not really *yu* is not the same as *yu*. This being so, the principle of 'no real unreality' is clear." (*Chao Lun*, ch. 2.)

In another essay, titled "On the Immutability of Things," Seng-chao says: "Most men's idea of mutability is that things in the past do not come down to the present. They therefore say that there is mutability and no immutability. My idea of immutability is also that things of the past do not come down to the present. Therefore I on the contrary say that there is immutability and no mutability. That there is mutability and no immutability is because things of the past do not come down to the present. That there is immutability and no mutability is because things of the past do not vanish away with the past [i.e., though they do not exist today, they did exist in the past]. . . . If we search for past things in the past, they were not *wu* in the past. If we search for these past things in the present, they are not *yu* in the present. . . . That is to say, past things are in the past, and are not things that have receded from the present. Likewise present things are in the present, and are not something that have come down from the past. . . . The effect is not the cause, but because of the cause there is the effect. That the effect is not the cause shows that the cause does not come down to the present. And that, there being the cause, there is therefore the effect, shows that causes do not vanish in the past. The cause has neither come down nor has it vanished. Thus the theory of immutability is clear." (*Chao Lun*, ch. 1.)

The idea here is that things undergo constant change at every moment. Anything existing at any given moment is actually a new thing of that moment and not the same as the thing that has existed in the past. In the same essay Seng-chao says: "[There was a man by the name of] Fan-chih who, having become a monk in his early years, returned home when his hair was white. On seeing him the neighbors exclaimed at seeing a man of the past who was still alive. Fan-chih said: 'I look like the man of the past, but I am not he.'" At every moment there has been a Fan-chih. The Fan-chih of this moment is not a Fan-chih who has come down from the past, and the Fan-chih of the past was not a Fan-chih of the present who receded into the past. Juding from the fact that everything changes at every moment, we say that there is change but no permanence. And judging from the fact that everything at every moment remains with that moment, we say that there is permanence but no change.

This is Seng-chao's theory to substantiate the double truth on the second level. On this level, to say that things are *yu* and permanent, and to say that things are *wu* and mutable, are both common sense truth. To say that things are neither *yu* nor *wu*, neither permanent nor mutable, is the higher sense truth.

Seng-chao also gives arguments to substantiate the double truth on the third or highest level. This he does in an essay titled "On *Prajna* [i.e., Wisdom of the Buddha] Not Being Knowledge." *Prajna* is described by Seng-chao as Sage-knowledge, but, he says, this Sage-knowledge is really not knowledge. For knowledge of a thing consists in selecting a quality of that thing and taking that quality as the object of knowledge. But Sage-knowledge consists in knowing about what is called W*u* (Non-being), and this W*u* "transcends shapes and features" and has no qualities; hence it can never be the object of knowledge. To have knowledge of W*u* is to be one with it. This state of identification with W*u* is called *Nirvana*. *Nirvana* and *Prajna* are two aspects of one and the same state of affairs. As *Nirvana* is not something to be known, so *Prajna* is knowledge which is not knowledge. (*Chao Lun*, ch. 3.) Hence, on the third level of truth, nothing can be said and one must remain silent.

Philosophy of Tao-sheng

Seng-chao died when only thirty years old, so that his influence was less than it might otherwise have been. Tao-sheng (died 434), who was a fellow student with Seng-chao under Kumarajiva, was born at P'eng-ch'eng in the northern part of the present Kiangsu province. He became a monk of wide learning, great brilliancy, and eloquence, of whom it is said that when he spoke even the stones beside him nodded their heads in assent. In his later years he taught at Lu-shan in the present Kiangsi province, which was the center of Buddhist learning at that time, and the place where such great monks as Tao-an (died 385) and Hui-yüan (died 416) had lectured. Tao-sheng advanced many theories so new and revolutionary that once he was publicly banished from Nanking by the conservative monks.

Among these is the doctrine that "a good deed entails no retribution." His essay on this subject is now lost. But in the *Hung Ming Chi* or *Collected Essays on Buddhism*, a work compiled by Seng-yu (died 518), there is a treatise by Hui-yüan titled "On the Explanation of Retribution." This essay may represent some aspects of Tao-sheng's concept, though we cannot be sure. Its general idea is to apply the Taoist ideas of *wu-wei* and *wu-hsin* to metaphysics. As we have seen, *wu-wei* literally means non-action, but this non-action does not really signify no action; rather it signifies action that takes place without effort. When one acts spontaneously, without any deliberate discrimination, choice, or effort, one is practicing non-action. *Wu-hsin* also literally means no mind. When one practices *wu-wei* in the manner described above, one is also practicing *wu-hsin*. If, argues Hui-yüan, one follows the principles of *wu-wei* and *wu-hsin*, one then has no craving for or cleaving to things, even though one may pursue various activities. And since the effect or retribution of one's *Karma* is due to one's craving and cleaving or attachment, one's *Karma* under these circumstances will not entail any retribution. (*Chüan* 5.) This theory of Hui-yüan, regardless of whether it is the same as Tao-sheng's original idea or not, is an interesting extension to Buddhist metaphysics of a Taoist theory which originally possessed purely social and ethical significance. As such, it is certainly an important development in Chinese Buddhism, and one that was to be followed later by the Ch'an school.

Another theory of Tao-sheng is that Buddhahood is to be achieved by Sudden Enlightenment. His essay on this subject is also lost, but the theory is preserved in Hsieh Ling-yün's (died 433) *Pien Tsung Lun* or "Discussion of Essentials." It was developed in opposition to another theory, that of gradual attainment, according to which Buddhahood is to be achieved only through the gradual accumulation of learning and practice. Tao-sheng and Hsieh Ling-yün did not deny the importance of such learning and practice, but they maintained that its accumulation, no matter how great, is only a sort of preparatory work, which in itself is insufficient for one ever to achieve Buddhahood. Such achievement is an instantaneous act, like the leaping over of a deep chasm. Either one makes the leap successfully, in which case one reaches the other side and thus achieves Buddhahood in its entirety in a flash, or one fails in one's leap, in which case one remains as one was. There are no intermediate steps between.

The reason advanced for this theory is that to achieve Buddhahood means to be one with *Wu* (Non-being) or, as one might say, with the Universal Mind. The *Wu*, since it transcends shapes and features, is not a "thing" in itself, and so is not something that can be divided into parts. Therefore one cannot gain oneness with a part of it today and oneness with another part of it tomorrow. Oneness means oneness with the whole of it. Anything less than this is no longer oneness.

The *Pien Tsung Lun* records many arguments on this subject between Hsieh Ling-yün and others. One monk named Seng-wei argued that if the student is one with *Wu*, he will no longer speak about it, but if he is to learn about *Wu* in order to get rid of *Yu* (Being), this learning represents a process of gradual enlightenment. To this Hsieh Ling-yün answered that when a student is still in the realm of *Yu*, whatever he does is learning, but not Enlightenment. Enlightenmen itself is something beyond *Yu*, though a student must devote himself first to learning, in order to attain Enlightenment.

Seng-wei again asked: If a student devotes himself to learning and hopes thereby for identification with *Wu*, does he in this way make some advancement? If he does not, why does he pursue learning? But if he does, is this not gradual enlightenment? To this Hsieh Ling-yün answered that devotion to learning can have the positive achievement of suppressing the impure element of the mind. Though such suppression seems to be its extinction, in actual fact it is still not without impure attachment. It is only with Sudden Enlightenment that all attachments are gone.

Again Seng-wei asked: If a student devote himself to learning and practice, can he achieve a temporary identification with *Wu?* If he can, this temporary identification is better than no identification at all, and is it not gradual enlightenment? To this Hsieh Ling-yün answered that such temporary identification is a false one. A real identification is by its nature everlasting. Though the temporary identification seems to be a real identification, it is so only in the same sense that the suppression of the impure element of the mind seems to be its extinction.

All these arguments are endorsed by Tao-sheng in a letter also included in the *Pien Tsung Lun.* The latter is now to be found in the *Kuang Hung Ming Chi* or *Further Collections of Essays on Buddhism (chüan* 18), a work compiled by Tao-hsüan (596-667).

Another of Tao-sheng's theories is that every sentient being possesses the Buddha-nature or Universal Mind. His essay on this subject is also lost, but its ideas can be gathered from his commentaries on several Buddhist *Sutras.* According to these, every sentient being has the Buddha-nature; only he does not realize that he has it. This Ignorance (*Avidya*) is what binds him to the Wheel of Birth and Death. The necessity, therefore, is for him first to realize that he has the Buddha-nature originally within him, and then, by learning and practice, to "see" his own Buddha-nature. This "seeing" comes as a Sudden Enlightenment, because the Buddha-nature cannot be divided; therefore he either sees it as a whole or does not see it at all. Such "seeing" also means to be one with the Buddha-nature, because the Buddha-nature is not something that can be seen from outside. This is the meaning of Tao-sheng's statement: "By gaining freedom from illusion, one returns to the Ultimate, and by returning to the Ultimate, one attains the Original." * The state of attainment of the Original is the state of *Nirvana.*

But *Nirvana* is not something external to and altogether different from the Wheel of Birth and Death, nor is the reality of the Buddha-nature external to and altogether different from the phenomenal

---

* Quoted in the *Nieh-pan-ching Chi-chieh* or *Collected Commentaries to the Parinirvana Sutra, chüan* 1.

world. Once one gains Sudden Enlightenment, the latter is at once the former. Thus Tao-sheng says: "The Enlightenment of Mahayana Buddhism is not to be sought outside the Wheel of Birth and Death. Within it one is enlightened by the affairs of birth and death." * The Buddhists use the metaphor of "reaching the other shore" to express the idea of achieving Nirvana. Tao-sheng says: "As to reaching the other shore, if one reaches it, one is not reaching the other shore. Both not-reaching and not-not-reaching are really reaching. This shore here means birth and death; the other shore means Nirvana." (Ibid., chüan 9.) Again he says: "If one sees Buddha, one is not seeing Buddha. When one sees there is no Buddha, one is really seeing Buddha." (Ibid.)

This is perhaps also the meaning of another theory of Tao-sheng, that for Buddha there is no "Pure Land" or other world. The world of Buddha is simply here in this present world.

In an essay titled "The Treasure House," which has been traditionally attributed to Seng-chao but seems to be a forgery, it is said: "Suppose there is a man who, in a treasure house of golden utensils, sees the golden utensils, but pays no attention to their shapes and features. Or, even if he does pay attention to their shapes and features, he still recognizes that they are all gold. He is not confused by their varying appearances, and therefore is able to rid himself of their [superficial] distinctions. He always sees that their underlying substance is gold, and does not suffer any illusion. This is an illustration of what a sage is." (Ch. 3.)

This saying may not come from Seng-chao, but its metaphor has been constantly used by later Buddhists. The reality of the Buddha-nature is itself the phenomenal world, just as the golden utensils are themselves the gold. There is no other reality outside the phenomenal world, just as there is no other gold besides the golden utensils. Some people, in their Ignorance, see only the phenomenal world, but not the reality of the Buddha-nature. Other people, in their Enlightenment, see the Buddha-nature, but this Buddha-nature is still the phenomenal world. What these two kinds of people see is the same, but what one person sees in his Enlightenment has a significance quite different from what the other person sees in his

* Quoted in Seng-chao's Wei-mou-ching Chu or Commentary to the Vimalakirti Sutra, chüan 7.

Ignorance. This is the meaning of a common saying of Chinese Buddhism: "When ignorant, one is a common man; when enlightened, one is a sage."

Another theory of Tao-sheng is that even the *icchantika* (i.e., the being who opposes Buddhism) is capable of achieving Buddhahood. This is the logical conclusion of the assertion that every sentient being has the Buddha-nature. But it was in direct contradiction to the *Parinirvana Sutra*, as known at that time, and consequently Tao-sheng, because he uttered it, was banished for some time from the capital, Nanking. Many years later, however, when the complete text of the *Parinirvana Sutra* was translated, Tao-sheng's theory was found to be confirmed by one of its passages. His biographer, Hui-chiao (died 554), wrote: "Because his interpretation of the *icchantika* came to be established by Scriptural evidence, his theories of Sudden Enlightenment and that a good deed entails no retribution, also came to be highly honored by the Buddhists of the time." (*Kao-seng Chüan* or *Biographies of Eminent Buddhist Monks, chüan* 7.)

Hui-chiao also reports another saying of Tao-sheng: "The symbol serves to express an idea, and is to be discarded once the idea has been understood. Words serve to explain thought, and ought to be silenced once the thoughts have been absorbed. . . . It is only those who can grasp the fish and discard the fishing net that are qualified to seek the truth." (*Ibid.*) This figure of speech refers to a saying in the *Chuang-tzu* which says: "The fishing net serves to catch fish. Let us take the fish and forget the net. The snare serves to catch rabbits. Let us take the rabbit and forget the snare." (Ch. 26.) Chinese philosophical tradition makes use of a term called the "net of words." According to this tradition, the best statement is one that does not "fall into the net of words."

We have seen that in Chi-tsang's theory of the three levels of double truth, when one reaches the third level one simply has nothing to say. On that level there is no danger of falling into the net of words. When Tao-sheng speaks of the Buddha-nature, he almost falls into this net, because by speaking of it as the Mind, he gives people the impression that the limitations of definition can be imposed on it. In this respect he is influenced by the *Parinirvana Sutra*, which emphasizes the Buddha-nature, and so he approaches the *Hsing tsung* or School of Universal Mind.

Thus, as we shall see in the next chapter, by the time of Tao-sheng, the theoretical background for Ch'anism had been prepared. The Ch'an Masters themselves, however, were needed to put the theories described in the present chapter into high relief.

In what has been told here we can also find the germ of the Neo-Confucianism of several centuries later. The theory of Tao-sheng that every man can become a Buddha reminds us of the theory of Mencius that every man can become a Yao or Shun (two traditional sage-kings). (*Mencius*, VIb, 2.) Mencius also stated that by fully developing our mind, we come to know our nature; and by fully developing our nature, we come to know Heaven. (*Mencius*, VIIa, 1.) But what he called mind and nature are both psychological and not metaphysical. By giving them a metaphysical interpretation along the line suggested by Tao-sheng's theory, one arrives at Neo-Confucianism.

The idea of the Universal Mind is a contribution of India to Chinese philosophy. Before the introduction of Buddhism, there was in Chinese philosophy only the mind, but not the Mind. The *Tao* of the Taoists is the "mystery of mysteries," as Lao Tzu put it, yet it is not Mind. After the period dealt with in this chapter, there is, in Chinese philosophy, not only mind, but also Mind.

CHAPTER 22

CH'ANISM: THE PHILOSOPHY

OF SILENCE

THE Chinese term *Ch'an* (Japanese reading: *Zen*) or *Ch'an-na* is a phonetic rendering of the Sanskrit *Dhyana*, which is usually translated in English as Meditation. The traditional account of the origin of the Ch'an or Zen school is that the Buddha, in addition to his Scriptures, possessed an esoteric teaching that was transmitted independently of written texts. This teaching he transmitted personally to one of his disciples, who in turn transmitted it to his own disciple. In this way, it was handed down until it reached Bodhidharma, who is supposed to have been the twenty-eighth Patriarch in India, and who came to China some time between 520 and 526, where he became the first *Tsu* (Patriarch, literally, Ancestor) of the Ch'an school in China.

Traditional Account of the Origin of Ch'anism

There Bodhidharma transmitted the esoteric teaching to Hui-k'o (486-593), who was China's second Patriarch. The teaching was thus perpetuated until a major split in the school occurred, caused by the two chief disciples of the fifth Patriarch, Hung-jen (605-675). One of them, Shen-hsiu (died 706), became the founder of the Northern school; the other, Hui-neng (638-713), founded the Southern school. The Southern school soon surpassed the Northern one in popularity, so that Hui-neng came to be recognized as the sixth Patriarch, the true successor of Hung-jen. All the later influential groups in Ch'anism took their rise from the disciples of Hui-neng.*

How far we can depend on the earlier part of this traditional ac-

* For the traditional account, see Yang Yi (974-1020), *Ch'uan Teng Lu* or *Record of the Transmission of the Light, chüan* 1.

count is much questioned, for it is not supported by any documents dated earlier than the eleventh century. It is not our purpose in this chapter to make a scholarly examination of this problem. Suffice it to say that no scholar today takes the tradition very seriously. Indeed, as we have already seen in the last chapter, the theoretical background for Ch'anism had already been created in China by such men as Seng-chao and Tao-sheng. Given this background, the rise of Ch'anism would seem to have been almost inevitable, without looking to the almost legendary Bodhidharma as its founder.

The split in the Ch'an school caused by Shen-hsiu and Hui-neng is, however, a historical fact. The difference between these founders of the Northern and Southern schools represents the earlier difference between the *Hsing tsung* (Universal Mind school) and *K'ung tsung* (Empty school) that was described in the last chapter. This can be seen in Hui-neng's own autobiography. From this work we learn that Hui-neng was a native of the present Kwangtung province and became a student of Buddhism under Hung-jen. The account continues that one day Hung-jen, realizing that his time was nearly over, summoned his disciples together and told them that a successor must now be appointed; this successor would be the disciple who could write the best poem summarizing the teaching of Ch'anism. Shen-hsiu then wrote a poem which read:

> The body is like unto the *Bodhi*-tree,
> And the mind to a mirror bright;
> Carefully we cleanse them hour by hour
> Lest dust should fall upon them.

To refute this idea, Hui-neng then wrote the following poem:

> Originally there was no *Bodhi*-tree,
> Nor was there any mirror;
> Since originally there was nothing,
> Whereon can the dust fall?

It is said that Hung-jen approved Hui-neng's poem and appointed him as his successor, the sixth Patriarch.*

Shen-hsiu's poem emphasized the Universal Mind or Buddha Nature spoken of by Tao-sheng, while Hui-neng's emphasized the *Wu*

* See the *Liu-tsu T'an-ching* or *Sutra Spoken by the Sixth Patriarch, chüan* 1.

(Non-being) of Seng-chao. There are two phrases that often occur in Ch'anism. One is, "The very mind is Buddha"; the other, "not-mind, and not-Buddha." Shen-hsiu's poem is the expression of the first phrase, and Hui-neng's of the second.

The First Principle Is Inexpressible

In later times the Ch'an school in its major development followed the line set by Hui-neng. In it the combination already begun between the Empty school and Taoism reached its climax. What the Empty school called higher sense truth on the third level, the Ch'anists called the First Principle. As we have seen in the last chapter, on this third level one simply cannot say anything. Hence the First Principle is by its very nature inexpressible. The Ch'an Master Wen-yi (died 958) was once asked: "What is the First Principle?" To which he answered: "If I were to tell you, it would become the second principle." (*Wen-yi Ch'an-shih Yü-lu* or *Sayings of the Ch'an Master Wen-yi*.)

It was the principle of the Ch'an Masters to teach their disciples only through personal contact. For the benefit of those who did not have opportunity for such contact, however, written records were made of the sayings of the Masters, which were known as *yü lu* (recorded conversations). This was a practice that was later taken over by the Neo-Confucianists. In these records, we often find that when a student ventured to ask some question about the fundamental principles of Buddhism, he would often be given a beating by his Ch'an Master, or some quite irrelevant answer. He might, for example, be told that the price of a certain vegetable was then three cents. These answers seem very paradoxical to those who are not familiar with the purpose of Ch'anism. But this purpose is simply to let the student know that what he asks about is not answerable. Once he understands that, he understands a great deal.

The First Principle is inexpressible, because what is called the **Wu** is not something about which anything can be said. By calling it "Mind" or any other name, one is at once giving it a definition and thus imposing on it a limitation. As the Ch'anists and Taoists both say, one thereby falls into the "net of words." Ma-tsu or the Patriarch Ma (died 788), a disciple of the disciple of Hui-neng, was once asked: "Why do you say that the very mind is Buddha?" Ma-tsu answered: "I simply want to stop the crying of children." "Suppose they do stop crying?" asked the questioner. "Then not-mind, not-Buddha," was the answer.*

Another student asked Ma-tsu: "What kind of man is he who is not linked to *all* things?" The Master answered: "Wait until in one gulp you can drink up all the water in the West River, then I will tell you." (*Ibid.*) Such an act is obviously impossible and by suggesting it Ma-tsu meant to indicate to the student that he would not answer his question. His question, in fact, was really not answerable, because he who is not linked to *all* things is one who transcends *all* things. This being so, how can you ask what kind of man he is?

There were Ch'an Masters who used silence to express the idea of *Wu* or the First Principle. It is said, for example, that when Hui-chung (died 775) was to debate with another monk, he simply mounted his chair and remained silent. The other monk then said: "Please propose your thesis so I can argue." Hui-chung replied: "I have already proposed my thesis." The monk asked: "What is it?" Hui-chung said: "I know it is beyond your understanding," and with this left his chair. (*Record of the Transmission of the Light, chüan* 5.) The thesis Hui-chung proposed was that of silence. Since the First Principle or *Wu* is not something about which anything can be said, the best way to expound it is to remain silent.

From this point of view no Scriptures or *Sutras* have any real connection with the First Principle. Hence the Ch'an Master Yi-hsüan (died 866), founder of a group in Ch'anism known as the Lin-chi school, said: "If you want to have the right understanding, you must not be deceived by others. You should kill everything that you meet internally or externally. If you meet Buddha, kill Buddha. If you meet the Patriarchs, kill the Patriarchs. . . . Then you can gain your emancipation." (*Recorded Savings of Ancient Worthies, chüan* 4.)

Method of Cultivation

The knowledge of the First Principle is knowledge that is non-knowledge; hence the method of cultivation is also cultivation that is non-cultivation. It is said that Ma-tsu, before he became a dis-

* Yi-tsang (of the Sung dynasty), *Ku-tsun-hsü Yü-lu* or *Recorded Sayings of Ancient Worthies. chüan* 1.

ciple of Huai-jang (died 744), lived on the Heng Mountain (in present Hunan province). There he occupied a solitary hut in which, all alone, he practiced meditation. One day Huai-jang began to grind some bricks in front of the hut. When Ma-tsu saw it, he asked Huai-jang what he was doing. He replied that he was planning to make a mirror. Ma-tsu said: "How can grinding bricks make a mirror?" Huai-jang said: "If grinding bricks cannot make a mirror, how can meditation make a Buddha?" By this saying Ma-tsu was enlightened and thereupon became Huai-jang's disciple. (*Recorded Sayings of Ancient Worthies, chüan* 1.)

Thus according to Ch'anism, the best method of cultivation for achieving Buddhahood is not to practice any cultivation. To cultivate oneself in this way is to exercise deliberate effort, which is *yu-wei* (having action). This *yu-wei* will, to be sure, produce some good effect, but it will not be everlasting. The Ch'an Master Hsi-yün (died 847), known as the Master of Huang-po, said: "Supposing that through innumerable lives a man has practiced the six *paramitas* [methods of gaining salvation], done good and attained the Buddha Wisdom, this will still not last forever. The reason lies in causation. When the force of the cause is exhausted, he reverts to the impermanent." (*Recorded Sayings of Ancient Worthies, chüan* 3.)

Again he said: "All deeds are essentially impermanent. All forces have their final day. They are like a dart discharged through the air; when its strength is exhausted, it turns and falls to the ground. They are all connected with the Wheel of Birth and Death. To practice cultivation through them is to misunderstand the Buddha's idea and waste labor." (*Ibid.*)

And yet again: "If you do not understand *wu hsin* [absence of a purposeful mind], then you are attached to objects, and suffer from obstructions. . . . Actually there is no such thing as *Bodhi* [Wisdom]. That the Buddha talked about it was simply as a means to educate men, just as yellow leaves may be taken as gold coins in order to stop the crying of children. . . . The only thing to be done is to rid yourself of your old *Karma*, as opportunity offers, and not to create new *Karma* from which will flow new calamities." (*Ibid.*)

Thus the best method of spiritual cultivation is to do one's tasks without deliberate effort or purposeful mind. This is exactly what the Taoists called *wu-wei* (non-action) and *wu-hsin* (no-mind). It is what Hui-yüan's theory signifies, as well as, probably, the statement of Tao-sheng that "a good deed does not entail retribution." This method of cultivation does not aim at doing things in order to obtain resulting good effects, no matter how good these effects may be in themselves. Rather it aims at doing things in such a way as to entail no effects at all. When all one's actions entail no effect, then after the effects of previously accumulated *Karma* have exhausted themselves, one will gain emancipation from the Wheel of Birth and Death and attain *Nirvana*.

To do things without deliberate effort and purposeful mind is to do things naturally and to live naturally. Yi-hsüan said: "To achieve Buddhahood there is no place for deliberate effort. The only method is to carry on one's ordinary and uneventful tasks: relieve one's bowels, pass water, wear one's clothes, eat one's meals, and when tired, lie down. The simple fellow will laugh at you, but the wise will understand." (*Recorded Sayings of Ancient Worthies, chüan 4.*) The reason why those who try to achieve Buddhahood so often fail to follow this course is because they lack self-confidence. Yi-hsüan said: "Nowadays people who engage in spiritual cultivation fail to achieve their ends. Their fault is not having faith in themselves. . . . Do you wish to know who are the Patriarchs and Buddha? All of you who are before me are the Patriarchs and Buddha." (*Ibid.*)

Thus the way to practice spiritual cultivation is to have adequate confidence in one's self and discard everything else. All one should do is to pursue the ordinary tasks of one's everyday life, and nothing more. This is what the Ch'an Masters call cultivation through non-cultivation.

Here a question arises: Granted that this be so, then what is the difference between the man who engages in cultivation of this kind and the man who engages in no cultivation at all? If the latter does precisely what the former does, he too should achieve *Nirvana*, and so there should come a time when there will be no Wheel of Birth and Death at all.

To this question it may be answered that although to wear clothes and eat meals are in themselves common and simple matters, it is still not easy to do them with a completely non-purposeful mind and thus without any attachment. A person likes fine clothes, for example, but dislikes bad ones, and he feels pleased when others admire his clothes. These are all the attachments that result from wearing clothes. What the Ch'an Masters emphasized is that spiritual cultivation does not require special acts, such as the ceremonies and prayers of institutionalized religion. One should simply try to be without a purposeful mind or any attachments in one's daily life; then cultivation results from the mere carrying on of the common and simple affairs of daily life. In the beginning one will need to exert effort in order to be without effort, and to exercise a purposeful mind in order not to have such a mind, just as, in order to forget, one at first needs to remember that one should forget. Later, however, the time comes when one must discard the effort to be without effort, and the mind that purposefully tries to have no purpose, just as one finally forgets to remember that one has to forget.

Thus cultivation through non-cultivation is itself a kind of cultivation, just as knowledge that is not knowledge is nevertheless still a form of knowledge. Such knowledge differs from original ignorance, and cultivation through non-cultivation likewise differs from original naturalness. For original ignorance and naturalness are gifts of nature, whereas knowledge that is not knowledge and cultivation through non-cultivation are both products of the spirit.

Sudden Enlightenment

The practice of cultivation, no matter for how long, is in itself only a sort of preparatory work. For Buddhahood to be achieved, this cultivation must be climaxed by a Sudden Enlightenment, such as was described in the last chapter as comparable to the leaping over of a precipice. Only after this leaping has taken place can Buddhahood be achieved.

Such Enlightenment is often referred to by the Ch'an Masters as the "vision of the *Tao*." P'u-yüan, known as the Master of Nan-ch'üan (died 830), told his disciple: "The *Tao* is not classifiable as either knowledge or non-knowledge. Knowledge is illusory consciousness and non-knowledge is blind unconsciousness. If you really comprehend the indubitable *Tao*, it is like a wide expanse of emptiness, so how can distinctions be forced in it between right and wrong?" (*Recorded Sayings of Ancient Worthies, chüan* 13.) Comprehension of the *Tao* is the same as being one with it. Its wide expanse of emptiness is not a void; it is simply a state in which all distinctions are gone.

This state is described by the Ch'an Masters as one in which "knowledge and truth become undifferentiable, objects and spirit form a single unity, and there ceases to be a distinction between the experiencer and the experienced." (*Ibid., chüan* 32.) "A man who drinks water knows by himself whether it is cold or warm." This last expression first appeared in the *Sutra Spoken by the Sixth Patriarch* (Hui-neng), but it was later widely quoted by the other Ch'an Masters, meaning that only he who experiences the non-distinction of the experiencer and the experienced really knows what it is.

In this state the experiencer has discarded knowledge in the ordinary sense, because this kind of knowledge postulates a distinction between the knower and the known. Nevertheless, he is not without knowledge, because his state differs from that of blind unconsciousness, as Nan-ch'üan calls it. This is what is called the knowledge that is not knowledge.

When the student has reached the verge of Sudden Enlightenment, that is the time when the Master can help him the most. When one is about to make the leap, a certain assistance, no matter how small, is a great help. The Ch'an Masters at this stage used to practice what they called the method of "stick or yell" to help the leap to Enlightenment. Ch'an literature reports many incidents in which a Master, having asked his student to consider some problem, suddenly gave him several blows with a stick or yelled at him. If these acts were done at the right moment, the result would be a Sudden Enlightenment for the student. The explanation would seem to be that the physical act, thus performed, shocks the student into that psychological awareness of enlightenment for which he has long been preparing.

To describe Sudden Enlightenment, the Ch'an Masters use the metaphor of "the bottom of a tub falling out." When this happens, all its contents are suddenly gone. In the same way, when one is suddenly enlightened, he finds all his problems suddenly solved. They are solved not in the sense that he gains some positive solution for them, but in the sense that all the problems have ceased any longer to be problems. That is why the *Tao* is called "the indubitable *Tao*."

The Attainment of Non-attainment

The attainment of Sudden Enlightenment does not entail the attainment of anything further. The Ch'an Master Ch'ing-yüan, known as the Master of Shu-chou (died 1120), said: "If you now comprehend it, where is that which you did not comprehend before? What you were deluded about before is what you are now enlightened about, and what you are now enlightened about is what you were deluded about before." (*Recorded Sayings of Ancient Worthies, chüan* 32.) As we have seen in the last chapter, the real is the phenomenal, according to Seng-chao and Tao-sheng. In Ch'anism there is the common expression that "the mountain is the mountain, the river is the river." In one's state of delusion, one sees the mountain as the mountain and the river as the river. But after Enlightenment one still sees the mountain as the mountain and the river as the river.

The Ch'an Masters also use another common expression: "Riding an ass to search for the ass." By this they mean a search for reality outside of the phenomenal, in other words, to search for *Nirvana* outside of the Wheel of Birth and Death. Shu-chou said: "There are only two diseases: one is riding an ass to search for the ass; the other is riding an ass and being unwilling to dismount. You say that riding an ass to search for the ass is silly and that he who does it should be punished. This is a very serious disease. But I tell you, do not search for the ass at all. The intelligent man, understanding my meaning, stops to search for the ass, and thus the deluded state of his mind ceases to exist.

"But if, having found the ass, one is unwilling to dismount, this disease is most difficult to cure. I say to you, do not ride the ass at all. You yourself are the ass. Everything is the ass. Why do you ride on it? If you ride, you cannot cure your disease. But if you do not ride, the universe is as a great expanse open to your view. With these two diseases expelled, nothing remains to affect your mind. This is spiritual cultivation. You need do nothing more." (*Ibid.*) If one insists that after attaining Enlightenment one will still attain something else, this is to ride an ass and be unwilling to dismount.

Huang-po said: "[If there be Enlightenment], speech or silence, activity or inactivity, and every sight and sound, all pertain to Buddha. Where should you go to find the Buddha? Do not place a head on top of a head or a mouth beside a mouth." (*Recorded Sayings of Ancient Worthies, chüan* 3.) If there be Enlightenment, everything pertains to Buddha and everywhere there is Buddha. It is said that one Ch'an monk went into a temple and spat on the statue of the

Buddha. When he was criticized, he said: "Please show me a place where there is no Buddha." (*Record of the Transmission of the Light, chüan* 27.)

Thus the Ch'an sage lives just as everyone else lives, and does what everyone else does. In passing from delusion to Enlightenment, he has left his mortal humanity behind and has entered sagehood. But after that he still has to leave sagehood behind and to enter once more into mortal humanity. This is described by the Ch'an Masters as "rising yet another step over the top of the hundred-foot bamboo." The top of the bamboo symbolizes the climax of the achievement of Enlightenment. "Rising yet another step" means that after Enlightenment has come, the sage still has other things to do. What he has to do, however, is no more than the ordinary things of daily life. As Nan-ch'uan said: "After coming to understand the other side, you come back and live on this side." (*Recorded Sayings of Ancient Worthies, chüan* 12.)

Although the sage continues living on this side, his understanding of the other side is not in vain. Although what he does is just what everyone else does, yet it has a different significance to him. As Huihai, known as the Master of Pai-ch'ang (died 814), said: "That which before Enlightenment is called lustful anger, is after Enlightenment called the Buddha Wisdom. The man is no different from what he was before; it is only that what he does is different." (*Recorded Sayings of Ancient Worthies, chüan* 1.) It would seem that there must be some textual error in this last sentence. What Pai-ch'ang apparently intended to say was: "What the man does is no different from what he did before; it is only that the man himself is not the same as he was."

The man is not the same, because although what he does is what everyone else does, he has no attachment to anything. This is the meaning of the common Ch'an saying: "To eat all day and yet not swallow a single grain; to wear clothes all day and yet not touch a single thread." (*Recorded Sayings of Ancient Worthies, chüan* 3 and 16.)

There is yet another common saying: "In carrying water and chopping firewood: therein lies the wonderful *Tao*." (*Record of the Transmission of the Light, chüan* 8.) One may ask: If this is so, does not the wonderful *Tao* also lie in serving one's family and the state? If we were to draw the logical conclusion from the Ch'an doctrines that have been analyzed above, we should be forced to answer yes. The Ch'an Masters themselves, however, did not give this logical answer. It was reserved for the Neo-Confucianists, who are the subject of our next several chapters, to do so.

CHAPTER 23

NEO-CONFUCIANISM:
THE COSMOLOGISTS

In 589, after centuries of division, China was again unified by the Sui dynasty (590-617). The Sui, however, soon gave way to the powerful and highly centralized dynasty of T'ang (618-906). Both culturally and politically the T'ang was a golden age in China, which equalled and in some ways surpassed that of Han.

The examination system for the selection of officials, in which the Confucian Classics held a pre-eminent position, was reestablished in 622. In 628 Emperor T'ai-tsung (627-649) ordered that a Confucian temple be established in the Imperial University, and in 630 he again ordered scholars to prepare an official edition of the Confucian Classics. As part of this work, standard commentaries on the Classics were selected from among the numerous commentaries that had been written before that time, and official subcommentaries were written to elucidate these standard commentaries. The resulting Classical texts, with their official commentaries and subcommentaries, were then commanded by the Emperor to be taught in the Imperial University. In this way Confucianism was reaffirmed as the official teaching of the state.

But Confucianism had by this time already lost the vitality which it had once manifested in the form of such men as Mencius, Hsün Tzu, and Tung Chung-shu. The original texts were there, and their commentaries and subcommentaries were even more numerous than before, yet they failed to meet the spiritual interest and needs of the age. After the revival of Taoism and the introduction of Buddhism, people had become more interested in metaphysical problems and in what I call super-moral values, or, as they were then phrased, the problems of the nature and Destiny (of man). As we have seen in chapters four, seven, and fifteen, discussions on such problems are not lacking in such Confucian works as the *Confucian Analects*, the *Mencius*, the *Doctrine of the Mean*, and especially the *Book of Changes*. These, however, needed a genuinely new interpretation and elucidation in order to meet the problems of the new age, and this type of interpretation was as yet lacking despite the efforts of the Emperor's scholars.

Han Yü and Li Ao

It was not until the latter part of the T'ang dynasty that there arose two men, Han Yü (768-824) and Li Ao (died c. 844), who really tried to reinterpret such works as the *Ta Hsüeh* or *Great Learning* and *Chung Yung* or *Doctrine of the Mean*, in such a way as would answer the problems of their time. In his essay titled *Yüan Tao* or "On the Origin and Nature of the Truth," Han Yü wrote: "What I call the *Tao* is not what has hitherto been called the *Tao* by the Taoists and the Buddhists. Yao [a traditional sage-king of antiquity] transmitted the *Tao* to Shun [another traditional sage-king supposed to be the successor of Yao]. Shun transmitted it to Yü [successor of Shun and founder of the Hsia dynasty]. Yü transmitted it to [Kings] Wen and Wu and the Duke of Chou [the three founders of the Chou dynasty]. Wen and Wu and the Duke of Chou transmitted it to Confucius, and Confucius transmitted it to Mencius. After Mencius, it was no longer transmitted. Hsün [Tzu] and Yang [Hsiung] selected from it, but without reaching the essential portion; they discussed it, but without sufficient clarity." (*Ch'ang-li Hsien-sheng Chi*, or *Collected Works of Han Yü*, chüan 11.)

And Li Ao, in an essay titled "On the Restoration of the Nature," writes very similarly: "The ancient Sages transmitted this teaching to Yen Tzu [i.e., Yen Hui, the favored disciple of Confucius]. Tzu-ssu, the grandson of Confucius, received the teaching of his grandfather and composed the *Doctrine of the Mean* in forty-seven sections which he transmitted to Mencius. . . . Alas, though writings dealing with the nature and Destiny are still preserved, none of the scholars understand them, and therefore they all plunge into Taoism and Buddhism. Ignorant people say that the followers of the Master [i.e., of Confucius] are incapable of investigating the theories on the nature and Destiny, and everybody believes them. When some one asked me about this, I transmitted to him what I knew. . . . My

hope is that this long obstructed and abandoned Truth may be transmitted in the world." (*Li Wen-kung Chi* or *Collected Works of Li
Ao, chüan* 2.)

The theory of the transmission of the Truth from Yao and Shun
downward, though already roughly suggested by Mencius (*Mencius*
VIIb, 38), was evidently reinspired in Han Yü and Li Ao by the
Ch'an theory that the esoteric teaching of the Buddha had been
transmitted through a line of Patriarchs to Hung-jen and Hui-neng.
At a later time one of the Ch'eng brothers (see chapter 24) even
stated unequivocally that the *Chung Yung* or *Doctrine of the Mean*
was the esoteric teaching of Confucius. (Quoted by Chu Hsi in his
introduction to his *Commentary* on the *Chung Yung*.) It was widely
believed that the transmission of the Truth had become interrupted
after Mencius. Li Ao, however, apparently felt that he himself possessed a certain understanding of it, and that through his teaching he
could thus act as a continuator of Mencius. To do this became the
ambition of all Neo-Confucianists after Li Ao's time. All of them
accepted Han Yü's theory of the orthodox line of transmission of
the *Tao* or Truth, and maintained that they were themselves links
in that transmission. Their claim is not without justification, because,
as we shall see in this and the following chapters, Neo-Confucianism
is indeed the continuation of the idealistic wing of ancient Confucianism, and especially of the mystic tendency of Mencius. That is
the reason why these men have been known as the *Tao hsüeh chia*
and their philosophy as the *Tao hsüeh*, i.e., the Study of the *Tao* or
Truth. The term Neo-Confucianism is a newly coined western
equivalent for *Tao hsüeh*.

There are three lines of thought that can be traced as the main
sources of Neo-Confucianism. The first, of course, is Confucianism
itself. The second is Buddhism, together with Taoism via the medium
of Ch'anism, for of all the schools of Buddhism, Ch'anism was the
most influential at the time of the formation of Neo-Confucianism.
To the Neo-Confucianists, Ch'anism and Buddhism are synonymous
terms, and, as stated in the last chapter, in one sense Neo-Confucianism may be said to be the logical development of Ch'anism. Finally,
the third is the Taoist religion, of which the cosmological views of
the *Yin-Yang* School formed an important element. The cosmology
of the Neo-Confucianists is chiefly connected with this line of
thought.

These three lines of thought were heterogeneous and even in many respects contradictory. Hence it took time for philosophers to make a unity out of them, especially since this unity was not simply an eclecticism, but a genuine system forming a homogeneous whole. Therefore although the beginning of Neo-Confucianism may be traced back to Han Yü and Li Ao, its system of thought did not become clearly formed until the eleventh century. This was the time when the Sung dynasty (960-1279), which reunited China after a period of confusion following the collapse of the T'ang, was at the height of its splendor and prosperity. The earliest of the Neo-Confucianists were chiefly interested in cosmology.

Cosmology of Chou Tun-yi

The first cosmological philosopher is Chou Tun-yi, better known as the Master of Lien-hsi (1017-73). He was a native of Tao-chou in the present Hunan province, and in his late years lived on the famous mountain, Lu-shan, the same place where Hui-yüan and Tao-sheng had taught Buddhism, as described in chapter twenty-one. Long before his time, some of the religious Taoists had prepared a number of mystic diagrams as graphic portrayals of the esoteric principles by which they believed a properly initiated individual could attain to immortality. Chou Tun-yi is said to have come into possession of one of these diagrams, which he thereupon reinterpreted and modified into a diagram of his own designed to illustrate the process of cosmic evolution. Or rather, he studied and developed the ideas found in certain passages in the "Appendices" of the *Book of Changes*, and used the Taoist diagram by way of illustration. His resulting diagram is called the *T'ai-chi T'u* or *Diagram of the Supreme Ultimate*, and his interpretation of it is called the *T'ai-chi T'u Shuo* or *Explanation of the Diagram of the Supreme Ultimate*. The *Shuo* or *Explanation* can be read quite intelligibly without referring to the diagram itself.

The text of the *Explanation* reads as follows: "The Ultimateless [*Wu Chi*]! And yet the Supreme Ultimate [*T'ai Chi*]! The Supreme Ultimate through Movement produces the Yang. This Movement, having reached its limit, is followed by Quiescence, and by this Quiescence, it produces the Yin. When Quiescence has reached its limit, there is a return to Movement. Thus Movement and Quiescence, in alternation, become each the source of the other. The distinction between the *Yin* and *Yang* is determined and the Two Forms [i.e., the *Yin* and *Yang*] stand revealed.

"By the transformations of the *Yang* and the union therewith of the *Yin*, Water, Fire, Wood, Metal and Soil are produced. These Five Ethers [*ch'i*, i.e., Elements] become diffused in harmonious order, and the four seasons proceed in their course.

"The Five Elements are the one *Yin* and *Yang*; the *Yin* and *Yang* are the one Supreme Ultimate; and the Supreme Ultimate is fundamentally the Ultimateless. The Five Elements come into being, each having its own particular nature.

"The true substance of the Ultimateless and the essence of the Two [Forms] and Five [Elements] unite in mysterious union, so that consolidation ensues. The principle of *Ch'ien* [the trigram symbolizing the *Yang*]becomes the male element, and the principle of *K'un* [the trigram symbolizing the *Yin*] becomes the female element. The Two Ethers [the *Yin* and *Yang*] by their interaction operate to produce all things, and these in their turn produce and reproduce, so that transformation and change continue without end.

"It is man alone, however, who receives these in their highest excellence and hence is the most intelligent [of all beings]. His bodily form thereupon is produced and his spirit develops intelligence and consciousness. The five principles of his nature [the five constant virtues corresponding to the Five Elements] react [to external phenomena], so that the distinction between good and evil emerges and the myriad phenomena of conduct appear. The sage regulates himself by means of the mean, correctness, human-heartedness, and righteousness, and takes Quiescence as the essential. [Chou Tun-yi himself comments on this: 'Having no desire, he is therefore in the state of Quiescence.'] Thus he establishes himself as the highest standard for mankind. . . ." (*Chou Lien-hsi Chi* or *Collected Works of Chou Tun-yi, chüan* 1.)

In the *Book of Changes*, "Appendix III," it is said: "In the *Yi* there is the Supreme Ultimate, which produces the Two Forms." Chou Tun-yi's *Explanation* is a development of the idea of this passage. Brief though it is, it provides the basic outline for the cosmology of Chu Hsi (1130-1200), one of the greatest, if not the greatest, of the Neo-Confucianists, about whom I shall have more to say in chapter twenty-five.

Method of Spiritual Cultivation

The ultimate purpose of Buddhism is to teach men how to achieve Buddhahood—a problem that was one of the most vital to the people of that time. Likewise, the ultimate purpose of Neo-Confucianism is to teach men how to achieve Confucian Sagehood. The difference between the Buddha of Buddhism and the Sage of Neo-Confucianism is that while the Buddha must promote his spiritual cultivation outside of society and the human world, the Sage must do so within these human bonds. The most important development in Chinese Buddhism was its attempt to depreciate the other-worldliness of original Buddhism. This attempt came close to success when the Ch'an Masters stated that "in carrying water and chopping firewood, therein lies the wonderful *Tao*." But, as I said in the last chapter, they did not push this idea to its logical conclusion by saying that in serving one's family and the state therein also lies the wonderful *Tao*. The reason, of course, is that, once they had said this, their teaching would have ceased to be Buddhism.

For the Neo-Confucianists, too, how to achieve Sagehood is one of the main problems, and Chou Tun-yi's answer is that one should "be quiescent," which he further defines as a state of *wu-yü* or "having no desires." In his second major treatise, the *T'ung Shu* or *General Principles of the Book of Changes*, we find that by *wu-yü* he means much the same as the *wu-wei* (having no effort) and *wu-hsin* (having no mind) of Taoism and Ch'anism. The fact that he uses *wu-yü*, however, instead of these other two terms, shows how he attempts to move away from the other-worldliness of Buddhism. So far as the terms are concerned, the *wu* in *wu-yü* is not so all inclusive as that in *wu hsin*.

In the *T'ung Shu* Chou Tun-yi writes: "*Wu-yü* results in vacuity when in quiescence, and straightforwardness when in movement. Vacuity in quiescence leads to enlightenment, and enlightenment leads to comprehension. [Likewise] straightforwardness in movement leads to impartiality, and impartiality leads to universality. One is almost [a sage when one has] such enlightenment, comprehension, impartiality, and universality." (*Collected Works, chüan* 5.)

The word *yü* used by the Neo-Confucianists always means selfish desire or simply selfishness. Sometimes they prefix it by the word *ssu* (selfish), in order to make their meaning clearer. Chou Tun-yi's idea in this passage may be illustrated by a passage from the *Mencius*, often quoted by the Neo-Confucianists: "If today men suddenly see a child about to fall into a well, they will without exception experience a feeling of alarm and distress. This will not be as a way whereby to gain the favor of the child's parents, nor whereby they may seek the praise of their neighbors and friends, nor are they so because they dislike the reputation [of being unvirtuous]." (*Mencius*, IIa, 6.)

According to the Neo-Confucianists, what Mencius here describes is the natural and spontaneous response of any man when placed in such a situation. Man is by nature fundamentally good. Therefore his innate state is one in which he has no selfish desires in his mind, or as Chou expresses it, one of "vacuity in quiescence." As applied to conduct, it will lead to an immediate impulse to try to save the child, and this sort of intuitive conduct is what Chou calls "straightforwardness in movement." If, however, the man does not act on his first impulse, but pauses instead to think the matter over, he may then consider that the child in distress is a son of his enemy, and therefore he should not save it, or that it is the son of his friend and therefore he should save it. In either case, he is motivated by secondary selfish thoughts and thereby loses both his original state of vacuity in quiescence and the corollary state of straightforwardness in movement.

When the mind lacks all selfish desires it becomes, according to the Neo-Confucianists, like a brilliant mirror, which is always ready to reflect objectively any object that comes before it. The brilliancy of the mirror is compared with the mind's "enlightenment," and its readiness to reflect with the mind's "comprehension." When the mind lacks any selfish desires, its natural response to external stimuli results in actions that are straightforward. Being straightforward, they are impartial, and being impartial, they are carried out without discrimination. Such is their nature of universality.

This is Chou Tun-yi's method of achieving Sagehood, and consists, like that of the Ch'an monks, of living naturally and acting naturally.

Cosmology of Shao Yung

Another cosmological philosopher to be mentioned in this chapter is Shao Yung, known as the Master of Pai-ch'üan (1011-77). He was a native of the present Honan province. Though in a way somewhat

different from that of Chou Tun-yi, he too developed his cosmological theory from the *Book of Changes,* and, like Chou, made use of
diagrams to illustrate his theory.

In chapter eighteen we have seen that the Han dynasty saw the
appearance of a number of *wei shu* or apocrypha, which were supposed to complement the original Six Classics. In the *Yi Wei,* or
Apocryphal Treatise on the Book of Changes, the theory is developed
of the "influence" of each of the sixty-four hexagrams upon a certain
period of the year. According to this theory, each of the twelve
months is under the jurisdiction of several of the hexagrams, one of
which plays a leading role in the affairs of that month and is hence
known as its "sovereign hexagram." These sovereign hexagrams are
Fu ☷☳ , *Lin* ☷☱ , *T'ai* ☷☰ , *Ta Chuang* ☳☰ , *Chüeh* ☱☰ ,
Ch'ien ☰☰ , *Kou* ☰☴ , *Tun* ☰☶ , *P'i* ☰☷ , *Kuan* ☴☷ ,
Po ☶☷ , and *K'un* ☷☷ . The reason for their importance is that
they graphically represent the waxing and waning of the *Yang* and
Yin principles throughout the year.

In these hexagrams, as we have seen in chapter twelve, the unbroken lines represent the *Yang,* which is associated with heat, while
the broken lines represent the *Yin,* which is associated with cold. The
hexagram *Fu* ☷☳ , with five broken lines above and one unbroken
line below, is the "sovereign hexagram" of that month in which the
Yin (cold) has reached its apogee and the *Yang* (heat) then begins
to reappear. That is the eleventh month of the traditional Chinese
calendar, the month in which the winter solstice occurs. The hexagram *Ch'ien* ☰☰ , with its six unbroken lines, is the "sovereign
hexagram" of the fourth month, in which the *Yang* is at its apogee.
The hexagram *Kou* ☰☴ , with five unbroken lines above and one
broken line below, is the "sovereign hexagram" of the fifth month,
in which the summer solstice is followed by the rebirth of the *Yin.*
And the hexagram *K'un* ☷☷ , with its six broken lines, is the "sovereign hexagram" of the tenth month, in which the *Yin* is at its
apogee, just before the rebirth of the *Yang* which follows the winter
solstice. The other hexagrams indicate the intermediate stages in the
waxing and waning of the *Yin* and *Yang.*

The twelve hexagrams *in toto* constitute a cycle. After the influence of the *Yin* has reached its apogee, that of the *Yang* appears at
the very bottom of the following hexagram. Rising upward, it becomes steadily greater month by month and hexagram by hexagram,

until it reaches its apogee. Then the *Yin* again appears at the bottom of the following hexagram, and grows in its turn until it too reigns supreme. It is followed in turn by the reborn *Yang*, and thus the cycle of the year and of the hexagrams begins again. Such is the inevitable course of nature.

It is to be noticed that Shao Yung's theory of the universe gives further illumination to the theory of the twelve sovereign hexagrams. As in the case of Chou Tun-yi, he deduces his system from a statement in "Appendix III" of the *Book of Changes* which reads: "In the *Yi* there is the Supreme Ultimate. The Supreme Ultimate produces the Two Forms. The Two Forms produce the Four Emblems, and the Four Emblems produce the eight trigrams." To illustrate this process, Shao Yung made a diagram as follows:

Greater	Greater	Lesser	Lesser	Lesser	Lesser	Greater	Greater
Softness	Hardness	Softness	Hardness	*Yin*	*Yang*	*Yin*	*Yang*

Softness	Hardness	*Yin*	*Yang*

Quiescence	Movement

The first or lower tier of this diagram shows the Two Forms, which, in Shao Yung's system, are not the *Yin* and *Yang* but Movement and Quiescence. The second tier, looked at in conjunction with the first, shows the Four Emblems. For instance, by combining the unbroken line beneath *Yang* in the middle tier, with the unbroken line beneath Movement below, we obtain two unbroken lines which are the emblem of the *Yang*. That is to say, the *Yang* is not, for Shao Yung, represented by a single unbroken line ———— , but by two unbroken lines ════ . Likewise, by combining the broken line beneath *Yin* in the central tier with the unbroken line beneath Movement below, we obtain one ·broken line above and one unbroken line below, which are the emblem of *Yin*. That is to say, the emblem of the *Yin* is not —— —— but ══ ══ .

In the same way, the third or highest tier looked at in conjunction with both the central and lower tier, represents the eight trigrams. For instance, by combining the unbroken line beneath Greater *Yang* above with the unbroken line beneath *Yang* in the middle and the unbroken line beneath Movement below, we obtain a combination of three unbroken lines, which is the trigram for *Ch'ien*, ☰ . Likewise, by combining the broken line beneath Greater *Yin* above with the unbroken line beneath *Yang* in the middle and the unbroken line beneath Movement below, we obtain the combination of one broken line above and two unbroken lines below, which is the trigram for *Tui*, ☱ . And still again, by combining the unbroken line beneath Lesser *Yang* above with the broken line beneath *Yin* in the middle and the unbroken line beneath Movement below, we obtain the trigram for *Li*, ☲ . By following the same process through the other combinations, we obtain the entire eight trigrams in the following sequence: *Ch'ien* ☰ , *Tui* ☱ , *Li* ☲ , *Chen* ☳ , *Sun* ☴ , *K'an* ☵ , *Ken* ☶ , and *K'un* ☷ . Each of these trigrams represents a certain principle or influence.

The materialization of these principles results in Heaven, Earth, and all things of the universe. As Shao Yung says: "Heaven is produced from Movement and Earth from Quiescence. The alternating interplay of Movement and Quiescence gives utmost development to the course of Heaven and Earth. At the first appearance of Movement, the *Yang* is produced, and this Movement having reached its apogee, the *Yin* is then produced. The alternating interplay of the *Yang* and *Yin* gives utmost development to the functioning aspect of Heaven. With the first appearance of Quiescence, Softness is produced, and this Quiescence having reached its apogee, Hardness is then produced. The alternating interplay of Hardness and Softness gives utmost development to the functioning aspect of Earth." * The terms Hardness and Softness are, like the others, borrowed by Shao Yung from "Appendix III" of the *Book of Changes*, which says: "The Way of Heaven is established with the *Yin* and *Yang*. The Way of Earth is established with Softness and Hardness. The Way of Man is established with human-heartedness and righteousness."

Shao Yung writes further: "The Greater *Yang* constitutes the sun, the Greater *Yin* the moon, the Lesser *Yang* the stars, the Lesser *Yin* the zodiacal spaces. The interplay of the sun, moon, stars, and zodiacal spaces gives utmost development to the substance of Heaven.

* *Kuan-wu P'ien* or "Observation of Things," Inner Chapter, in the *Huang-chi Ching-shih* or *Cosmological Chronology*, ch. 11a.

The Greater Softness constitutes water, the Greater Hardness fire, the Lesser Softness soil, and the Lesser Hardness stone. The interplay of water, fire, soil, and stone gives utmost development to the substance of Earth." (*Ibid.*)

This is Shao Yung's theory of the origin of the universe, deduced strictly from his diagram. In this diagram, the Supreme Ultimate itself is not actually shown, but it is understood as being symbolized by the empty space beneath the first tier of the diagram. Shao Yung writes: "The Supreme Ultimate is a Unity which does not move. It produces a Duality, and this Duality is spirituality. . . . Spirituality produces numbers, the numbers produce emblems, and the emblems produce implements [i.e., individual things]." (*Ibid.*, ch. 12b.) These numbers and emblems are illustrated in the diagram.

Law of the Evolution of Things

By adding a fourth, fifth, and sixth tier to the above diagram, and following the same procedure of combination that was used there, we arrive at a diagram in which all the sixty-four hexagrams (derived from combination of the eight primary trigrams) are shown. If this diagram is then cut into two equal halves, each of which is bent into a half circle, and if the two half circles are then joined together, we have another of Shao's diagrams, known as "the circular diagram of the sixty-four hexagrams."

Upon examining this diagram (here, for the sake of simplicity, reduced from sixty-four to the twelve "sovereign hexagrams"), we see that these twelve appear in it in their proper sequence as follows (looking from the center, and progressing clockwise from above):

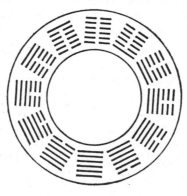

This sequence is automatically arrived at by what is called "the method of doubling," because, as we have seen, the number of emblems in each tier in the diagram is always double that of the tier immediately below, so that combination of all six tiers results in the sixty-four hexagrams at the top. This simple progression makes the diagram appear as both something natural and at the same time mysterious. As a result, it was hailed by most of the Neo-Confucianists as one of the greatest discoveries of Shao Yung, in which could be found the universal law governing the evolution of all things, and the key to the mystery of the universe.

This law not only applies to the alternation of the seasons throughout the year, but also to the alternation of day and night every twenty-four hours. According to Shao Yung and the other Neo-Confucianists, the *Yin* can be interpreted as merely the negation of the *Yang*. Hence, if the *Yang* is the constructive force of the universe, the *Yin* is its destructive principle. Interpreting the *Yin* and *Yang* in this sense, the law represented by the diagram indicates the way in which all things of the universe go through phases of construction and destruction. Thus, the first or lowest line of the hexagram *Fu* ䷗ shows the beginning of the phase of construction, and in hexagram *Ch'ien* ䷀ we find the completion of this phase. The first line of the hexagram *Kou* ䷫ shows the beginning of the phase of destruction, and in hexagram *K'un* ䷁ this phase is completed. In this way the diagram graphically illustrates the universal law that everything involves its own negation, a principle that was stressed both by Lao Tzu and the "Appendices" of the *Book of Changes*.

The world as a whole is no exception to this universal law. Thus Shao Yung maintains that with the first line of the hexagram *Fu*, the world comes into existence. With the hexagram *T'ai*, the individual things that belong to it begin to be produced. Mankind then appears, and with the hexagram *Ch'ien* the golden age of civilization is reached. There follows a process of continuous decay, until with the hexagram *Po* all individual things disintegrate, and with the hexagram *K'un* the whole world ceases to be. Thereupon another world begins with the first line of the recurring hexagram *Fu*, and the whole process is repeated. Each world which is thus created and destroyed has a duration of 129,600 years.

Shao Yung's major work is the *Huang-chi Ching-shih*, which is an elaborate chronological diagram of our existing world. According to its chronology, the golden age of our world has already passed away. It was the age of Yao, the traditional philosopher king of China who reputedly ruled in the twenty-fourth century B.C. We today are now in an age corresponding to the hexagram *Po*, the time of the beginning of decline of all things. As we have seen in chapter fourteen, most Chinese philosophers have considered the process of history to be one of continuous degeneration, in which everything of the present falls short of the ideal past. Shao Yung's theory gives this view a metaphysical justification.

The theory that everything involves its own negation sounds Hegelian. But according to Hegel, when a thing is negated, a new thing commences on a higher level, whereas according to Lao Tzu and the "Appendices" of the *Book of Changes*, when a thing is negated, the new thing simply repeats the old. This is a philosophy characteristic of an agrarian people, as I pointed out in chapter two.

Cosmology of Chang Tsai

The third cosmological philosopher to be mentioned in this chapter is Chang Tsai, known as the Master of Heng-ch'ü (1020-77). He was a native of the present Shensi province. He too, though from yet another point of view, developed a cosmological theory based on the "Appendices" of the *Book of Changes*. In this he especially emphasized the idea of *Ch'i*, a concept which became more and more important in the cosmological and metaphysical theories of the later Neo-Confucianists. The word *ch'i* literally means gas or ether. In Neo-Confucianism its meaning is sometimes more abstract and sometimes more concrete, according to the different systems of the particular philosophers. When its meaning is more abstract, it approaches the concept of matter, as found in the philosophy of Plato and Aristotle, in contrast to the Platonic Idea or the Aristotelian form. In this sense, it means the primary undifferentiated material out of which all individual things are formed. When, however, its meaning is concrete, it means the physical matter that makes up all existing individual things. It is in this concrete sense that Chang Tsai speaks of *Ch'i*.

Chang Tsai, like his predecessors, bases his cosmological theory on the passage in "Appendix III" of the *Book of Changes* that states:

"In the *Yi* there is the Supreme Ultimate which produces the Two Forms [i.e., the *Yin* and *Yang*]." For him, however, the Supreme Ultimate is nothing other than the *Ch'i*. In his main work, the *Cheng Meng* or *Correct Discipline for Beginners*, he writes: "The Great Harmony is known as the *Tao* [by which he here means the Supreme Ultimate]. Because in it there are interacting qualities of floating and sinking, rising and falling, movement and quiescence, therefore there appear in it the beginnings of the emanating forces which agitate one another, overcome or are overcome by one another, and contract or expand, one with regard to the other." (*Chang-tzu Ch'üan-shu* or *Collected Works of the Master Chang, chüan* 2.)

The Great Harmony is a name for the *Ch'i* in its entirety, which Chang Tsai also describes as "wandering air." (*Ibid.*) The qualities of floating, rising, and movement are those of the *Yang*, while those of sinking, falling, and quiescence are those of the *Yin*. The *Ch'i*, when influenced by the *Yang* qualities, floats and rises, while when influenced by the *Yin* qualities, it sinks and falls. As a result the *Ch'i* is constantly either condensing or dispersing. Its condensation results in the formation of concrete things; its dispersion results in the dissolution of these same things.

In the *Cheng Meng*, Chang Tsai writes: "When the *Ch'i* condenses, its visibility becomes apparent so that there are then the shapes [of individual things]. When it disperses, its visibility is no longer apparent and there are no shapes. At the time of its condensation, can one say otherwise than that this is but temporary? But at the time of its dispersing, can one hastily say that it is then non-existent?" (*Ibid.*) Thus Chang Tsai tries to get away from the Taoist and Buddhist idea of *Wu* (Non-being). He says: "If one knows the Void is the *Ch'i*, one knows that there is no *Wu*." The Void is not really an absolute vacuum; it is simply the *Ch'i* in its state of dispersion in which it is no longer visible.

One particularly famous passage of the *Cheng Meng* has become known as the *Hsi Ming* or "Western Inscription," because it was separately inscribed on the western wall of Chang Tsai's study. In this passage Chang maintains that since all things in the universe are constituted of one and the same *Ch'i*, therefore men and all other things are but part of one great body. We should serve *Ch'ien* and *K'un* (by which Chang means Heaven and Earth) as we do our own parents, and regard all men as we do our brothers. We should extend the virtue of filial piety and practice it through service to the universal parents. Yet, no extraordinary acts are needed for this service. Every moral activity, if one can understand it, is an activity that serves the universal parents. If, for instance, one loves other men simply because they are members of the same society as one's own, then one is doing his social duty and is serving society. But if one loves them not merely because they are members of the same society, but also because they are children of the universal parents, then by loving them one not only serves society, but at the same time serves the parents of the universe as a whole. The passage concludes with the saying: "In life I follow and serve [the universal parents], and when death comes, I rest." (*Ibid.*)

This essay has been greatly admired by later Neo-Confucianists, because it clearly distinguished the Confucian attitude towards life from that of Buddhism and of Taoist philosophy and religion. Chang Tsai writes elsewhere: "The Great Void [i.e., the Great Harmony, the *Tao*] cannot but consist of *Ch'i*; this *Ch'i* cannot but condense to form all things; and these things cannot but become dispersed so as to form [once more] the Great Void. The perpetuation of these movements in a cycle is inevitable and thus spontaneous." (*Ibid.*, *chüan* 2.) The sage is one who fully understands this course. Therefore, he neither tries to be outside it, as do the Buddhists, who seek to break the chain of causation and thus bring life to an end; nor does he try to prolong his life, as do the religious Taoists, who seek to nurture their body and thus remain as long as possible within the human sphere. The sage, because he understands the nature of the universe, therefore knows that "life entails no gain nor death any loss." (*Ibid.*) Hence he simply tries to live a normal life. In life he does what his duty as a member of society and as a member of the universe requires him to do, and when death comes, he "rests."

He does what every man should do, but because of his understanding, what he does acquires new significance. The Neo-Confucianists developed a point of view from which all the moral activities valued by the Confucianists acquire a further value that is super-moral. They all have in them that quality that the Ch'anists called the wonderful *Tao*. It is in this sense that Neo-Confucianism is actually a further development of Ch'anism.

CHAPTER 24

NEO-CONFUCIANISM:
THE BEGINNING OF THE
TWO SCHOOLS

Neo-Confucianism came to be divided into two main schools, which, by happy coincidence, were initiated by two brothers, known as the two Ch'eng Masters. Ch'eng Yi (1033-1108), the younger brother, initiated a school which was completed by Chu Hsi (1130-1200) and was known as the Ch'eng-Chu school or *Li hsüeh* (School of Laws or Principles). Ch'eng Hao (1032-1085), the elder brother, initiated another school which was continued by Lu Chiu-yüan (1139-1193) and completed by Wang Shou-jen (1473-1529), and was known as the Lu-Wang school or *Hsin hsüeh* (School of Mind) The full significance of the difference between the two schools was not recognized at the time of the two Ch'eng Masters themselves, but Chu Hsi and Lu Chiu-yüan began a great controversy which has been carried on until the present day.

As we shall see in the following chapters, the main issue between the two groups was really one of fundamental philosophical importance. In terms of Western philosophy, it was one as to whether the laws of nature are or are not legislated by the mind or Mind. That has been the issue between Platonic realism and Kantian idealism, and may be said to be *the* issue in metaphysics. If it were solved, there would not be much other controversy left. In this chapter I am not going to discuss this issue in detail, but only to suggest its beginnings in the history of Chinese philosophy.

Ch'eng Hao's Idea of Jen

The Ch'eng brothers were natives of the present Honan province. The elder of them, Ch'eng Hao, was known as Master Ming-tao, and the younger, Ch'eng Yi, as the Master of Yi-ch'uan. Their father was a friend of Chou Tun-yi and the cousin of Chang Tsai. Hence in their youth the Ch'eng brothers received some teaching from Chou Tun-yi, and later they constantly held discussions with Chang Tsai. Furthermore, they lived not far from Shao Yung, with whom they often met. The close contact between these five philosophers was certainly a very happy incident in the history of Chinese philosophy.

Ch'eng Hao greatly admired Chang Tsai's *Hsi Ming* or "Western Inscription," because its central theme of the oneness of all things is also the main idea in his philosophy. According to him, oneness with all things is the main characteristic of the virtue of *jen* (human-heartedness). He says: "The learner needs first to comprehend *jen*. The man of *jen* is undifferentiably one with all things. Righteousness, propriety, wisdom, and good faith, all these are *jen*. Get to comprehend this truth and cultivate it with sincerity and attentiveness, that is all that is required. . . . The *Tao* has nothing that stands in contrast to it; even the word great is inadequate to express it. The function of Heaven and Earth is our function. Mencius said that all things are complete within us. We must reflect and realize that this is really so. Then it is a source of immense joy. If we reflect and do not realize that it is really so, then there are still two things [the self and not-self] that stand in contrast with each other. Even if we try to unite the self and not-self, we still do not form a unity, and so how can there then be joy? In the 'Correcting of the Ignorant' [another name for Chang Tsai's *Hsi Ming*] there is a perfect statement of this unity. If we cultivate ourselves with this idea, there is nothing further required to be done. We must do something, and never stop and never forget, yet never help to grow, doing it without the slightest effort. This is the way of spiritual cultivation." (*Erh-Ch'eng Yi-shu* or *Literary Remains of the Two Ch'engs, chüan* 24.)

In chapter seven I have fully discussed the statement of Mencius referred to by Ch'eng Hao in the above quotation. One must do something, but "never help to grow"; this is Mencius' method for cultivating the Great Morale, a method which was greatly admired by the Neo-Confucianists. According to Ch'eng Hao, one must first understand the principle that one is originally one with all things. Then all one needs to do is to keep this in mind and act in accordance with it sincerely and attentively. Through the accumulation of such practices, one will really come to feel that one is one with all things. The statement that one must act in accordance with this principle sincerely and attentively means that there is something one must do. There must, however, be no artificial striving to achieve the unity. In this sense, one must be "without the slightest effort."

The difference between Ch'eng Hao and Mencius is that the former gives to *jen* a much more metaphysical interpretation than does the latter. "Appendix III" of the *Book of Changes* contains the statement: "The supreme virtue of Heaven and Earth is *sheng*." The word *sheng* here may mean simply production or to produce; it may also mean life or to give birth to life. In chapter fifteen I translated *sheng* as to produce, because that seems to be the meaning that best harmonizes with the ideas of the "Appendices." But according to Ch'eng Hao and other Neo-Confucianists, *sheng* really means life or to give birth to life. According to them there is a tendency toward life in all things, and this tendency constitutes the *jen* of Heaven and Earth.

It so happens that the expression "not-*jen*" is a technical term for paralysis in Chinese medicine. Ch'eng Hao says: "The doctor describes the paralysis of a man's arms or legs as not-*jen*; this is a very good description [of the disease]. The man of *jen* takes Heaven and Earth as being one with himself. To him there is nothing that is not himself. Having recognized them as himself, what cannot he do for them? If there is no such relationship with the self, it follows that there is no connection between the self and others. If the hand or foot are not-*jen*, it means that the *ch'i* [vital force] is not circulating freely and the parts [of the body] are not connected with each other." (*Ibid., chüan* 2a.)

Thus, according to Ch'eng Hao, metaphysically there is an inner connection between all things. What Mencius called the "feeling of commiseration" or the "unbearing mind" is simply an expression of this connection between ourselves and other things. It often happens, however, that our "unbearing mind" is obscured by selfishness, or, to use the Neo-Confucian term, by selfish desires or simply desires. Hence the original unity is lost. What is necessary is simply to remember that originally there is a oneness between oneself and all things, and to act accordingly with sincerity and attentiveness. In this way the original unity will be restored in due course. Such is the general idea of the philosophy of Ch'eng Hao, which Lu Chiu-yüan and Wang Shou-jen later developed in detail.

Origin of the Ch'eng-Chu Idea of Li

In chapter eight we have seen that already in early times Kung-sun Lung made clear the distinction between universals and things. He insisted that whiteness is whiteness even though nothing is in itself white in the world. It would seem that he had some idea of the Platonic distinction of the two worlds, the eternal and the temporal, the intelligible and the visible. This idea was not developed by later philosophers, however, and the philosophy of the School of Names did not become a main current in Chinese thought. On the contrary, this thought moved in another direction, and it took more than one thousand years for Chinese philosophers to turn their attention once more to the problem of eternal ideas. The two main thinkers to do so are Ch'eng Yi and Chu Hsi.

The philosophy of Ch'eng Yi and Chu Hsi, however, is not a continuation of the School of Names. They paid no attention to Kung-sun Lung or to the *ming-li* (principles based on the analysis of names) discussed by the Neo-Taoists whom we have treated in chapter nineteen. They developed their idea of *Li* (abstract Principles or Laws) directly from the "Appendices" of the *Book of Changes.* I have pointed out in chapter fifteen that a distinction exists between the *Tao* of Taoism and the *tao* of the "Appendices." The *Tao* of Taoism is the unitary first "that" from which all things in the universe come to be. The *tao* of the "Appendices," on the contrary, are multiple, and are the principles which govern each separate category of things in the universe. It is from this concept that Ch'eng Yi and Chu Hsi derived the idea of *Li.*

The immediate stimulus for Ch'eng Yi and Chu Hsi, however, seems to be the thought of Chang Tsai and Shao Yung. In the last chapter we have seen that Chang Tsai explained the appearance and disappearance of concrete particulars in terms of the condensation and dispersion of the *Ch'i.* The condensation of the *Ch'i* results in the formation and appearance of things. But this theory fails to explain the reason for the different *categories* of things. Granted that a flower and a leaf are both condensations of the *Ch'i,* we are still at a loss as to why a flower is a flower and a leaf a leaf. It is here that Ch'eng Yi's and Chu Hsi's idea of *Li* comes in. According to them, the universe as we see it is a result not only of the *Ch'i* but also of the *Li.* Different categories of things exist, because the condensation of the *Ch'i* takes place in different ways in accordance with different *Li*. A flower is a flower, because it is the condensation of the *Ch'i* taking place in accordance with the *Li* of the flower; and a leaf is a leaf, because it is the condensation of the *Ch'i* taking place in accordance with the *Li* of the leaf.

Shao Yung's diagrams also helped to suggest the idea of *Li*. According to Shao, what the diagrams represent is the law that governs the transformations of individual things. This law is antecedent not only to the diagrams, but also to the existence of individual things. Shao maintained that before the trigrams were first drawn by their discoverer, the *Book of Changes* already ideally existed. One of the Ch'eng Masters says: "[In one of his poems], Yao-fu [i.e., Shao Yung] writes: 'Before the drawing [of the trigrams by Fu Hsi, a traditional sage supposed to have lived in the twenty-ninth century B.C.], there was already the *Book of Changes*.' . . . This idea has never been said before." (*Literary Remains of the Two Ch'engs, chüan* 2a.) This theory is the same as that of the new realists, who maintain that there is a Mathematics before there is mathematics.

Ch'eng Yi's Concept of Li

The combination of the philosophy of Chang Tsai and Shao Yung suggests the distinction between what the Greek philosophers called the form and the matter of things. This distinction Ch'eng Yi and Chu Hsi made very clear. For them, just as for Plato and Aristotle, all things in the world, if they are to exist at all, must be the embodiment of some principle in some material. If a certain thing exists, there must be for it a certain principle. If there be a certain principle, however, there may or may not exist a corresponding thing. The principle is what they call *Li*, and the material is what they call *Ch'i*. The latter, for Chu Hsi, is much more abstract than is the *Ch'i* in Chang Tsai's system.

Ch'eng Yi also distinguishes between what is "within shapes" and what is "above shapes." The origin of these two terms is traceable to "Appendix III" of the *Book of Changes*: "What is above shapes is called the *Tao*; what is within shapes is called the implements." In the system of Ch'eng Yi and Chu Hsi, this distinction corresponds to that between the abstract and concrete in Western philosophy. The *Li* are the *Tao* which is "above shapes," or, as we would say, abstract; while the "implements," by which Ch'eng Yi and Chu Hsi mean particular things, are "within shapes," or, as we would say, concrete.

According to Ch'eng Yi, the *Li* are eternal, and can neither be added to nor reduced. As he says: "Existence or non-existence, addition or reduction, cannot be postulated about *Li*. All *Li* are complete in themselves; in them there can never be deficiency." (*Literary Remains of the Two Ch'engs, chüan* 2a.) Again he says: "All the *Li* are pervasively present. We cannot say that the *tao* of kingship was more when Yao [a traditional sage-king] exemplified it as a king, nor can we say that the *tao* of sonship was more when Shun [the successor of Yao, known for his filial piety] exemplified it as a son. These [the *Li*] remain what they are." (*Ibid.*) Ch'eng Yi also describes the world "above shapes" as "void, with nothing in it, yet filled with all." (*Ibid.*) It is void because in it there are no concrete things; yet it is filled with all the *Li*. All the *Li* are there eternally, no matter whether or not instances of them occur in the actual world, nor does it matter whether we human beings know of them or not.

Ch'eng Yi's method of spiritual cultivation is expressed in his famous statement: "In cultivation one needs attentiveness; in the advancement of learning, one needs the extension of knowledge." (*Literary Remains of the Two Ch'engs, chüan* 18.) The word "attentiveness" is a translation of the Chinese word *ching*, which may also be translated as seriousness or earnestness. We have seen that Ch'eng Hao also said that the "learner" must first understand that all things are originally one, and then cultivate this understanding with sincerity and attentiveness. Attentiveness is the key word used by Neo-Confucianists after this time to describe their method of spiritual cultivation. It replaces the word used by Chou Tun-Yi for this process, which was a different word also pronounced *ching* but meaning quiescence. The replacement of "quiescence" by "attentiveness" in the methodology of spiritual cultivation marks further the departure of Neo-Confucianism from Ch'anism.

As pointed out in chapter twenty-two, effort is needed for the process of cultivation. Even if one's ultimate aim is to be effortless, it requires an initial effort to attain the effortless state. This, however, the Ch'anists do not state, nor is it expressed by Chou Tun-yi's quiescence. Use of the word attentiveness, however, brings this idea of effort into the foreground.

In cultivation one must be attentive, but attentive to what? This is a controversial question between the two schools of Neo-Confucianism, which I will return to in the next two chapters.

Method of Dealing with the Emotions

In chapter twenty I said that Wang Pi maintained the theory that the sage "has emotions but is without ensnarement." It is also said in the *Chuang-tzu*: "The mind of the perfect man is like a mirror. It does not move with things, nor does it anticipate them. It responds to things, but does not retain them. Therefore the perfect man is able to deal successfully with things but is not affected by them." (Ch. 7.) Wang Pi's theory of the emotions seems to be an extension of this statement of Chuang Tzu.

The Neo-Confucian method of dealing with the emotions follows the same line as Wang Pi's. Its essential is the disconnecting of the emotions from the self. Ch'eng Hao says: "The normality of Heaven and Earth is that their mind is in all things, yet of themselves they have no mind. The normality of the sage is that his emotion follows the nature of things, yet of himself he has no emotion. Therefore, for the superior man nothing is better than being impersonal and impartial, and responding to things spontaneously as they come. The general trouble with man is that he is selfish and rationalistic. Being selfish, he cannot take action as a spontaneous response. Being rationalistic, he cannot take intuition as his natural guide. When the sage is pleased, it is because the thing is there which is rightly the object of pleasure. When the sage is angry, it is because the thing is there which is rightly the object of anger. Therefore the pleasure and anger of the sage are not connected with his mind, but with things." (*Ming-tao Wen-chi* or *Collected Writings of Ch'eng Hao*, *chüan* 3.)

This is a part of Ch'eng Hao's "Letter on the Calmness of the Nature," which was written to Chang Tsai. The impersonalness, impartiality, and action with spontaneity and without self-rationalization, of which Ch'eng Hao speaks, are the same as the vacuity and straightforwardness spoken of by Chou Tun-yi. The same illustration from Mencius that was used in connection with Chou Tun-yi can be applied here.

According to Ch'eng Hao's view, it is natural that even the sage should sometimes experience pleasure or anger. But since his mind has an impersonal, objective, and impartial attitude, when these feelings come, they are simply objective phenomena in the universe, and are not especially connected with his self. When he is pleased or angry, it is simply the external things, deserving of either pleasure or anger, that produce corresponding feelings in his mind. His mind is like a mirror on which anything may be reflected. As a result of this attitude, when the object has gone, the emotion it produced goes with it. In this way the sage, though he has emotions, is without ensnarement. Let us return to the illustration mentioned earlier. Suppose a man sees a child about to fall into a well. If he follows his natural impulse, he will immediately rush forward to save the child. His success will certainly give him pleasure and his failure will equally certainly cause him sorrow. But since his action is impersonal and impartial, once the affair is finished, his emotion is also gone. Thus he has emotions, but is without ensnarement.

Another illustration commonly used by the Neo-Confucianists is that of Yen Hui, the favorite disciple of Confucius, of whom the latter said: "Hui did not transfer his anger." (*Analects*, VI, 2.) When a man is angry, he often abuses other people and destroys things that apparently have nothing to do with his emotion at all. This is called "transferring anger." He transfers his anger from something that is the object of his anger to something that is not. The Neo-Confucianists took this statement of Confucius very seriously, and considered this quality of Yen Hui as the most significant in the great Confucian disciple, whom they considered next to Confucius himself in spiritual perfection. Thus Ch'eng Yi comments: "We must understand why it is that Yen Hui did not transfer his anger. In a bright mirror, a beautiful object produces a beautiful reflection, while an ugly object produces an ugly one. But the mirror itself has no likes or dislikes. There are some people who, being offended in their home, discharge their anger in the street. But the anger of the sage operates only in accordance with the nature of things; it is never he himself who possesses the anger. The superior man is the master of things; the small man is their slave." (*Literary Remains of the Two Ch'engs, chüan* 18.)

Thus according to the Neo-Confucianists, the reason why Yen Hui did not transfer his anger is because his emotion was not connected with the self. A thing might act to produce some emotion in his mind, just as an object may appear in a mirror, but his self was not connected with the emotion. Therefore there was nothing to be transferred to other objects. He responded to the thing that produced the emotion in his mind, but he himself was not ensnared by it. He was considered to be a happy man, and for that, was greatly admired by the Neo-Confucianists.

The Search for Happiness

In chapter twenty I have said that Neo-Confucianism attempted to find happiness in *ming-chiao* (morals, institutions). The search for happiness, indeed, is one of the professed aims of the Neo-Confucianists. Ch'eng Hao says, for example: "When we studied under Chou [Tun-yi], he always asked us to find out wherein lay the happiness of K'ung [Confucius] and Yen [Hui], and what they found enjoyable." (*Literary Remains of the Two Ch'engs, chüan* 2a.) There are, in fact, many passages in the *Analects* recording the happiness of Confucius and his disciple. Those commonly quoted by the Neo-Confucianists include the following:

"Confucius said: 'With coarse rice to eat, with only water to drink, and my bended arm for a pillow, I am happy in the midst of these things. Riches and honor acquired by means that I know to be wrong are to me as a floating cloud.'" (*Analects*, VII, 15.)

About Yen Hui, Confucius said: "Incomparable indeed was Hui. A handful of rice to eat, a gourdful of water to drink, and living in a mean street: these, others would have found unbearably depressing, but for Hui's happiness they made no difference at all. Incomparable indeed was Hui." (*Ibid.*, VI, 9.)

Another passage says that once when Confucius was sitting with several of his disciples, he asked each of them to express his desires. One replied that he would like to be minister of war in a certain state, another to be minister of finance, and still another to be master of ceremonies. But the fourth, Tseng Tien, paid no attention to what others were saying, but continued to strum his lute. When the others had finished, Confucius asked him to speak. He replied: "[My desire would be], in the last month of spring, with the dress of the season all complete, along with five or six young men, and six or seven boys, to go to wash in the river Yi, enjoy the breezes among the rain altars, and return home singing." Whereupon Confucius said: "I am with Tien." (XI, 25.)

Commenting on the first two passages, Ch'eng Yi says that there is nothing to be enjoyed in eating coarse rice and drinking water *per se*. What the passages mean is simply that Confucius and Yen Hui remained happy, despite the fact that they had only this meager fare. (See *Ch'eng-shih Ching-shuo* or *Notes on the Classics by the Ch'engs, chüan* 6.) This comment is correct in itself, but the question remains what it was that did constitute their happiness.

A certain man once asked Ch'eng Yi: "Why is it that the happiness of Yen Hui remained unaffected [by external hardships]?" Ch'eng Yi answered: "[Do you know] what it was that Yen Hui enjoyed?" The man replied: "He enjoyed the *Tao*." To which Ch'eng Yi said: "If Yen Hui enjoyed the *Tao*, he was not Yen Hui." (*Erh-Ch'eng Wai-shu* or *External Collection of Sayings of the Two Ch'engs, chüan* 7.) This statement is very much like that of the Ch'an Masters, which is why Chu Hsi, editor of the *Literary Remains of the Two Ch'engs*, did not include it there but placed it instead into the subsidiary work known as the *External Collection*. Nevertheless, the saying contains some truth. The happiness of the sage is a natural outcome of his state of mind, described by Chou Tun-yi as "vacuous in quiescence and straightforward in movement," and by Ch'eng Hao as "impersonal, impartial, and responding to things spontaneously." He does not enjoy the *Tao*; he simply enjoys what he himself is.

This view of the Neo-Confucianists can be seen by their interpretation of the third passage from the *Analects* quoted above. Chu Hsi's comment on this passage reads: "The learning of Tseng Tien would seem to have attained to the complete elimination of selfish desires, and to the Heavenly Laws in their pervasiveness, which are to be found everywhere without the slightest deficiency. This is why, both in activity and at rest, he was so simple and at ease. Speaking about his intention, he simply based himself on his existing station [in society and the universe] and enjoyed the ordinary state of affairs. He did not have the slightest idea of living according to [the views of] others, but lived according to himself. His mind was so vast that it lay in a single stream with Heaven and Earth, in which all things enjoy themselves. This mysterious sense is behind his words and can be dimly seen [by us]. The other three disciples only paid

attention to the lesser branches of affairs, so that they could bear
no comparison with the mood of Tseng Tien. That is why the Master
[Confucius] deeply approved of him." (*Lun-yü Chi-chu* or *Collected
Comments on the Analects, chüan* 6.)

In chapter twenty I have said that the essential quality of *feng
liu* is to have a mind that transcends the distinctions of things and
lives in accord with itself, rather than with others. According to
Chu Hsi's interpretation, Tseng Tien was precisely a person of this
kind. He was happy, because he was *feng liu*. In this statement of
Chu Hsi we also see the romantic element in Neo-Confucianism.
The Neo-Confucianists, as I have said, tried to seek happiness in
ming chiao, but at the same time, according to them, *ming chiao*
is not the opposite of *tzu jan* (nature, natural), but rather its development. This, the Neo-Confucianists maintained, was the main
thesis of Confucius and Mencius.

Did the Neo-Confucianists themselves succeed in carrying out
this idea? They did, and their success can be seen in the following
translation of two poems, one by Shao Yung and the other by
Ch'eng Hao. Shao Yung was a very happy man and was referred
to by Ch'eng Hao as a *feng liu* hero. He named his house the *An
Lo Wo* or Happy Nest, and called himself the Master of Happiness.
His poem, titled "Song on Happiness," reads:

> The name of the Master of Happiness is not known.
> For thirty years he has lived on the bank of the Lo river.
> His feelings are those of the wind and moon;
> His spirit is on the river and lake.
>
> (To him there is no distinction)
> Between low position and high rank,
> Between poverty and riches.
> He does not move with things nor anticipate them.
> He has no restraints and no taboos.
> He is poor but has no sorrow,
> He drinks, but never to intoxication.
> He gathers the springtime of the world into his mind.
> He has a small pond on which to read poems,
> He has a small window under which to sleep;
> He has a small carriage with which to divert his mind,
> He has a great pen with which to enjoy his will.

He sometimes wears a sun hat;
He sometimes wears a sleeveless shirt;
He sometimes sits in the forests;
He sometimes walks on the river bank.
He enjoys seeing good men;
He enjoys hearing about good conduct;
He enjoys speaking good words;
He enjoys carrying out a good will.

He does not flatter the Ch'an Masters;
He does not praise the man of occult arts.
He does not leave his home,
Yet he is one with Heaven and Earth.
He cannot be conquered by a great army;
He cannot be induced by a great salary.
Thus he has been a happy man,
For sixty-five years.*

Ch'eng Hao's poem, titled "Autumn Days," reads:

In these late years there is nothing that comes
    That is not easy and simple;
Each morning through my window shines the sun,
    As I awake.
All creatures run their course in true content,
    As I calmly observe.
The pleasure of each season through the year,
    I enjoy with others.
Beyond Heaven and Earth and all that has shape,
    The *Tao* is there.
The winds and clouds about me shift and change,
    My thought is there.
By riches and high estate, I am not to be polluted;
Neither poverty nor low rank can affect my happiness.
    A man like this is a hero indeed! †

Men such as these are heroes in the sense that they cannot be conquered. Yet they are not such in the ordinary sense. They are what is known as the *feng liu* hero.

* *Yi-ch'uan Chi-jang Chi, chüan* 14.
† *Collected Writings of Ch'eng Hao, chüan* 1.

Among the Neo-Confucianists there were some who criticized Shao Yung to the effect that he made too much display of his happiness. But no such criticism is ever made about Ch'eng Hao. In any case we find here a combination of Chinese romanticism (*feng liu*) and classicism (*ming chiao*) at its best.

CHAPTER 25

NEO-CONFUCIANISM:
THE SCHOOL OF PLATONIC IDEAS

ONLY twenty-two years after the death of Ch'eng Yi (1033-1108),
Chu Hsi (1130-1200) was born in the present Fukien province. The
political change that took place during these twenty years is tremendous. The Sung dynasty, although culturally outstanding, was
militarily never as strong as the Han and T'ang dynasties, and was
under constant threat from outside tribes in the north and north-
west. Its greatest catastrophe came when it lost its capital, the
present city of Kaifeng, to the Jurchen, a Tungusic tribe from
the northeast, and was compelled to reestablish itself south of the
Yangtze River in 1127. This event marked the division of the Sung
dynasty into two lesser parts: the Northern Sung (960-1126) and
the Southern Sung (1127-1279).

Position of Chu Hsi in Chinese History

Chu Hsi, better known simply as Chu Tzu or the Master Chu,
was a philosopher of subtle argument, clear thinking, wide knowledge and voluminous literary output. His *Recorded Sayings* alone
amount to 140 *chüan* or books. With him, the philosophic system of
the Ch'eng-Chu school, also known as the *Li hsüeh* or School of *Li*,
reached its culmination. Though the supremacy of this school was
several times to be disputed, notably by the Lu-Wang school and
by certain scholars of the Ch'ing dynasty, it remained the most
influential single system of philosophy until the introduction of
Western philosophy in China in recent decades.

In chapter seventeen I have said that the dynastic governments
of China ensured the supremacy of their official ideology through
the examination system. Persons who took the state examinations

were required to write essays based on the official versions and commentaries of the Confucian Classics. In chapter twenty-three I also said that one of the major acts of Emperor T'ai-tsung of the T'ang dynasty was to determine the official version and "correct meaning" of the Classics. During the Sung dynasty, the great statesman and reformer, Wang An-shih (1021-1086), prepared "new interpretations" to some of these Classics, and in 1075 Emperor Shen-tsung ordered that Wang's interpretations should be made official. This order, however, was soon cancelled when the political rivals of Wang An-shih gained control of the government.

It is to be remembered that the Neo-Confucianists considered the *Confucian Analects*, the *Mencius*, the *Chung Yung* or *Doctrine of the Mean*, and the *Ta Hsüeh* or *Great Learning*, as the most important texts, which they grouped together, giving to them the collective title of the *Four Books*. For these Chu Hsi wrote a *Commentary*, which he considered to be the most important of his writings. It is said that even on the day before his death, he was still working on a revision of this *Commentary*. He also wrote *Commentaries* on the *Book of Changes* and the *Shih Ching* or *Book of Odes*. In 1313 Emperor Jen-tsung of the Yüan, the Mongol dynasty that succeeded the Sung, ordered that the *Four Books* should be the main texts used in the state examinations, and that their official interpretation should follow Chu Hsi's commentaries. The same governmental indorsement was given to Chu Hsi's commentaries on the other Classics; persons hoping for success in the examinations had to interpret these works in accordance with Chu's commentaries. This practice was continued throughout the Ming and Ch'ing dynasties, until the abolition of the state examination system in 1905, when the government tried to introduce a modern educational system.

As pointed out in chapter eighteen, one of the main reasons why Confucianism gained supremacy in the Han dynasty was its success in combining speculative thought with scholarship. In Chu Hsi himself these two aspects of Confucianism are outstandingly exemplified. His wide knowledge and learning made him a notable scholar, and his deep insight and clear thinking made him a philosopher of the first rank. It is no accident that he has been the dominant figure in Chinese thought during the last several centuries.

Li *or Principle*

In the last chapter we have examined Ch'eng Yi's theory of *Li*, i.e., Principles or Laws. By Chu Hsi this theory was made still clearer. He says: "What are *hsing shang* or above shapes, so that they lack shapes or even shadows, are *Li*. What are *hsing hsia* or within shapes, so that they have shapes and body, are things." (*Chu-tzu Yü-lei* or *Classified Recorded Sayings of the Master Chu, chüan* 95.) A thing is a concrete instance of its *Li*. Unless there be such-and-such a *Li*, there cannot be such-and-such a thing. Chu Hsi says: "When a certain affair is done, that shows there is a certain *Li*." (*Ibid., chüan* 101.)

For everything, whether it be natural or artificial, there is its *Li*. In the *Recorded Sayings,* one passage reads: "(Question:) 'How can dried and withered things also possess the nature?' (Answer:) 'They all possess *Li* from the first moment of their existence. Therefore it is said: In the universe there is not a single thing that is without its nature.' Walking on the steps, the Master [Chu Hsi] continued: 'For the bricks of these steps there is the *Li* of bricks.' And sitting down, he said: 'For the bamboo chair, there is the *Li* of the bamboo chair. You may say that dried and withered things have no life or vitality, yet among them, too, there are none that do not have *Li*.'" (*chüan* 4.)

Another passage reads: "(Question:) 'Do things without feeling also possess *Li*?' (Answer:) 'Most certainly they possess *Li*. For example, a ship can go only on water, while a cart can go only on land.'" (*Ibid.*) And still another passage reads: "(Question:) 'Is there *Li* in dried and withered things?' (Answer:) 'As soon as a thing exists, the *Li* is inherent in it. Even in the case of a writing brush—though it is not produced by nature but by man, who takes the long and soft hairs of the hare to make it—as soon as that brush exists, *Li* is inherent in it." (*Ibid.*) The *Li* that is inherent in the writing brush is the nature of that brush. The same is true of all other kinds of things in the universe: each kind has its own *Li*, so that whenever the members of a certain kind of thing exist, the *Li* of that kind is inherent in them and constitutes their nature. It is this *Li* that makes them what they are. Thus according to the Ch'eng-Chu school, not all categories of objects possess mind, i.e., are sentient; nevertheless, all of them do possess their own particular nature, i.e., *Li.*

For this reason, there are the *Li* for things already before the concrete things themselves exist. In a letter answering Liu Shu-wen, Chu Hsi writes: "There are *Li*, even if there are no things. In that case there are only such-and-such *Li*, but not such-and-such things." (*Chu Wen-kung Wen-chi* or *Collected Literary Writings of Chu Hsi, chüan* 46.) For instance, even prior to the human invention of ships and carts, the *Li* of ships and carts are already present. What is called the invention of ships and carts, therefore, is nothing more than the discovery by mankind of the *Li* of ships and carts, and the construction of these objects accordingly. All *Li* are present even before the formation of the physical universe. In the *Recorded Sayings* one passage reads: "(Question:) 'Before heaven and earth had yet come into existence, were all the things of later times already there?' (Answer:) 'Only the *Li* were there.'" (*Chüan* 1.) The *Li* are always there; that is to say, they are eternal.

T'ai Chi *or the Supreme Ultimate*

For every kind of thing there is the *Li,* which makes it what it ought to be. The *Li* is the *chi* of that thing, i.e., it is its ultimate standard. (The word *chi* originally was a name for the ridge pole at the peak of the roof of a building. As used in Neo-Confucianism, it means the highest ideal prototype of things.) For the universe as a whole, there must also be an ultimate standard, which is supreme and all embracing. It embraces the multitude of *Li* for all things and is the highest summation of all of them. Therefore it is called the Supreme Ultimate or *T'ai Chi.* As Chu Hsi says: "Everything has an ultimate, which is the ultimate *Li.* That which unites and embraces the *Li* of heaven, earth, and all things is the Supreme Ultimate." (*Recorded Sayings, chüan* 94.)

He also says: "The Supreme Ultimate is simply what is highest of all, beyond which nothing can be. It is the most high, most mystical, and most abstruse, surpassing everything. Lest anyone should imagine that the Supreme Ultimate has bodily form, Lien-hsi [i.e., Chou Tun-yi] has said of it: 'The Ultimateless, and yet also the Supreme Ultimate.' That is, it is in the realm of no things that there is to be found the highest *Li.*" (*Chu-tzu Ch'üan-shu,* or *Com-*

plete Works of the Master Chu, chüan 49.) From these statements
we see that the position of the Supreme Ultimate in Chu Hsi's system corresponds to the Idea of the Good or to God in the systems of
Plato and Aristotle respectively.

There is one point in Chu Hsi's system, however, that makes his
Supreme Ultimate more mystical than Plato's Idea of the Good or
Aristotle's God. This is the fact that, according to Chu Hsi, the
Supreme Ultimate is not only the summation of the *Li* of the universe as a whole, but is at the same time immanent in the individual
examples of each category of things. Every particular thing has inherent in it the *Li* of its particular category of things, but at the same
time the Supreme Ultimate in its entirety is inherent in it too. Chu
Hsi says: "With regard to heaven and earth in general, the Supreme
Ultimate is in heaven and earth. And with regard to the myriad
things in particular, the Supreme Ultimate is in every one of them
too." (*Recorded Sayings, chüan* 94.)

But if this is so, does not the Supreme Ultimate lose its unity? Chu
Hsi's answer is no. In the *Recorded Sayings* he says: "There is but
one Supreme Ultimate, which is received by the individuals of all
things. This one Supreme Ultimate is received by each individual
in its entirety and undivided. It is like the moon shining in the
heavens, of which, though it is reflected in rivers and lakes and thus
is everywhere visible, we would not therefore say that it is divided."
(*Ibid.*)

We know that in Plato's philosophy there is a difficulty in explain-
ing the relation between the intellectual and sensible worlds, and between the one and the many. Chu Hsi, too, has this difficulty, which
he meets with an illustration which is really a metaphor of constant
use in Buddhism. The question as to how the *Li* of a whole class
of things is related to the individual things within that class, and as
to whether this relationship may also involve a division of the *Li*, is
not raised. If it were, I think Chu Hsi would meet it with the same
illustration.

Ch'i *or Matter*

If there were nothing but *Li*, there could be nothing more than a
world that is "above shapes." Our own concrete physical world, however, is made possible by the presence of *Ch'i* upon which is im-

posed the pattern of the *Li*. "In the universe," says Chu Hsi, "there are *Li* and *Ch'i*. The *Li* is the *Tao* that pertains to 'what is above shapes,' and is the source from which all things are produced. The *Ch'i* is the material [literally, instrument] that pertains to 'what is within shapes,' and is the means whereby things are produced. Hence men or things, at the moment of their production, must receive this *Li* in order that they may have a nature of their own. They must receive this *Ch'i* in order that they may have their bodily form." ("Reply to Huang Tao-fu," *Collected Literary Writings, chüan* 58.)

Again he says: "It seems to me that the *Ch'i* depends upon the *Li* for its operation. Thus when there is an agglomeration of *Ch'i*, the *Li* is also present within it. It is so, because the *Ch'i* has the capacity to condense and thus form things; but the *Li* lacks volition or plan, and has no creative power. . . . The *Li* constitutes only a pure, empty, and vast world, without shapes or traces, and so incapable of producing anything. But the *Ch'i* has the capacity to undergo fermentation and condensation, and thus bring things into existence. And yet, whenever the *Ch'i* exists, the *Li* is present within it." (*Recorded Sayings, chüan* 1.) Here we see how Chu Hsi says what Chang Tsai should have said but did not. Any individual thing is a condensation of *Ch'i*, but it is not only an individual thing; it is at the same time a member of some category of objects. As such, it is not merely a condensation of the *Ch'i*, but is a condensation that takes place in accordance with the *Li* for that category of objects as a whole. That is why, whenever there is a condensation of the *Ch'i*, *Li* must always necessarily be present within it.

The question as to the relative priority of *Li* and *Ch'i* is one much discussed by Chu Hsi and his disciples. On one occasion he says: "Before the instances of it exist, there is the *Li*. For example, before there exist any sovereign and subject, there is the *Li* of the relationship between sovereign and subject. Before there exist any father and son, there is the *Li* of the relationship between father and son." (*Recorded Sayings, chüan* 95.) That there is a *Li* prior to the instances of it in our physical universe, is certainly clear from Chu Hsi's statement. But is *Li* in general also prior to *Ch'i* in general? Chu Hsi says: "*Li* is never separable from *Ch'i*. Nevertheless, *Li* pertains to 'what is above shapes,' whereas *Ch'i* pertains to 'what is within shapes.' Hence if we speak of 'what is above shapes' and 'what is within shapes,' how can there not be priority and posteriority?" (*Ibid.*, *chüan* 1.)

Elsewhere there is a passage: "(Question:) 'When there is *Li*, there is then *Ch'i*. It seems that we cannot say that either one is prior to the other.' (Answer:) 'In reality, *Li* is prior. We cannot say, however, that there is *Li* to-day and *Ch'i* to-morrow. Yet there must be a priority of the one to the other'." (*Complete Works*, *chüan* 49.) From these passages we can see that what Chu Hsi has in mind is that as a matter of fact "there is no *Li* without *Ch'i* and no *Ch'i* without *Li*." (*Recorded Sayings*, *chüan* 1.) There is no time when there is no *Ch'i*. And since *Li* is eternal, it is absurd to speak about it as having a beginning. Hence the question as to whether it is *Li* or *Ch'i* that comes into being first is really nonsensical. Nevertheless, to speak about the beginning of *Ch'i* is only a *factual* absurdity, while to speak about the beginning of *Li* is a *logical* one. In this sense it is not incorrect, as between *Li* and *Ch'i*, to say that there is priority and posteriority.

Another question is this: As between *Li* and *Ch'i*, which is it that Plato and Aristotle would have called the "First Mover"? *Li* cannot be so, because it "lacks volition or plan, and has no creative power." But though *Li* itself does not move, yet in the "pure, empty, and wide world" of *Li* there are the *Li* of movement and the *Li* of quiescence. The *Li* of movement does not itself move, nor does the *Li* of quiescence itself rest, but as soon as the *Ch'i* "receives" them, the latter begins to move or rest. The *Ch'i* that moves is called the *Yang*; the *Ch'i* that rests is called the *Yin*. Thus, according to Chu Hsi, the dualistic elements that are the fundamentals of the universe in Chinese cosmology are produced. He says: "Whereas the *Yang* is in movement and the *Yin* in quiescence, the Supreme Ultimate is neither in movement nor in quiescence. But there are the *Li* of movement and of quiescence. These *Li* are invisible, and become manifest to us only when there are the movement of the *Yang* and the quiescence of the *Yin*. The *Li* rests upon the *Yin* and *Yang* just as a man rides on a horse." (*Complete Works*, *chüan* 49.) Thus the Supreme Ultimate, like God in the philosophy of Aristotle, is not moved, yet at the same time is the mover of all.

The interaction of the *Yin* and *Yang* results in the production of the Five Elements, and from these the physical universe as we know it is produced. In his cosmological theory, Chu Hsi endorses most of the theories of Chou Tun-yi and Shao Yung.

Nature and Mind

From the above we see that, according to Chu Hsi, when an individual thing comes into existence, a certain Li is inherent in it, which makes it what it is and constitutes its nature. And a man, like other things, is a concrete particular produced in the concrete world. Hence what we call human nature is simply the Li of humanity that is inherent in the individual. The saying of Ch'eng Yi that "the nature is Li" is endorsed and commented on by Chu Hsi in many places. The Li here spoken of is not Li in its universal form; it is simply the Li that is inherent in the individual. This explains the rather paradoxical saying of Ch'eng Hao: "When something is said about the nature, it is then already not the nature." By this he simply means that it is then the individualized Li, and not Li in its universal form.

A man, in order to have concrete existence, must be the embodiment of Ch'i. The Li for all men is the same, and it is the Ch'i that makes them different. Chu Hsi says: "Whenever there is Li, then there is Ch'i. Whenever there is Ch'i there must be Li. Those who receive a Ch'i that is clear, are the sages in whom the nature is like a pearl lying in clear cold water. But those who receive a Ch'i that is turbid, are the foolish and degenerate in whom the nature is like a pearl lying in muddy water." (Recorded Sayings, chüan 4.) Thus any individual, besides what he receives from Li, also has what he receives from Ch'i, and this is what Chu Hsi calls the physical endowment.

Such is Chu Hsi's theory of the origin of evil. As pointed out by Plato long ago, every individual, in order to have concreteness, must be an embodiment of matter, by which, consequently, he is implicated, so that he necessarily falls short of the ideal. A concrete circle, for example, can only be relatively and not absolutely round. That is the irony of the concrete world, in which man is no exception. Chu Hsi says: "Everything depends on its physical endowment. Li, on the other hand, is nothing but good, for since it is Li, how can it be evil? What is evil lies in the physical endowment. Mencius' doctrine asserts absolutely that the nature is good. In this he apparently takes account only of the nature per se but not of the Ch'i, and thus in this respect his statement is incomplete. The Ch'eng school, however, supplements this with the doctrine of the physical nature, and so in it we get a complete and all-round view of the problem." (*Complete Works, chüan* 43.)

The term "physical nature" here means the nature as it is found actually inherent in the physical endowment of an individual. As thus found, it always strives for the ideal, as Plato would say, but always falls short of it and cannot attain it. *Li* in its originally universal form, however, Chu Hsi calls "the nature of Heaven and Earth," by way of distinction. This distinction was already made by Chang Tsai and is followed by Ch'eng Yi and Chu Hsi. According to them, the use of this distinction completely solves the old controversy as to whether human nature is good and bad.

In Chu Hsi's system, nature is different from mind. In the *Recorded Sayings*, one passage reads: "(Question:) 'Is the mental faculty in man the mind or the nature?' (Answer:) 'The mental faculty is the mind but not the nature. The nature is nothing but *Li*.'" (*Chüan* 5.) Another passage reads: "(Question:) 'With regard to consciousness: is it the mental faculty of the mind that is thus conscious, or is it the action of the *Ch'i*?' (Answer:) 'It is not wholly *Ch'i*. There is first the *Li* of consciousness; but by itself it cannot exercise consciousness. There can be consciousness only when the *Ch'i* has agglomerated to form physical shapes, and the *Li* has united with the *Ch'i*. The case is similar to that of the flame of this candle. It is because the latter receives this rich fat that we have so much light.'" (*Ibid.*)

Thus the mind, just as all other individual things, is the embodiment of *Li* with *Ch'i*. The distinction between mind and nature is that mind is concrete and nature is abstract. Mind can have activities, such as thinking and feeling, but nature cannot. But whenever such an activity takes place in our mind, we can deduce that there is a corresponding *Li* in our nature. Chu Hsi says: "In discussing the nature, it is important first of all to know what kind of entity the nature is. Master Ch'eng put it well when he said: 'Nature is *Li*.' Now if we regard it as *Li*, then surely it is without shapes and features. It is nothing but principle. In man the principles of humanheartedness, righteousness, propriety, and wisdom belong to the nature. They are principles only. It is because of them that we are capable of having commiseration, that we can be ashamed of wrongdoing, that we can be courteous, and that we can distinguish between what is right and wrong. Take as an illustration the nature of drugs: some have cooling and some heating properties. But in the drugs themselves you cannot see the shapes of these properties. It is only by the result that follows upon taking the drug that we know what its property is; and this constitutes its nature." (*Complete Works, chüan* 42.)

In chapter seven we have seen how Mencius maintained that in human nature there are four constant virtues which manifest themselves as the "four beginnings." In the above quotation Chu Hsi gives a metaphysical justification to this theory of Mencius, which is primarily psychological. According to Chu, the four constant virtues pertain to *Li* and belong to the nature, while the four beginnings are the operations of the mind. We cannot know the abstract except through the concrete. We cannot know our nature except through our mind. As we shall see in the next chapter, the Lu-Wang school maintained that the mind is the nature. This is one of the main issues between the two schools.

Political Philosophy

If every kind of thing in this world has its own *Li*, then for the state, as an organization having concrete existence, there must also be the *Li* of statehood or government. If the state is organized and governed in accordance with this *Li*, it will be stable and prosperous; if not, it will become disorganized and fall into disorder. According to Chu Hsi, this *Li* is the principle of government as taught and practiced by the former sage-kings. But it is not something subjective. It is eternally there, no matter whether or not it is taught or practiced. Regarding this point, Chu had some warm debates with his friend Ch'en Liang (1143-1194), who held a different point of view. Arguing with him, he wrote: "During a period of fifteen hundred years, the *Tao* [the principle of government], as handed down by Yao and Shun [two traditional sage-kings] . . . and Confucius, has never been put into practice for even a single day in the world. But beyond human intervention, it is eternally there. It is simply what it is, and is eternal and immortal. It cannot perish, even though men have done violence to it during the last fifteen hundred years." ("Reply to Ch'en Liang," *Collected Literary Writings, chüan* 36.) "The *Tao*," he said again, "does not cease to be. What ceases to be is man's practice of it." (*Ibid.*)

As a matter of fact, not only have the sage-kings governed their states in accordance with the *Tao*, but all persons who have achieved something in politics must, to a certain degree, have followed the same *Tao*, even though sometimes unconsciously or incompletely. Chu Hsi writes: "I always think that this *Li* [principle of government] is one and the same both in times past and present. Those who follow it, succeed; those who violate it, fail. Not only did the sages of antiquity practice it, but even among the heroes of modern times, none can have any achievement without following this *Li*. Herein, however, is a difference. The ancient sages, being cultivated in the wisest way in what is fundamental, could hold the golden mean, and therefore what they did was all entirely good from the beginning to the end. The so-called heroes of modern times, however, have never undergone such cultivation, and have only moved in the world of selfish desires. Those of them who were talented have succeeded in coming into a seeming agreement [with the *Li*], each making accomplishment to the extent that he followed this *Li*. There is one aspect in which all the so-called heroes are the same; that is, what they do can never be completely in accordance with the *Li*, and therefore is not perfectly good." (*Ibid.*)

To illustrate Chu Hsi's theory, let us take as an example the building of a house. A house must be built in accordance with the principles of architecture. These principles eternally remain, even if in the physical world itself no house is actually built. A great architect is a man who fully understands these principles and makes his plans in accordance with them. For example, the house he builds must be strong and durable. Not only great architects, however, but all who want to build a house, must follow the same principles, if their houses are to be built at all. Such non-professional architects, however, may simply follow these principles through intuition or practical experience, without understanding or even knowing about them. As a result, the houses they build cannot completely accord with the principles of architecture and therefore cannot be of the best. Such is the difference between the government of the sage-kings and that of the lesser so-called heroes.

As we have seen in chapter seven, Mencius maintained that there are two kinds of government: that of the *wang* or king and that of the *pa* or military lord. Chu Hsi's argument with Ch'en Liang is a continuation of the same controversy. Chu Hsi and other Neo-Confucianists maintain that all governments from the Han and T'ang dynasties downward have been those of *pa*, because their rulers have all governed in their own interests and not in the interests of the people. Here again, therefore, Chu Hsi follows Mencius, but, as before, gives a metaphysical justification to the latter's theory, which is primarily political.

Method of Spiritual Cultivation

The Platonic idea that we cannot have a perfect state "until the philosopher becomes king or the king philosopher," is shared by most Chinese thinkers. In the *Republic*, Plato dwells at great length upon the education of the philosopher who is to become king. And Chu Hsi too, as we have seen, says that the sage-kings of antiquity were cultivated in the wisest way in what is fundamental. What is this method of cultivation? Chu Hsi has already told us that in every man, and indeed in everything, there is the Supreme Ultimate in its entirety. Since the Supreme Ultimate is the totality of the *Li* of all things, hence these *Li* are all within us, but, because of our physical endowment, they are not properly manifested. The Supreme Ultimate that is within us is like a pearl in turbid water. What we have to do is to make this pearl become visible. The method for so doing is, for Chu Hsi, the same as that taught by Ch'eng Yi, which, as we have seen in the last chapter, is twofold: "The extension of knowledge through the investigation of things," and "the attentiveness of the mind."

This method has its basis in the *Ta Hsüeh* or *Great Learning*, which was considered by the Neo-Confucianists as "the beginner's door for entering the life of virtue." As we have seen in chapter sixteen, the method of self-cultivation as taught by the *Great Learning* begins with the "extension of knowledge" and "investigation of things." According to the Ch'eng-Chu school, the purpose of the "investigation of things" is to extend our knowledge of the eternal *Li*.

Why does not this method start with the investigation of *Li* instead of things? Chu Hsi says: "The *Great Learning* speaks of the investigation of things but not of the investigation of *Li*. The reason is that to investigate *Li* is like clutching at emptiness in which there is nothing to catch hold. When it simply speaks of 'the investigation of things,' it means that we should seek for 'what is above shapes' through 'what is within shapes'." (*Complete Works, chüan* 46.) In other words, *Li* are abstract and things are concrete. We investigate the abstract through the concrete. What we as a result come to see lies both within the eternal world and within our own nature. The more we know *Li*, the more our nature, ordinarily concealed by our physical endowment, becomes visible to us.

As Chu Hsi says: "There is no human intelligence [utterly] lacking knowledge, and no single thing in the world without *Li*. But because the investigation of *Li* is not exhaustive, this knowledge is in some ways not complete. This is why the first instruction of the *Great Learning* is that the student must, for all the separate things in the world, by means of the *Li* which he already understands, proceed further to gain exhaustive knowledge of those [with which he is not yet familiar], thus striving to extend [his knowledge] to the farthest point. When one has exerted oneself for a long time, finally one morning a complete understanding will open before one. Thereupon there will be a thorough comprehension of all the multitude of things, external or internal, fine or coarse, and every exercise of the mind will be marked by complete enlightenment." (*Commentary on the Great Learning*, ch. 5.) Here we have again the theory of Sudden Enlightenment.

This seems to be enough in itself, so why should it be supplemented by the "attentiveness of the mind?" The answer is that without such attentiveness, the investigation of things is likely to be simply a kind of intellectual exercise and thus will not lead to the desired goal of Sudden Enlightenment. In investigating things we must keep in mind that what we are doing is to make visible our nature, to cleanse the pearl so that it can shine forth. In order to be enlightened, we must always think about Enlightenment. This is the function of the attentiveness of mind.

Chu Hsi's method of spiritual cultivation is very like that of Plato. His theory that in our nature there are the *Li* of all things, is very like Plato's theory of a previous knowledge. According to Plato, "We acquire knowledge before birth of all the essences." (*Phaedo* 75.) Because there is this previous knowledge, therefore he who "has learned to see the beautiful in due course and succession," can "suddenly perceive a nature of wondrous beauty." (*Symposium* 211.) This, too, is a form of Sudden Enlightenment.

CHAPTER 26

NEO-CONFUCIANISM:

THE SCHOOL OF UNIVERSAL MIND

As we have seen in chapter twenty-four, the Lu-Wang school, also known as the *Hsin hsüeh* or Mind school, was initiated by Ch'eng Hao and completed by Lu Chiu-yüan and Wang Shou-jen. Lu Chiu-yüan (1139-1193), popularly known as the Master of Hsiang-shan, was a native of the present Kiangsi province. He and Chu Hsi were friends, despite their widely divergent philosophic views. Their verbal and written debates on major philosophical problems evoked great interest in their day.

Lu Chiu-yüan's Conception of the Mind

Both Lu Chiu-yüan and Wang Shou-jen are said to have become convinced of the truth of their ideas as a result of experiencing Sudden Enlightenment. One day, it is said, Lu was reading an ancient book in which he came upon the two words *yü* and *chou*. An expositor remarked: "What comprises the four points of the compass together with what is above and below: this is called *yü*. What comprises past, present, and future: this is called *chou*." Thereupon Lu Chiu-yüan experienced an instantaneous enlightenment and said: "All affairs within the universe come within the scope of my duty; the scope of my duty includes all affairs within the universe." (*Lu Hsiang-shan Ch'üan-chi* or *Collected Works of Lu Hsiang-shan, chüan* 33.) And on another occasion he said: "The universe is my mind; my mind is the universe." (*Ibid., chüan* 36.)

Whereas Chu Hsi endorses Ch'eng Yi's saying that "the nature is *Li*," Lu Chiu-yüan replies that "the mind is *Li*." (*Collected Works, chüan* 12.) The two sayings differ only by one word, yet in them lies the fundamental division between the two schools. As we have seen in the last chapter, the mind, in Chu Hsi's system, is conceived of as the concrete embodiment of *Li* as found in *Ch'i;* hence it is not the same as the abstract *Li* itself. Chu Hsi, consequently, can only say that the nature is *Li*, but not that the mind is *Li*. But in Lu Chiu-yüan's system, on the contrary, the mind itself *is* the nature, and he considers the presumed distinction between nature and mind as nothing more than a verbal one. Regarding such verbal distinctions, he says: "Scholars of to-day devote most of their time to the explanation of words. For instance, such words as feeling, nature, mind, and ability all mean one and the same thing. It is only accidental that a single entity is denoted by different terms." (*Collected Works, chüan* 35.)

Yet as we have seen in the last chapter, Chu Hsi's distinction between nature and mind is certainly far from a verbal one, for from his point of view, there actually exists such a distinction in reality. This reality as seen by him, however, is not the same as that seen by Lu Chiu-yüan. For the former, reality consists of two worlds, the one abstract, the other concrete. For the latter, however, it consists of only one world, which is the mind or Mind.

But the sayings of Lu Chiu-yüan give us only a sketchy indication of what the world system of the Mind school is. For a more complete exposition, we must turn to the sayings and writings of Wang Shou-jen.

Wang Shou-Jen's Conception of the Universe

Wang Shou-jen (1472-1528) was a native of the present Chekiang province, and is generally known as the Master of Yang-ming. He was not only an outstanding philosopher, but was also notable as a practical statesman of high capacity and moral integrity. In his early years he was an ardent follower of the Ch'eng-Chu school; and, determined to carry out Chu Hsi's teaching, once started to investigate the principle or *Li* of bamboo. He concentrated his mind upon the bamboo day and night for seven consecutive days, yet failed to discover anything. Finally he was forced to give up the attempt in great despair. Afterward, however, while living amid primitive surroundings in the mountains of southwest China, to which he had been temporarily exiled because of political intrigue at court, enlightenment came to him suddenly one night. As a result, he gained a new under-

standing of the central idea of the *Great Learning,* and from this viewpoint reinterpreted this work. In this way he completed and systema-
tized the teaching of the Mind school.

In the *Ch'uan Hsi Lu* or *Record of Instructions,* which is a selection of Wang Shou-jen's recorded sayings made by one of his disciples, one passage reads: "While the Master was taking recreation at
Nan-chen, one of our friends, pointing at the flowers and trees on a
cliff, said: 'You say there is nothing under heaven that is external to
the mind. What relation, then, do these high mountain flowers and
trees, which blossom and drop of themselves, have to my mind?' The
Master replied: 'When you do not see these flowers, they and your
mind both become quiescent. When you see them, their color at once
becomes clear. From this fact you know that these flowers are not
external to your mind.'" (Pt. 3.)

Another passage reads: "The Master asked: 'According to you, what
is the mind of Heaven and Earth?' The disciple answered: 'I have
often heard that man is the mind of Heaven and Earth.' 'And what
is it in man that is called his mind?' 'It is simply the spirituality or consciousness.' 'From this we know that in Heaven and Earth there is one
spirituality or consciousness. But because of his bodily form, man has
separated himself from the whole. My spirituality or consciousness is
the ruler of Heaven and Earth, spirits and things. . . . If Heaven,
Earth, spirits, and things are separated from my spirituality or consciousness, they cease to be. And if my spirituality or consciousness is
separated from them, it ceases to be also. Thus they are all actually one
body, so how can they be separated?'" (Pt. 3.)

From these sayings we gain an idea of Wang Shou-jen's conception of the universe. In this conception, the universe is a spiritual
whole, in which there is only one world, the concrete actual world
that we ourselves experience. Thus there is no place for that other
world of abstract *Li,* which Chu Hsi so much emphasized.

Wang Shou-jen also maintains that mind is *Li:* "Mind is *Li.* How
can there be affairs and *Li* outside the mind?" (*Record of Instructions,* pt. 1.) Again: "The substance of the mind is the nature and
the nature is *Li.* Therefore, since there is the mind of filial love,
hence there is the *Li* of filial piety. If there were no such a mind,
there would be no such a *Li.* And since there is the mind of loyalty
to the sovereign, hence there is the *Li* of loyalty. If there were no
such a mind, there would be no such a *Li.* How can *Li* be outside

our mind?" (*Ibid.*, pt. 2.) From these sayings we can see still more clearly the difference between Chu Hsi and Wang Shou-jen and between the two schools they represent. According to Chu Hsi's system, we can only say that since there is the *Li* of filial piety, therefore there is the mind of loving one's parents; and since there is the *Li* of loyalty, therefore there is the mind of loyalty to one's sovereign. We cannot, however, say the converse. But what Wang Shou-jen said is precisely this converse. According to Chu Hsi's system, all the *Li* are eternally there, no matter whether there is mind or not. But according to Wang Shou-jen's system, if there is no mind, there will be no *Li*. Thus the mind is the legislator of the universe and is that by which the *Li* are legislated.

"The Illustrious Virtue"

With this conception of the universe, Wang Shou-jen gives a metaphysical justification to the *Great Learning*. As we have seen in chapter sixteen, this work speaks of what are later called the "three major cords" and eight "minor wires." The three "cords" are "to manifest the illustrious virtue, love people, and rest in the highest good." Wang Shou-jen defines great learning as the learning of the great man. Regarding the "manifestation of the illustrious virtue," he writes: "The great man is an all-pervading unity, which is one with Heaven, Earth, and all things. He considers the world as one family, and the Middle Kingdom as one man. Those who emphasize the distinction of bodily forms and thus make cleavage between the self and others are the small men. The reason that the great man is able to be one with Heaven, Earth, and all things, is not that he is thus for some purpose, but because the human-heartedness of his mind is naturally so. The mind of the small man is exactly the same, only he himself makes it small. When the small man sees a child about to fall into a well, he will certainly experience a feeling of alarm and distress. This shows that in his love he is one with the child. And when he hears the pitiful cry or sees the frightened appearance of a bird or beast, he will certainly find it unbearable to witness them. This shows that in his love he is one with birds and beasts. . . . From all this it may be seen that the original unity lies in the small man [as well as the great man]. Even the small man has his heavenly nature, the light of which cannot be obscured. Therefore it is called the illustrious virtue. . . . Thus when there is no obscuring caused by selfish desires, even the small man has the love for the whole, just as does the great man. But when there is this obscuring, even the mind of the great man is divided and hampered, just as is the small man. The learning of the great man serves simply to clear away the obscuring and thus to manifest the illustrious virtue, so as thus to restore the original unity of Heaven, Earth, and all things. It is not possible to add anything to this original state." *

Regarding the second of the "three cords" in the *Great Learning,* that of "loving people," Wang Shou-jen writes: "To manifest the illustrious virtue is to establish the nature of the unity of Heaven, Earth, and all things; to love people is to exercise the function of that unity. Therefore the manifestation of the illustrious virtue consists in loving people, and to love people is to manifest the illustrious virtue. If I love my own father, the fathers of some other men, and the fathers of all men, my love will be truly extended with my love of these fathers. . . . Beginning with all these human relationships, and reaching to mountains, rivers, spirits and gods, birds and beasts, grasses and trees, all should be loved in order to extend our love. In this way there is nothing that is not manifested in our illustrious virtue; and then we are really one with Heaven, Earth and all things." (*Ibid.*)

Regarding the third "cord," that of "resting in the highest good," he writes: "The highest good is the highest standard for the manifesting of the illustrious virtue and loving people. Our original nature is purely good. What cannot be obscured in it is the manifestation of the highest good and of the nature of the illustrious virtue, and is also what I call intuitive knowledge. When things come to it, right is right, wrong is wrong, important is important, and inferior is inferior. It responds to things and changes with circumstances, yet it always attains the natural mean. This is the highest standard for the actions of man and of things, to which nothing can be added, and from which nothing can be reduced. If there is any addition or reduction, that is selfishness and a petty kind of rationalization, and is not the highest good." (*Ibid.*)

* *Ta Hsüeh Wen* or *Questions on the Great Learning* in the *Wang Wen-ch'eng-kung Ch'üan-shu* or *Complete Works of Wang Shou-jen, chüan* 26.

Intuitive Knowledge

Thus the three "main cords" are reduced to a single "cord," that of the manifestation of the illustrious virtue, which is simply the original nature of our mind. All of us, whether good or bad, fundamentally have the same mind, which can never be wholly obscured by our selfishness, and always manifests itself in our immediate intuitive reaction to things. A case in point is the feeling of alarm which we all automatically experience upon suddenly seeing a child about to fall into a well. In our first reaction to things, we know naturally and spontaneously that the right is right and the wrong is wrong. This knowing is the manifestation of our original nature, and for it Wang uses the term "intuitive knowledge" (literally, "good knowledge"). All we need to do is simply to follow the dictates of this knowledge and go unhesitatingly forward. For if we try to find excuses for not immediately following these dictates, we are then adding something to, or reducing something from, the intuitive knowledge, and are thus losing the highest good. The act of looking for excuses is a rationalization which is due to selfishness. As we have seen in chapters twenty-three and twenty-four, Chou Tun-yi and Ch'eng Hao expressed the same theory, but Wang Shou-jen here gives it a more metaphysical basis.

It is said that when Yang Chien (died 1226) first met Lu Chiu-yüan, he asked the later what our original mind is. It may be noted in passing that this term, "original mind," was originally a Ch'anist one, but it also came to be used by the Neo-Confucianists of the Lu-Wang school. Answering the question, Lu Chiu-yüan recited the passage in the *Mencius* about the "four beginnings." Yang Chien said that he had read this passage since boyhood, but still did not know of what the original mind consists. He was then an official, and during the conversation was called upon to attend to some official business, in the course of which he had to pass a verdict on a certain lawsuit. When the business was concluded, he turned to Lu Chiu-yüan again with the same question. Lu then said: "Just now in announcing your verdict, the right you knew to be right, and the wrong you knew to be wrong. That is your original mind." Yang said: "Is there anything else?" To which Lu in a very loud voice answered: "What else do you want?" Thereupon Yang was suddenly enlightened and thus became the disciple of Lu. (*Tz'u-hu Yi-shu* or *Literary Remains of Yang Chien, chüan* 18.)

Another story says that a follower of Wang Shou-jen once caught a thief in his house at night, whereupon he gave him a lecture about intuitive knowledge. The thief laughed and asked: "Tell me, please, where is my intuitive knowledge?" At that time the weather was hot, so the thief's captor invited him first to take off his jacket, then his shirt, and then continued: "It is still too hot. Why not take off your trousers too?" At this the thief hesitated and replied: "That does not seem to be quite right." Thereupon his captor shouted at him: "There is your intuitive knowledge!"

The story does not say whether the thief gained enlightenment as a result of this conversation, but it and the preceding story certainly are typical of the Ch'an technique of initiating a student to Enlightenment. They show that every man possesses that intuitive knowledge which is the manifestation of his original mind, and through which he immediately knows that right is right and wrong is wrong. Everyone, in his original nature, is a sage. That is why the followers of Wang Shou-jen were in the habit of saying that "the streets are full of sages."

What they meant by this is that every man is potentially a sage. He can become an actual sage if he but follow the dictates of his intuitive knowledge and act accordingly. What he needs to do, in other words, is to carry his intuitive knowledge into practice, or, in Wang Shou-jen's terminology, to extend his intuitive knowledge. Thus the "extension of intuitive knowledge" became the key term in Wang's philosophy, and in his later years he mentioned only these words.

"The Rectification of Affairs"

It will be remembered that the *Great Learning* also speaks of "eight minor wires," which are the eight steps to be followed in the spiritual cultivation of the self. The first two of them are the "extension of knowledge" and "investigation of things." According to Wang Shou-jen, the extension of knowledge means the extension of the intuitive knowledge. Cultivation of the self is nothing more than the following of one's intuitive knowledge and putting it into practice.

The Chinese term for the "investigation of things" is *ko wu*, and it is Ch'eng Yi and Chu Hsi who interpret it as having this meaning. According to Wang Shou-jen, however, *ko* means to rectify and *wu* means affairs. *Ko wu*, therefore, does not mean "investigation of things," but "rectification of affairs." The intuitive knowledge, he maintains, cannot be extended through the techniques of contemplation and meditation taught by the Buddhists. It must be extended through our daily experience in dealing with ordinary affairs. Thus he says: "The activity of the mind is called *yi* [will, thought], and the objects toward which *yi* is directed are called *wu* [things, affairs]. For instance, when the object of one's *yi* is the serving of one's parents, then this serving of one's parents is the *wu*. And when the object of one's *yi* is the serving of the sovereign, then this serving of the sovereign is the *wu*." (*Record of Instructions*, pt. 1.) The *wu* may be right or wrong, but as soon as this can be determined, our intuitive knowledge will immediately know it. When our intuitive knowledge knows a thing to be right, we must sincerely do it, and when our intuitive knowledge knows it to be wrong, we must sincerely stop doing it. In this manner we rectify our affairs and at the same time extend our intuitive knowledge. There is no other means of extending our intuitive knowledge except through the rectification of our affairs. That is why the *Great Learning* says: "The extension of knowledge consists in the rectification of affairs."

The next two steps of the "eight wires" are "sincerity of thought [*yi*] and rectification of the mind." According to Wang Shou-jen, sincerity of thought is nothing more than the rectification of affairs and the extension of intuitive knowledge, both being carried out with the utmost sincerity. When we try to find excuses for not following the dictates of our intuitive knowledge, we are insincere in thought, and this insincerity is the same as what Ch'eng Hao and Wang Shou-jen call selfishness and rationalization. When our thought is sincere, our mind is rectified; the rectification of the mind is no other than sincerity in thought.

The next four steps of the "eight wires" are the cultivation of the self, regulation of the family, setting in order of the state and bringing of peace to the world. According to Wang Shou-jen, the cultivation of the self is the same as the extension of the intuitive knowledge. For how can we cultivate ourselves without extending our intuitive knowledge? And in cultivating ourselves what should we do besides extending our intuitive knowledge? In extending our intuitive knowledge, we must love people, and in loving people, how can we do otherwise than regulate our family, and contribute our best to creating order in our state, and bringing peace to the world? Thus all the "eight wires" may after all be reduced to a single "wire," which is the extension of the intuitive knowledge.

What is the intuitive knowledge? It is simply the inner light of our mind, the original unity of the universe, or, as the *Great Learning* calls it, the illustrious virtue. Hence the extension of the intuitive knowledge is nothing else than the manifestation of the illustrious virtue. Thus all the ideas of the *Great Learning* are reduced to the one idea expressed in the key words, the extension of the intuitive knowledge.

To quote Wang Shou-jen again: "The mind of man is Heaven. There is nothing that is not included in the mind of man. All of us are this single Heaven, but because of the obscurings caused by selfishness, the original state of Heaven is not made manifest. Every time we extend our intuitive knowledge, we clear away the obscurings, and when all of them are cleared away, our original nature is restored, and we again become part of this Heaven. The intuitive knowledge of the part is the intuitive knowledge of the whole. The intuitive knowledge of the whole is the intuitive knowledge of the part. Everything is the single whole." (*Record of Instructions*, pt. 1.)

Attentiveness of the Mind

Thus Wang Shou-jen's system follows the same lines as those of Chou Tun-yi, Ch'eng Hao and Lu Chiu-yüan, but he expresses it in more systematic and precise terms. The fact that the "cords" and "wires" of the *Great Learning* fit so well into his system brings both conviction to himself and authority to others.

The system and its method of spiritual cultivation are simple and direct—qualities which themselves give it a powerful appeal. What we need is first of all the understanding that each and every one of us possesses the original mind, which is one with the universe. This understanding is referred to by Lu Chiu-yüan as "first establishing the most important," a phrase he borrows from Mencius. On one occasion he said: "Recently there have been people who have criticized me by saying that apart from the single statement in which I lay emphasis upon first establishing the most important, I have no other tricks to offer. When I heard this, I exclaimed: 'Quite so!' " (*Collected Works, chüan* 34.)

In chapter twenty-four it was pointed out that, according to the Neo-Confucianists, spiritual cultivation requires that one should be attentive; but attentive to what? According to the Lu-Wang school, one must "first establish the most important," and then be attentive to it. And it is the criticism of this school that the Ch'eng-Chu school, without "first establishing the most important," starts immediately and haphazardly with the task of investigating things. Under these conditions, even attentiveness of mind cannot lead to any results in spiritual cultivation. This procedure is compared by the Lu-Wang school to starting a fire for cooking, without having any rice in the pot.

To this, however, the Ch'eng-Chu school would reply that unless one begins with the investigation of things, how can anything be definitely established? If one excludes this investigation of things, the only way left of "establishing the most important" is through instantaneous Enlightenment. And this the Ch'eng-Chu school regarded as more Ch'anist than Confucianist.

In chapter twenty-four, we have seen that Ch'eng Hao also says that the student must first understand *jen* (human-heartedness), which is the unity of all things, and then cultivate it with sincerity and attentiveness. Nothing else requires to be done. We merely need have confidence in ourselves and go straight forward. Lu Chiu-yüan remarks in similar strain: "Be courageous, be zealous, break open the net, burn the thorns in your path, and wash away the mire." (*Ibid.*) When so doing, even the authority of Confucius need no longer necessarily be respected. As Lu states again: "If in learning one gains a comprehension of what is fundamental, then the Six Classics become but one's footnotes." (*Ibid.*) In this respect we see clearly that the Lu-Wang school is a continuation of Ch'anism.

Criticism of Buddhism

Yet both the Lu-Wang and Ch'eng-Chu schools strongly criticize Buddhism. In this criticism, the difference between the two is again revealed. Thus Chu Hsi says: "When the Buddhists speak of 'emptiness,' this does not mean that they are [entirely] incorrect. But they must know that in this emptiness there are the *Li*. For if we are merely to say that we are 'empty,' without understanding that there are still the real *Li*, what is the use [of such a doctrine]? The case is like that of a pool of clear water, the cold clearness of which extends to the very bottom. When it is first seen, it will appear to have no water in it at all, and a person will then say that this pool is only 'empty.' If this person does not put in his hand to feel whether there is coldness or warmth, he will not know that there is water within. And such, precisely, is the view of the Buddhists." (*Recorded Sayings, chüan* 126.) Again he says: "The Confucianists consider *Li* as without birth and indestructible. The Buddhists consider spirituality and consciousness as without birth and indestructible." (*Ibid.*) According to Chu Hsi, the Buddhists are not without justification in saying that the concrete world is empty, because things in the concrete world do change and are impermanent. But there are also the *Li*, which are eternal and not subject to change. In this sense, then, the universe is not empty. The Buddhists do not know that the *Li* are real, because they are abstract, just as some men do not see the water in the pool, because it is colorless.

Wang Shou-jen also criticizes Buddhism, but from quite a different point of view: "When the Taoists [i.e., the religious Taoists] speak of *hsü* [vacuity, unrealness], can the Confucian sage add to it a hair of *shih* [actualness, realness]? And when the Buddhists speak of *wu* [non-being, non-existence], can the Confucian sage add to it a hair of *yu* [being, existence]? But when the Taoists speak of *hsü*, their motive is to preserve life, whereas when the Buddhists speak of *wu*, their motive is to escape the suffering of life and death. When they add these ideas to the original nature of the mind, their original meaning of *hsü* and *wu* is somewhat lost, and thereby the original nature of the mind is not freed from obstruction. The Confucian sage simply restores the original condition of the intuitive knowledge and adds to it no idea whatsoever. . . . Heaven, Earth, and all things all lie within the function and activity of our intuitive knowledge. How, then, can there be anything outside it to hinder or obstruct it?" (*Record of Instructions*, pt. 3.)

Again he says: "The claim of the Buddhists that they have no attachment to phenomena shows that they do have attachment to them. And the fact that we Confucianists do not claim to have no attachment to phenomena, shows that we do not have attachment to them. . . . The Buddhists are afraid of the troubles involved in human relationships, and therefore escape from them. They are forced to escape because they are already attached to them. But we Confucianists are different. There being the relationship between father and son, we respond to it with love. There being the relationship between sovereign and subject, we respond to it with righteousness. And there being the relationship between husband and wife, we respond to it with mutual respect. We have no attachment to phenomena." (*Ibid.*)

If we follow this argument, we can say that the Neo-Confucianists more consistently adhere to the fundamental ideas of Taoism and Buddhism than do the Taoists and Buddhists themselves. They are more Taoistic than the Taoists, and more Buddhistic than the Buddhists.

CHAPTER 27

THE INTRODUCTION OF
WESTERN PHILOSOPHY

Every system of philosophy is likely to be misunderstood and misused, and so it was with the two schools of Neo-Confucianism.
According to Chu Hsi, one must in principle start with the investigation of things in order to understand the eternal *Li* or Laws, but this
principle Chu Hsi himself did not strictly carry out. In the record of
his sayings, we see that he did make certain observations on natural
and social phenomena, but most of his time was devoted to the study
of, and comment on, the Classics. He not only believed that there
are eternal *Li*, but also that the utterances of the ancient sages are
these eternal *Li*. So in his system there is an element of authoritarianism and conservatism, which became more and more apparent as the
tradition of the Ch'eng-Chu school went on. And the fact that this
school became the official state teaching did much to increase this
tendency.

Reaction Against Neo-Confucianism

The Lu-Wang school is a revolution against this conservatism, and
in the time of Wang Shou-jen, the revolutionary movement was at
its highest. In a very simple way, it appealed directly to the intuitive
knowledge of every man, which is the inner light of his "original
mind." Though never recognized by the government, as was the
Ch'eng-Chu school, the Lu-Wang school became as influential as the
former.

But the philosophy of Wang Shou-jen was also misunderstood and
misused. According to Wang, what the intuitive knowledge immediately knows is the ethical aspect of our will or thought. It can only
tell us what we ought to do, but not *how* to do it. It lacks what

319

Americans would now call "know-how." In order to know how to do what we ought to do in certain situations, Wang said that we have to study practical methods of action in relation to the existing state of affairs. Later on, however, his followers seemed to come to the belief that the intuitive knowledge can itself tell us everything, including the "know-how." This is absurd, and the followers of the Lu-Wang school have certainly suffered the consequences of this absurdity.

At the end of the last chapter we have seen that Wang Shou-jen used the Ch'an method of argument to criticize Buddhism. This is precisely the sort of argument that is most likely to be misused. A satiric story tells us that when a scholar once paid a visit to a certain Buddhist temple, he was treated with only scant respect by the monk in charge. While he was there, however, the temple was also visited by a prominent official, to whom the monk showed the greatest respect. After the official had gone, the scholar asked the monk the reason for this difference. The monk answered: "To respect is not to respect, and not to respect is to respect." The scholar immediately gave him a hearty blow on the face. The monk protested angrily: "Why do you beat me?" To which the scholar replied: "To beat is not to beat, and not to beat is to beat." This story became current after the time of Wang Shou-jen, and no doubt was intended to criticize him and the Ch'anists.

The Ming dynasty (1368-1643), under which Wang Shou-jen lived and had his influence, was a native Chinese dynasty which replaced the Yüan or Mongol dynasty (1280-1367). In due course it in turn was overthrown as a result of internal revolts coupled with invasion from the outside, and was replaced by the Ch'ing dynasty (1644-1911), under which, for the second time in Chinese history, all of China was ruled by an alien group, this time the Manchus. The Manchus, however, were far more sympathetic to Chinese culture than the Mongols had been, and the first two-thirds of their dynasty was, on the whole, a period of internal peace and prosperity for China, during which, in certain respects, Chinese culture made important advances, though in other respects it was a period of growing cultural and social conservatism. Officially, the Ch'eng-Chu school was even more firmly entrenched than before. Unofficially, however, the Ch'ing dynasty witnessed an important reaction against both this school and the Lu-Wang school. The leaders of this reaction accused both schools of having, under the influence of Ch'anism and Taoism, misinterpreted the ideas of Confucius, and of thus having lost the practical aspect of original Confucianism. One of the attackers said: "Chu Hsi was a Taoist monk, and Lu Chiu-yüan was a Buddhist monk." This accusation, in a sense, is not entirely unjustified, as we have seen in the last two chapters.

From the point of view of philosophy, however, it is entirely irrelevant. As was pointed out in chapter twenty-three, Neo-Confucianism is a synthesis of Confucianism, Buddhism, philosophical Taoism (through Ch'anism), and religious Taoism. From the point of view of the history of Chinese philosophy, such a synthesis represents a development, and therefore is a virtue rather than a vice.

In the Ch'ing dynasty, however, when the orthodox position of Confucianism was stronger than ever before, to assert that Neo-Confucianism was not the same as pure Confucianism was equal to asserting that Neo-Confucianism was false and wrong. According to its opponents, indeed, the harmful effects of Neo-Confucianism were even greater than those of Buddhism and Taoism, because its seeming agreement with original Confucianism could more easily deceive people and so lead them astray.

For this reason the scholars of the Ch'ing dynasty started a "back-to-the-Han" movement, meaning by this a return to the commentaries that the scholars of the Han dynasty had written on the early Classics. They believed that because these Han scholars lived nearer in time to Confucius and before the introduction of Buddhism into China, their interpretations of the Classics must therefore be purer and closer to the genuine ideas of Confucius. Consequently, they studied numerous writings of the Han scholars which the Neo-Confucianists had discarded, and termed this study the *Han hsüeh* or learning of the Han dynasty. It was so called in contrast to that of the Neo-Confucianists, which they termed the *Sung hsüeh* or learning of the Sung dynasty, because the major schools of Neo-Confucianism had flourished in this dynasty. Through the eighteenth century until the beginning of the present century, the controversy between the Ch'ing adherents of the *Han hsüeh* and *Sung hsüeh* has been one of the greatest in the history of Chinese thought. From our present point of view, it was really one as between the philosophical and scholarly interpretation of the ancient texts. The scholarly interpretation emphasized what it believed was their actual meaning; the philosophical interpretation emphasized what it believed they *ought* to have meant.

Because of the emphasis of the *Han hsüeh* scholars on the scholarly interpretation of ancient texts, they made marked developments in such fields as textual criticism, higher criticism, and philology. Indeed, their historical, philological, and other studies became the greatest single cultural achievement of the Ch'ing dynasty.

Philosophically, the contribution of the *Han hsüeh* scholars was less important, but culturally, they did much to open the minds of their time to the wider reaches of Chinese literary achievement. During the Ming dynasty, most educated people, under the influence of Neo-Confucianism, a knowledge of which was required for success in the state examinations, devoted their whole attention to the "Four Books" (the *Confucian Analects, Mencius, Great Learning,* and *Doctrine of the Mean*). As a result, they knew but little about other literature. Once the Ch'ing scholars became interested in the scholarly reevaluation of the ancient texts, however, they could not confine themselves simply to the Confucian Classics. These, to be sure, engaged their first attention, but when the work in this field had been done, they began to study all the other ancient texts of the schools other than orthodox Confucianism, including such writings as the *Mo-tzu, Hsün-tzu* and *Han-fei-tzu,* which had long been neglected. They worked to correct the many corruptions that had crept into the texts, and to explain the ancient usage of words and phrases. It is owing to their labors that these texts are today so much more readable than they were, for example, in the Ming dynasty. Their work did much to help the revival of interest in the philosophical study of these philosophers that has taken place in recent decades under the stimulus of the introduction of Western philosophy. This is a topic to which we shall now turn.

Movement for a Confucian Religion

It is not necessary to examine here precisely the manner in which the Chinese first came in contact with Western culture. Suffice it to say that already toward the end of the Ming dynasty, i.e., in the latter part of the sixteenth century and early part of the seventeenth, many Chinese scholars became impressed by the mathematics and astronomy that were introduced to China at that time by Jesuit missionary-scholars. If Europeans call China and surrounding areas the Far East, the Chinese in the period of early Sino-European contacts referred to Europe as the Far West or T'ai Hsi. In earlier centuries they had spoken of India as "the West"; hence they could only refer to countries to the west of India as the "Far West." This term has now been discarded, but it was in common usage as late as the end of the last century.

In chapter sixteen I said that the distinction which the Chinese have traditionally made between themselves and foreigners or "barbarians" has been more cultural than racial. Their sense of nationalism has been more developed in regard to culture than to politics. Being the inheritors of an ancient civilization, and one geographically far removed from any other of comparable importance, it has been difficult for them to conceive how any other people could be cultured and yet live in a manner different from themselves. Hence whenever they have come into contact with an alien culture, they have been inclined to despise and resist it—not so much as something alien, but simply because they have thought it to be inferior or wrong. As we have seen in chapter eighteen, the introduction of Buddhism stimulated the foundation of religious Taoism, which came as a sort of nationalistic reaction to the alien faith. In the same way, the introduction of Western culture, in which Christian missionaries played a leading part, created a very similar reaction.

In the sixteenth and seventeenth centuries, as just noted, the missionary scholars impressed the Chinese not so much by their religion as by their attainments in mathematics and astronomy. But later, especially during the nineteenth century, with the growing military, industrial, and commercial predominance of Europe, and the coincident decline of China's political strength under the Manchus, the impetus of Christianity became increasingly felt by the Chinese. After several major controversies had broken out in the nineteenth century between missionaries and Chinese, a movement for a native Confucian religion to counteract the growing impact of the West was started at the very end of that century by the famous statesman and reformer, K'ang Yu-wei (1858-1927). This event was no mere accident—even from the point of view of the inner development of Chinese thought—because the scholars of the Han hsüeh had already paved the way.

In chapters seventeen and eighteen, we saw that the Han dynasty was dominated by two schools of Confucianism: one the Old Text and the other the New Text school. With the revival during the Ch'ing dynasty of the study of the works of the Han scholars, the old controversy between these two schools was also revived. We have also seen that the New Text school, headed by Tung Chung-shu, believed Confucius to have been the founder of an ideal new dynasty, and later even went so far as to consider him as a supernatural being having a mission to perform on this earth, a veritable god among men. K'ang Yu-wei was a leader of the Ch'ing adherents of the New Text school in the *Han hsüeh*, and found in this school plenty of material for establishing Confucianism as an organized religion in the proper sense of the word.

In studying Tung Chung-shu, we have already read Tung's fantastic theory about Confucius. The theory of K'ang Yu-wei is even more so. As we have seen, in the *Ch'un Ch'iu* or *Spring and Autumn Annals*, or rather in the theory of its Han commentators, as well as in the *Li Chi* or *Book of Rites*, there is the concept that the world passes through three ages or stages of progress. K'ang Yu-wei now revived this theory, interpreting it to mean that the age of Confucius had been the first age of decay and disorder. In our own times, he maintained, the growing communications between East and West, and the political and social reforms in Europe and America, show that men are progressing from the stage of disorder to the second higher stage, that of approaching peace. And this in turn will be followed by the unity of the whole world, which will be the realization of the last stage of human progress, that of great peace. Writing in 1902, he said: "Confucius knew all these things beforehand." (*Lun-yü Chu* or *Commentary to the Analects, chüan* 2.)

K'ang Yu-wei was the leader of the notable political reforms of 1898, which, however, lasted only a few months, and were followed by his own flight abroad, the execution of several of his followers, and renewed political reaction on the part of the Manchu government. In his opinion, what he was advocating was not the adoption of the new civilization of the West, but rather the realization of the ancient and genuine teachings of Confucius. He wrote many commentaries on the Confucian Classics and read his new ideas into them. Besides these, he also in 1884 wrote a book titled the *Ta T'ung Shu* or *Book of the Great Unity*, in which he gave a concrete picture of the utopia that will be realized in the third stage of human progress, according to the Confucian scheme. Although this book is so bold and revolutionary that it will startle even most utopian writers, K'ang Yu-wei himself was far from being a utopian. He insisted that his program could not be put into practice except in the highest and last stage of human civilization. For his immediate practical political program he insisted on merely instituting a constitutional monarchy. Thus throughout his life he was hated first by the conservatives because he was too radical, and later by the radicals because he was too conservative.

But the twentieth century is not one of religion, and together with, or in addition to, the introduction of Christianity into China, there also came modern science, which is the opposite of religion. Thus the influence of Christianity *per se* has been limited in China, and the movement for a Confucian religion suffered an early death. Nevertheless, with the overthrow of the Ch'ing dynasty and its replacement by the Republic in 1912, there was a demand by K'ang Yu-wei's followers, when the first Constitution of the Republic was drafted in 1915, that it state that the Republic adopt Confucianism as the state religion. A vigorous controversy developed over this point, until a compromise was reached, the Constitution asserting that the Chinese Republic would adopt Confucianism, not as a state religion, but as the fundamental principle for ethical discipline. This Constitution was never put into practice, and no more has since been heard about Confucianism as a religion in the sense intended by K'ang Yu-wei.

It is to be noted that up to 1898, K'ang Yu-wei and his comrades knew very little, if anything, about Western philosophy. His friend T'an Ssu-t'ung (1865-1898), who died a martyr's death when the political reform movement failed, was a much more subtle thinker than K'ang himself. He wrote a book titled *Jen Hsüeh* or *Science of Jen* (human-heartedness), which introduces into Neo-Confucianism some ideas taken from modern chemistry and physics. In the beginning of his work, he lists certain books to be read before one studies his *Science of Jen*. In that list, among books on Western thought, he mentions only the *New Testament* and "some treatises on mathematics, physics, chemistry, and sociology." It is plain that men of his time knew very little about Western philosophy, and that their knowledge of Western culture, in addition to machines and warships, was confined primarily to science and Christianity.

Introduction of Western Thought

The greatest authority on Western thought at the beginning of the present century was Yen Fu (1853-1920). In his early years he was sent to England by the government to study naval science, and while there read some of the works on the humanities current at the time. After returning to China, he translated into Chinese the following works: Thomas Huxley, *Evolution and Ethics*; Adam Smith, *An Enquiry into the Nature and Causes of the Wealth of Nations*; Herbert Spencer, *The Study of Sociology*; John Stuart Mill, *On Liberty*, and half of his *A System of Logic*; E. Jenks, *A History of Politics*; Montesquieu, *Esprit des Lois*; and an adapted translation of Jevons, *Lessons in Logic*. Yen Fu began to translate these works after the first Sino-Japanese war of 1894-95. After that he became very famous and his translations were widely read.

There are three reasons to account for this popularity. The first is that China's defeat in the Sino-Japanese war, following a series of earlier humiliations at the hands of the West, shook the confidence of the Chinese people in the superiority of their own ancient civilization, and therefore gave them a desire to know something about Western thought. Before that time they fancied that Westerners were only superior in science, machines, guns, and warships, but had nothing spiritual to offer. The second reason is that Yen Fu wrote comments on many passages of his translations, in which he compared certain ideas of his author with ideas in Chinese philosophy, in order to give a better understanding to his readers. This practice is something like the *ko yi* or interpretation by analogy, which was mentioned in chapter twenty in connection with the translation of Buddhist texts. And the third reason is that in Yen Fu's translations, the modern English of Spencer, Mill, and others was converted into Chinese of the most classical style. In reading these authors in his translation, one has the same impression as that of reading such ancient Chinese works as the *Mo-tzu* or *Hsün-tzu*. Because of their traditional respect for literary accomplishment, the Chinese of Yen Fu's time still had the superstition that any thought that can be expressed in the classical style is *ipso facto* as valuable as are the Chinese classical works themselves.

But the list of his translations shows that Yen Fu introduced very little Western philosophy. Among them, the ones really concerned with the subject are Jevons' *Lessons in Logic* and Mill's *System of Logic*, of which the former was an abridged summary, and the latter was left unfinished. Yen Fu recommended Spencer as the greatest Western philosopher of all time, thus showing that his knowledge of Western philosophy was rather limited.

There was another scholar of Yen Fu's time who in this respect had a better understanding and deeper insight, but who did not become known to the public until after he gave up the study of philosophy. He was Wang Kuo-wei (1877-1927), a scholar renowned as one of the greatest historians, archaeologists, and literary writers of recent times. Before he was thirty, he had already studied Schopenhauer and Kant, in this respect differing from Yen Fu, who studied almost none but English thinkers. But after he became thirty, Wang Kuo-wei gave up the study of philosophy, for a reason mentioned in one of his writings titled "A Self-Account at the Age of Thirty." In this he says:

"I have been tired of philosophy for a considerable time. Among philosophical theories, it is a general rule that those that can be loved cannot be believed, and those that can be believed cannot be loved. I know truth, and yet I love absurd yet great metaphysics, sublime ethics, and pure aesthetics. These are what I love most. Yet in searching for what is believable, I am inclined to believe in the positivistic theory of truth, the hedonistic theory of ethics, and the empiricist theory of aesthetics. I know these are believable, but I cannot love them, and I feel the other theories are lovable, but I cannot believe in them. This is the great vexation that I have experienced during the past two or three years. Recently my interest has gradually transferred itself from philosophy to literature, because I wish to find in the latter direct consolation." *

He says again that such men as Spencer in England and Wundt in Germany are but second-rate philosophers, their philosophies being but a syncretism of science or of earlier systems. Other philosophers known to him at that time were only historians of philosophy. He said that he himself could become a competent historian of philosophy, if he continued to study it. "But," said he, "I cannot be a pure philosopher, and yet I do not like to be an historian of philosophy.

* *Ching-an Wen-chi* or *Collected Literary Writings of Wang Kuo-wei, Second Collection.*

This is another reason why I am tired of philosophy." (*Ibid.*)

I have quoted Wang Kuo-wei at length, because judging from these quotations, I think he had some insight into Western philosophy. He knew, as a Chinese expression says, "what is sweet and what is bitter in it." But on the whole, at the beginning of this century, there were very few Chinese who knew anything about Western philosophy. When I myself was an undergraduate student in Shanghai, we had a course on elementary logic, but there was no one in Shanghai at the time capable of teaching such a course. At last a teacher was found who asked us to buy a copy of Jevons' *Lessons in Logic* and to use it as a textbook. He asked us to read it in the way a teacher of English expects his pupils to go through an English reader. When we came to the lesson on judgment, he called on me to spell the word "judgment," in order to make sure that I would not insert an "e" between the "g" and "m"!

Before long we were at the mercy of another teacher who conscientiously tried to make the course a real one on logic. There are many exercises at the end of Jevons' book which this teacher did not ask us to do, but I nonetheless prepared them on my own account. It so happened that there was one exercise that was beyond my understanding, which I requested the teacher to expound after class. After discussing it with me for half an hour without being able to solve it, he finally said: "Let me think it over and I shall do it for you the next time I come." He never came again, and for this I felt rather sorry, for I had no desire to embarrass him.

The University of Peking was then the only national university in China which was supposed to have three departments of philosophy: Chinese, Western, and Indian. But as the University was then constituted, there was only the one department of Chinese philosophy. In 1915 it was stated that a department of Western philosophy would be established, since a professor had been engaged who had studied philosophy in Germany and presumably could teach courses in that subject. I accordingly went to Peking in that year and was admitted as an undergraduate, but to my disappointment the professor who was to have taught us had just died, and I had therefore to study in the department of Chinese philosophy.

In this department we had professors who were scholars representing the Old Text, New Text, Ch'eng-Chu, and Lu-Wang schools. One of them, a follower of the Lu-Wang school, taught us a course on the history of Chinese philosophy, a two-year course meeting four hours a week. He began with the traditional sage-kings, Yao and Shun, and by the end of the first semester had gone only as far as the Duke of Chou—that is to say, about five centuries before Confucius. We asked him how long, if he continued at this rate, it would take to finish the course. "Well," he replied, "in the study of philosophy there is no such thing as finishing or not finishing. If you want this course to be finished, I can finish it in one word; if you do not want it to be finished, it can never be finished."

Introduction of Western Philosophy

John Dewey and Bertrand Russell were invited in 1919-20 to lecture at the University of Peking and other places. They were the first Western philosophers to come to China, and from them the Chinese for the first time received an authentic account of Western philosophy. But what they lectured about was mostly their own philosophy. This gave their hearers the impression that the traditional philosophical systems had all been superseded and discarded. With but little knowledge of the history of Western philosophy, the great majority of the audience failed to see the significance of their theories. One cannot understand a philosophy unless one at the same time understands the earlier traditions which it either approves or refutes. So these two philosophers, though well received by many, were understood by few. Their visit to China, nevertheless, opened new intellectual horizons for most of the students at that time. In this respect, their stay had great cultural and educational value.

In chapter twenty-one I have said that there is a distinction between Chinese Buddhism and Buddhism in China, and that the contribution of Buddhism to Chinese philosophy is the idea of Universal Mind. In the introduction of Western philosophy there have been similar cases. Following the visit of Dewey and Russell, for example, there have been many other philosophical systems that, at one time or another, have become popular in China. So far, however, almost all of them have simply represented Western philosophy in China. None has yet become an integral part of the development of the Chinese mind, as did Ch'an Buddhism.

So far as I can see, the permanent contribution of Western philosophy to Chinese philosophy is the method of logical analysis. In chapter twenty-one I have said that Buddhism and Taoism both use the negative method. The analytic method is just the opposite of this, and hence may be called the positive method. The negative method attempts to eliminate distinctions and to tell what its object is not, whereas the positive method attempts to make distinctions and tell what its object *is*. It is not very important for the Chinese that the negative method of Buddhism was introduced, because they had it already in Taoism, though Buddhism did serve to reinforce it. The introduction of the positive method, however, is really a matter of the greatest importance. It gives the Chinese a new way of thinking, and a change in their whole mentality. But as we shall see in the next chapter, it will not replace the other method; it will merely supplement it.

It is the method, not the ready-made conclusions of Western philosophy, that is important. A Chinese story relates that once a man met an immortal who asked him what he wanted. The man said that he wanted gold. The immortal touched several pieces of stone with his finger and they immediately turned to gold. The immortal asked the man to take them but he refused. "What else do you want?" the immortal asked. "I want your finger," the man replied. The analytic method is the finger of the Western philosophers, and the Chinese want the finger.

That is the reason why among the different branches of philosophical study in the West, the first to attract the attention of the Chinese was logic. Even before Yen Fu's translation of J. S. Mill's *System of Logic*, Li Chih-tsao (died 1630) had already translated with the Jesuit Fathers a mediaeval textbook on Aristotelean logic. His translation was titled *Ming-li T'an* or *An Investigation of Ming-li*. We have seen in chapter nineteen that *ming-li* means the analysis of principles through the analysis of names. Yen Fu translated logic as *ming hsüeh* or the Science of Names. As we have seen in chapter eight, the essence of the philosophy of the School of Names as represented by Kung-sun Lung is precisely the analysis of principles through the analysis of names. But in that chapter I also pointed out that this philosophy is not exactly the same as logic. There is a similarity, however, and when the Chinese first heard something about Western logic, they immediately noticed the similarity, and so connected it with their own School of Names.

Up to recent times the most fruitful result of the introduction of

Western philosophy has been the revival of the study of Chinese philosophy, including Buddhism. There is nothing paradoxical in this statement. When one encounters new ideas that are unfamiliar, it is only natural that one should turn to familiar ones for illustration, comparison, and mutual confirmation. And when one turns to these ideas, armed with the analytic method, it is only natural that one should make an analysis of them. We have already seen at the beginning of this chapter that for the study of the ancient schools of thought other than Confucianist, the scholars of the *Han hsüeh* paved the way. Their interpretation of the ancient texts was primarily textual and philological, rather than philosophical. But that is exactly what is needed before one applies the analytic method to analyze the philosophical ideas of the various ancient Chinese schools of thought.

Because logic was the first aspect of Western philosophy that attracted the attention of the Chinese, it is natural that among the ancient Chinese schools, the School of Names was also the first to receive detailed study in recent years. Dr. Hu Shih's book, *The Development of the Logical Method in Ancient China*, since its first publication in 1922 has been one of the important contributions to this study. Scholars like Liang Ch'i-ch'ao (1873-1930) have also contributed much to the study of the School of Names and of the other schools.

The interpretation and analysis of the old ideas through use of the analytic method characterized the spirit of the age up to the outbreak of the Sino-Japanese war in 1937. Even Christian missionaries could not escape from the influence of this spirit. This may be why many missionaries in China have translated Chinese philosophical works and written books on Chinese philosophy in Western languages, whereas few have translated Western philosophical works and written books on Western philosophy in Chinese. Thus in the philosophical field they seem to have conducted what might be called a reverse form of missionary work. It is possible to have reverse missionary work, just as it is possible to have reverse lend-lease.

CHAPTER 28

CHINESE PHILOSOPHY IN THE
MODERN WORLD

AFTER all that has been said about the evolution and development of Chinese philosophy, readers may be inclined to ask such questions as: What is contemporary Chinese philosophy like, especially that of the war period? What will Chinese philosophy contribute to the future philosophy of the world? As a matter of fact, I have often been asked these questions, and have been somewhat embarrassed by them, because it is difficult to explain what a certain philosophy is to someone who is unfamiliar with the traditions that it either represents or opposes. However, now that the reader has gained some acquaintance with the traditions of Chinese philosophy, I am going to try to answer these questions by continuing the story of the last chapter.

The Philosopher and the Historian of Philosophy

In so doing, I propose to confine myself to my own story, not at all because I think this is the only story worth telling, but because it is the story I know best and it can, perhaps, serve as a sort of illustration. This, I think, is better than merely giving a list of names and "isms," without any fuller exposition of any of them, a procedure which results in no kind of picture at all. By simply saying that a philosopher is a certain "ist," and nothing more, one usually creates misunderstanding instead of understanding.

My own larger *History of Chinese Philosophy*, the second and last volume of which was published in 1934, three years before the outbreak of the Sino-Japanese war, and the first volume of which was translated into English by Dr. Bodde and published in Peiping in 1937, three months after the war began, is an expression of that spirit of the age mentioned by me at the end of the last chapter. In that work I utilized the results of the studies of the *Han hsüeh* scholars on the texts of the ancient philosophers, and at the same time applied the analytic method to clarify the ideas of these philosophers. From the point of view of the historian, the use of this method has its limits, because the ideas of the ancient philosophers, in their original form, may not be as clear as in the presentation of their modern expositor. The function of a history of philosophy is to tell us what the words of the philosophers of the past actually meant to these men themselves, and not what we think they ought to mean. In my *History* I have tried my best to keep my use of the analytic method within its proper limits.

From the point of view of the pure philosopher, however, to clarify the ideas of the philosophers of the past, and push their theories to their logical conclusions in order to show their validity or absurdity, is certainly more interesting and important than merely to find out what they themselves thought about these ideas and theories. In so doing there is a process of development from the old to the new, and this development is another phase of the spirit of the age mentioned above. Such a work, however, is no longer the scholarly one of an historian, but the creative one of a philosopher. I share the feeling of Wang Kuo-wei, that is to say, I do not like to be simply an historian of philosophy. Therefore after I had finished the writing of my *History*, I immediately prepared for new work. But at this juncture the war broke out in the summer of 1937.

Philosophical Production in Wartime

Before the war, the philosophy departments of the University of Peking, from which I graduated, and of Tsing Hua University, where I am now teaching, were considered to be the strongest in China. Each of them has had its own tradition and emphasis. Those of the University of Peking have been toward historical studies and scholarship, with an idealistic philosophical trend, which, in terms of Western philosophy, is Kantian and Hegelian, and, in terms of Chinese philosophy, is Lu-Wang. The tradition and emphasis of Tsing Hua, on the contrary, have been toward the use of logical analysis for the study of philosophical problems, with a realistic philosophical trend,

which, in terms of Western philosophy, is Platonic in the sense that
the philosophy of neo-realism is Platonic, and in terms of Chinese
philosophy, is Ch'eng-Chu.

These two universities are both situated in Peiping (formerly
known as Peking), and on the outbreak of the war they both moved
to the southwest, where they combined with a third, the Nankai
University of Tientsin, to form the Southwest Associated University
throughout the entire war period. Together, their two Philosophy
Departments formed a rare and wonderful combination, comprising
nine professors representing all the important schools both of Chinese and Western philosophy. At first, the Associated University as
a whole was situated in Changsha in Hunan province, but our Philosophy Department, together with the other Departments of the
humanities, was separately located in Hengshan, known as the South
Holy Mountain.

We stayed there only about four months before moving again to
Kunming, farther southwest, in the spring of 1938. These few
months, however, were spiritually very stimulating. We were then in
a national crisis which was the greatest in our history, and we were in
the same place where Huai-jang had tried to grind a brick into a mirror, as mentioned in chapter twenty-two, and where Chu Hsi had
also once lived. We were sufferers of the same fate met by the Southern Sung dynasty, that of being driven southward by a foreign army.
Yet we lived in a wonderful society of philosophers, writers, and
scholars, all in one building. It was this combination of the historical
moment, the geographical location, and the human gathering, that
made the occasion so exceptionally stimulating and inspiring.

During these few months, myself and my colleagues, Professors
T'ang Yung-t'ung and Y. L. Chin, finished books on which we had
been working. T'ang's book is the first part of his *History of Chinese
Buddhism*. Chin's book is titled *On the Tao,* and mine the *Hsin Li-
hsüeh* or *New Li-hsüeh*. Chin and myself have many ideas in common, but my work is a development of the Ch'eng-Chu school, as
the title indicates, while his is the result of an independent study of
metaphysical problems. Later in Kunming I wrote a series of other
books: the *Hsin Shih-lun*, also titled *China's Road to Freedom;* the
Hsin Yüan-jen or *New Treatise on the Nature of Man;* the *Hsin
Yüan-tao*, also titled *The Spirit of Chinese Philosophy*, which has
been translated from the manuscript by Mr. E. R. Hughes of Oxford

University and is published in London; and the *Hsin Chih-yen* or *New Treatise on the Methodology of Metaphysics.* (All these, in their original Chinese editions, have been published by the Commercial Press, Shanghai.) In the following, I shall try to summarize some of their results, as an illustration of one trend in contemporary Chinese philosophy, and in so doing we may perhaps get a partial glimpse of what Chinese philosophy can contribute to future philosophy.

Philosophical, or rather metaphysical, reasoning starts with the experience that something exists. This something may be a sensation, an emotion, or anything else. From the statement: "Something exists," I have in my *Hsin Li-hsüeh* deduced all the metaphysical ideas or concepts not only of the Ch'eng-Chu school but also of the Taoists. They are all considered in such a way that they are simply the logical implications of the statement that something exists. It is not difficult to see how the ideas of *Li* and *Ch'i* are deducible from this statement, and other ideas are also treated in the same way. For instance, the idea of Movement is treated by me not as a cosmological idea for some actual initial movement of the world, but as a metaphysical idea implied in the idea of existence itself. To exist is an activity, a movement. If we think about the world in its static aspect, we will say with the Taoists that before anything comes into being there must first be the being of Being. And if we think about the world in its dynamic aspect, we will say with the Confucianists that before anything comes to exist, there must first be Movement, which is simply another way of speaking of the activity of existing. In what I call men's pictorial form of thinking, which is really imagination, men imagine Being or Movement as God, the Father of all things. In imaginative thought of this kind, one has religion or cosmology, but not philosophy or metaphysics.

Following the same line of argument, I have been able in my *Hsin Li-hsüeh* to deduce all the metaphysical ideas of Chinese philosophy and to integrate them into a clear and systematic whole. The book was favorably received because in it critics seemed to feel that the structure of Chinese philosophy was more clearly stated than hitherto. It was considered as representing a revival of Chinese philosophy, which was taken as the symbol of a revival of the Chinese nation.

In the Ch'eng-Chu school, as we have seen in the last chapter, there is a certain element of authoritarianism and conservatism, but this is avoided in my *Hsin Li-hsüeh*. In my opinion, metaphysics can know only that there are the *Li*, but not the content of each *Li*. It is the business of science to find out the content of the individual *Li*, using the scientific and pragmatic method. The *Li* in themselves are absolute and eternal, but as they are known to us, that is, in the laws and theories of science, they are relative and changeable.

The realization of the *Li* requires a material basis. The various types of society are the realization of the various *Li* of social structure, and the material basis each *Li* requires for its realization is the economic foundation of a given type of society. In the sphere of history, therefore, I believe in an economic interpretation, and in my book, *China's Road to Freedom*, I apply this interpretation to Chinese civilization and history, as I also have in chapter two of the present book.

I think Wang Kuo-wei's trouble in philosophy has been due to his failure to realize that each branch of knowledge has its own sphere of application. One does not need to believe in any theory of metaphysics, if that theory does not make much assertion about matters of fact. If it does make such assertions, however, it is bad metaphysics, which is the same as bad science. This does not mean that a good metaphysical theory is unbelievable, but only that it is so evident that one does not need to say that he believes in it, just as one need not say that one believes in mathematics. The difference between metaphysics and mathematics and logic is that in the latter two one does not need to start with the statement that something exists, which is an assertion about matters of fact, and is the only one that metaphysics need make.

The Nature of Philosophy

The method I use in the *Hsin Li-hsüeh* is wholly analytic. After writing that book, however, I began to realize the importance of the negative method which has been mentioned in chapter twenty-one. At present, if someone were to ask me for a definition of philosophy, I would reply paradoxically that philosophy, especially metaphysics, is that branch of knowledge which, in its development, will ultimately become "the knowledge that is not knowledge." If this be so, then the negative method needs to be used. Philosophy, especially metaphysics, is useless for the increase of our knowledge regarding matters of fact, but is indispensable for the elevation of our mind. These few points are not merely my own opinion, but, as we have previously seen, represent certain aspects of the Chinese philosophical tradition. It is these aspects that I think can contribute something to future world philosophy. In the following I shall try to develop them a little further.

Philosophy, as well as other branches of knowledge, must start with experience. But philosophy, especially metaphysics, differs from these other branches in that its development will lead it ultimately to that "something" which transcends experience. In this "something" there is that which cannot logically be sensed, but can only be thought. For instance, one can sense a square table, but cannot sense squareness. This is not because one's sense organ is insufficiently developed, but because squareness is a *Li*, which logically can only be thought but not sensed.

In the "something" there is also that which not only cannot be sensed, but strictly speaking, cannot even be thought. In chapter one I said that philosophy is systematic reflective thinking on life. Because of its reflective nature, it ultimately has to think on "something" that logically cannot be the object of thought. For instance, the universe, because it is the totality of all that is, cannot logically be the object of thought. As we have seen in chapter nineteen, the Chinese word *T'ien* or Heaven is sometimes used in this sense of totality, as when Kuo Hsiang says: "Heaven is the name of all things." Since the universe is the totality of all that is, therefore when one thinks about it, one is thinking reflectively, because the thinking and the thinker must also be included in the totality. But when one thinks about that totality, the totality that lies in one's thought does not include the thought itself. For it is the object of the thought and so stands in contrast to it. Hence the totality that one is thinking about is not actually the totality of all that is. Yet one must first think about totality in order to realize that it is unthinkable. One needs thought in order to be conscious of the unthinkable, just as sometimes one needs a sound in order to be conscious of silence. One must think about the unthinkable, yet as soon as one tries to do so, it immediately slips away. This is the most fascinating and also most troublesome aspect of philosophy.

What logically cannot be sensed transcends experience; what neither be sensed nor thought of transcends intellect. Concerning what transcends experience and intellect, one cannot say very much. Hence philosophy, or at least metaphysics, must be simple in its nature. Otherwise it again becomes simply bad science. And with its simple ideas, it suffices for its function.

The Spheres of Living

What is the function of philosophy? In chapter one I suggested that, according to Chinese philosophical tradition, its function is not the increase of positive knowledge of matters of fact, but the elevation of the mind. Here it would seem well to explain more clearly what I mean by this statement.

In my book, *The New Treatise on the Nature of Man*, I have observed that man differs from other animals in that when he does something, he understands what he is doing, and is conscious that he is doing it. It is this understanding and self-consciousness that give significance for him to what he is doing. The various significances that thus attach to his various acts, in their totality, constitute what I call his sphere of living. Different men may do the same things, but according to their different degrees of understanding and self-consciousness, these things may have varying significance to them. Every individual has his own sphere of living, which is not quite the same as that of any other individual. Yet in spite of these individual differences, we can classify the various spheres of living into four general grades. Beginning with the lowest, they are: the innocent sphere, the utilitarian sphere, the moral sphere, and the transcendent sphere.

A man may simply do what his instinct or the custom of his society leads him to do. Like children and primitive people, he does what he does without being self-conscious or greatly understanding what he is doing. Thus what he does has little significance, if any, for him. His sphere of living is what I call the innocent sphere.

Or man may be aware of himself, and be doing everything for himself. That does not mean that he is necessarily an immoral man. He may do something, the consequences of which are beneficial to others, but his motivation for so doing is self-benefit. Thus everything he does has the significance of utility for himself. His sphere of living is what I call the utilitarian sphere.

Yet again a man may come to understand that a society exists, of which he is a member. This society constitutes a whole and he is a part of that whole. Having this understanding, he does everything for the benefit of the society, or as the Confucianists say, he does everything "for the sake of righteousness, and not for the sake of personal profit." He is the truly moral man and what he does is moral action in the strict sense of the word. Everything he does has a moral significance. Hence his sphere of living is what I call the moral sphere.

And finally, a man may come to understand that over and above society as a whole, there is the great whole which is the universe. He is not only a member of society, but at the same time a member of the universe. He is a citizen of the social organization, but at the same time a citizen of Heaven, as Mencius says. Having this understanding, he does everything for the benefit of the universe. He understands the significance of what he does and is self-conscious of the fact that he is doing what he does. This understanding and self-consciousness constitute for him a higher sphere of living which I call the transcendent sphere.

Of the four spheres of living, the innocent and the utilitarian are the products of man as he is, while the moral and the transcendent are those of man as he ought to be. The former two are the gifts of nature, while the latter two are the creations of the spirit. The innocent sphere is the lowest, the utilitarian comes next, then the moral, and finally the transcendent. They are so because the innocent sphere requires almost no understanding and self-consciousness, whereas the utilitarian and the moral require more, and the transcendent requires most. The moral sphere is that of moral values, and the transcendent is that of super-moral values.

According to the tradition of Chinese philosophy, the function of philosophy is to help man to achieve the two higher spheres of living, and especially the highest. The transcendent sphere may also be called the sphere of philosophy, because it cannot be achieved unless through philosophy one gains some understanding of the universe. But the moral sphere, too, is a product of philosophy. Moral actions are not simply actions that accord with the moral rule, nor is moral man one who simply cultivates certain moral habits. He must act and live with an understanding of the moral principles involved, and it is the business of philosophy to give him this understanding.

To live in the moral sphere of living is to be a *hsien* or morally perfect man, and to live in the transcendent sphere is to be a *sheng* or sage. Philosophy teaches the way of how to be a sage. As I pointed out in chapter one, to be a sage is to reach the highest perfection of man as man. This is the noble function of philosophy.

In the *Republic*, Plato said that the philosopher must be elevated from the "cave" of the sensory world to the world of intellect. If the philosopher is in the world of intellect, he is also in the transcendent sphere of living. Yet the highest achievement of the man living in this sphere is the identification of himself with the universe, and in this identification, he also transcends the intellect.

Previous chapters have already shown us that Chinese philosophy has always tended to stress that the sage need do nothing extraordinary in order to be a sage. He cannot perform miracles, nor need he try to do so. He does nothing more than most people do, but, having high understanding, what he does has a different significance to him. In other words, he does what he does in a state of enlightenment, while other people do what they do in a state of ignorance. As the Ch'an monks say: "Understanding—this one word is the source of all mysteries." It is the significance which results from this understanding that constitutes his highest sphere of living.

Thus the Chinese sage is both of this world and the other world, and Chinese philosophy is both this-worldly and other-worldly. With the scientific advancement of the future, I believe that religion with its dogmas and superstitions will give way to science; man's craving for the world beyond, however, will be met by the philosophy of the future—a philosophy which is therefore likely to be both this-worldly and other-worldly. In this respect Chinese philosophy may have something to contribute.

The Methodology of Metaphysics

In my work, *A New Treatise on the Methodology of Metaphysics*, I maintain that there are two methods, the positive and the negative. The essence of the positive method is to talk about the object of metaphysics which is the subject of its inquiry; the essence of the negative method is not to talk about it. By so doing, the negative method reveals certain aspects of the nature of that something, namely those aspects that are not susceptible to positive description and analysis.

In chapter two I have indicated my agreement with Professor Northrop that philosophy in the West started with what he calls the concept by postulation, whereas Chinese philosophy started with what he calls concept by intuition. As a result, Western philosophy has naturally been dominated by the positive method, and Chinese philosophy by the negative one. This is especially true of Taoism, which started and ended with the undifferentiable whole. In the *Lao-tzu* and *Chuang-tzu*, one does not learn what the *Tao* actually *is*, but only what it is not. But if one knows what it is not, one does get some idea of what it is.

This negative method of Taoism was reinforced by Buddhism, as we have seen. The combination of Taoism and Buddhism resulted in Ch'anism, which I should like to call a philosophy of silence. If one understands and realizes the meaning and significance of silence, one gains something of the object of metaphysics.

In the West, Kant may be said to have used the negative method of metaphysics. In his *Critique of Pure Reason*, he found the unknowable, the noumenon. To Kant and other Western philosophers, because the unknowable is unknowable, one can therefore say nothing about it, and so it is better to abandon metaphysics entirely and stop at epistemology. But to those who are accustomed to the negative method, it is taken for granted that, since the unknowable is unknowable, we should say nothing about it. The business of metaphysics is not to say something about the unknowable, but only to say something about the fact that the unknowable is unknowable. When one knows that the unknowable is unknowable, one does know, after all, something about it. On this point, Kant did a great deal.

The great metaphysical systems of all philosophy, whether negative or positive in their methodology, have crowned themselves with mysticism. The negative method is essentially that of mysticism. But even in the cases of Plato, Aristotle, and Spinoza, who used the positive method at its best, the climaxes of their systems are all of a mystical nature. When the philosopher in the *Republic* beholds and identifies himself with the Idea of the Good, or the philosopher in the *Metaphysics* with God "thinking on thinking," or the philosopher in the *Ethics* finds himself "seeing things from the point of view of eternity" and enjoying the "intellectual love of God," what can they do but be silent? Is their state not better described by such phrases as "not one," "not many," "not not-one," "not not-many"?

Thus the two methods do not contradict but rather complement one another. A perfect metaphysical system should start with the positive method and end with the negative one. If it does not end with the negative method, it fails to reach the final climax of philosophy. But if it does not start with the positive method, it lacks the clear thinking that is essential for philosophy. Mysticism is not the opposite of clear ˙thinking, nor is it below it. Rather, it is beyond it. It is not anti-rational; it is super-rational.

In the history of Chinese philosophy, the positive method was never fully developed; in fact, it was much neglected. Therefore, Chinese philosophy has lacked clear thinking, which is one of the reasons why it is marked by simplicity. Lacking clear thinking, its simplicity has been quite naive. Its simplicity as such is commendable, but its naiveté must be removed through the exercise of clear thinking. Clear thinking is not the end of philosophy, but it is the indispensable discipline that every philosopher needs. Certainly it is what Chinese philosophers need. On the other hand, the history of Western philosophy has not seen a full development of the negative method. It is the combination of the two that will produce the philosophy of the future.

A Ch'an story describes how a certain teacher used to stick out his thumb when he was asked to explain the Buddhist *Tao*. On such occasions, he would simply remain silent, but would display his thumb. Noticing this, his boy attendant began to imitate him. One day the teacher saw him in this act, and quick as lightning chopped off the boy's thumb. The boy ran away crying. The teacher called him to come back, and just as the boy turned his head, the teacher again stuck out his own thumb. Thereupon the boy received Sudden Enlightenment.

Whether this story is true or not, it suggests the truth that before the negative method is used, the philosopher or student of philosophy must pass through the positive method, and before the simplicity of philosophy is reached, he must pass through its complexity.

One must speak very much before one keeps silent.

BIBLIOGRAPHY

Compiled by the Editor

GENERAL

This bibliography is intended to be suggestive rather than exhaustive, and is wholly confined to books and articles in English. For a much more comprehensive bibliography, see Wing-tsit Chan, *An Outline and an Annotated Bibliography of Chinese Philosophy* (Yale University, Far Eastern Publications, 1959). The University of Hawaii Press publishes a quarterly journal, *Philosophy East and West* (Vol. 1, 1951, onward), which contains many articles and book reviews on Chinese philosophy.

By far the most comprehensive and authoritative survey of Chinese philosophy is Fung Yu-lan's *A History of Chinese Philosophy*, translated from the Chinese by Derk Bodde (2 vols.; Princeton University Press, 1952-53; 2d printing, 1959-60). A brief but stimulating summary is by H. G. Creel, *Chinese Thought: From Confucius to Mao Tse-tung* (University of Chicago Press, 1953; paperback ed., a Mentor book, New York: New American Library, 1960). For an extremely original and thought-provoking, though sometimes controversial, analysis from the point of view of science, see Joseph Needham's monumental *Science and Civilisation in China*, Vol. 2, *History of Scientific Thought* (Cambridge University Press, 1956).

Anthologies—only the first of which is devoted wholly to philosophy—include E. R. Hughes, *Chinese Philosophy in Classical Times* (Everyman's Library, London: Dent, and New York: Dutton, 1942); W. Theodore De Bary, Wing-tsit Chan, and Burton Watson, *Sources of Chinese Tradition* (Columbia University Press, 1960); and Lin Yutang, *The Wisdom of China and India* (New York: Random House, 1942). Wing-tsit Chan's *A Source Book in Chinese Philosophy* is promised for publication—probably in 1961—by Princeton University Press.

343

Four symposia—all save the first centered more on the interplay between thought and institutions than on philosophy per se—are Arthur F. Wright, ed., *Studies in Chinese Thought* (University of Chicago Press, 1953); John K. Fairbank, ed., *Chinese Thought and Institutions* (same, 1957); David S. Nivison and Arthur F. Wright, eds., *Confucianism in Action* (Stanford University Press, 1959); and Arthur F. Wright, ed., *The Confucian Persuasion* (same, 1960). An interesting study of early Confucianism, Taoism, and Legalism is Arthur Waley's *Three Ways of Thought in Ancient China* (London: Allen & Unwin, 1939; paperback ed., an Anchor Book, New York: Doubleday, 1956). Hu Shih's *The Development of the Logical Method in Ancient China* (Shanghai: Oriental Book Co., 3d ed., 1928) was epoch-making at the time of its appearance in 1922, but has now been largely superseded.

CHAPTER 1: THE SPIRIT OF CHINESE PHILOSOPHY

For a more extended summary of salient features in Chinese philosophy, see Derk Bodde, "Harmony and Conflict in Chinese Philosophy," in the above-cited *Studies in Chinese Thought*, pp. 19-80.

CHAPTER 2: THE BACKGROUND OF CHINESE PHILOSOPHY

For theories concerning the environmental and social background of Chinese civilization, see Wolfram Eberhard, *Conquerors and Rulers: Social Forces in Medieval China* (Leiden: E. J. Brill, 1952) and Owen Lattimore, *Inner Asian Frontiers of China* (New York: American Geographical Society, 2d ed., 1951).

CHAPTER 3: THE ORIGIN OF THE SCHOOLS

This is the summary of a theory expounded by Fung Yu-lan in a Chinese-language *Supplement* to the Chinese edition of his *History of Chinese Philosophy*, Vol. 1.

CHAPTER 4: CONFUCIUS, THE FIRST TEACHER

The standard English translation of the *Confucian Analects* is still that in James Legge, *The Chinese Classics*, Vol. 1 (Hong Kong: 1861;

2d ed., Oxford: Clarendon Press, 1893). A more recent and very in teresting version is by Arthur Waley, *The Analects of Confucius* (London: Allen & Unwin, 1938). For a brilliant, though sometimes controversial, study of Confucius and of the development of Confucianism after his time, see H. G. Creel, *Confucius, The Man and the Myth* (New York: John Day, 1949).

CHAPTER 5: MO TZU, THE FIRST OPPONENT OF CONFUCIUS

On Mo Tzu, see Y. P. Mei, transl., *The Ethical and Political Works of Motse* (London: Probsthain, 1929), and Y. P. Mei, *Mo Tse, The Neglected Rival of Confucius* (London: Probsthain, 1934).

CHAPTER 6: THE FIRST PHASE OF TAOISM: YANG CHU

For the "Yang Chu" chapter in the *Lieh-tzu,* see below under ch. 20.

CHAPTER 7: THE IDEALISTIC WING OF CONFUCIANISM: MENCIUS

The standard translation of the *Mencius* is in James Legge, *The Chinese Classics,* Vol. 2 (Hong Kong: 1861; 2d ed., Oxford: Clarendon Press, 1895).

CHAPTER 8: THE SCHOOL OF NAMES

Attempts to translate the corrupt and exceedingly difficult *Kung-sun Lung-tzu* have been made by Alfred Forke, "The Chinese Sophists," *Journal of the [North] China Branch of the Royal Asiatic Society,* Vol. 34 (1901-02), pp. 1-85; Max Perleberg, *The Works of Kung-sun Lung-tzu* (Hong Kong, 1952); Y. P. Mei, "The *Kung-sun Lung-tzu,*" *Harvard Journal of Asiatic Studies,* Vol. 16 (1953), pp. 404-37; A. C. Graham, "Kung-sun Lung's Essay on Meanings and Things," *Journal of Oriental Studies,* Vol. 2 (1955), pp. 282-301. See also Graham, "The Composition of the Kungsuen Long Tzyy," *Asia Major,* n.s. Vol. 5 (1956), pp. 147-83.

CHAPTER 9: THE SECOND PHASE OF TAOISM: LAO TZU

Of the innumerable translations of the *Lao-tzu* (also known as the *Tao Te Ching*), two of the best are Arthur Waley, *The Way and Its*

Power (New York and Boston: Houghton Mifflin, 1935; paperback ed., an Evergreen book, New York: Grove Press, 1958), and J. J. L. Duyvendak, *Tao Te Ching, The Book of the Way and Its Virtue* (London: John Murray, 1954). For an extremely interesting analysis of Lao Tzu's ideas, followed by an account of the historical evolution of Taoism, see Holmes Welch, *The Parting of the Way, Lao Tzu and the Taoist Movement* (Boston: Beacon Press, 1957).

CHAPTER 10: THE THIRD PHASE OF TAOISM: CHUANG TZU

The best translation, but covering only the first seven chapters, is Fung Yu-lan, *Chuang Tzu, A New Selected Translation with an Exposition of the Philosophy of Kuo Hsiang* (Shanghai: Commercial Press, 1933). A complete but unsatisfactory translation is that of Herbert A. Giles, *Chuang Tzu, Mystic, Moralist, and Social Reformer* (Shanghai: Kelly & Walsh, 2d revised ed., 1926).

CHAPTER 11: THE LATER MOHISTS

No complete translation of the writings of the later Mohists has yet been attempted in English.

CHAPTER 12: THE "YIN-YANG" SCHOOL AND
EARLY CHINESE COSMOGONY

For translations of the *Book of Changes*, see below under ch. 15. For the *Yüeh Ling* or "Monthly Commands," see translation of James Legge in *Sacred Books of the East* (Oxford: Clarendon Press, 1885), Vol. 27, pp. 249-310, and for the *Hung Fan* or "Grand Norm," see Legge's translation in *ibid.* (2d ed., 1899), Vol. 3, pp. 139-48.

CHAPTER 13: THE REALISTIC WING OF CONFUCIANISM:
HSÜN TZU

On Hsün Tzu, see H. H. Dubs, transl., *The Works of Hsüntze* (London: Probsthain, 1928), and H. H. Dubs, *Hsüntze, The Moulder of Ancient Confucianism* (London: Probsthain, 1927). For the *Li Chi* or *Book of Rites*, see translation of James Legge in *Sacred Books of the East* (Oxford: Clarendon Press, 1885), Vols. 27-28.

CHAPTER 14: THE LEGALIST SCHOOL

See J. J. L. Duyvendak, transl., *The Book of Lord Shang, A Classic of the Chinese School of Law* (London: Probsthain, 1928); W. K. Liao, transl., *The Complete Works of Han Fei Tzu, A Classic of Chinese Legalism* (2 vols.; London: Probsthain, 1939, 1959); D. Bodde, *China's First Unifier: A Study of the Ch'in Dynasty as Seen in the Life of Li Ssu* (280?-208 B.C.) (Leiden: E. J. Brill, 1938).

CHAPTER 15: CONFUCIANIST METAPHYSICS

The *Book of Changes* has been translated by James Legge in *Sacred Books of the East*, Vol. 16 (Oxford: Clarendon Press, 2d ed., 1899); also by Richard Wilhelm into German and from this by Cary F. Baynes into English, as *The I Ching or Book of Changes* (2 vols.; New York: Pantheon Books, 1950). Legge's translation of the *Doctrine of the Mean* appears in *The Chinese Classics*, Vol. 1 (cited above under ch. 4); also in his *Li Ki*, in *Sacred Books of the East*, Vol. 28 (Oxford: Clarendon Press, 1885), pp. 301-29. Another translation is that of E. R. Hughes, *The Great Learning and the Mean-in-Action* (New York: Dutton, 1943).

CHAPTER 16: WORLD POLITICS AND WORLD PHILOSOPHY

On the *Great Learning*, see translation of James Legge in *The Chinese Classics*, Vol. 1, and in *Sacred Books of the East* (both cited above under ch. 15), Vol. 28, pp. 411-24; also that of E. R. Hughes (cited above under ch. 15). Some of the ideas and events treated in this chapter are also discussed in D. Bodde, *China's First Unifier* (cited above under ch. 14). See, as well, items in L. C. Porter, compiler, with translations by Porter and Fung Yu-lan, *Aids to the Study of Chinese Philosophy* (Peiping: Yenching University, 1934).

CHAPTER 17: THE THEORIZER OF THE HAN EMPIRE: TUNG CHUNG-SHU

On Tung Chung-shu, see also Yao Shan-yu, "The Cosmological and Anthropological Philosophy of Tung Chung-shu," *Journal of the North China Branch of the Royal Asiatic Society*, Vol. 73 (1948), pp. 40-68. On the *Li Yün* or "Evolution of Rites," see translation of James Legge in *Sacred Books of the East* (Oxford: Clarendon Press, 1885), Vol. 27, pp. 364-93.

CHAPTER 18: THE ASCENDANCY OF CONFUCIANISM AND REVIVAL OF TAOISM

On the Burning of the Books, see D. Bodde, *China's First Unifier* (cited above under ch. 14). On the apocrypha, see Tjan Tjoe Som, *Po Hu T'ung, The Comprehensive Discussions in the White Tiger Hall*, Vol. 1 (Leiden: E. J. Brill, 1949), pp. 100-20. On the ascendancy of Confucianism, see H. H. Dubs, "The Victory of Han Confucianism," in Dubs, transl., *History of the Former Han Dynasty*, Vol. 2 (Baltimore: Waverly Press, 1944), pp. 341-53. On Wang Ch'ung, see Alfred Forke, transl., *Lun-Heng* (2 vols.; London: Luzac, 1907, 1911).

CHAPTER 19: NEO-TAOISM: THE RATIONALISTS

See also the account of Kuo Hsiang in Fung Yu-lan, *Chuang Tzu* (cited above under ch. 10), pp. 145-57.

CHAPTER 20: NEO-TAOISM: THE SENTIMENTALISTS

The material in this chapter is almost entirely new. For the "Yang Chu" chapter in the *Lieh-tzu*, see Anton Forke, transl., *Yang Chu's Garden of Pleasure* (London: John Murray, 1912).

CHAPTER 21: THE FOUNDATION OF CHINESE BUDDHISM

A brief but excellent survey of the impact of Buddhism on Chinese civilization is by Arthur F. Wright, *Buddhism in Chinese History* (Stanford University Press, 1959). For a short summary of the philosophical aspects of Chinese (and Japanese) Buddhism, see J. Takakusu, *The Essentials of Buddhist Philosophy* (University of Hawaii Press, 1947). On Seng-chao, see Walter Liebenthal, transl., *The Book of Chao* (Peiping: Catholic University of Peking, 1948). See also many other articles by Liebenthal on early Chinese Buddhism, including, on Tao-sheng, "The World Conception of Chu Tao-sheng," *Monumenta Nipponica*, Vol. 12, Nos. 1-2 (1956), pp. 65-103; Nos. 3-4 (1956), pp. 73-100.

CHAPTER 22: CH'ANISM, THE PHILOSOPHY OF SILENCE

Of the enormous modern flow of literature—good, bad and indifferent—stimulated by Ch'an (Zen) Buddhism, mention should be made of the prolific writings of D. T. Suzuki, including his *Manual of Zen Buddhism* (Kyoto: Eastern Buddhist Society, 1935), and *Essays in Zen Buddhism* (London: Luzac, 1st series, 1927, 2d series, 1933, 3d series, 1934). See also Hu Shih, "Development of Zen Buddhism in China," *Chinese Social and Political Science Review*, Vol. 15 (1931), pp. 475-505.

CHAPTER 23: NEO-CONFUCIANISM: THE COSMOLOGISTS

On this and the next two chapters, see also the account—lively but marred by factual inaccuracies—by Carsun Chang, *The Development of Neo-Confucian Thought* (New York: Bookman Associates, 1957).

CHAPTER 24: NEO-CONFUCIANISM: THE BEGINNING OF
THE TWO SCHOOLS

On the Ch'eng brothers, see the excellent study by A. C. Graham, *Two Chinese Philosophers; Ch'eng Ming-tao and Ch'eng Yi-ch'uan* (London: Lund Humphries, 1958).

CHAPTER 25: NEO-CONFUCIANISM: THE SCHOOL OF
PLATONIC IDEAS

On Chu Hsi, see J. Percy Bruce, transl., *The Philosophy of Human Nature, by Chu Hsi* (London: Probsthain, 1922), and J. Percy Bruce, *Chu Hsi and His Masters, An Introduction to Chu Hsi and the Sung School of Chinese Philosophy* (London: Probsthain, 1923).

CHAPTER 26: NEO-CONFUCIANISM: THE SCHOOL OF
UNIVERSAL MIND

On Lu Chiu-yüan, see Siu-chi Huang, *Lu Hsiang-shan, A Twelfth Century Chinese Idealist Philosopher* (New Haven: American Oriental Society, 1944). On Wang Shou-jen, see Frederick Goodrich Henke, transl., *The Philosophy of Wang Yang-ming* (London and Chicago: Open Court Publishing Co., 1916).

CHAPTER 27: THE INTRODUCTION OF WESTERN PHILOSOPHY

For a general survey of thought during the Ch'ing dynasty (1644-1911), see Liang Ch'i-ch'ao, *Intellectual Trends in the Ch'ing Period,* translated from the Chinese by Immanuel C. Y. Hsü (Harvard University Press, 1959). On the "Han Learning" and some of its major philosophical exponents, see articles by Mansfield Freeman in *Journal of the North China Branch of the Royal Asiatic Society,* Vol. 57 (1926), pp. 70-91; Vol. 59 (1928), pp. 78-110; Vol. 64 (1933), pp. 50-71. On K'ang Yu-wei, see Laurence G. Thompson, transl., *Ta T'ung Shu, The One-World Philosophy of K'ang Yu-wei* (London: Allen & Unwin, 1958). On the ideological impact of the West on China, see, *inter alia,* Joseph R. Levenson, *Confucian China and Its Modern Fate: The Problem of Intellectual Continuity* (University of California Press, 1958).

CHAPTER 28: CHINESE PHILOSOPHY IN THE MODERN WORLD

Fung Yu-lan's *Hsin Yüan-tao* has been translated by E. R. Hughes as *The Spirit of Chinese Philosophy* (London: Kegan Paul, 1947) For surveys of Chinese philosophical (and religious) developments in recent years, see Wing-tsit Chan, "Trends in Contemporary Philosophy," in H. F. MacNair, ed., *China* (University of California Press, 1946), pp. 312-30, and Chan, *Religious Trends in Modern China* (Columbia University Press, 1953); also O. Brière, *Fifty Years of Chinese Philosophy, 1898-1950,* translated from the French by Laurence G. Thompson (London: Allen & Unwin, 1956).

INDEX

351